PAKISTAN

AT THE CROSSCURRENT OF HISTORY

RELATED TITLES FROM ONEWORLD

Argentina: A Short History, Colin M. Lewis, ISBN 1–85168–300–3
Britain: A Short History, T.A. Jenkins, ISBN 1–85168–266–X
Egypt: A Short History, James Jankowski, ISBN 1–85168–240–6
India and South Asia: A Short History, David Ludden,
    ISBN 1–85168–237–6
Ireland: A Short History, Joseph Coohill, ISBN 1–85168–238–4
Japan: A Short History, Mikiso Hane, ISBN 1–85168–239–2
Morocco: A Short History, C.R. Pennell, ISBN 1–85168–303–8
The Palestine Israeli Conflict: A Beginners Guide, Dan Cohn-Sherbok and
    Dawoud El-Alami, ISBN 1–85168–332–1
Pre-Industrial Societies: Anatomy of the Pre-Modern World, Patricia
    Crone, ISBN 1–85168–311–9
Russia: A Short History, Abraham Ascher, ISBN 1–85168–242–2
Slavery and Freedom in Colonial Brazil, A.J.R. Russell-Wood,
    ISBN 1–85168–288–0
Turkey: A Short History, Feroz Ahmad, ISBN 1–85168–241–4

PAKISTAN

AT THE CROSSCURRENT OF HISTORY

Lawrence Ziring

ONEWORLD
OXFORD

PAKISTAN: AT THE CROSSCURRENT OF HISTORY

Oneworld Publications
(Sales and Editorial)
185 Banbury Road
Oxford OX2 7AR
England
www.oneworld-publications.com

ISBN 1–85168–327–5

Cover design by Design Deluxe
Cover photograph: The Pakistani Army base
in Mushong © Siem Vaessen/Corbis Sygma
Typeset by LaserScript, Mitcham, UK
Printed and bound in China by Sun Fung Offset Binding Co. Ltd

For Anya Ranae
That her generation will possess wisdom

CONTENTS

MAPS

PREFACE

Pakistan: At the Crosscurrent of History was completed approximately six years after publication of my Golden Jubilee volume *Pakistan in the Twentieth Century*, published by Oxford University Press in 1997. This smaller volume traces many of the events described in that earlier work, but the focus of *Pakistan in the Twentieth Century* did not anticipate the ongoing impact on Pakistan's overall development of its venture into Afghanistan well after the last Soviet soldier departed from the neighboring mountain state. When that more detailed history was nearing completion the Taliban had not yet occupied Kabul and therefore it was not yet clear what their role would be in that troubled country, let alone what Pakistani leaders, notably in the army, intended to accomplish by their intimate association with militant Islamic students. Also not clarified at the time was the role to be played by the non-Afghan Muslims (especially Arabs) and thousands of Pakistani volunteers who had filtered back into Afghanistan following the Red Army withdrawal. The latter's assistance in the consolidation of Taliban gains as well as in transforming the country from a loosely knit and conflicted tribal order into a centralized Islamic emirate could not have been foreseen. Nor was it possible to predict Osama bin Laden's return to Afghanistan in 1996, or, for that matter, the extent to which Taliban and bin Laden's al-Qaeda intertwined. Pakistan's continuing role in Afghanistan was expressed in

Islamabad's security interests, but here again it was not yet public information the extent to which Pakistan, the Taliban, and al-Qaeda, had overlapping interests. Also not realized at the time was the shift in the importance given to Pakistan's Islamist organizations, how they related to Muslim movements elsewhere, or how they became central to Pakistan's political experience. Since they were never successful at the polls, it was only later that one could argue that the real power of the Islamists did not turn on success or failure in the electoral process. Pakistan's conventional political parties, that is, the more secular organizations, had become less significant in a country forced to accept frequent and extended periods of military rule. Moreover, only later was it fathomed how far the traditional political parties had been neutered by the Pakistan army, and, in light of this development, how the Islamists were able to elevate their profile by more intimate association with the country's armed forces. Kashmir factored into this equation. An old problem, the Kashmir issue was ready made for the Islamists and also connected them and the Pakistan armed forces with the Taliban and al-Qaeda. Nor could anyone have forecast the events of September 11, 2001. The destruction of the World Trade Center in New York City and the bombing of the Pentagon in Washington trailed back to Afghanistan, and hence to Pakistan as well.

It is generally assumed that the events of September 11, 2001 changed the world. They certainly changed Pakistan. If Pakistan was ever judged remote and on the margins of history, 9/11 altered attitudes and perceptions, and for a great many brought an end to such thoughts. For contemporary observers of the world condition, Pakistan today is a pivotal country, a demonstrated nuclear power since 1998, that can no longer be taken for granted or denied access to the inner sanctum of world powers. Pakistan's past and present are equally important because neither one or the other alone can inform the concerned world about the challenges burdening that large Muslim country. To understand Pakistan today is to read the history of the country from its roots in the early years of the twentieth century to the current period a century later. This volume represents almost two years of labor and more than four decades of exposure to this fascinating land. The book is meant to edify the uninformed as well as to assist the scholar in charting the course of Pakistan's history.

The book, like so many other brief histories, has required compression, and therefore much is left unsaid. Nevertheless, the essential details are to be found in this text, as well as the author's attempt to interpret what events mean and what they are likely to indicate for the future. There is much therefore in this small volume to inform as well as to provoke thinking. It is impossible to spend so much of your life chronicling a nation and not to be left with impressions and some rather strong points of view. This volume therefore is also an interpretive essay, intended to broaden understanding, but also meant to explore consequences. So I have avoided using the usual format of including citations and footnotes. My objective was the production of a quick read, a book that could be read as one would read a story rather than a scholarly tract. I decided when I began that the book should be read without interruptions. Whatever needed saying would be incorporated in the ongoing narrative, and readers sufficiently energized could then find more detailed discussions in other works already or yet to be written. Mindful, however, of my obligations to the academic community, I have included a list of sources used or consulted in every chapter through chapter 9. Chapters 10 and 11, however, were prepared exclusively from electronic sources; a list of websites and writers that have provided me with a chronology of events as well as influenced my analysis is found at the end of chapter 11.

Finally, let me note that writing *Pakistan: At the Crosscurrent of History* has been a long, difficult, even grueling experience. As with other books, much of my life and the lives of those around me has been sacrificed to see this writing to a conclusion. I owe much to all of those who, knowingly or not, gave up something to allow me to complete the project. I am especially aware of the impact on my wife, Raye, who not only stoically put up with my moods but also gave me her unstinting support. Moreover, Raye has always been there with technical advice and assistance and she came to my rescue in this effort more than once. And, indeed, it must be said again. Authors are often indebted to their editors and it is for me to acknowledge the encouragement and work done in the production of this book by two very special people at Oneworld Publications: Victoria Roddam, who shepherded the book through all its phases, and Rebecca Clare, whose expert handling of the manuscript made my task so much lighter. Finally, I want this book to be a reminder to Pakistanis that there are people like this writer who have devoted themselves to the study of Pakistan, not for personal gain, but to assist in the development of what is still a very new nation. Through it all, for so many, many years, my affection for the Pakistani people has never wavered. I trust they find something in this small volume that is instructive and positive, but most important helps in the reformulation of ideas about what it means to be a Pakistani at the dawn of a new millennium. With this thought in mind it must be said that any errors of fact or interpretation are my responsibility alone.

Lawrence Ziring

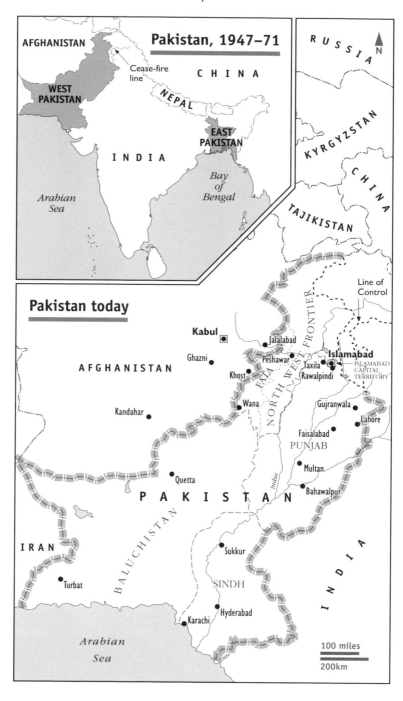

Pakistan, 1947–71

AFGHANISTAN

WEST PAKISTAN

Cease-fire line

CHINA

NEPAL

EAST PAKISTAN

INDIA

Bay of Bengal

Arabian Sea

Pakistan today

RUSSIA

N

KYRGYZSTAN

CHINA

TAJIKISTAN

Line of Control

Kabul

Jalalabad

Ghazni

Peshawar

Islamabad

Taxila

ISLAMABAD CAPITAL TERRITORY

AFGHANISTAN

Khost

Rawalpindi

NORTH WEST FRONTIER

FATA

Wana

Gujranwāla

Lahore

Kandahar

Faisalabad

PUNJAB

Multan

Quetta

Bahawalpur

Indus

PAKISTAN

IRAN

BALUCHISTAN

Sukkur

INDIA

Turbat

SINDH

Hyderabad

Karachi

Arabian Sea

100 miles

200km

THE ORIGINS OF PAKISTAN

Pakistan has been precariously balanced between past and present, between tradition and modernity, between Islamism and secularism throughout its brief history. A product of the age of European imperialism, the country emerged as an independent state with a relatively forward-looking outlook that was essentially the vision of Mohammad Ali Jinnah. Jinnah, respectfully referred to as the "Quaid-i-Azam" (Great Leader), represented the modern Muslim man of his generation. A figure comfortable in the ways and dress of the European colonizers, Jinnah was an English-trained barrister and one of British India's more successful lawyers. Riveted by the English common law, he found its teachings the rock bed of a civilized society. Moreover, as a Muslim of liberal persuasion, Jinnah was convinced that the secular legal tradition he proclaimed as his own was the *sine qua non* in the building of a modern community. Motivated by a deep sense of history, Jinnah concluded early in his life that the British would one day depart from India and leave the management of the country to its native population. Therefore, he was all the more convinced of the need to bridge deep and abiding differences between the major religious and cultural communities, especially the Hindu and Muslim.

All of Jinnah's talent and energy in the first half of his life was devoted to the building of a foundation that was centered on an accommodation between Hindus and Muslims. Himself a student

1

of liberal Hindu thinkers, Jinnah shied away from exclusive Muslim ritual and found in the eclectic human experience the central idea that forecast the melding of peoples irrespective of their separate and distinct traditions and culture. Fervently committed to the intertwining of communities, Jinnah became an active member of the Indian National Congress and labored toward the goal of Hindu–Muslim amity and cooperation. Not oblivious to the pulls of his Islamic faith, or to the great cultural gaps that separated the monotheistic Muslim from the idol-worshipping Hindu, Jinnah nevertheless strove to create the political and legal conditions that promised a stable and cooperative relationship between members of different religious traditions and practices.

Like other prominent leaders of his generation, Jinnah was born into the age of self-determination, a period wherein peoples long under alien rule would assert their right to administer their own affairs. Self-determination, like so many other forces that influenced the course of events in the subcontinent, had emerged from Western experience. Self-determination was the promise as well as the vehicle to the realization of national ambitions. It also meant there would be no returning to the conditions prevailing before the British conquest of India. The Mughal Empire would not be resurrected, nor would Indian Hindus reclaim their Maurya and Gupta experiences. The twentieth century beckoned the formation of the nation-state, and India could not avoid its destiny as a contemporary member of the family of nations.

Jinnah was one of a number of Indian luminaries to project a life experience anchored on secular ideas and philosophy. But more than other Muslims of his day he was able to articulate the meaning and importance of social coalescence. Muslim competitors for political leadership were numerous, but their postures were more limited, their declarations more circumspect, and their pronounced objectives more aggressively expressed. Jinnah stood out from these other major Muslim actors and their movements. Furthermore, he embraced the totality of the subcontinent. He identified with no particular region and he reached out to anyone wishing to associate with a more positive and constructive outlook. In the years before World War I, Jinnah did not considerhimself a spokesman for Muslims alone. He believed the time had arrived for Indian leaders to speak rationally and objectively to all the people of India.

Mahatma Gandhi was a great boost to the self-government movement launched by the Indian National Congress following the Great War. Returning to India from South Africa shortly after the onset of hostilities in Europe, Gandhi epitomized the Indian quest for shared governance. Unlike Jinnah, however, Gandhi, although also a barrister in the English tradition, was less concerned with the rule of law. Gandhi's success was not within the confines of the courtroom but in rallying the multitudes against colonial authority. His street tactics, notably his several passive resistance campaigns, in fact involved challenging and undermining existing colonial law. Moreover, the Mahatma's appeal was aimed directly at the subcontinent's illiterate or semi-educated population, which he mobilized to pressure the British in every public venue. Jinnah, by contrast, had addressed his appeal to the literati, to educated Indian leaders who understood his sophisticated idiom and acknowledged the need to educate their followers in the manners of modernity. Gandhi was less interested in laying a legal foundation for the reconciliation of disparate communities than he was in leading a huge popular movement against British rule.

Gandhi knew what he was against more than what he was for. He related more to the impoverished multitude, notably among the Hindus, who found purpose for their lives as well as common cause in the struggle for national freedom. Jinnah's more aristocratic approach was exaggerated by Gandhi's earthy, popular, and soon worldwide persona, and Jinnah was virtually unknown outside British India. Moreover, the popular media dramatized Gandhi's every action and they recorded his determined, often personalized efforts (for example, his many fasting episodes) to embarrass colonial authority. Jinnah's more elegant style evoked no such attention and he found himself in a zero-sum game with the Mahatma that he was destined to lose. Distressed by the failure of his reserved strategy, Jinnah retired from the political contest in the late 1920s and sought refuge in England. In so doing, he left the self-determination struggle to Mahatma Gandhi and the Congress Party. Jinnah found solace in the sedate English surroundings that had nurtured his early manhood, but he knew he had left the future of the subcontinent to be shaped by a frail man clad in a loincloth and carrying little more than a walking stick.

Jinnah and Gandhi and the struggle for a secular state

The Muslim League was organized in Dacca in 1906 as an immediate reaction to events in Bengal that had witnessed the formation of what was to be a short-lived Muslim-dominant province. In larger measure, the expansion of Muslim League influence was a direct response by concerned Indian Muslim leaders to the growing importance of political organizations such as the Indian National Congress, but even more so to the emergence of militant Hinduism. The Hindu Mahasabha violently opposed the Bengal partition and played a singular role in forcing the British to rescind their earlier order. Arguing against the formation of a Muslim-dominant province, the Mahasabha had launched a campaign of terror that took its toll of the innocent and enflamed communal passions. The Indian National Congress did little to thwart or condemn the perpetrators of social disorder in Bengal, and the Muslim League became further convinced of its need to speak for all of India's endangered Muslims.

Jinnah, without abandoning his membership in the Congress, joined the Muslim League in 1913 in a display of Muslim solidarity, but his instincts were aimed at identifying moderates in both parties who, like himself, wished to neutralize the extremists. Mindful of the prevailing bitterness between Hindus and Muslims, as well as their capacity for displays of uncontrolled violence, Jinnah saw no other option than for men and women of reason and education to stand, if necessary, with the colonial authority in the maintenance of law and order. Citing the prevailing conditions and the difficulties in restraining pent-up animosities, Jinnah forcefully opposed both Hindu and Muslim demagogues but saved his speechmaking and bridge building for the more erudite leaders who were demanding a share in the governance of India. For his consistency of effort and level-headed behavior Jinnah won the appellation "Ambassador of Unity" from both Hindus and Muslims.

The Lucknow Pact of 1916 was heralded as promoting Hindu–Muslim amity within the subcontinent. Fashioned and managed by Jinnah, the agreement between the Indian National Congress and the All-India Muslim League declared it the intention of both organizations to work toward common goals. Both eschewed violence and promoted the tranquility of India as fervently as they pursued shared government status with the colonial authority. The "Memorandum of the Nineteen," calling for a substantial measure of self-government, that was presented to the Viceroy's council by Hindu and Muslim notables was acknowledged to have been drafted at Jinnah's initiative. These moments would be recorded as the high point in Congress–Muslim-League cooperation.

An enormous British Indian army had been raised for battle in Europe during World War I. Thousands of Indians died in the trenches in France and Belgium, and an even greater number were wounded in the service of the Empire. Britain had promised its Indian subjects a degree of self-government in return for their war service, and the leaders of the political parties had reason to expect that pledge would be honored. British policy after the war, however, also sought to muffle opposition to British authority, and in 1919 this had resulted in the passing of anti-sedition acts. Instead of being granted more rights, Indians found themselves constrained and even oppressed under a colonial action known as the Rowlatt Act.

Jinnah saw Gandhi as chiefly responsible for this turn of events. Gandhi had returned to India in 1915 and had quickly moved to the forefront of the Congress movement. Hardly a year after the signing of the Lucknow Pact, the Mahatma introduced his *satyagraha* campaign of passive resistance, a mass movement that enlisted the poorest of India's peasants to oppose the British planter class. Arrested and jailed, Gandhi's popularity soared as he polished his program of open defiance to colonial authority. Gandhi symbols and actions appealed to essentially Hindu religious sensibilities and left the Muslim leaders wondering how they fitted into the larger scheme of independence. Jinnah was particularly distressed, having invested so much in the more secular argument that he hoped would nullify the influence of particularistic, and especially the more militant, religiously directed interest groups like the Hindu Mahasabha.

Gandhi, however, had captured the imagination of people far and wide. He was acknowledged as the leader of the spreading anti-imperialist struggle. Gandhi also challenged the might of the British-inspired industrial class. Moreover, Gandhi's preaching of non-violence did not prevent his followers from disrupting the colonial economy or closing down India's industrial centers. Labor strikes focused attention on poor working conditions, on long working hours for little pay, and on overbearing management that was indifferent to the plight of their workers. Work stoppages that lasted more than a year occurred in all the major cities. Sustained unrest and a variety of mob actions led directly to the Rowlatt Act of 1919. Rowlatt was aimed at containing the disturbances, but it had quite the opposite effect. Mass protests against the Act were immediate and widespread and virtually paralyzed the entire colony. Moreover, coming as it did, just months after the end of World War I, the Rowlatt Act was hardly what Indians anticipated after their contribution to the war effort.

The quest for Hindu–Muslim amity was swallowed up in the events that followed. Gandhi rejected Jinnah's accommodative strategy, asserting it served colonial interests, and a few short years after his return from South Africa the Mahatma turned India away from a more deliberate and patient course to one more revolutionary and bombastic. Gandhi addressed the issues of passive resistance, of *ahimsa* and non-violence, but he had enlisted the multitudes in his campaign and his mass movement unleashed intense bitterness against British authority. Jinnah could only look on with foreboding, seeing his dream for a transitional and methodical transfer of power dashed even before it had been set in train. The British crackdown on the Gandhi led and inspired demonstrations was forceful and crude, such as in the notorious Jalianwalabagh massacre.

Jinnah condemned Gandhi's tactics, but at the 1920 Nagpur session of the Indian National Congress, his was the only dissident voice against the Gandhian policy of non-cooperation. It now was apparent to Jinnah that the Congress no longer reflected the ideals of the liberal Congress leader Gopal Krishna Gokhale, who had died almost six years earlier. Gandhi, Jinnah argued, was leading India down the wrong channel, and was feeding the frenzy of the uninformed and emotional segments of the Indian population. By contrast, Jinnah believed the masses needed more deliberate leaders. Political education, he opined, would require years not months. If "Home Rule" were to be a positive experience, it must begin with a workable structure of governance that could be embraced by all those considered agents of change. In Jinnah's opinion, Gandhi's resurrection of traditional Hindu symbols could mobilize and energize but they could not prepare the people for responsible self-government.

Gandhi's objective was to outmaneuver and isolate Jinnah. Moreover, Gandhi had already extended his hand to the Muslims of the subcontinent distressed over the World War I defeat of the Ottoman Empire. The occupation of the Sublime Porte at Constantinople, site of the Islamic Caliphate, by combined European forces caused major distress among Indian Muslims. Arguing that he spoke for Muslims as well as Hindus, the Mahatma condemned the actions of the European imperialists, and in particular the British. Gandhi used the occasion to denounce the Montagu–Chelmsford Reforms that promised a degree of self-government. He was also critical of the Government of India Act of 1919, calling it little more than a colonial ruse aimed at sustaining the Empire. The dyarchy aspects of the 1919 Act gave the British Viceroy veto power over indigenous decision making and Gandhi decried the entire episode as a sham perpetrated by shameless opportunists. Gandhi never believed himself more justified in rallying the masses. His bona fides intact as a leader of all Indians, Gandhi also played a prominent role in the Caliphate Movement that Indian Muslims had organized with the goal of freeing the Ottoman Sultan/Caliph from European bondage. Gandhi's call was to the subcontinent's Muslims to give up their domicile and possessions in India. He urged them to do battle with the "heathen" that threatened Islam's holy places in the Arabian Peninsula and had made a captive of the Caliph of Islam. Gandhi's association with a key Muslim cause met with a positive response from tens of thousands of India's Islamic faithful. It also was meant to make him more popular with Muslims than Mohammad Ali Jinnah.

Jinnah had stood in opposition to the Caliphate Movement, which he argued was full of false promises. He saw Gandhi's tactics as deceptive and designed to deflect Muslims from the real issues. He also accused Gandhi and the Caliphate organizers of misleading an ignorant but emotionally charged people. So incensed was he that Muslims were being led astray by unscrupulous plotters within the Congress Party that he used this opportunity to quit his long-standing membership in the Indian National Congress. Jinnah shifted his own actions to mirror those of Gandhi. Long a proponent of open and fair elections, Jinnah had supported the competitive nature of elections and been critical of elections along communal lines. Now, however, he was prepared to adopt the 1909 Morley–Minto Reforms that called for separate electorates for the different religious communities. Jinnah's justification for this about-face was his disgust with the Gandhi-led self-rule strategy. Still a believer in the secular dimensions of national unity, Jinnah nevertheless was persuaded to address the more narrowly expressed Muslim causes. Events forced Jinnah to ponder the ineluctable and multiethnic character of Indian society. It was the beginning of a thought process that would lead inevitably to the articulation of his "two-nation theory," and the later justification for the creation of an independent Muslim state. Jinnah, however, had not yet given up the idea of a unified India nurtured by a developing civil society.

Once a secretary to Dadabhai Naoroji, a founder of the Congress Party, Jinnah was deeply committed to constitutional principles, and showed particular reverence for the legal process. He also condemned mass movements and street demonstrations, arguing they produced nothing in the way of meaningful change. His association with the Hindu militant and extremist B.J. Tilak, whom he represented in open court, centered on his affection for the law. His attachment to G.K. Gokhale, perhaps the staunchest believer in English liberalism, convinced him that goodwill and common cause could achieve impossible goals. Despite obvious differences between Hindus and Muslims, Jinnah was not swayed from the belief that, with good faith, Indian leaders of opposed persuasions could guide their followers along a common path of social progress and reform. Jinnah's essential goal remained the nurturing of a polity along democratic lines. This meant weaning the illiterate masses from the religious obscurantism so illustrated by the subcontinent's caste-ridden society and sectarian clashes. The evolution of the secular state was the *sine qua non* in the realization of a modern India, and for Jinnah the process could not be rushed, nor the British contribution ignored.

Jinnah's task was not only to inject a modicum of contemplation into the struggle for freedom; he had to convince members of the Muslim League that their patience and fortitude in the face of Gandhi's provocative actions were absolute requirements. Jinnah recognized a pressing need to learn the ways of modern self-government, and only the British example offered that experience. Gandhi's boycotting of the colonial councils had limited exposure to the nuances of contemporary administration. What Gandhi preached and taught was not constitutional limitations on the uses of power but rebellion and the rejection of authority. For Jinnah, therefore, mob rule was especially frightening. How might a polyglot, largely poor, and illiterate society find equilibrium when the British departed the scene? Without that balancing force, Muslims, Sikhs, Hindus, and others would be left to their own devices; and, without an appropriate understanding of the give and take of politics, how were the many nations that called India their home to find peace and harmony?

Jinnah's commitment to the rule of law informed him that only a legal structure, familiar and acceptable to the vast and diverse majority, offered the promise of an India renewed through democratic tradition. Neither Hinduism, nor Islam, nor Sikhism, nor any other strongly held faith was organized along lines conducive to progressive change. India would build its future along lines that allowed for the assimilation of all groups, large and small, or the subcontinent would shatter into its many divisions. Mere contemplation of such a consequence was too horrific to ignore. Jinnah therefore was forced to conclude that Gandhi's tactics could not go unchallenged.

Jinnah, however, could not do battle with the international media that were mesmerized by Gandhi's personality. The likes of Mahatma Gandhi had never been seen before. In the heyday of empire, the picture of a small, gaunt man, armed only with a walking stick, doing battle with the great British Empire was a story to be told. Sensational journalism had begun to emerge toward the end of the nineteenth century and it flowered after World War I. Gandhi was an intriguing character whose activities were documented in significant detail by the world press. Radio was in its infancy, but Gandhi's voice could be magnified in the most unlikely places. Moreover, the nascent movie industry was nurtured on short subjects and the early newsreels often depicted the Mahatma in many of his numerous ministrations. Thus, people in distant places may have known little about the more specific struggle for Indian freedom, but they quickly formed opinions about M.K. Gandhi. Gandhi's stubbornness had become so celebrated via the media that his very manner worked its way into common speech. It was not uncommon for children, defying their parents' authority, to be accused of acting like "Mahatma Gandhi." Having entered the popular consciousness, Gandhi had become a worldwide phenomenon as well as a symbol of popular resistance.

Gandhi's speeches and exploits were recorded by some of the most eminent American and European journalists and photographers of the period. By contrast, Jinnah received almost no attention outside the subcontinent. His cause was at best ignored. His actions too often led to the conclusion that he was little more than a lackey of colonial authority. Indeed, even among Muslims, notably those with dominant roles in the many different regions of the subcontinent, Jinnah was seen as either a threat or a nuisance. Regional leaders and virtual potentates had gained strength as a consequence of the Government of India Act of 1919. Power had devolved to the many local communities and authority was already well established within them when Gandhi emerged to lead the Home Rule campaign. Many Muslim leaders identified with Gandhi and the Congress Party. By contrast, they saw little connection between themselves and a Muslim League dominated by Mohammad Ali Jinnah.

Gandhi's campaign against the British colonial system could not be derailed. The Mahatma had taken control of the Home Rule League and had turned it into the *Swaraj* or freedom movement. Sidelined by these events, Jinnah took little part in political affairs in the early 1920s, or even after his election to the Central Legislative Assembly in 1923. Continuing his campaign for Muslim–Hindu unity, he received little attention and less interest from the Indian National Congress, now thoroughly a nationalist organization. In 1925, Jinnah assumed a role on the committee concerned with the Indianization of the colonial army and the establishment of a military training college in India similar to that of Sandhurst in Great Britain. Jinnah visited Britain to study first-hand the needs of such an institution, and on returning to India he was again elected to the Central Legislative Assembly. Jinnah labored in the cause of fair Muslim representation in any future constitutional system but still he received little if any attention from his counterparts in the Congress. In 1928, Sir John Simon led a group of parliamentarians to India to advise on subsequent reforms regarding self-government, but Jinnah saw little coming from their visit and shortly after the group's arrival he left India for England.

A despondent Jinnah took up domicile in the country that nurtured his intellectual soul, and there was little evidence he would ever return to India. Before his departure Jinnah had had one more major confrontation with Gandhi and the Congress at the Calcutta All-Parties Conference. Pleading for consideration of Muslim sensibilities, Jinnah warned the Congress leaders that ignoring minimum Muslim demands for representation in a future Indian government would have disastrous consequences. The Moltilal Nehru Report was before the conference during this confrontation and Jinnah noted its flawed framework in not giving appropriate recognition to the more than one hundred million Muslims residing within the country. In the end, however, all his demands and suggestions were rejected. Jinnah, in fact, faced verbal attacks from some of the conferees. It was made clear that they thought he neither represented the Muslims of India nor had the right to speak for them. It is reported that his sense of loss was so deep that he left the session without uttering another word. Jinnah could only conclude that he had witnessed more than the death of Hindu–Muslim unity. While he was in this state of depression Jinnah's young wife, only twenty-nine years old, died after a long illness.

One more activity, however, drew Jinnah's attention before he abandoned the political world altogether. Condemning the Simon Commission, Jinnah called upon the new British Prime Minister, Ramsay MacDonald, to assemble a conference in London so that India's political representatives could meet with British officials to discuss the future of India. The Round Table Conference of 1930 was a direct consequence of this action and Jinnah was one of fifty-eight delegates representing the subcontinent. Gandhi chose not to attend. The Aga Khan led the Muslim delegation and

Jinnah was appropriately respectful of his leadership. Lasting several weeks, the Round Table succeeded in establishing the principle of self-government for all of India's people, but further discussion was needed. Hence the decision was taken to assemble again some time in 1931. Jinnah remained in England when the conference ended and assumed the life of a barrister before the Privy Council Bar. His sister, Fatima, whom he had guided in her educational pursuits, joined him in London, and the two siblings became inseparable from that day forward. Miss Jinnah, as she was known, had left a dental practice to be with her brother. She became his principal confidante for the remainder of his life.

The second Round Table Conference convened in London in 1931. This time Gandhi attended, sensing something of importance might emerge that required his reaction. The British representatives addressed the issue of minority rights in an independent India and argued the need to resolve the communal problem before self-government was achieved. This was not what the Mahatma wanted to hear. Believing Britain was deliberately delaying the proceedings, the Congress delegation accused Whitehall of continuing its "divide and rule" policy by placating the Muslims. Seeing that the British Prime Minister presided over the minorities committee, and that the Aga Khan also was a prominent committee member chosen by the British, Gandhi lashed out against the colonial hypothesis that only a resolution of the Hindu–Muslim question could move the subcontinent toward independence. Gandhi insisted on the reverse order. He argued for the earliest British withdrawal so that the different communities could be free to find their own formula for social harmony. After one side's demands were rejected by the other, and after four difficult months of inconclusive wrangling, Gandhi abruptly left the conference and returned to India. The Round Table Conference dragged on another six months without resolving anything, and the only agreement was a general call for another session some time in 1932 or 1933. That conference never materialized.

Gandhi returned to India disgruntled and empty-handed. Civil disobedience was renewed, and strikes and protest meetings again paralyzed the country. The British government answered the demonstrators with even more repressive measures than earlier. Gandhi was again arrested. A Congress Party meeting was banned by the authorities and many Congress delegates were imprisoned. Jinnah observed the sustained conflict in India from his retreat in England, noting that it was a predictable outcome of the Round Table failure. Gandhi's appeal to the Hindu untouchables grew during this period. So too his effort at reaching out to the Christian community. It was also during this sequence that the violence-prone peasant movement spread to include the Indian south. Gandhi insisted on wearing the anti-feudal mantle, and his verbal attack on the landlord class won him still more adherents. So too his call for provincial autonomy gained the fancy of the Muslims in the North West Frontier. Followers of Abdul Ghaffar Khan found common cause with Gandhi, who had even demonstrated sympathy with the Khudai Khidmatgar's secessionist Pakhtunistan Movement.

Ghaffar Khan publicly announced his alliance with Gandhi. Their cooperative endeavor was also a sign that Hindus and Muslims could find common ground and that opposing British rule was at the heart of their joint struggle. Jinnah's tactics, it was said, were more about "divide and rule" than true unity. So intimate was the relationship forged by Gandhi and Ghaffar Khan that it was not long before the latter was being referred to as the "Frontier Gandhi." Alliances such as this one with the tribal Pushtuns placed the Congress firmly on the Afghan frontier, and in position to influence the Afghan monarchy in Kabul, which also had a vendetta against the British. The Muslim League had few supporters among the Pushtuns and Afghans, and Gandhi's tactics centered on neutralizing the League's claim to speak for all of the subcontinent's Muslims. Similar Congress activities penetrated the Muslim-dominant Punjab, where opposition to the Muslim League was nurtured by Congress support for the growing provincial Unionist Party. By the early 1930s, Jinnah, from his self-imposed exile in England, was forced to acknowledge that his quest for a unified, independent India, comfortable with constitutional principles as well as social and political pluralism, had to be abandoned.

The emergence of the Pakistan movement

Mohammad Iqbal is credited with the first serious reference to an independent Muslim state in the subcontinent. An acknowledged philosopher and poet, Iqbal cited the need for a separate Muslim homeland at the 1930 meeting of the Muslim League. Associated with Jinnah and moved by his legal and political work, Iqbal nevertheless questioned Jinnah's insistence on the unity of India. Iqbal's reasoning was simple. The Muslims had suffered ignominy following the abolition of the Mughal system in the nineteenth century, and British rule had revived the Hindus, who subsequently had organized themselves into a formidable political force. Moreover, Hindus had taken advantage of British offers of English education and had achieved considerable station within the colonial government. Muslim refusal to follow the Hindu example had caused the community to lose position in the colonial regime and by the twentieth century the economic and political gap between Hindus and Muslims had widened appreciably.

Arguing that neither the British formula nor the Jinnah notion of unity could lead to anything but civil war, Iqbal proposed the formation of a Muslim state to be forged from the Punjab, North West Frontier Province and the territories of Sind and Balochistan. Iqbal discussed his ideas with Jinnah during the latter's domicile in England but in the end they agreed to disagree. Moreover, Jinnah saw the issue of a separate Muslim state in the northwestern region of the subcontinent as a non-starter. Gandhi was the driving force in the effort to dislodge the British and he and the Congress Party were hardly prepared to yield to Iqbal's demand any more than they would adopt Jinnah's vision. Moreover, Congress alliances with the Khudai Khidmatgar in the North West Frontier Province and the Unionists in the Punjab had left the Muslim League with little leverage in those regions. Jinnah cautioned Iqbal not to provoke a war between Muslims, or else even the more limited gains obtained under British rule could be lost.

Jinnah acknowledged Iqbal's sentiments and understood the source of his philosophy. Still, he was inclined to look at the practical aspects of the Muslim problem and he could not envision a viable Muslim state as described by the renowned poet. Balochistan was still a wild, arid border region and Sindh had not yet been split off from the Bombay presidency. The North West Frontier Province was a rugged mountain area along the Afghan border, its inhabitants largely tribal, and, with the exception of a limited settled area around Peshawar, it was subject to no known central authority. Only the Punjab represented the contemporary world of South Asia and there the Muslims had to find communion with the Sikhs in addition to the resident Hindus. The more Jinnah pondered the idea of an independent Muslim nation comprised from such a mixture, the more he was convinced that his quest for national unity was the only option when the British left India. Indeed, Jinnah raised the issue of the remaining Muslim population inhabiting the subcontinent. Far more numerous then their brethren in the northwest, the Muslims of the Ganges plain extending into the eastern province of Bengal also needed to be factored into the thinking of those who would partition the subcontinent between Hindu and Muslim. Tens of millions of Muslims could not be ignored. Nor could they be accommodated within Iqbal's "independent" Muslim state. Struggle as he would with the notion of a Muslim majority state, Jinnah returned again and again to the need for a constitutional arrangement that would guarantee the interests of all the people of the subcontinent.

Jinnah assumed the life of an English gentleman, watched over by his sister. He endeavored to put the subcontinent behind him. In July 1933, however, the subcontinent appeared at his door in the person of Nawabzada Liaquat Ali Khan, a leader of the Muslim League whose residence in Delhi had doubled as the headquarters of the party. A graduate of Aligarh and Oxford, and a lawyer by training, Liaquat had turned to politics on a full-time basis after returning to India. Jinnah had only met Liaquat in 1928, when he was subjected to the stings of his detractors at the Calcutta Congress. Liaquat, twenty years Jinnah's junior, was impressed with his stolid and firm performance in the face of the harshest opposition. Liaquat had singled Jinnah out as the only one capable of reorganizing and breathing life into a deeply wounded Muslim League. Liaquat informed Jinnah that Gandhi had aroused the Hindu masses and had virtually no opposition in pressing his campaign. Muslims, he noted, had a greater sense of danger than ever before. Liaquat made convincing argument that the times called for an exceptional leader who could embrace the diversity of the subcontinent's Muslims. He insisted the only person fitting that role was Mohammad Ali Jinnah.

Reluctant to cut his ties to England but moved by Liaquat's plea, Jinnah agreed to return to India to see for himself if the

Muslims who claimed to need his leadership really wanted it. Liaquat did his homework before Jinnah's arrival, and arranged for a number of Muslim leaders to meet with him when he returned to India. Jinnah was moved by the positive reception, and sensed a new opportunity to reintroduce his thinking into the political scene. Gandhi's profile dominated the subcontinent and only a substantial Muslim personality could attract the attention of the millions of uncommitted Muslims. Only Jinnah was capable of straddling the Muslims of western and eastern India. Jinnah questioned his personal capacity, refused to yield to flattery, but in the end was prepared to assume the role destiny had again thrust in his path. Jinnah counseled his colleagues that the road would be difficult, but that if they worked together the Muslim League might yet take its place alongside the Indian National Congress.

Jinnah returned to England to terminate his practice before the Privy Council and to sell his home. In January 1935, he returned to India with his sister and took up the charge given him by the members of the Muslim League. The timing of his arrival in India was in large part a consequence of the King's Royal Assent to the Government of India Act of 1935 that granted more self-government. The Act signified a decline in British power and seemed to point to the future independence of India. It devolved more powers to the indigenous population, and eliminated dyarchy, but the center maintained special powers that were aimed at protecting the public peace. Federation was made the preferred structure for a unified India, but the many princely states, sensing their demise, rejected the arrangement. The number of Indian provinces increased to eleven and, in the Communal Award, India's minority population were apportioned seats in separate communal electorates. Moreover, no provincial ministry could prevent ministers being named from the minority parties.

Jinnah was not in agreement with the Award but believed it had to be accepted it in order to build a constitutional order. To demonstrate his desire to work the new system, Jinnah went to the Punjab, where Muslims and Sikhs clashed over the ownership of a mosque that had been seized by the latter community. With calm demeanor and an appeal to legal reasoning Jinnah successfully gained the understanding of the conflicted parties. It was his first test under the new system and he was buoyed by the welcome both he and his methods received from opposed Muslim and Sikh groups. Jinnah was therefore firm in the belief that his rational approach was more appropriate, and he became even more determined to challenge Gandhi's radical strategy.

Elections were forecast to give operational meaning to the 1935 Act. Congress had not waited for the passage of the Act, but as early as 1934 had set up a Parliamentary Board to formulate policy and select candidates. The Muslim League, by contrast, was slow to react and it was not until two years later that they created a similar body. Jinnah was made president of the League's Central Election Board and he had the task of enlivening the party and getting Muslims to leave their more familiar associations for membership in the League. The major challenge was in those areas where the Muslims were in the majority and where there was little fear of Hindu domination. The Muslim League's appeal would have to center on these populations. Moreover, Jinnah was of two minds. He believed the Muslim League was the only organization that had any chance of uniting all the Muslims of the subcontinent. On the other hand, he continued to believe that an Indian polity constructed over a firm constitutional foundation would guarantee a future India that was both united and democratic.

The immediate question, therefore, was how to represent the central purpose of the Muslim League when the essential goal was a unified, independent India, not different from that said to be the objective of the Congress Party. As already noted, the Congress appeared to be the preference of the Muslims of the North West Frontier Province and the Punjab. These provinces saw greater opportunities in a non-communal party, much like the one Jinnah had originally promoted. Adding to Jinnah's dilemma, Sind province was established in 1936 as a direct consequence of the 1935 Act. Its leaders also followed a course away from the Muslim League. In fact, it was only in Bengal, the remaining Muslim-dominant region, that Jinnah could expect a loyal following. Jinnah's major Muslim supporters therefore emerged from the Hindu-dominant regions of northern India. It was in those areas that the fear "Islam in Danger" was most pronounced. It was also there that the dominance of the Congress Party was most in evidence.

Jinnah's appeal to Muslims to join the League was further tasked upon his return from exile in England. Gandhi's passive resistance movement was now a mighty force, and the Mahatma was capable of shutting down the country at a single command. Assuming the role of a mystic and following a life of extreme asceticism, Gandhi had transferred the mundane chores of running the Congress to disciples, notably to Pandit Jawaharlal Nehru, the son of Moltilal, still a young and vibrant personality in his middle forties. Gandhi's age was no doubt a factor in his strategy. Believing it would be two or three years before Britain would consider releasing its Indian colony, Gandhi could not imagine taking the political helm of the new state. Grooming younger men for that task was imperative, and what better opportunity than the elections scheduled for 1937?

Jinnah made the mistake of underestimating Nehru. He also saw the Mahatma's action in pressing Nehru to the head of the Congress as either a clever ruse as cover for his own pre-eminence, or a failure of judgment. Jinnah later acknowledged his error. Thirty million people cast ballots in the 1937 election, thirty percent representing Muslim choices. When the votes were tallied the Muslim League was almost eliminated as a competitive organization. Under the separate electorate system the Muslim League garnered no more than five percent of the Muslim votes. By contrast, the Congress Party took control of almost all the provincial legislatures. Nehru's voice was heard throughout India when he declared that there were only two parties in the country, that is, the Indian National Congress and the British colonial authority. Jinnah had anticipated defeat, but not on such an ignominious scale. A weaker personality might have admitted defeat and moved on. Moreover, the Congress victory spoke to the issue of unity and the many Muslims who had voted for Gandhi's party had also demonstrated a desire for full integration. The League's loss was also Jinnah's loss and the future of the communal party, as Nehru had implied, was much in doubt.

Jinnah, however, had come too far to admit defeat. The country had voted for the Congress, but the question regarding constitutional order and a loyal opposition was still to be addressed. A separate, independent Muslim state was not the immediate goal, but a political organization that articulated the concerns and needs of Muslims was more needed than ever in the face of a Congress monopoly. Jinnah therefore drew inspiration from defeat and recognized the necessity of changing tactics. Jinnah decided he would be the voice of the subcontinent's Muslims even if the Muslim League were not the choice of the Muslim majority. Jinnah continued to represent the League but it was his personality that dominated Muslim thought and actions. Jinnah sought a role that transcended the Muslim League. He alone carried the party and in spite of its poor showing he insisted that the League be acknowledged as an "equal" partner with the Congress. Jinnah never intended to match the Congress in numbers and his call for a form of parity was more a qualitative response to the significance of the Indian Muslim minority. Jinnah's interpretation of events was audacious and unexpected in light of the election results. On the Congress side there were expressions of outrage. Nehru was among the first to cite the arrogance of the Muslim League leader who, though thoroughly defeated, would assume so defiant a posture.

The Congress argued that it was the only genuine national party and as such should control all the ministries in all the provinces. Muslims were offered opportunities to participate but only as Congress members, and with the understanding that the Muslim League would be disbanded. Jinnah's insistence that the Congress include League members in the government was brushed aside. Such a big winner in the elections, Congress was determined to proceed without the Muslim League. Jinnah and his colleagues perceived mortal danger in the Congress attitude. Everything seemed to confirm Muslim League fears that the Congress rhetoric stressing secularism was a mere cover for Hindu hegemony. The Muslim League fell back on its "Islam in Danger" theme, indeed with more justification than earlier. Jinnah was now more determined to take up the cause of Muslim rights. According to official Muslim League statements, the election revealed the true Hindu machinations. Jinnah also wanted the British to know that one hundred million Muslims had to be taken seriously no matter how many more Hindus resided in the subcontinent.

The Congress demonstrated superior organization, but it failed to address Muslim concerns, let alone aspirations. The moment called for stable and efficient authority, but it also required compassionate and sensitive leaders. Avoiding communal warfare was the highest priority. For the Muslim League separation seemed the only real alternative. Iqbal's perception of a Muslim state, carved from the Muslim majority areas of the subcontinent, was revisited. Jinnah was compelled to entertain the idea of partition, and the view that if it were done, it had better be done under British colonial auspices, not as a consequence of civil war. The campaign for an independent state was not what any of the parties had seriously contemplated, but it was now the dominating issue.

Gandhi and Nehru acknowledged that Jinnah was a resolute foe. Neither side was prepared to yield, however, and their stubborn posturing prevented the search for a workable solution. Gandhi described Jinnah's bellicose statements following the League's losses in the 1937 elections an "act of war." Jinnah cited Congress hysteria and its total lack of diplomacy. In this acrimonious environment, all the principals were oblivious to the storm clouds forming over the European continent. In 1938 the British Prime Minister, Neville Chamberlain, journeyed to Munich in an attempt to appease Adolf Hitler. Despite the pledges and capitulation, however, Germany could not be satiated. In September 1939 Germany invaded Poland, precipitating World War II. While Gandhi and Jinnah struggled over the issue of their independence, India suddenly found itself a belligerent in a worldwide conflict. Congress, however, refused to be committed to India's participation in the war without its formal approval and it ordered all its elected officials to quit their posts in the provincial governments. Gandhi resurrected the non-cooperation movement and took to the streets. Hard pressed on the war front, Britain was called to divert resources to law and order operations in the subcontinent.

Where the colonial authority saw increased danger, Jinnah read opportunity in the Congress call to abandon posts in the provincial governments. Jinnah called for celebration and declared a "Day of Deliverance" from Hindu tyranny. He also took the contrary position to that of the Congress and ordered his followers to do everything in their power to support the British war effort. Although Jinnah's position was read as submission to colonial power, tens of thousands of Indian Muslims heeded his command. Muslim League ranks swelled with new recruits, drawn particularly from student ranks. Jinnah wasted little time in indoctrinating the young members who soon became the vanguard of a revitalized Muslim League. The All-India Muslim Students Federation was a consequence of these events and branches of the organization sprouted all over the country.

Jinnah was now broadly acclaimed the Muslim peoples' "Great Leader," their Quaid-i-Azam. He also drew greater attention from the British government. Jinnah's declarations of support were welcome in Whitehall and Muslim assistance in the war translated into more serious consideration from the British Viceroy. Jinnah turned his sights from his fruitless struggle with the Congress to the British colonial government, recognizing that the leverage gained at the beginning of the war could return rich dividends when the hostilities finally ended. In 1937, a year before his death, Iqbal had called Jinnah the only person capable of saving the Muslims from a terrible fate. Jinnah had taken that responsibility to heart, and his strategy in the pursuit of an independent Muslim state now entered a critical phase.

A Government of India Amending Act passed the British parliament after the declaration of war against Germany. This was followed by a Defence of India Ordinance on September 3, 1939 in which the Viceroy was sanctioned the necessary power to rule India by decree. The colonial authority declared it would not tolerate street demonstrations or anything disturbing the public peace. The harshest penalties were reserved for those challenging authority and those who by their acts gave comfort and support to the enemy. The suspension of the Indian federation followed. Congress responded with its own declaration stating that it was opposed to German fascism but also would not relent in its campaign to remove the yoke of British imperialism.

Congress spokesmen insisted the 1935 election made it the voice of the Indian nation and that it alone expressed the true sentiments of all Indians. Indians, it was repeated, wanted no part in a European war, and the Congress intended to press that message worldwide. Congress, however, did not confine itself to public statements of policy. Protest meetings degenerated into street riots, causing numerous deaths and considerable destruction of property. Given the intensification of civil strife, the Viceroy summoned

Gandhi to demand that he call off those determined to further destabilize the colony. The Mahatma, however, had no intention of reducing the pressure. Given the opportunity, he repeated the Congress policy that India refused to be committed to a war not of its making or concern. War and peace, he counseled, must be a matter for the Indian people to decide. The British government did not have the right to impose a war on the nation and India's human and material resources could not be used for imperial purposes. Gandhi reiterated his belief that the imperial *status quo* could never be the objective of the war and that Congress could only reconsider its anti-war policy if Britain agreed to a date for its withdrawal from the subcontinent. The British government had long suffered Gandhi's stubborn behavior, but it now judged the Mahatma's inflexibility a threat to its war effort. Gandhi, however, refused to yield to entreaties or counter-threats or fear of imprisonment. He was convinced the time was right for India to regain its independence.

Jinnah, in sharp contrast to Congress leaders, offered the British his cooperation. The Muslim League was brought into line with wartime policy and in return for its support the party anticipated more intimate association with the colonial authority. The Viceroy noted the cooperation of the Muslim population and agreed to an expansion of his Executive Council to include Mohammad Ali Jinnah, whom the British now described as one of the colony's more popular leaders. Angry Congress leaders cited still another version of Britain's divide and rule policy, and condemned what they judged to be the reintroduction of the communal issue. In October 1939, the Congress ordered all serving officials to tender their resignations in the colonial government and to join in a countrywide action of non-cooperation. Jinnah heralded the moment as a turning point in the Muslim League struggle with the Congress, and with the 1937 election virtually nullified, fear of a "Congress Raj" had also dissipated. The Muslim League was renewed by these events. With newfound strength it began to prepare itself for future contests with the Congress Party.

Jinnah had crossed his personal Rubicon. It was no longer a question of melding Congress and Muslim League objectives. The two political movements had passed a crossroads and now trod very separate paths. Jinnah understood that his re-energized party, full of young cohorts, wanted nothing less than a self-governing Muslim country. His challenge was not whether or not he should press for an independent Muslim state, but what form it would take. Through it all Jinnah remained the essential pragmatist. He rejected anything even remotely related to the formation of a political order founded on the notion of an Islamic state. Jinnah's philosophy of politics and government highlighted the liberalism of the Western or European tradition. His thought rooted in constitutionalism and legal guarantees of fundamental rights, Jinnah sought the protection of the subcontinent's minority population and the weakest members of society. More secure in the belief that such could not be realized in a unified India, Jinnah now turned his attention to a more exclusive national context, even if that meant pressing ahead with the partition of India.

Congress officials saw Jinnah's actions and statements as anti-democratic and authoritarian. By supporting the colonial authority he had virtually denied the freedom movement. In hinting at partition he had fallen in with separatists calling for the vivisection of the subcontinent. Jinnah of course saw his actions in a different light. The colonial experience had elevated people from conventions that were not only archaic, but also anarchic. Hindus could not be expected to conform to Muslim traditions, nor were Muslims capable of associating themselves with Hindu rituals and precepts. Britain had come to dominate India because it brought a different philosophy of rule and, more importantly, a system of law that could be applied uniformly to all, irrespective of separate lifestyles and cultural practices. Colonialism was demeaning but it also had a constructive side in an environment where a diverse people had demonstrated an inability to find common identity. For all its alien character, there was in the British experience an opportunity for people at variance with one another to transcend their differences and, in the course of events, to accommodate one another. The British had in fact introduced the notion of civil society to the subcontinent's people. For Jinnah it was now a question of finding the structural and procedural underpinnings for the formation of such a civil society. Civil society for Jinnah preceded full-blown democracy. Without a foundation based on civil society, democracy was little more than a sham perpetrated by either fools or demagogues. Thus, late in 1939 the Muslim

League, under Jinnah's command, passed a resolution of satisfaction with the Viceroy's statement concerning the loyalty of the monarchy's subjects. As League president, Jinnah gave the colonial government the League's "fullest assurance of cooperation" in the pursuance of the war.

For the Congress this was nothing less than capitulation. Gandhi personally pleaded with Jinnah to call off "Deliverance Day" activities, to silence negative statements directed against the country's Hindus, and to open a new round of conversations with the Congress. But events had already outdistanced calls for cooperation. The Congress could not abandon its anti-war position, and the Muslim League was too committed to the idea of a separate Muslim homeland to accept the idea of a unified state. The ground was now prepared for the Muslim League convention in Lahore, where on March 23, 1940 a resolution was passed that called for the formation, in the not too distant future, of a Muslim state or states where the Muslims were the majority.

Muslim leaders from the Muslim-dominant provinces, who earlier had identified with their own provincial or regional parties, now found reason to join the Muslim League. Sikandar Hyat Khan, a Punjabi with a reputation for independent thought and action, Fazlul Huq, the "Tiger of Bengal," and Mohammad Saadullah of Assam were in attendance. All had asked members of their respective parties to join the League. Jinnah was now their acknowledged leader in the national struggle with the Congress, and it came as no surprise when Jinnah chose Fazlul Huq to propose the Lahore (Pakistan) Resolution before this great east–west assembly of Muslims. The resolution was deliberately left ambiguous. There had been a number of publicized schemes for a Muslim or Islamic state in the subcontinent. Rehmat Ali, the student who in 1933 invented the name "Pakistan" while studying in Britain, had founded the Pakistan National Movement in that same year. In 1940 he published a pamphlet titled "The Millat of Islam and the Menace of Indianism" in which he called for the creation of a Pak Commonwealth. The Commonwealth idea seemed to replicate the long-defunct Mughal Empire. Jinnah, however, would have none of such schemes. His general policy was aimed at restraining the more rabid among his followers while maintaining an idea of a self-governing Muslim entity which said little about Islamic guidelines and much about the need to establish a contemporary secular nation-state.

The geographic structuring of the Muslim state or states began to take form with the Sir Abdullah Haroon Committee, which met to finalize its work in November 1940. The committee called for the formation of a Muslim state in the northwestern portion of India and another in the northeast. It also left the impression that the Nizam of Hyderabad, although ruling over a predominantly Hindu population, would be given consideration as the leader of a third Muslim region. Jinnah, however, was unprepared for any precipitous action that left him with little room for maneuver. A realist, he recognized that pie-in-the-sky propositions only made it more difficult to negotiate change with the colonial authority, as well as the Congress Party. Jinnah had adopted the two-nation theory as his own, but the timing was not right to declare the unity of India an impossible objective. At least not until such time as all the parties had agreed to a mutual parting of the ways and guarantees were in place to protect the innocent who would be caught between opposed forces in the great divide.

Although opinion would be forever divided on who was most responsible for the partition of British India, Jinnah wanted it known that he had fought for a united India to the last, not under a particular flag, but as one completely committed to the rule of law. Much has been made of Jinnah's late-hour rejection of a federal scheme for India that would leave it with a strong center. It is suggested that Jinnah was concerned that a Hindu majority would so dominate the center that the Muslim periphery would never reap the harvest of development. What is clear is not Jinnah's denial of a strong center in a federal system, but rather the plight of the minority, no matter how secure regionally, under the subcontinent's overriding viceregal tradition. In other words, Jinnah was looking for the safeguards in a federal system that would protect the minorities from the majority's arbitrary use of power. Confidence-building measures had not fared well in the struggle for Indian freedom, and indeed the struggle had been more a matter of internecine strife than of skirmishes with the colonial government.

Jinnah preferred a more measured pace in contrast to his followers who enthusiastically attempted to rush events to a conclusion. Jinnah sensed the need for time. Even the envisioned

Muslim state would require the blending of a variety of cultures, aspirations, and mindsets in the several Muslim majority areas. Provision also needed to be made for Muslims remaining in India as well as Hindus and Sikhs who would fall within the Muslim state. The vast majority of people residing in all areas of the subcontinent were undereducated or illiterate, so fashioning a workable polity from the impoverished many and the few enlightened or materially advantaged people of the subcontinent was an incredible challenge. Events, however, did not favor Jinnah's patient approach. The wars in and outside India were creating a scenario that Jinnah could neither control nor direct. Like so many other high-positioned actors, he was conditioned and influenced by events, hardly their master.

The British role in the emergence of Pakistan

Two wars buffeted British India in the early 1940s. One was the global contest that allied Germany and Japan against the British Empire, and the other was the struggle to free India from the colonial grasp of a distant European power. Of the two, the latter was the far more complicated because it involved the long-term future of the subcontinent and the nadir of the British Empire. The war had not gone well for the British. Forced to retreat in the Pacific and Asia, the Empire had been made to yield its colonies stretching from Hong Kong to Malaya and Singapore, to Burma and the borders of India. The Japanese advance had been as swift as it was methodical. The British fleet had been virtually neutralized as a successful fighting instrument, and the combined British colonial forces were unable to prevent Japan from leapfrogging into South Asia. Only the entry of American forces into the war after the Japanese attack on Pearl Harbor in December 1941 offered the British a ray of hope that their fortunes might yet be saved. In the European theater of conflict, Britain had been left to fight Germany alone when France surrendered. Again it was only the assistance provided by the United States that offered a glimmer of hope, despite a heroic defense of the British Isles by the Royal Air Force.

With Britain on the defensive worldwide, the colonial authority in India was in a difficult position to ward off demands for independence. The Congress, however, was especially troublesome because of its anti-war program. Gandhi did not suspend his campaign, but, to the contrary, increased the pressure. It was not extraordinary for people in high position to question Britain's capacity to fight a successful war against the Axis powers. In India, the Congress, Gandhi included, had decided early on that Britain would indeed lose the contest and thus would be forced to give up its colonies, notably those already overrun by the Japanese army. In some Indian circles the approaching Japanese were to be considered liberators, and at the very least they would force the British to yield their South Asian possession sooner than expected. At the extreme, there was the old Congress leader Subas Chandra Bose, who linked up with Japanese forces in Southeast Asia to form the Indian National Army (INA), raised largely from captured Indian army troops. His accidental death did not end that scheme but without him the plan eventually fizzled. If nothing more, the attempt to create an INA to serve alongside Japanese forces illustrated the effort some Indians made to terminate British rule in the subcontinent.

Britain's determined resistance, combined with major benefits derived from American and Soviet victories, ultimately saved the Empire. Nevertheless it was obvious London would have to give serious consideration to yielding its most prominent possessions. With Winston Churchill at the helm of Britain's war policies, in 1942 Sir Stafford Cripps was sent to India to discuss the Indian question. Cripps cited the Japanese advance through Southeast Asia and the Dutch Indies and its penetration of Burma as posing a direct threat to both Australia and India. Gandhi's campaign of civil disobedience also had an echo in the speeches of the popular ascetic Vinoba Bhave. Their combined tactics had seriously undermined the British war effort, especially as troops scheduled for the war with Japan had to be diverted to police the local scene in India. Churchill, no friend of the Mahatma, would publicize later his belief that Gandhi had stabbed Great Britain in the back.

Jinnah and the Muslim League did not break their resolve to support the colonial authority, however. While sustaining their call for a Muslim homeland, Jinnah's followers did not adopt the Axis cause and many Muslims served faithfully in the imperial army.

The same could be said of Hindu units, but there was no mistaking British policy to favor the Muslim soldiers after the losses suffered in Southeast Asia and the subsequent formation of the INA. Congress Hindus verbalized their disgust with Muslim League tactics, which were described as disingenuous and meant only to reap advantages in their quest for an independent Muslim state. Declaring the Muslim League a fascist organization and indicating it could do nothing to enhance the British role in India, Congress leaders called upon Britain not to be fooled by a party of "weaklings." With the dialog between the two major Indian parties at a new level of bitterness it was questionable how the Cripps mission could ease conditions and, at the very least, get the Congress to call off its program of disruption.

Cripps, Lord Privy Seal of the Empire and a member of the British War Cabinet, brought with him a set of proposals that called for the earliest realization of the goal of self-government for India. The object of the proposals was the establishment of a new Indian Union that would constitute India as a dominion within the British Empire. India in effect would receive the same treatment as the other dominions, e.g. Canada and Australia, which meant taking charge of its domestic and external affairs in return for a demonstration of allegiance to the Crown. Much of what Cripps offered, however, would not take effect until the war had ended and peace had been restored. Pending those events, India would elect a body that would be charged with framing a constitution for the entire country. His Majesty's government would also call for the participation of India's princely states in these constitutional deliberations.

The proposals also focused attention on the demands made by the Muslim League when it specified that non-acceding, i.e. the Muslim-dominant, provinces might desire to form their own constitution-making body. In other words, Cripps wanted it known that his government was duty bound to protect the rights of all racial and religious minorities and, in so doing, to permit them to establish a political edifice more suitable to their needs. If in fact the Muslim provinces decided on a separate course, it would be left to the newly created Indian Union, obviously under Congress leadership, to negotiate a settlement that would be mutually acceptable to all the parties.

Congress reaction to the Cripps proposals was swift and negative. In their collective judgment Britain continued to play divide and rule politics and the party let it be known it would not accept the proposals. Within a period of less than three weeks, Cripps announced the failure of his mission. Noting that he never had suggested supporting the Pakistan demand, that he continued to believe in a united India, he nevertheless let the Congress and Muslim League leaders understand that the Empire was engaged in a great war and that the defense of India could not be left in indigenous hands. The Congress position was clearly stated. If Britain insisted on a dominant role in India, Pakistan was likely to be ceded to the Muslims, Khalistan would be created for the Sikhs, and even India's depressed castes might be offered autonomy. The British purpose, it was said, was nothing less than the vivisection of the subcontinent. Congress critics of the Cripps proposals pointed to the fact that a Constituent Assembly would be created to write a constitution and it would be formed on the basis of separate electorates, the reservation of seats for women, tribal people, etc., and, not less important, restricted franchise.

The Cripps proposals did not please any of the arrayed groups. The Hindu Mahasabha was totally opposed. So too the Sikhs. They failed to see their objectives realized, especially if the Muslims were given first consideration in territories they jointly inhabited. But even the Muslim League had its doubts. The execution of all the features of the proposals would hardly grant the Muslims the security they desired against a Hindu-dominated government. Jinnah declared in an Allahabad session of the Muslim League that the proposals would keep "the Musalmans tied to the chariot-wheel of Hindustan." Therefore, when Cripps left India for Britain the proposals were withdrawn. Although some of the items were to be revisited at a later date, the mission had had an entirely negative effect on Indian politics. The major communities were even more at loggerheads, more prone to do violence to one another, and most reluctant to consider a compromise formula that might bridge their differences.

Subsequently, the Congress Working Committee passed a resolution on July 14, 1942 demanding the immediate withdrawal of British power from the subcontinent. Displaying no concern about the Japanese penetration of Assam and Bengal, the Congress leaders had obviously concluded that Japanese pressure would accelerate the British withdrawal, leaving the Indians to sort out their future. If Congress projections proved accurate, in the absence of the British Raj the Muslim League would lose its purpose and the demand for Pakistan would be muted. But for the Congress to believe that Britain had had enough of its South Asian colony, or that the British imperial army would surrender to Japan, was ludicrous. Moreover, an American force was beginning to operate in Burma, and another was feverishly constructing a road to China. The Allied forces in the Pacific in July 1942 had launched their first serious engagement against Japanese bases in the South Pacific and the battle for Guadalcanal had signaled the start of a counter-offensive that was destined to move toward the Japanese islands.

The Allies had created the China–Burma–India theater of operations and Lord Louis Mountbatten had been established as its commanding officer. Britain had fallen back from Singapore and Rangoon but its new resistance point was Calcutta. The Royal Air Force had established a presence in the city's downtown area from where it launched raids against Japanese positions and, more significantly, defended India's skies from Japanese air attacks. If the Indian National Congress anticipated Britain would yield India as it had Malaya they were badly mistaken. The conflict was far from over and with stretched supply lines Japan would find it rougher going making war in eastern India. Significantly, the Japanese advance through Asia stalled at India's eastern borders and, though the Congress might sustain its civil disobedience campaign, the future of India would wait on the termination of hostilities as Cripps had indicated earlier.

The quest for Pakistan took on more credibility following the failure of the Cripps mission. At the same time the Congress Party more vehemently rejected all discussion about a separate Pakistan state. Joined by Shyama Prasad Mookerjee and his Hindu Mahasabha, the Congress agreed to send key members to different regions of the country to preach defiance of any British order that would seriously consider secessionist movements. Mookerjee had a long history of inciting fear among Muslims, and his position alongside the Congress did nothing to reduce the feeling of foreboding felt by Muslims in different areas of the subcontinent.

The Mahasabha leader said that nothing would be permitted to stand in the way of India's progress toward independence and that his organization would resist any attempt to transform the country into a chessboard of rival enclaves.

Jinnah was perceived as riding a strong wave of British support. His critics accused him and his aides of the intoxication that comes from too much power. Jinnah's demand for one-third Muslim representation on India's Executive Council and Chaudhri Khaliquzzaman's comment that Pakistan was only the beginning of a process of greater Muslim power from South to Southwest Asia were offered as evidence. Hindus were put on notice that if the Muslim League were allowed to succeed, Hindu India would be reduced to a small island in a vast Muslim sea. Mutual fears therefore influenced the course of events. Each side envisaged the worst if the other achieved its desired goal, and few among the principals in this drama were prepared to give ground or seek compromise.

When the tide of war turned in favor of the Allied cause, Congress protestations against the colonial authority waned rapidly. Civil disobedience was still a formidable Congress weapon but the British were in an improved position to cope with the situation, and the question of independence had become the question of what form independence would take. The major Congress concern was the leverage gained by the Muslim League in the course of the war. Informed opinion more and more held the position that Britain was certain to partition the colony between Hindus and Muslims, or at least between the two most vocal of the national organizations, the Indian National Congress and the Muslim League. Gandhi had made his case for Indian freedom; about that there was no real debate in Whitehall. The remaining question was what to do with Jinnah's demand for a separate Muslim majority state, the country that all now referred to as Pakistan.

From 1942 until the end of World War II in 1945, Jinnah and his colleagues offered numerous dissertations on the reasons for establishing Pakistan. History and culture were only part of the argument. The attempt to achieve the unity of Hindus and Muslims had been strenuously pursued without success. Too much had happened since Gandhi had returned from South Africa during

World War I. The subcontinent had been transformed. Popular movements had sprung up throughout the country and demands were now legion from numerous organizations across an expanded political spectrum. Few movements could be treated seriously, and even fewer could be given serious consideration if the character of the subcontinent were to be preserved. Moreover, too much blood had been shed in maintaining the Empire, and even at that moment of its certain dissolution the British hoped that retreat could be made with dignity. The freeing of the colonies was seen in the course of events, but so too was the formation of the Commonwealth that would bind the new states to one another and, most important, to the once and future mother country.

The Labor government under the leadership of Prime Minister Clement Attlee had replaced Churchill's wartime government in 1945. The war in the Pacific had not yet ended. One of Attlee's first acts, however, was to declare his intention to give India its freedom. The Viceroy, Lord Wavell, was recalled to London for direct discussions with his superiors about the manner of the transfer of power and when it might be feasible. Wavell returned to India with a set of proposals that were described as the "Wavell Plan." The plan called for the creation of a new Executive Council that was fully representative of India's principal communities and that would include an equal proportion of caste Hindus and Muslims. Finance, home and foreign affairs were to be made Indian concerns, and Britain agreed to appoint a High Commissioner (an ambassador) in India, thus giving the country virtual sovereign status. The newly constituted Executive Council would be expected to give its full support to the continuing war against Japan, and would assume the role of an interim government until such time as a permanent constitution was drafted and promulgated. To implement the proposals the Viceroy called a meeting of representatives from a variety of organizations to meet at the hill station of Simla on June 25, 1945. Lord Wavell also announced the release of incarcerated Congress Working Committee officials, as well as those imprisoned as a consequence of the Quit India Movement.

Jinnah had pondered the meaning of the Labor Party takeover in Britain. He did not have the same relationship with Attlee that he had developed with Churchill. Nor was Attlee as sensitive to the Muslim role in the war. He therefore began to see signs of betrayal in the Wavell Plan, not in the matter of India's independence, but in how the Muslims were to be safeguarded in a country controlled and dominated by Hindus. Fearful that British tactics were aimed at dividing the Muslims and turning them against themselves, Jinnah insisted on speaking for all the subcontinent's Muslim population. He therefore demanded the right of the Muslim League to nominate all Muslims serving on the Executive Council. Lord Wavell, however, refused to entertain such power being granted to a single organization. As Viceroy, he insisted on his right to name the representatives, but Jinnah refused to be sidetracked.

Jinnah's intransigence was a response to the Congress decision to appoint Muslims to the Executive Council, a policy that Jinnah believed was still another version of "divide and rule." Maulana Kalam Azad, a Congress leader of vast reputation and a Gandhi follower of long standing, accused Jinnah of dictatorial practices. So too did Malik Khizar Hayat Khan Tiwana, the Unionist leader in the Punjab, who found Jinnah's demand an outrageous declaration and beyond the pale of democratic behavior. Such Muslim voices were aimed at the British as much as they were directed toward Jinnah. The Muslim League leader would have to expect stiff opposition to his claim that he spoke for all Muslims. Although blame for the breakdown of the Simla conference was directed at Jinnah, it also could be said that the Congress was not disturbed by that breakdown. The Wavell Plan, by giving numerous organizations a place on the Executive Council, reduced the Congress's representation, but the party's political role was little diminished. The Congress in fact was even more ready to do business with the Crown.

Lord Wavell's continuing discussions in London led to the second Wavell Plan, but it was even less successful than the first and was rejected by all the parties. In February 1946 the Attlee government tried yet again. What was described as a "Cabinet Mission," led by Lord Pethick Lawrence and including Sir Stafford Cripps and A.V. Alexander, First Lord of the Admiralty, journeyed to India for the purpose of finding a formula for an Indian constitution. Nehru's immediate reaction was less than positive. He called upon the British to declare India's independence.

A constitution could be drafted later. Jinnah on the other hand voiced his opposition to a single constitution-making body. Despite this early opposition, however, the Cabinet Mission remained optimistic, and efforts were launched to speak openly and frankly with an array of Indian leaders representing different regions as well as cultures and political interests. The talks, however, were reduced to the principals, Gandhi and the Congress leaders insisting they could not accept the partition of India, and Jinnah arguing there could be no other solution. Despite the impasse the Cabinet Mission persisted and finally agreed to focus its attention on the Congress and the Muslim League. Another call went out to meet at Simla in what was described as a tripartite conference that would include the two major parties and the British government. Like the previous Simla meeting, however, this one too failed to examine the issues before it was disbanded.

Not willing to accept yet another failure, the Cabinet Mission and the Viceroy presented their own plan for the transfer of power. Their plan called for a Union of India that embodied all of the country, including the princely states. The Union would be responsible for foreign affairs, defense, communications, and finance, and its executive institution and legislature would be constituted along parliamentary lines. Questions arising in the legislature involving the communal issue would have to be resolved by a majority of the representatives from both the Hindu and Muslim communities, as well as a majority of all members present and voting. Powers not granted the Union would devolve to the provinces. Princely states would likewise retain those powers not considered Union subjects. Constitutional issues engaging the Union and the provinces or the Union and the states would be subject to review after ten years, and each ten-year period following. The Cabinet Mission then called for the formation of a constitution-making body that would be drawn from the recently elected provincial legislatures. Each province was to be allotted seats in proportion to its population.

As constitution making moved forward, an interim government was to be formed with full powers to direct government policy. The system envisioned was essentially unitary; the hope being that Hindus and Muslims could find common ground based on the principal of secularism and that there would be no need to pursue the idea of separate states drawn along communal lines. Pethick-Lawrence referred to the nightmare of dividing the subcontinent into Hindu and Muslim dominant regions. Pakistan, he asserted, could not be formed without including a forty-percent Hindu minority within its borders. Citing the Muslim majority in Bengal, Pethick-Lawrence was quick to point out that Calcutta, the great commercial metropolis, was populated by far more Hindus than Muslims. Also puzzling to the Cabinet Mission was the status of the Indian army that had just distinguished itself in World War II.

Partitioning the subcontinent also meant dividing the Indian army. How might India be defended if the army was divided and one section was given control of strategic areas to the detriment of the other? In summary: the Cabinet Mission appeared to reject the establishment of Pakistan while at the same time allowing the individual provinces a considerable amount of latitude in deciding whether to accept or reject the idea of Union.

On June 6, 1946, the Muslim League Council, to the surprise of many, accepted the Cabinet Mission scheme. It agreed to join the constitution-making body with the understanding that the provinces retained the option to abandon the Union under terms specified earlier. Much was made dependent on the final determination of the constitution-making effort. Jinnah also accepted the proposed interim government and insisted on the observance of a formula for parity between the Congress and the Muslim League. The Congress was already on record opposing parity. In fact, the Congress had further reason to oppose the Cabinet Mission plan. Separate electorates were sustained against Congress objections. The Congress also found the Viceroy's decision to prevent the Congress from appointing Muslims to the interim government unacceptable. These decisions were made to appease Jinnah, complained Congress officials, and they would not accept them. When the Viceroy announced his list of members for the interim government on June 16, none of the Congress complaints had been addressed. The Muslim League had been given parity with the Congress and all the Congress members were either Hindus, Sikhs or Christians. As a consequence, more Muslims were appointed than Hindus. Congress therefore announced it could not support the interim government and would not serve in it. Congress did agree to participate in the

Constituent Assembly, however, and hoped thereby to introduce a political order that was more consistent with its ideology and practices.

The colonial government declared its satisfaction that a constitution-making body would be established, but without prior warning reversed its original position. It declared it had decided to bypass the interim government idea in favor of a caretaker unit until such time as the constitutional issues were resolved. Jinnah saw still another betrayal in the British action. Lord Wavell was accused of having backed away from an earlier statement that the interim government would be formed even if only one of the two parties agreed to its terms. Moreover, Jinnah had believed that his discussions with the Viceroy and the members of the Cabinet Mission had resulted in firm agreement. Under the terms of the original understanding, Congress rejection and Muslim League approval meant the latter would form the interim government. Wavell, however, had reneged on his pledge. Instead he called upon Nehru to form the interim government with or without Muslim League compliance. The only conclusion Jinnah could draw was that Wavell had gone too far in placating the Muslim League and that the Attlee government was duty bound to go with the Congress.

Jinnah was devastated. When Nehru subsequently asked Jinnah to join his caretaker government, the Muslim leader angrily declined. The Cabinet Mission proposals had been turned on their head. In the final analysis, the Congress was provided *carte blanche*. The Muslim League was left with the option of either joining Nehru's administration or leaving the field to its rivals. After further discussions with the Viceroy, the League agreed to join Nehru's cabinet on a limited basis. Liaquat Ali Khan, I.I. Chundrigar, Sardar Abdur Rab Nishtar, Ghazanfar Ali Khan, and Jogendarnath Mandal (a Hindu) accepted portfolios in the name of the League. The decision of the League to assume roles in the government, however, did not extend to participation in the Constituent Assembly. The League boycotted these sessions, thus making constitution making impossible.

Observing the failure of all efforts at compromise, Prime Minister Attlee, with advice from members of his Cabinet Mission, decided that nothing Britain could do would bring the parties together. Britain at this time, so soon after the termination of hostilities, was burdened by the daunting task of clearing the rubble and reconstructing its cities after six years of conflict. The Empire's economy needed priming, and a way of life was in dire need of rehabilitation. A victim even more than a victor in the war just ended, Britain also was in a poor position to administer its possessions. India had been Britain's proudest conquest, but the subcontinent was ablaze from one end to the other with unrestrained mobs seeking advantages from a weakened imperial system. Anarchy was not uncommon, especially in Bengal. In 1946, the Muslim League observed "Direct Action Day," and set off displays of lawlessness seldom experienced in the volatile subcontinent. Looting and murder in Calcutta spread into the Bengal hinterland and produced the atrocities visited upon Noakhali and other locations.

Gandhi made a personal visit to Noakhali but his attempt at pacification proved fruitless. Killings ranged over Bihar province, into Uttar Pradesh, and fueled violence in Punjab as well as on the North West Frontier. Those seeking a simple explanation for the mayhem placed responsibility on Jinnah and the Muslim League, but it was also obvious that the weighty events of the prior decades were piled too high over a much weakened colonial edifice. British authority was either too feeble or too indifferent, and it failed to take the actions necessary to quell the disorder. Concluding that it could no longer keep the peace or broker a compromise formula acceptable to all the parties, London finally bowed to pressure and announced it had decided to break up the Empire. With something resembling a lament, on February 20, 1947, Attlee declared his government would transfer power to the Indian people at the earliest possible date. Britain in fact had made plans to leave India no later than June 1948. Lord Wavell was ordered back to London and Lord Earl Mountbatten was named the new and last Viceroy of India.

Mountbatten wasted no time in warning the Congress and Muslim League leaders that any further delay in arriving at a constitutional settlement would leave him with no other option than to determine how and in what manner the final transfer of power would take place. Moreover, Mountbatten was eager to expedite the process. Patience exhausted, Moutbatten quickly announced that the date for Britain's withdrawal had been changed at his order. Instead of June 1948, the transfer and retreat would occur in August 1947. Unprepared for this change in schedule and fearing another reversal, Jinnah again issued a call for "Direct Action." This time there would be no ambiguities. The call was for the formation of an independent Pakistan.

Conditions again were explosive as mobs took to the streets attacking members of rival religious and ethnic groups. Numerous atrocities occurred in the name of divine sanction. Law and order was virtually impossible to maintain. Again, responsibility for the slaughter and destruction centered on the actions of the Muslim League, and especially Mohammad Ali Jinnah. Many organizations were affected by the Mountbatten decision, however. More than the League had a stake in the future India and the Viceroy had left so little time to register so many interests. Among the major claimants to power were the Sikhs. Playing a significant role in the Punjab, the Sikh Akali Dal challenged the Muslim claim to dominate the Punjab. Moreover, the Muslim League had only recently substituted themselves for the Unionists, and the Sikhs accused the League of manipulating the Sikhs' Punjabi identity. The Sikhs therefore insisted on a homeland of their own, a place they called "Khalistan." The Balkanization of the subcontinent was not what the British had in mind. The Sikhs were denied a separate state. Confronted with the choice of living in either a Hindu- or Muslim-dominant country, the Sikhs rebelled but vented virtually all their anger against Punjabi Muslims.

Having only assumed the office of Viceroy on March 24, by June 3, 1947 Mountbatten had seen and heard enough to convince him to make short work of his commission. The Viceroy announced the methods for the transfer of power in a broadcast to the nation. In so far as Hindus and Muslims could not be reconciled, the areas where the Muslims were in the majority would be allowed to form a separate dominion. A Constituent Assembly would be created for that dominion, but first the colonial authority would divide the provinces of Punjab and Bengal so that Hindu- and Sikh-dominant regions would fall within the Indian Union. In other words, the eastern Punjab, which stretched from Amritsar to a region close to the Indian capital, would be denied to Pakistan. By the same token, Calcutta and West Bengal would be awarded to India. Frontiers were to be completed in the shortest possible time. In the case of the North West Frontier Province, which earlier had elected a Congress government, the Viceroy ordered the holding of a plebiscite to gauge the will of the Pashtun people. Finally, the Assamese territory of Sylhet, because of its Muslim character, was to be merged with Bengal if agreed by a popular referendum. Boundary commissions were to be established almost immediately to define the frontiers between the two new dominions of India and Pakistan. By the order of the Viceroy, India was given immediate dominion status.

Few celebrated Mountbatten's decisions. The Congress saw only distress in the "vivisection" of the subcontinent. More extreme nationalists perceived unending conflict. Muslims found much to question in the formation of a "truncated and moth-eaten" Pakistan. Whatever the politicians had intended by their long, arduous struggle, it clearly was not reflected in the Viceroy's announcement. Too little time and too much hatred prevented the major actors from arriving at a better formula. Faced with a *fait accompli*, they could only stumble into an uncertain future. In the end, it was a distant European power that determined the fate of the subcontinent's multitudes. Sir Cyril Radcliffe was rushed from London to Delhi to chair the two territorial commissions that determined the division of Punjab and Bengal, and the British parliament approved the India Independence Bill on July 1, 1947 without a single dissenting vote. On schedule, Great Britain terminated its rule over the subcontinent and in two ceremonies transferred authority to the Indian National Congress and the Muslim League on August 14–15, 1947. With the India Independence Act approved by the British parliament, not only India and Pakistan were established as sovereign, independent dominions. The rulers of the princely states, more than six hundred of them, were also given the option of declaring their independence.

Defining the Pakistan ethos

India and Pakistan were a consequence of unresolved conflict between the very recipients of the transfer of power. The colonial institution, by contrast, departed India in grand style, without a display of anger, and with much ceremony and pomp. Unlike in other colonies gaining independence following World War II, national self-determination was never clearly defined in the Indian subcontinent. Independence did not arrive at the end of a colonial war of liberation. The triangular character of the struggle for freedom was more an internal test of strength between two major indigenous contenders, one of which was prepared to wait upon the evolution of events while the other was determined to achieve self-government at the earliest moment. There also were numerous lesser actors, all stressing their claim to an independent course. However, only the Indian National Congress led by Mahatma Gandhi and the Muslim League of Mohammad Ali Jinnah addressed national interests. All the others were regional in one form or another, and in such cases the British were prepared to acknowledge only the royal satrapies with whom the Crown had separate treaties that entitled them to self-governing status.

The government of India moved quickly to terminate the sovereignty of these princely states, with the exception of Kashmir, where the Hindu Maharajah was determined to sustain his authority over a predominantly Muslim population. In the Hindu-dominant princely state of Hyderabad, however, where the Muslim Nizam also intended to continue his independent ways, the Indian government forcefully removed the ruler and seized his kingdom. Kashmir therefore was the exception. The Muslim-dominant character of the state had made the Maharajah an anachronism. Moreover, conflict, so frequent and historic a circumstance between the Dogra Hindu kingdom of Kashmir and the tribal Pushtuns of the adjoining northern areas, assumed another dimension after partition. Unable to defend his kingdom from tribal invasions without external assistance, the Maharajah called upon India for help. India agreed to answer that distress call only if the potentate agreed to accede to the Indian Union, which, it is argued, he did before fleeing the region. With the Maharajah no longer a player, the contest was now between the two new dominions, both claiming their right to annex the mountain territory, one by the nature of the resident Muslim population, the other by legal accession. Thus, the conflict between the Indian National Congress and the Muslim League was extended well past the moment of the British transfer. Instead of the rival major parties reconciling their differences with the end of colonialism, the struggle that had characterized their pre-independence experience was perpetuated.

Kashmir was transformed into the symbol of both Indian and Pakistani resolve. India, already teeming with millions of Muslims, saw no reason to deny itself control of a state because of its Muslim majority. Arguing a secular program, India refrained from ideological distinctions. Nor did it seek to emphasize ethnic and racial differences. Stressing a collective principle, India postured as an open democracy, capable of representing diversity and promising its minorities both security and equal opportunity. Pakistan assumed a different approach that seemed to challenge the Indian example. Pakistan was a country created by Muslims for Muslims in a turbulent environment. Moreover, prior to and following partition, the different communities faced assaults by legions of radicals and fanatics on all sides. Minorities were all at risk despite the pleadings of the leaders who had labored so long and so fervently for independence.

In the immediate aftermath of partition, the communal warfare that had begun years before was carried to an extreme. The slaughter of the innocent on both sides of the great divide mounted with each passing day. Instruments of law and order were made more helpless by the nature of the transfer of power, or else by an utter lack of preparation. Moreover, British forces were unavailable for the task of taming such a rabid display of calumny. Atrocities were attributed to all sides in the equation, not simply Hindu versus Muslim and vice versa. Sikhs were a prominent force in the Punjab, where the slaughter became the most intense. Acts of arbitrary and malicious violence were directed against the weakest elements across the whole north of the subcontinent. How many millions had their lives terminated during this period will never be known. Refugees were estimated to number between fifteen and twenty million. India may have avoided formal war in achieving its freedom, but it could not avoid the human toll consequent upon the inability or stubborn reluctance of the political parties to find a compromise formula. The fate of many innocents was sealed and the two new dominions, now independent nation-states, became immediate enemies. The hateful venom released in the orgy of partition infected India–Pakistan relations from that time forward.

Each saw the other as a determined foe, and each was equally determined to defend itself from the other at any cost.

In Pakistan the cost was the vision of the country's founder, Mohammad Ali Jinnah. In his quest for Pakistan, Jinnah had been opposed by many Muslim groups. Not the least of this opposition was the collection of Muslim clerics, the *ulema*. In the period leading up to independence the most prominent member of this self-proclaimed body was Maulana Abul Kalam Azad, a long-time member of the Congress and a soul mate of Mahatma Gandhi. Long before Pakistan gained independence he had taken the role of a full-time politician, his main task to reject the formation of Pakistan. No less significant was the Deoband School of Islam, also associated with the Congress Party. The Deoband's control of the Delhi Jamiat-i-Ulema-i-Hind made it a potent force in the politics of the subcontinent, and its fire was directed against Jinnah, whom it, like the Hindus, saw as a lackey of the British Raj. Deoband's fundamentalism was expressed in its anti-British position. The members of the Muslim religious elite therefore considered Jinnah a heretic and an unbeliever. They had devoted years to the cause of freeing the Muslims from colonial rule and had long concluded that the British were the chief enemy of Islam, the subjugators of Muslims from Egypt to India. For the Deoband, therefore, the British hold on India was the fundamental reason for the decline of Islamic civilization. Jinnah had reached out to the Jamiat in the 1935 elections, but they failed to honor his appeal for their votes. Maulana Abul Ala Maudoodi, founder of the Jamaat-i-Islami, was another Muslim cleric who rejected Jinnah and the call for an independent Pakistan. Jinnah was made the target of personal attacks in which holy scripture was used to vilify him. Jinnah nevertheless persisted in his efforts; the vulgarity of the assaults made upon him only steeled his resolve. The Muslim devotees were so blinded by their fury that they opposed every maneuver, every utterance made by the Quaid-i-Azam.

Jinnah believed his cause was a Muslim cause despite the diatribe of his religious opponents. Moreover, given the intensity of this assault upon his person as well as his leadership, Jinnah was more convinced that only a secular formula, as found in Europe, and notably in the British experience, could provide Pakistan with a firm foundation. "The Congress *ulema* repeated the Hindu slander *ad nauseam* that Pakistan was the brain child of the British." The *ulema* therefore may have denied the Muslim League but they adopted with alacrity the Indian cause in promoting an independent Pakhtunistan. The *ulema* opposed the referendum in Muslim-dominant Sylhet, but they worked strenuously to hold the region for India. Before his death even Mohammad Iqbal had found it necessary to strike out against the Deobandi fundamentalists. He accused them of malicious and retrograde actions that inflicted great harm on Muslims everywhere. With support drawn from people like Iqbal and with the vituperative assault on his Muslim identity unrelenting, Jinnah forcefully argued a secular vision for Pakistan. Moreover, it was because no other Muslim League leader possessed the mettle to articulate a secular objective that Jinnah, despite poor health, assumed the role of the country's first head of state.

Bibliography

Akhilananda, Swami, *Hindu Psychology: Its Meaning for the West*, New York: Harper, 1946.

Bahadur, Lal, *The Muslim League, Its History, Activities and Achievements*, Agra: Agra Book Store, 1954.

Bin Sayeed, Khalid, *Pakistan: The Formative Phase*, Karachi: Pakistan Publishing House, 1960.

Bolitho, Hector, *Jinnah: The Creator of Pakistan*, London: John Murray, 1954.

Chaudhrui, Nirad C., *The Autobiography of an Unknown Indian*, London: Macmillan, 1951.

Chaudhuri, Nirad C., *The Continent of Circe: An Essay on the Peoples of India*, New York: Oxford University Press, 1966.

Coupland, R., *Indian Politics, 1936–1942*, London: Oxford University Press, 1944.

Coupland, R., *The Indian Problem: Report on the Constitutional Problem in India*, New York: Oxford University Press, 1944.

Faruqi, Ziya-ul-Hasan, *The Deoband School and the Demand for Pakistan*, Bombay: Asia Publishing, 1963.

Firishta, Muhammad Kasim, *History of the Rise of the Muhammadan Power in India*, Calcutta: Susil Gupta, 1958.

Gandhi, M.K., *Gandhi's Autobiography: The Story of My Experiments with Truth*, Washington: Public Affairs Press, 1948.

Hossain, Syed Mohammad, *Our Difficulties and Wants in the Path of the Progress of India*, London: W.H. Allen, 1884.

Hunter, W.W., *The Indian Musalmans*, 2nd edn., London: Trubner, 1872.

Moon, Penderel, *Divide and Quit*, Berkeley: University of California Press, 1962.

Mosley, Leonard, *The Last Days of the British Raj*, New York: Harcourt, Brace & World, 1961.

Nehru, Jawaharlal, *Toward Freedom: The Autobiography of Jawaharlal Nehru*, New York, John Day, 1941.

Park, Richard L. and Tinker, Irene, eds., *Leadership and Political Institutions in India*, Princeton: Princeton University Press, 1959.

Qureshi, Ishtiaq Husain, *Ulema in Politics*, Karachi: Ma'Aref, 1974.

Shah, A.B. and Rao, C.R.M, eds., *Tradition and Modernity in India*, Bombay: Manaktalas, 1965.

Sharan, Parmatma, *The Imperial Legislative Council of India*, Delhi: S. Chand, 1961.

Smith, Donald Eugene, *India as a Secular State*, Princeton: Princeton University Press, 1963.

Smith, Donald Eugene, ed., *South Asian Politics and Religion*, Princeton: Princeton University Press, 1966.

Smith, Wilfred Cantwell, *Modern Islam in India: A Social Analysis*, Lahore: Sh. Muhammad Ashraf, 1943.

Stephens, Ian, *Pakistan*, New York: Frederick A. Praeger, 1963.

Symonds, Richard, *The Making of Pakistan*, London: Faber & Faber, 1950.

Tinker, Hugh, *South Asia: A Short History*, 2nd edn., Honolulu: University of Hawaii Press, 1990.

Wolpert, Stanley, *Tilak and Gokhale: Revolution and Reform in the Making of Modern India*, Berkeley: University of California Press, 1961.

Wolpert, Stanley, *Jinnah of Pakistan*, New York: Oxford University Press, 1984.

2

POLITICAL ASPIRATIONS

Although in failing health, Mohammad Ali Jinnah assumed the role of Governor General of Pakistan. By contrast, Gandhi chose to avoid public office and devoted himself to healing the deep wounds of communalism. Jinnah, however, had little choice. With his newborn country already at the brink of self-destruction, it was only his presence at the helm of affairs that stirred his followers to more substantial efforts. In major part, Pakistan comprised those regions of British India that were poor and undeveloped. Denied West Bengal, whatever industrial capacity might have been awarded the new state had been given to India. Pakistan had no choice but to accept East Bengal, a jute-growing hinterland and home of more than forty million of the subcontinent's most deprived peasantry. Pakistan's western wing, separated from East Bengal by one thousand miles of hostile India, was awarded only half of the Punjab, with India in position to disrupt some of the vital river sources feeding Pakistan's agricultural lands. Moreover, Sind province in the southeast was among the most backward areas of the subcontinent, and the North West Frontier Province, still very much a tribal preserve, though strategically important, otherwise possessed little in the way of economic product. Balochistan was still a tribal preserve ruled by local patriarchs. Barren and sparsely populated, its natural resources awaited discovery. "Truncated and moth-eaten" was Jinnah's characterization of the new Pakistan. Few questioned that description. Pakistan may have been a consequence of hard bargaining, but the Viceroy's take-it-or-leave-it offer and his rush to judgment left no room for further negotiation.

Jinnah confronted a war over Kashmir on the day independence was granted. Moreover, the British Indian army had yet to be satisfactorily divided and, even with a British general at the head of the new Pakistan army, the military stores that India was to transfer to Pakistan had not materialized. Logistically, the war in Kashmir favored the Pakistanis but their ill-equipped and still to be structured force could only do token damage to a more intact and formidable Indian army, also led by an Englishman. Thus, Pakistani forces occupied a portion of the disputed territory, but the predominantly Muslim Vale, the heartland of the Kashmiri nation, proved beyond reach.

Jinnah also was challenged by a massive flow of Muslim refugees who had fled their homes in India. Caring for the millions who spilled over Pakistan's borders in the weeks and months immediately following partition strained the very meager resources of the young nation, and the vast majority of these misbegotten went unattended. Hundreds of thousands flooded the sleepy resort and fishing seaport of Karachi, which had been made Pakistan's capital. In need of basic assistance they constructed shelters that were little more than hovels, and set out to besiege government officials in a desperate attempt to gain relief. Jinnah was humbled by the sight of the huddled and suffering refugees but was forced to acknowledge his inability to alleviate their plight.

Pakistan had virtually nothing from which to construct a government, let alone a treasury to serve the needs of an ever-expanding citizenry. The basic necessities were either non-existent or in extremely short supply. Buildings had to be commandeered for government use, and office furniture was a rarity. The government was even limited in pencils and writing paper and simply keeping track of needs and demands was often more than officials could manage. Jinnah's central role in assembling and running the new administration therefore was unavoidable. Only the Quaid-i-Azam engendered the confidence that succored the former colonial bureaucrats who opted for Pakistan.

The colonial civil service was the only professional instrument of government, and few Muslim civil servants had had much if any experience in managing departments and agencies, or, for that matter, taking charge of day-to-day operations. Suddenly advanced into high positions, they took their cues from Jinnah, who spurred them on to higher levels of achievement. The selflessness exhibited by government officials in those first trying weeks, and the discipline and professionalism of the career officers were a tribute to Jinnah's looming presence. So much had been sacrificed and so many depended upon the integrity of those in key positions that no one was permitted to consider failure an option. It has been said that without the leadership of Mohammad Ali Jinnah, Pakistan would never have achieved independence. It also was said that without Jinnah's leadership in those initial months after independence the nation would not have survived.

The center and the periphery

Jinnah's tasks were even more formidable than intimated above. The Quaid had to contend with a country made up of disparate regions that had only recently accepted the rule of the Muslim League. Provincial and local leaders were well entrenched in all the western provinces at the time of independence. A number had favored the Congress and were more inclined to follow Gandhi than Jinnah. The Pakistan Movement had gained strength in central India where Muslims were in the minority. In the territories that became Pakistan, Muslims were in the majority and the cry "Islam in Danger" did not have the same import. The Muslim League had to win the favor of numerous regional leaders, and it was evident from the start that many could not be influenced to follow the party line. For the holdouts the Muslim League was an alien organization with a message that threatened their personal independence. As far back as 1919, when dyarchy was first introduced in the subcontinent, local leaders had assumed positions of significant power. With the independence of Pakistan they were expected to share and in some cases to relinquish their prerogatives to rivals who now identified with the Muslim League. Moreover, the League monopolized power in the federal government, and with Jinnah's looming presence the critics had reason to describe the nation as a budding dictatorship, hardly a democracy.

It is said of the Quaid-i-Azam that had he wanted to be crowned a king, the people would have rewarded him with his wish and would have dutifully shown homage to his command. Although that may have been true of those who idolized Jinnah, who saw in him their only hope and future, it was not true for many of the established local leaders who saw in his awesome powers a zero-sum game they could not win. Such was the case in the North West Frontier Province, which had opted for Pakistan in consequence of a pre-partition plebiscite. Former opponents of the Muslim League like Abdul Qayyum Khan had joined the party in return for rich rewards. It was leaders like Abdul Qayyum that brought down the pro-Congress administration of Dr. Khan Sahib, the brother of Abdul Ghaffar Khan. Both brothers were staunch foes of the Muslim League. Each attempted to rally his constituents but they could not stymie the momentum of the Jinnah-driven Muslim League. Similar divisions obtained in the Punjab. The Unionist leader, Khizr Hyat Khan Tiwana, was forced from power by his Muslim League adversaries Mian Mumtaz Daultana and the Khan of Mamdot. Political intrigue in Sindhi politics followed a similar course when Mohammad Ayub Khuhro, the venerable Karachi leader, fell out of Jinnah's favor and an aggressive campaign was launched to separate him from his constituents.

Although the Muslim League had won Pakistan, and Mohammad Ali Jinnah was celebrated as a vaunted personality, the infighting between those coveting power and those seeking to protect it sapped the vitality of the party. Moreover, Jinnah was called to expend considerable energy in managing internecine squabbling. This also was true in East Bengal, where the Muslim League had originated and the party had popular recognition. The Muslim League had formed the last government before partition, and after the bifurcation of Bengal a decision had to be made about who would lead the party in that portion of the province granted to Pakistan. Personality conflicts in the provinces of the western region therefore were duplicated in the eastern province. No less important, following partition the All-India Muslim League split into two organizations, the Pakistan Muslim League and the India Muslim League. The All-India Muslim League had been the domain of urban leaders, and their cosmopolitan outlook was well known. The formation of the Pakistan Muslim League, by contrast, had a rural cast of leaders representing feudal interests. Relating to feudal landlords required gifts even Jinnah did not possess. Moreover, Jinnah was too burdened by affairs of state to continue as party president. The latter task was transferred to Chaudhri Khaliquzzaman, a former member of the Congress Party and a political refugee from India. Although a loyal Jinnah confidant he was without roots in the new Pakistan and generally perceived as a weak personality. Put to the test he could not effectively challenge the influence of the feudal landlords who quickly came to dominate the League and use it for their own purposes.

In East Bengal, the picture was different but it too presented a formidable challenge to Muslim League interests. The last chief minister of Undivided Bengal was H.S. Suhrawardy, an urbane Muslim Leaguer and an adroit politician. He had urged Jinnah to resist the partition of Bengal, pleading with him to retain Calcutta as an integral part of Pakistan. In the rush to independence, and in the face of stiff Hindu resistance, however, Jinnah accepted the British plan to divide and quit. Jinnah had been advised to ignore Suhrawardy. The former chief minister was accused of promoting a united and therefore independent Bengal, separate from Pakistan, to serve his own interests. By poisoning the relationship between Jinnah and Suhrawardy, the Dacca leaders saw greater gains for themselves. Indeed, the rivalry between the Dacca-based Nazimuddin and the Calcutta-based Suhrawardy had intensified in the years leading up to Pakistan's independence. Nazimuddin had preceded Suhrawardy as chief minister in Bengal, only to be dismissed for malpractice by the reigning British Viceroy. Nazimuddin was succeeded as chief minister by Suhrawardy, who successfully revitalized a Bengal ravaged by war and famine. However, Jinnah, challenged by the colonial power as well as the Congress Party, ignored that recent history. At the time of decision, he accepted the partition of Bengal, urged on by the nawabs of Dacca and knowing they would be the major beneficiaries. Dacca, therefore, not Calcutta, became the capital of the new Pakistani Bengal. Suhrawardy, in spite of his election to the Pakistan Constituent Assembly, was confined to India, banned from traveling in East Bengal or making speeches in the province.

Forced to resign his membership in the Muslim League, Suhrawardy was nonetheless determined to remain in politics as well as gain access to the new Muslim country. In the contest between Suhrawardy and Nazimuddin, Jinnah chose the weaker, less capable of the two personalities, but the ramifications of that decision were little grasped at that particular moment.

Although in declining health, and with a myriad of issues crowding his agenda, Jinnah was forced to expend much of his energy in attempts to pacify dissident elements in all the provinces. He journeyed to the North West Frontier Province and the Punjab to ask for reconciliation among conflicted local leaders, but with little if any success. In Sind, he ordered a crackdown on dissident voices and reserved much of his criticism for Ayub Khuhro, who was accused of entertaining personal power motives. Jinnah was even compelled to make the arduous trip to East Bengal, where he was called to address an aroused population, notably the students, that claimed a place for the Bengali language alongside that of Urdu. Jinnah pleaded with the crowd to understand his language policy and why it was necessary to create a uniform language for a nation divided by geography as well as culture. Although there were expressions of willingness to follow the guidance of the Quaid-i-Azam, in reality the issue was not resolved.

Jinnah governed Pakistan by dint of a determined personality but it required all his charismatic qualities to hold the nation to the course he had envisaged long before the creation of the state. Jinnah wanted Pakistan to become a modern, secular, democratic state, sustained by the rule of law and popularly supported institutions. This was the model he presented to the nation when he called for tolerance between the different religious communities and under-standing between the provinces. Confronted by an aggressive Indian neighbor on the one side and a hostile Afghan kingdom on the other, Jinnah cited the need for a strong center but he also recognized a need to satisfy local claims for autonomy. The needs of the center and the periphery would be identified in constitution making and that responsibility lay with the Constituent Assembly. He counseled patience as this effort was being launched. He acknowledged that the work would take time and that reason and compromise must prevail. Jinnah's words were important but so too was his presence.

Unfortunately for the nation he inspired, Jinnah's frail body was consumed by his labors both in achieving independence and in sustaining the fledgling nation. Weak and desperately in need of rest he retreated to the Balochistan hills, where he passed the last weeks of his life. Flown back to Karachi for emergency medical treatment, he died on September 11, 1948 in a disabled ambulance not far from the aircraft that had returned him to the capital city.

The Jinnah legacy

Jinnah's supreme role in the creation of Pakistan carried over into the country's consolidation phase. Pakistan was an idea, or, more accurately, an experiment. The idea of an independent Muslim state and the demand voiced by the Muslim League failed to outline the structure or character of the new entity. Even Jinnah had failed to explain how a congeries of disparate and relatively poor territories, housing diverse nationalities, could be forged into a united nation. Moreover, the speed with which Mountbatten and Radcliffe divided British India left no time to work through relationships with the people who held significant, if spatially circumscribed, dominance in the regions that emerged as Pakistan in August 1947. Whatever compromises were necessary had to be reached after the transfer of power and in the midst of catastrophic events. By accepting the demanding role of head of state, Jinnah transformed the Governor General's office from one of ritual and ceremony to a central institution responsible for the survival of state and nation. Jinnah was the living embodiment of Pakistan, the single national personality that demanded attention from both followers and detractors. As Father of the Nation, Jinnah was irreplaceable. Nevertheless, within a year following Pakistan's independence a successor had to be found. Jinnah's mantle was placed on the shoulders of Liaquat Ali Khan. Liaquat was that yeoman member of the Muslim League who had coaxed Jinnah to leave his London exile and return to India. Liaquat, however, was in no way a facsimile of Mohammad Ali Jinnah. A member of the *mohajir* or refugee community that had left India for Pakistan, he was denied a political constituency in his adopted country. Although he had been named the country's first Prime

Minister, he was ill-equipped to assume the heavy role of Pakistan's supreme leader.

During Jinnah's brief tenure as Pakistan's Governor General, Prime Minister Liaquat Ali Khan was literally shorn of the power to administer the needs of his government. Obscured by the Quaid-i-Azam, he was given the title "Quaid-i-Millet" or "Leader of the Nation," but this added little to his powers in dealing with difficult or alienated personalities in and outside the League. Jinnah had been so much the center of attention that the parliamentary institution received little notice. The Constituent Assembly that doubled as the legislature in fact deferred to the Quaid in all matters of state. Thus was perpetuated the colonial tradition wherein the Viceroy dominated all aspects of political life. Whether deliberate or not, Jinnah's inability to delegate effectively reinforced and perpetuated the subcontinent's viceregal tradition. The office of the chief executive loomed large over that of the legislative institution and law making was either made perfunctory or thwarted by the Governor General, who never yielded his emergency powers.

Liaquat either failed to give due consideration to the special powers of the Governor General, or believed he could reduce the power of the latter office by giving new importance to the parliamentary institution. After Jinnah's death, Liaquat chose to remain Prime Minister, but in the absence of the state's founder his government was unprepared for the tasks confronting it. Jinnah wanted a constitutionally empowered parliament that insured Pakistan would be a democracy. Liaquat shared that view and in remaining Prime Minister he knew he had to exorcise the viceregal tradition. However, he did not have the ties to the power brokers and he did not have the means with which to neutralize those planning to maneuver around his authority. Moreover, the regional leaders controlled powerful constituencies, and even Jinnah's attempt to mediate rivalries in Punjab, Sindh, and the North West Frontier Province had not been successful. Jinnah's death therefore was an open invitation to ambitious provincial leaders to challenge national policy. Liaquat neither possessed the necessary bargaining skills, nor fully comprehended local issues. Consumed by constitution making, he held to the belief that a formal contract between the center and the periphery would allow him to govern.

Never fully versed in the thinking of the Quaid-i-Azam and hardly one capable of pressing policies he was uncomfortable with, Liaquat abdicated much of his power to those he believed could offset other personal weaknesses. He clothed himself in the religious tradition and fell victim to those more intent in pursing particular goals than in bolstering the Prime Minister's authority. Thus Liaquat allowed himself to become ensnared in a web of secular cum religious demands that defined his leadership and shifted Pakistan to a course avoided by the Quaid-i-Azam. Jinnah's secular propensities were virtually ignored. Pakistan was a country created for Muslims by Muslims who sensed danger to their circumstances in an India dominated by the Hindu majority. "Islam in Danger" and Jinnah's two-nation theory became the focus for Muslim League claims and policies. Jinnah, however, framed the Muslim argument in terms of distributing political power; religious practices were never in jeopardy and he saw no justification for including Muslim clerics in matters of governance. Liaquat did not enjoy Jinnah's acumen or prestige. Moreover, in the absence of a national constituency and subject to the pulls of regional strongmen, he judged he had little choice other than to exaggerate his Islamic goals and enlist the services of the mullahs.

The Objectives Resolution of 1949 was drafted to frame Pakistan as a Muslim state. Islam was made the unifying focus for the citizens of Pakistan and the nation set its constitutional course to guarantee the country would conform to Muslim teaching and principles. Secular aspects of nation building were allowed to recede into the background. Jinnah's goal of balancing different nationalities and religions, as well as bridging distant regions, also was forgotten. Instead, emphasis was given to Pakistan becoming a model Islamic republic. This turn of events whetted the appetite of those least responsible for the creation of the independent nation. Religious orders metamorphosed into political parties and, even if they counted few joiners on their membership rolls, their weight in public policy was considerable. The masses, otherwise apolitical, were hardly unreligious and could be expected to answer calls expressing their predisposed Muslim identity. Thus, constitution making was made more difficult by the shift in favor of Islamic guidelines. Defining a proper Muslim was made the central issue in the allocation of power; issues of distributive justice and representative government became little more than sideshows.

The Constituent Assembly's struggle to draft a constitution was protracted. The Basic Principles Committee issued a report on the formation of the constitutional system but a common formula did not materialize. A majority of Pakistan's population resided in East Bengal and the latter's spokesmen insisted on an allocation of parliamentary seats that reflected its numerical majority. Immediately, however, the power brokers in the Punjab, citing a larger contribution to national development, demanded a resolution that went beyond demographics. Moreover, Punjabis argued that East Pakistan's majority was a consequence of the high percentage of Bengali Hindus in the province. By contrast, the provinces of West Pakistan had far fewer remaining Hindus. Punjabis also cited their almost entirely Muslim community following the Sikh population's flight to India. If the western Pakistani provinces had more Muslim residents, then the East Bengal claim to greater representation was without merit. According to this Islamic litmus test, East Pakistan was not entitled to majority status in a future federal parliament. One person one vote did not obtain in a country guided by Islamic principles and practices, according to opinion in the western provinces. In East Bengal, however, the matter was seen differently. More disposed to secular thinking, the Bengalis saw the attempt to count only Muslims as a tactic aimed at denying them their basic rights.

This debate was so intense that constitution making could not proceed. The Punjabi Chief Minister, Mian Mumtaz Daultana, chided Liaquat on the representation issue and insisted that he would not approve a report that reduced the level of Punjabi expression. He demanded that the Prime Minister personally travel to the Punjab to sell the Basic Principles Report to his people. Although warned not to travel to the Punjab, Liaquat believed in the matter so much that he decided to go anyway. That decision proved fatal. In October 1951, as he rose to speak to an unruly Punjabi crowd, the Prime Minister was shot and died almost immediately. Liaquat's assassin was killed on the spot by a nearby police officer, making it impossible to learn whether the murderer had acted alone or was the instrument of a wider conspiracy. The immediate consequence of the assassination was not only the loss of one of the few intimates of the Quaid-i-Azam, but the virtual collapse of the federal government. Power now devolved to the provinces, where the traditional patriarchs held sway and where the Islamists were expected to capitalize on their recently acquired political leverage.

Hardly four years after achieving independence, Pakistan was denied both its Quaid-i-Azam and its Quaid-i-Millet. Khwaja Nazimuddin, who had been ushered to Karachi from Dacca following Jinnah's death, had assumed the office of the Governor General. He was now urged to yield that post and become the country's new Prime Minister. Nazimuddin had been Liaquat's choice for Governor General because the Prime Minister wanted a weak head of state who would not interfere with his management of national affairs. In the time Nazimuddin had served in that capacity he had in fact followed all the wishes of the Prime Minister, and as Governor General he had confined his activities to ceremonial functions. Liaquat's goal was to depoliticize the office of the head of state and bring an end to the viceregal tradition. That goal had not been fully realized at his death. Moreover, Pakistan harbored individuals who plotted to sustain the power of the Governor General and it was some of these people who convinced Nazimuddin to become Prime Minister. In a time of high crisis, Pakistan did not need so reserved a head of government. Nor did they require a puppet in the hands of ambitious personalities. Pakistanis had yet to develop a clear picture of who they were and where they were heading, but the forces that shape events are often revealed in the machinations of powerful individuals and such was the case following Liaquat's death.

The assassination of Liaquat Ali Khan left Pakistan at a crossroads. Nazimuddin became the Prime Minister and Ghulam Mohammad was named Pakistan's Governor General. The latter had never been a member of the Muslim League, nor did he demonstrate a flair for political give and take. A civil servant, Ghulam Mohammad had had a sterling career as a member of the Indian financial service. Before partition he had served in important capacities in India's nascent industries. Following independence Jinnah selected him to be Minister of Finance. It was Ghulam Mohammad who had the major responsibility for organizing Pakistan's treasury and his performance in that endeavor won him special recognition. Praised by the Quaid, Ghulam Mohammad looked forward to retirement when his services were no longer required. Moreover, by 1951, Ghulam Mohammad was in declining health and, many believed, little able to manage his work. His selection as Governor General therefore was a surprise. Although some rationalized he would make a respectable ceremonial head of state, others saw intrigue in the juxtaposition of the two men. For all his infirmity, Ghulam Mohammad was a determined taskmaster and a resolute professional. Only the naïve could believe the old civil servant would allow events to swirl around him and not react to them. Nazimuddin was familiar with Ghulam Mohammad's lifetime reputation as a no-nonsense administrator but nevertheless could not imagine he would intrude himself in parliamentary affairs. Nazimuddin saw his task as moving constitution making to a conclusion and he had expected the Governor General to be as supportive to him as previously he was to the Quaid-i-Azam. What the Prime Minister failed to realize, however, was that Ghulam Mohammad, not he, occupied the Quaid's office.

The Prime Minister confronted a mountain of unresolved issues, the contours of which became quickly apparent. A native Bengali, Nazimuddin was burdened by the language question that Jinnah had attempted to arrest in his hurried visit to East Bengal in 1948. Bengalis were among the more politically aroused elements of the Pakistan population and considerable passion was displayed in the effort to have Bangla established as a national language alongside Urdu. Jinnah had insisted on a single national language and had argued the case for Urdu in a country of many tongues. Apparently, Jinnah's death was a time for the Bengalis to re-energize their demand for more autonomy and greater cultural recognition, and although Liaquat chose to ignore Bengali sentiments, Nazimuddin could not. Nazimuddin traveled to Dacca not long after becoming Prime Minister and was called upon to make an important speech on the Paltan Maidan, a great open area in the heart of the city. Reading from a prepared text, he came upon the matter of the national language and reiterated Jinnah's declaration that the country could afford only one national tongue and that it had long been a settled fact that it would be Urdu. His Bengali audience could not believe that one of their own would speak so dispassionately about a matter so close to the hearts of those residing in the eastern province. The crowd registered their disfavor almost immediately and the Prime Minister had to endure a volley of criticism.

Nazimuddin later would argue that he had not read the speech before making it and that the language question had only been mentioned in the context of so many other challenges needing resolution. Although the Prime Minister sought to quickly distance himself from his own words, his explanation went unheeded. Indeed, it was those very words that the enemies of the Muslim League in East Bengal intended to use against him. Riots broke out in several areas of Dacca even before the Prime Minister could return to his residence in Karachi. The demonstrators labeled the Prime Minister a traitor to Bengal and its beloved culture. With the students in the vanguard of the protest, assaults were made on business and government structures in the city. The provincial Muslim League government of Nurul Amin was unsuccessful in preventing the anger from escalating, and when the police were called upon to respond to the protesters the violence intensified and was protracted over several days. Before calm could be restored, several students of Dacca University lay dead, the university was ordered closed, and the students were forced to retreat to their homes, many to distant villages scattered throughout the province. Word now spread that the Muslim League government had murdered scores of students and had turned its back on the Bengali complaint. Although this was an exaggeration, there was no mistaking the level of mayhem, and an aroused public turned to anti-Muslim-League politicians who were pleased to represent their sentiments.

Bengali nationalism was born on February 21, 1952, the day that marked the start of the Bengali language movement. Always thereafter known as "Shahid" or "Martyrs' Day," the students would celebrate the event each year. A monument was later erected outside the gates of Dacca University and that place became the central venue for the politicized student community that in time led the call for secession from Pakistan. More immediately, however, the language riots exposed the weakness in the Nazimuddin administration. If Nazimuddin could not maintain law and order among his own people, how could he be expected to manage the diverse population in the western provinces. Ghulam Mohammad and those who served him had concluded that Pakistan was little suited to parliamentary democracy, that its largely illiterate and divided population could not be melded into a unified nation, and that it would take extraordinary efforts to sustain the state. Jinnah's vision could not be translated into reality. Much attention centered on the actions of the country's politicians. Ghulam Mohammad was only one of many from the civil–military establishment to question their role. The higher administration questioned the politicians' acceptance of the national idea, and sensed the need to sustain the "steel frame" of colonial government in the face of what they judged to be divisive forces.

The "steel frame" included the civil administration and the army, the twin pillars that had supported British authority in India. Professional by calling as well as training and experience, it also represented the modernists in the Pakistan experience. Focused on the maintenance of law and order, the members of the civil–military establishment made themselves the holders of the Quaid's flame. The country had survived the initial years after partition as a consequence of their labors and dedication, and they now discerned a vast distance between themselves and the country's politicians, who for the most part were perceived as overly ambitious and venal. Moreover, members of the higher administration were wedded to the secular state and at every opportunity had sought to separate religion from politics. Acknowledging that the country was born into a world of expanding nation-states, Pakistani administrators and soldiers understood that the country's sectarian and ethnic problems could be exploited by the very people who had rejected Jinnah's quest for Pakistan. This concern deepened in the months following the Bengal language riots.

The violence factor

Unrest was sparked in the Punjab by the Majlis-i-Ahrar-i-Islam, supported by the Jamaat-i-Islami. The target of the religious organizations was the Ahmediyya community that resided in the province. The Ahrars opposed the Ahmediyya for what they claimed was a heretical position on Islam. Based in India and aligned with the Congress Party before partition, the Ahrars had described Pakistan as "palidistan," the "land of the filthy." The Jamaat, also an Indian organization, and under the leadership of Maulana Maudoodi, used similar words to describe the country of Jinnah's creation. Following independence, both organizations shifted their operations to Pakistan, however, and their criticism of the country's leaders and political system became a familiar refrain in the early years of the new state. Now, however, they aimed to shift the public's attention to their position, and their assault on the Ahmediyya was aimed at gaining adherents, as well as weakening and possibly bringing down the central government.

There was sufficient public distaste for the Ahmediyya, given their apparent questioning of Mohammad's role as the "Seal of the Prophets." The Ahmediyya were followers of one Ghulam Ahmed, a nineteenth-century Punjabi who claimed a form of revelation. Although Ghulam Ahmad's preachings were considered blasphemous by devout Muslims, the colonial authority had protected the Ahmediyya and had found its followers eager to pursue English educational opportunities. As a consequence, trained Ahmediyya were recruited for various forms of government service and when Pakistan became independent a number of them had attained high positions in the army, the bureaucracy, and the professions. Pakistan's first foreign minister was an Ahmediyya, Zafrullah Khan, who had been knighted by the Crown and had a distinguished career as a public official. Therefore when the riots broke out, much of the mob's venom focused on the high profile of Sir Zafrullah Khan.

The Ahrar and Jamaat leaders insisted that the government remove the Foreign Minister. They also called for the termination of Ahmediyya positions in the government, the army, and the civil bureaucracy. As tensions increased, the Punjab Muslim League, under the leadership of Mian Mumtaz Daultana, welcomed the assistance of the Islamists who had given the party their support in the 1951 provincial elections. And because Daultana refused to bring calm to the province or protect the Ahmediyya, Prime Minister Nazimuddin was drawn into the controversy. A pious Muslim, Nazimuddin's sympathies were thought to be with the Islamists, but as head of government he was duty bound to defend public order. Caught between his personal convictions and official responsibility, Nazimuddin hesitated before taking the actions needed to address the problem. Without a popular base in western Pakistan and repudiated in his own province, Nazimuddin feared losing still another constituency. The Ahrars had merged forces with a number of fundamentalist orders and had joined with the Muslim Parties Convention in calling for the excommunication of the Ahmediyya. Nazimuddin was personally sympathetic to these remonstrations and thus a reluctant enforcer of law and order. His decision to arrest the more radical and violent members of the religious community in Karachi was considered a desperate move, forced on him by the Governor General. But the real problem was in the Punjab, not Karachi. Protests had reached a critical stage, and Chief Minister Daultana again refused to act against the law breakers, arguing that grievances against the Ahmediyya were a popular issue.

Given this government indecision or complicity, the Punjab riots began officially on February 27, 1953, spearheaded by the fundamentalists but assisted by a wide array of the Punjabi public, drawn from both the educated as well as the illiterate classes. Karachi remained relatively quiet as a consequence of central government actions, but the widespread killing and destruction of property in the Punjab could not be ignored. Nazimuddin was forced to make an emergency visit to Lahore, where he forced the resignation of the Chief Minister, ordered the banning of many of the participant religious parties, and arrested hundreds of perpetrators. The Prime Minister nevertheless had not acted until the rioters had destroyed much of the province's vital infrastructure. Accused of hesitation and sympathy with the miscreants, Nazimuddin was forced to explain his consorting with the instigators of the disturbances.

The Punjab riots had brought into public view the Prime Minister's problems in managing the government. Nazimuddin's role in the Punjab riots was scrutinized, but so too was his decision to enlist the services of the *ulema* in constitution making. The latter decision had allowed the clerics to play an obstructionist role that further delayed the process. The country had also experienced significant economic dislocation, and with the devastation in the Punjab, Pakistan's declining economy could not be successfully addressed. Economic stagnation and political decay had raised questions about the politicians' capacity to govern; it also prompted the bureaucrats to revisit their history as the subcontinent's rulers. Impatient with the political bickering and the failure to place country above personal aspirations, the riots in the Punjab and Bengal were traced to political intrigue that if not checked could destroy the Pakistan experiment. Higher civil administrators noted the rise in social and religious tension and the inability of law enforcement to prevent anti-state behavior. Law and order could only be restored in the Punjab after the imposition of martial law, and future disturbances would no doubt call for similar measures. The civil–military establishment saw itself in a pivotal role. Pakistan needed saving from itself.

Governor General Ghulam Mohammad demanded that Nazimuddin purge his government. When Nazimuddin hesitated, Ghulam Mohammad dismissed the Prime Minister and his entire cabinet. Nazimuddin was not given opportunity to seek a vote of confidence in the legislature, and on April 17, 1953 all of Pakistan came under a limited form of civilian martial law. The viceregal tradition was resurrected along with the authoritarian trappings of the former colonial administration. Ghulam Mohammad's actions received the support of the country's armed forces, notably the head of the army, General Mohammad Ayub Khan, the Defense Secretary, Iskandar Mirza, and the Secretary General of the Civil Service, Chaudhri Mohammad Ali. Muslim League officials were appalled by the action and immediately appealed to the Pakistani judiciary. The judiciary's silence, however, allowed the assembling of a new cabinet, headed by the Pakistani ambassador to the United States, Mohammad Ali Bogra. Bogra's choice hinted at other moves by the civil–military establishment to link Pakistan more intimately with the United States. Indeed, Bogra had been working with General Ayub Khan and Defense Secretary Iskandar Mirza in a behind-the-scenes effort to secure American arms for the Muslim nation. Bogra had found the new Eisenhower government amenable to Pakistani overtures and both Vice-President Richard Nixon and Secretary of State John Foster Dulles were eager to assemble a cold war defensive alliance that stretched from Turkey to Pakistan. Bogra therefore found the Americans little concerned about the course of Pakistani politics and more than willing to do business with a Pakistan government that represented the views of Pakistan's civil–military complex.

The demise of the Muslim League

The Muslim League had suffered serious damage with the ouster of the Nazimuddin government, but the party faced another test when provincial elections were scheduled in East Bengal in 1954. The party had lost its popularity in the eastern province and was confronted with challenges from other organizations that lacked national appeal but nevertheless represented local sentiment. Moreover, after the deaths of Jinnah and Liaquat, the Muslim League had become prey to ambitious, self-aggrandizing members of the political fraternity. The language issue weighed heavily on Muslim League leaders and Chief Minister Nurul Amin had refused to hold by-elections for vacant seats, lest the party expose its weakness. Thus, the announcement of province-wide elections had energized the opposition's determination to put an end to Muslim League rule. The nature of the opposition challenge was signaled by the formation of a United Front.

The Front combined all the principal opposition organizations and their respective leaders. Most prominent were Fazlul Huq and H.S. Suhrawardy. The former had moved the Lahore (Pakistan) Resolution in 1940 and the latter had been the Muslim League's last chief minister of undivided Bengal. Both men had left the League and had to withstand attacks from their erstwhile colleagues. But they also had developed impressive followings and were respected leaders. Suhrawardy had been blocked from participating in Pakistani politics and efforts had been made to prevent him from making public appearances. Though he was arrested on several occasions, his determination to challenge the Muslim League leadership was undiminished. Suhrawardy was instrumental in the creation of the urban-based Awami League in 1949, and with the deaths of Jinnah and Liaquat, he envisaged an opportunity to build a new national partnership. The first major test of his organizational skills was the 1954 East Bengal elections. Fazlul Huq had labored on behalf of Bengali workers and peasants long before the independence of Pakistan, and his party, the Krishak Sramik (formerly the Krishak Praja), was especially strong in the villages of

East Bengal. Together Suhrawardy and Huq represented the most formidable challenge to Muslim League influence in the province.

Fazlul Huq and Suhrawardy led the United Front and their combined strategy succeeded beyond all their expectations. The Muslim League was demolished at the polls. The opposition secured 309 seats in the provincial legislature to a paltry ten for the Muslim League. The election in the only province where the Muslim League was judged native to the soil proved the final undoing of the party that had won Pakistan. With the civil–military bureaucracy dominating the party at the center and with provincial politicians vying for power in the western provinces, the termination of Muslim League rule in East Bengal pointed Pakistan in a new direction. In effect the break-up of the Muslim League ended the fiction of a unified polity. The Muslim League had been more a movement than a political party. Personalized by Jinnah, it forced the British to create an independent Pakistan, but the Pakistan that ultimately emerged from Muslim League efforts was never the vision of its principal founder. The regions that comprised the Pakistani nation were too disparate, too disrupted by the manner of the partition, to fit into a design reflecting national identity and collective purpose. Pakistan was an idea that was yet to be realized. Nonetheless, too much had been invested in its formation for the enterprise to be abandoned. If the political elements were unprepared for the challenge of nation building, the steel frame of colonial administration was eager to press ahead with the notion that the country was a reality and therefore had to be made viable.

Maintaining the fiction of a Muslim League party at the center of national affairs while the country was clearly rejecting the party at the grassroots became the task of the higher bureaucracy with assistance from the Pakistan army. The legitimacy of the bureaucratic *putsch* was made manifest in this exercise. But the politicians were not prepared to yield to the members of the colonial legacy. Sensing the need to curtail the powers of the center, especially the office of the Governor General, the politicians developed a strategy that they believed would enhance their influence and neutralize the administrators. Unrest in East Bengal, however, stymied these efforts. When the United Front was in the process of forming a government for East Bengal, labor unrest shattered the peace and, because of the heavy loss of life and destruction of property, the central government intervened. Fazlul Huq was in Calcutta during these events and, thanks to the nostalgia of returning to familiar haunts, he exchanged kind words with his Indian hosts. On returning to Dacca he found himself the target of opposition abuse, while members of the central government called his actions and statements in India treasonous. Because he had not prevented the rioting in the province's nascent industries and had demonstrated "questionable" loyalty to Pakistan the central government proceeded to nullify the election results and to impose martial law throughout East Bengal. The United Front government was dissolved even before it could officially be sworn in, and Iskandar Mirza was sent to the province and authorized to assume dictatorial powers. The Bengali population offered little resistance despite knowing that the heavy hand of West Pakistani interests had been laid upon them. No friend of the Muslim League, Mirza also opposed the leaders of the United Front. A point man for the civil–military power in Karachi, Mirza intended to guide the eastern province along lines that encouraged the maintenance of national unity, even if that meant suspending all fundamental guarantees of citizenship.

The objective of the civil administrators was a reformed Muslim League without politicians. Jinnah had transcended the party and had neutralized the politicians. The higher administrators saw no reason why they could not emulate that example, especially given the miserable track record of those who would clothe themselves in the Quaid-i-Azam's mantle. The collapse of Muslim League rule in East Bengal, soon to be re-designated "East Pakistan," meant the party could no longer pretend it was the country's preferred political organization. Although Jinnah's and Liaquat's images would continue to appear, and their words and statements to be repeated *ad nauseam*, the Muslim League they had nurtured ceased to be a real actor in the nation's public life. With the passing of the League went the loss of several objectives. National unity ceased to be a political enterprise, and, even more important, no party was available to help bridge the gulf between the Islamist and more fundamentalist members of the population and those who envisaged a modern nation based on Western principles of pluralism and open debate.

The political organizations that succeeded the Muslim League were too provincial or too weak to represent the diverse regions that comprised Pakistan. Nor were the politicians, perhaps with the exception of Suhrawardy, gifted in national politics. Pakistan was an inchoate dream at the time of independence, and only a small minority grasped the significance of national existence. The Muslim League's major task was to educate the masses about political life in the middle of the twentieth century. Time and patience were required to socialize a polyglot and unsophisticated people into a union of unknown character. The Muslim League had won Pakistan on the theme "Islam in Danger," and was called to make a bridge between the traditional Muslim world and the new times that spoke to the masses in progressive, secular terms. In the immediate aftermath of World War II, attention centered on reconstruction. Fascism had been defeated and the language of democracy and material progress dominated expression and purpose. For the new state of Pakistan the challenge was not only how to fit itself into a constellation of states determined to achieve new levels of physical well-being, but how to build a state that embodied all the properties of the most advanced nations. This was the challenge presented to the Muslim League. Viewed from a historical perspective, it was obviously impossible for a party re-engineered by Mohammad Ali Jinnah in the late 1930s to achieve such an aim.

Jinnah's passing only a year following partition had left the Muslim League without a true leader. Liaquat was made of lesser stuff and his assassination in the midst of controversy over constitution making merely emphasized this point. Without Jinnah's firm hand the Muslim League could not hold to the agenda established for it by the transfer of power. Pakistan's political elite lacked the stature to carry Jinnah's message forward. Their reference to Jinnah's intentions was an attempt to cover their inadequacies, not to elevate or sanctify their mission. These circumstances led the civil–military establishment to assume Jinnah's mantle and thereby leadership of the Muslim League. But in taking control of the party they also denied the Muslim League's legitimate right to speak for the people of Pakistan. In time the bureaucracy would find it difficult to accommodate a political calling. The politicians would again assert themselves, but never again would they have the opportunity to demonstrate their inclusive goals. Not only did the politicians fail to make the transition from regional to national politics, but the religious orders were given their opportunity to demonstrate that they too could play at politics.

When the politicians moved against the Governor General following the elections in East Bengal and attempted to curtail the powers of the office, Ghulam Mohammad was hardly prepared to grant them their demands. The head of state, utilizing his viceregal authority, notably Section 92A of the Government of India Act of 1935, argued that the Constituent Assembly threatened the well-being of the nation and he took the unprecedented step of dissolving the body. The Constituent Assembly had been elected before partition for the express purpose of drafting a constitution. It had not done so. Having already dismissed a sitting Prime Minister, Ghulam Mohammad was not about to allow an assembly, essentially composed of Muslim Leaguers, to undermine the state, especially when the party had already lost control of the constituent units that made up the state. Although the speaker of the Constituent Assembly brought the matter before the High Court seeking a reversal, the court refused to accommodate the plea. Nazimuddin had earlier brought his dismissal before the Queen but Her Royal Highness had ignored that request for a review. The High Court's action in rejecting the plea to sustain the constitution-making body proved a final blow. Pakistan became the responsibility of the civil–military bureaucracy. The bureaucrats would continue to play at politics for several years thereafter but in the end it would be the Pakistan army that would assume the governance of the nation.

Bibliography

Ahmad, Hazrat Mirza Bashir-ud-Din Mahmud, *Ahmadiyyat or the True Islam*, Rabwah, Pakistan: Ahmadiyya Muslim Foreign Mission Office, 1959.

Ahmad, Ziauddin, *Liaquat Ali Khan: Leader and Statesman*, Karachi: Oriental Committee, 1971.

Ali, Chaudhri Muhammad, *The Emergence of Pakistan*, Lahore: Research Society of Pakistan, 1973.

Aziz, K.K., *Party Politics in Pakistan*, 1947–1958, Islamabad: National Commission on Historical Research, 1976.

Callard, Keith, *Pakistan: A Political Study*, London: George Allen & Unwin, 1957.

Chaudhuri, M.A., *The Civil Service in Pakistan*, Dacca: National Institute of Public Administration, 1963.

Choudhury, G.W., *Constitutional Development in Pakistan*, 2nd edn, London: Longman, 1969.

Dil, Anwar and Dil, Afia, *Bengali Language Movement to Bangladesh*, Lahore: Ferozsons, 2000.

Goodnow, Henry Frank, *The Civil Service of Pakistan: Bureaucracy in a New Nation*, New Haven: Yale University Press, 1964.

Government of Pakistan, *Report of the Court of Inquiry, Punjab Disturbances of 1953*, Lahore: Government Printing: Punjab, 1954.

Hardy, P., *The Muslims of British India*, Cambridge: Cambridge University Press, 1972.

Human Relations Area Files, *Pakistan: Government and Politics*, Berkeley: University of California, 1956.

Jamaat-i-Islami, *An Analysis of the Munir Report*, Karachi: Pakistan Herald Press, 1956.

Khaliquzzaman, Choudhry, *Pathway to Pakistan*, Lahore: Longman, 1961.

Khuhro, Hamida, *Mohammad Ayub Khuhro: A Life of Courage in Politics*, Lahore: Ferozsons, 1998.

Qureshi, Ishtiaq Husain, *The Struggle for Pakistan*, Karachi: University of Karachi Press, 1963.

Von Vorys, Karl, *Political Development in Pakistan*, Princeton: Princeton University Press, 1965.

Wilcox, Wayne Ayres, *Pakistan: The Consolidation of a Nation*, New York: Columbia University Press, 1963.

3

THE MILITARY AND POLITICS

The transfer of power established Pakistan as a parliamentary democracy but no consideration was given to its colonial history or its traditional background. Pakistan evolved from a history long involved with authoritarian modes of governance. Medieval rule, patriarchy, and monarchy permeated the region. The years immediately before partition had offered little hint of democratic norms and processes. The war years, and the brief period following them, had hardly introduced modern, sophisticated institutions and systems of self-government. The British never seriously tutored their subjects in the art of responsible government; nor were the people who were sent to rule the subcontinent given that charge. Law and order was the essential requirement of colonial administration and by most measures that objective was realized. The British departure from the subcontinent was by all standards peaceful and orderly. The same could not be said for what the colonial authority left behind.

The transfer of power was an action demanded by the events following the close of World War II. Britain saw little value in holding on to a territory that demanded more of its resources than it had left to expend following the termination of hostilities in Europe. Quit and run, and divide and quit was the easiest way out of a messy set of circumstances. Little time and less thought were given to the consequences of the rapid British departure.

Whereas the new independent Indian Union rested its immediate future on an established structure and a relatively unified political organization, Pakistan had only Mohammad Ali Jinnah and the semblance of a political body that superficially represented the larger nation.

Given the expectations at the time of Pakistan's independence, all references to democratic process were at best the individual ruminations of people in and outside the region. It is doubtful anyone seriously pondered the task of building a nation-state whose purpose was serious democratic expression. Moreover, although Pakistan was achieved as a consequence of emotional pressures that reflected Muslim sentiment, none of the country's leaders had seriously considered the compatibility of Islamic practice and secular society. Jinnah, virtually alone, became the exponent of constitution making along secular lines. His vision involved the blending of multiple traditions, in particular the Islamic experience with those at variance with it. Jinnah addressed the pressing need to build a civil society, but he never developed a strategy for the merger of Muslims, Hindus, Sikhs, and Christians, let alone the integration of Bengalis with Punjabis, Pashtuns, Sindhis, Balochis, and the myriad of refugees flooding into the state from India. Moreover, by Jinnah's own insistence, Pakistan had been created from the demand that Muslims were a separate nation and therefore entitled to an independent homeland. Ordinary people could not be faulted if they believed Pakistan would allow them to live and dream as members of an exclusive faith. To argue after partition, as Jinnah did, that Pakistanis were neither Muslim nor Hindu nor Sikh, but citizens of an all-embracing secular state, had little meaning for the vast majority who now were expected to adopt a Pakistani identity.

The colonial authority may have departed the area with the bands playing and the flags flying, but for the people of the subcontinent partition was a wrenching and tragic experience. Much of the region was bathed in blood as communal warfare pitted rival communities against one another. The unleashing of the apocalypse rained havoc on peoples who had sustained an equilibrium under alien tutelage. Law and order were quickly made relics of the past as neighbor assaulted neighbor, and those who could flee did so in huge numbers. The millions of refugees created in the immediate aftermath of partition confirmed the enormous gap between intention and reality, between vision and probability.

For Pakistan it was clear from the outset that the country would emerge as a parochial state or die in the initial months following the transfer of power. Jinnah's vision of a secular state could not be articulated, let alone adopted, by the politicians who succeeded him on his death. Moreover, war in Kashmir between India and Pakistan and the failure to bring an end to that conflict sealed the fate of the democratic experiment even before it could be tested. Too much of the Muslim psyche was focused on the territory of Kashmir and from the beginning successive Pakistan governments would be measured by their commitment to liberating the Kashmiri Muslims from the clutches of the Hindus. Kashmir became the religious symbol, the litmus test for governments seeking legitimacy in an inchoate and deeply divided and troubled state. Pakistan as a secular state seemed doomed to failure even before the independent country could establish its bona fides.

'Therefore, even though Jinnah's death within a year after partition produced some expectation that an orderly and representative political system might be attempted, that expectation soon became a dim prospect. After the "Great Leader," establishing a viable political system, even in a state dominated by one party, proved elusive. Jinnah's vision had called for the establishment of a constitutional order but constitution making was impossible among rival regional interests that were more inclined to protect their peculiar domains than construct a viable state. Unable to reconcile their different claims and sensing a loss of personal power, the politicians that inherited the Pakistan state favored their own more limited purposes and allowed the nation to grope for its own ill-defined destiny. Political failure was written large in the civil–military actions that were aimed at preserving the country's territorial integrity. Challenged by hostile neighbors on the North West Frontier as well as in India and Kashmir, the nascent Pakistan army assumed primary responsibility for the country's preservation. And with the changing of the guard, the army came under indigenous leadership. As Pakistan's first Muslim army commander, General Mohammad Ayub Khan was given the role of chief defender of the Pakistan nation.

External defense, however, could not be achieved without a modicum of internal stability. The bureaucratic intrusion into the nation's political life that followed the assassination of Liaquat Ali Khan therefore was not unexpected.

The army leaders watched as the bureaucrats attempted to bolster the failing Muslim League by assuming positions in the party and the federal cabinet. Power sharing between politicians and public officials, however, proved a hopeless exercise. When the administrators moved to monopolize political power, the military establishment did not interfere. Nazimuddin's ouster from the Prime Minister's office was prelude to the dissolution of the Constituent Assembly, and the latter event virtually ended the parliamentary experiment. Although the High Court upheld the Governor General's dissolution order, it nevertheless called for a continuation of the constitution-making process, and a new Constituent Assembly, one more representative of prevailing political conditions, was assembled. Under pressure of the civil–military establishment, the Second Constituent Assembly wasted little time in writing a document that gave parity of representation between the two wings of the country, but not before the provinces of western Pakistan were amalgamated into "One Unit."

One Unit was a purely bureaucratic enterprise. It overrode western Pakistan's multiethnic base and was aimed at depriving the provincial politicians of their significant influence. Moreover, in creating one administrative province from the original four, the civil–military institution believed it could ease east–west antagonism and hence nurture national unity. One Unit as policy therefore was little debated and was approved in record time.

In the course of these events Ghulam Mohammad's health took a drastic turn. In what was little less than a civil coup, the country was placed in the hands of a "Cabinet of Talents." That cabinet included the nation's most powerful public officials. Iskandar Mirza left his autocratic office in East Pakistan to take up leadership of the body. Chaudhri Mohammad Ali, the Secretary General of the civil service, General Mohammad Ayub Khan, the head of the army, and H.S. Suhrawardy, the leader of the dominant opposition party in East Pakistan and the only Bengali with a claim to national recognition, were the other important players. Mirza quickly replaced the ailing Ghulam Mohammad as

Governor General and Chaudhri Mohammad Ali was named the country's new Prime Minister when the influential Punjabi leader, Mushtaque Ahmad Gurmani, vetoed Suhrawardy's candidacy for the latter position. Placing themselves at the heart of the decision-making process, the higher bureaucracy truly believed they could not only save the nation, but steer it on a course they imagined Jinnah had intended.

The bureaucrats had little success in filling the political vacuum. Nevertheless, under their aegis constitution making was accelerated and with the deliberations of the Second Constituent Assembly a draft constitution was approved against only token opposition. Promulgated in 1956, it was now the responsibility of the civil servants to bring the constitution into force. Chaudhri Mohammad Ali, however, could not meet this test and he was forced to step aside and allow H.S. Suhrawardy to assume the office of Prime Minister. As Law Minister, Suhrawardy had played a leading role in completing the constitution. He also was a seasoned veteran politician. Nonetheless, he had been drummed out of the Muslim League following partition, and thus considerable opposition challenged his administration. Suhrawardy tried to reconcile his detractors but he also addressed the hard issues, among them the contradictions in the Pakistan paradigm that pitted secularists against fundamentalists and vice versa. Suhrawardy also attempted to bridge the growing rift between the two wings of the country, and sought an appropriate distribution of development funds among the provinces. Nothing he did, however, quieted the criticism leveled against him. Assaults on his administration emanated from all quarters, but especially from remnants of the West Pakistan Muslim League, as well as from his own Bengali-based Awami League, which believed he had made too many compromises and was not sufficiently firm in representing Bengali interests.

Although the new constitution officially described Pakistan as an "Islamic Republic," and had been approved by the Constituent Assembly, few were satisfied, and the majority of opposition politicians found much to complain about. Many labeled the document unworkable or designed to perpetuate the power of the civil–military establishment. Reinforced in their views when Iskandar Mirza became Pakistan's first President, they cited the chief executive's special prerogatives and that nothing had been done to eliminate the powers associated with the viceregal tradition. Moreover, the office of the Prime Minister was made subordinate to that of the President and Suhrawardy's tenure as Prime Minister was never based upon parliamentary support but rather upon the extent to which his administration satisfied President Iskandar Mirza. To emphasize this point, Mirza made it clear to dissenters that he had little patience with them and would use the powers of his office to silence them whenever he judged it necessary.

The road to martial law

Iskandar Mirza was the embodiment of a secular leader but his views had little to do with Jinnah's vision. Mirza was the subcontinent's first Muslim to be trained at the Imperial Military Academy at Sandhurst. Born in West Bengal of Persian ancestry, he was descended from a line of soldiers but upon graduation he chose the civil rather than military service. Appointed a political officer on the North West Frontier, Mirza had represented the colonial authority in the tribal area on the border with Afghanistan. Known for his strong demeanor and no-nonsense administrative style, his reputation had gained the attention of those in the highest political circles when Pakistan became a reality. Made Defense Secretary, Mirza joined with General Mohammad Ayub Khan when the latter assumed command of the Pakistan army. The two men shared their thoughts about the needs of the new state and came to a common understanding on the course the nation must follow.

Mirza displayed little patience with politicians, had been a close observer of the politics in the different regions, and was most concerned with the ongoing rivalry between combative political organizations. Believing that political conflict only added to the state's weakness, President Mirza was determined to maneuver the politicians toward common goals or nullify their actions altogether. Although General Ayub's sentiments were similar, he wanted more time to establish the army as an acknowledged fighting force and hence left the political strategizing to his colleague. Mirza was a staunch believer in the nation-state and verbally abused those who showed less than total commitment. He was particularly outspoken in his criticism of the cleric-politicians because they had insisted on framing the public discourse in theological terms. For Mirza, there was no question that sovereignty was a man-made phenomenon and that references to God's sovereignty, as in the Objectives Resolution of 1949, only served to confuse as well as divide the nation. Religion, he argued, was a personal matter, and he refused to yield to those who claimed to speak for God and thereby justified their limited support for the state. A Mirza quote appearing in the *New York Times* on February 7, 1955 appeared to sum up his thinking on this matter: "We can't run wild on Islam; it is Pakistan first and last."

Mirza and Ayub were Muslims who did not need others to define their faith. Both found reasons to reject those who legitimated their actions through religious pronouncements to a blind following. The Punjab riots were too fresh to ignore and they had revealed how negative statements directed against people professing different belief systems could degenerate into social unrest and widespread mayhem. That there were divisive elements in Pakistan's body public came as no surprise, but leaders of a nation-state were expected to transcend personal preferences and work toward the greater good. For Mirza, and no less so Ayub, the first imperative lay in promoting national unity, even if that meant curtailing the activities of religious zealots. Pakistan had been only an idea for Mohammad Ali Jinnah. Hindus represented the most vocal opposition in the struggle to achieve an independent Muslim state, but they were hardly the only ones. Muslims too had questioned the utility of a state that claimed to speak for the Muslims of the subcontinent, especially if that state was interpreted as serving colonial interests. The Islamists of the pre-independence era were more focused on the need to deny Western and especially European influence than they were on promoting an Islamic polity. Hence their general support for the Indian National Congress and their disapproval of Jinnah's tactics. Looked at in the context of Pakistan's prehistory, it was Jinnah and the Muslim League, no matter how secular their vision, who reflected Muslim aspirations. But that was so much history. For both Mirza and Ayub, accustomed to working with people across cultures, and having been trained to protect and defend the sovereign state, account-ability, not religious commitment, was the primary standard.

The constitutional debate centering on the sovereignty question framed the problem faced by Mirza and those identifying with his administration. The Objectives Resolution had focused attention on the central issue behind the Pakistan Movement, no matter how muted by the Quaid-i-Azam. Pakistan had been created to give political expression to a new nation inhabited predominantly by Muslims. How the new citizen of Pakistan related to the national ethos was heavily influenced by their religious affiliation and the question loomed large of who spoke for Islam in a government insisting on civic virtues and secular processes. The issue went beyond politics to the matter of legal structures and popular representation. The sovereignty of state and people lost significance in the affirmation of belief. Monotheism is not only an all-encompassing principle, it also establishes the connection between God and humankind. God's will is eternal and immutable. Human law is frail, temporary, and always subject to challenge. God delegates sovereignty to mortal human beings, but God's will is not subject to challenge. In the end, therefore, Pakistan's 1956 constitution accepted the sovereignty of God, but temporal issues, in particular who should govern, were left to the ministrations of fallible men.

Mirza was such a fallible man. Unhappy with the need to accept the parliamentary system, he acceded to the pressures imposed by the constitution. He yielded to the need to play at politics by surrounding himself with strong personalities who could be expected to act in accordance with his ideas. His choice for the leadership of the new One Unit of West Pakistan was the frontier leader and opponent of the Muslim League, Dr. Khan Sahib. Mirza pulled another rabbit out of his hat when in September 1956, with the collaboration of Dr. Khan Sahib and the Punjabi Mushtaque Ahmed Gurmani, he prompted the formation of the Republican Party. Chaudhri Mohammad Ali, the Prime Minister, had also assumed the presidency of the Muslim League, and when he learned that many of the larger Punjabi landlords had resigned membership in his party in order to join the Republicans, he accused Mirza of betrayal. In the end, Mohammad Ali quit his post in the Muslim League and resigned the office of Prime

Minister. Suhrawardy was named to succeed as Prime Minister, but Sardar Abdur Rab Nishtar had gained control of the Muslim League. Mirza was determined to neutralize Nishtar, however, whom he believed would lead the party into the arms of religious radicals. Allying with the secular Suhrawardy was therefore seen as creating the necessary coalition between the West Pakistani Republicans and East Pakistan's Awami League. The alliance seemed to satisfy Suhrawardy's long quest for true parity between the two wings of Pakistan. But both Suhrawardy and especially Mirza saw it as sustaining Pakistan's experiment in secular nation building. Moreover, it appeared to make the Muslim League even more irrelevant.

Mirza's calculations, however, proved faulty. Suhrawardy was challenged by the Suez Crisis of 1956, when Israel, France, and Britain attacked Egypt, essentially over the question of whether the latter had the right to nationalize the Suez Canal. The reaction in Pakistan to the invasion of a Muslim country was both vituperative and violent. Suhrawardy rejected the demand to support Egypt, thus increasing the fury of the street demonstrations and further undermining his authority. Moreover, the Muslim League's more Islamist posturing paid off with a renewal of popular support. Nishtar and his colleagues berated the government and demanded Pakistan cut its Western-engineered alliances in the Baghdad Pact and South-East Asia Treaty Organization (SEATO). Suhrawardy was labeled a threat to the Islamic world and a lackey of neo-imperialists. When the Jamaat-i-Islami added its voice to the chorus of dissent, and even found common cause with the country's leftists and communists, Mirza sidestepped responsibility and allowed Suhrawardy to bear the brunt of the assault on government policy. Suhrawardy's Awami League also fractured over the incident and the Prime Minister's position was made even more tenuous. In the end, Suhrawardy's government was terminated and the President demonstrated how quickly he could form still another unlikely coalition, this time between his Republican Party and the Muslim League.

In the background of these developments Dr. Khan Sahib and Mirza began plotting a civil coup. Talk circulated about the formation of a "revolutionary council" that would result in the suspension of the constitution. In 1957, on still another front, provincial leaders, largely identified with the political left, formed the National Awami Party (NAP). The NAP became the principal rival of the Awami League in East Pakistan. Its national status, however, also threatened the survival of the Muslim League in West Pakistan. The NAP was an immediate and formidable presence. Maulana Bhashani broke with the Awami League and Suhrawardy over the Suez issue and assumed the Bengali leadership of the new party. The Balochi leader A.S. Achakzai represented the NAP in his region, Mian Iftikharuddin spoke for the Punjab, G.M. Syed led the Sindh contingent, and Abdul Ghaffar Khan assumed a similar role in the North West Frontier Province. Forced by the Pakistan army to reject the radical separatists – indeed the NAP had vowed to dissolve the One Unit of West Pakistan and restore the original provinces – Mirza was also ready to dismiss Suhrawardy. Ironically, Mirza's only choice for a new coalition partner was Abdur Rab Nishtar and his Muslim League. In spite of all his distaste for the Islamists, Mirza chose them for his partners in order to deny the goals of the NAP. Political double-dealing and the curious gyrations in Pakistani politics had reached an intolerable level. Mirza played the game as well as anyone, but his more serious thoughts were riveted on the necessity for a civilian-led *putsch*.

Mirza, however, had to contend with General Ayub Khan, who had also displayed increasing distress over Pakistan's sustained instability. Ayub had become even more disillusioned with the behavior of the country's politicians. He was no less incensed by Mirza's opportunism and unabashed ambition. Whereas Mirza, to some extent, was constrained by the political ambience, Ayub had no difficulty in separating himself from it. As a civilian in a constitutional system, Mirza needed to play at politics. Ayub could avoid doing so. The two men therefore began to tread different paths. Realizing Mirza and his immediate followers would need the army to effect a civilian coup, Ayub pondered whether it was in his or the army's interest to become an instrument of personalities they could not respect. Ayub began to think of reconstructing Pakistan from the ground up, that is, after discarding all the political baggage accumulated since Liaquat's assassination. Mirza's selection of the Muslim Leaguer I.I. Chundrigar to be the new Prime Minister was a case in point.

Mirza could not avoid allying with the Muslim League, and although he was able to bypass Nishtar, by selecting Chundrigar, Ayub believed the maneuvering was counterproductive. Calm had not been restored, popular confidence had reached its lowest level, deeper fissures had opened between East and West Pakistan, and now too a major controversy had erupted over the issue of separate or joint electorates. Separate electorates stretched back to the colonial Morley–Minto Reforms of 1909 and had become an integral feature of Muslim League politics. Joint electorates, a creature of the East Pakistan Awami League, which rejected the policy of defining political affiliation along religious lines, would include Hindus among its members. This dispute tore at the nation's social and political fabric, the Muslim League expressing the concern that Pakistan's survival was in question. Mirza saw the affair as a tempest in a teapot, since West Pakistan was home to so few Hindus. Moreover, elections were not a common experience in Pakistan. The nation had yet to manage its first national election campaign and the provincial elections were hardly affected by the electorate issue. Nevertheless, Mirza was forced to respond and, because proponents on each side were able to bring their emotional supporters into the streets, he decided to release his Muslim League partners. The Chundrigar government was dismissed and a fellow Republican and feudal leader, Malik Firoz Khan Noon, was called to form still another government.

Noon's cabinet included politicians from all the significant political parties of East and West, except Islamist organizations like the Muslim League, Jamaat-i-Islami, and Nizam-i-Islam. Even Dr. Khan Sahib and Suhrawardy, previously archenemies, found common ground on which to support the new government. Differences, however, had not diminished, and opportunism more than accommodation was the theme of this latest scenario. Moreover, central government activity could not obscure the intensification of crisis politics in the two provinces. East Pakistan was especially unstable as the principal provincial parties jockeyed for an advantage. Unable to reconcile the politicians, particularly those represented by Mujibur Rahman, the now established leader of the Awami League, Mirza made Fazlul Huq the governor of the province. Fazlul Huq acted on command in muzzling Mujib, but he could not prevent the violence that tore up the provincial legislature. Nor could Fazlul Huq prevent the mayhem from spilling into the streets. Strikes and riots had become commonplace, taxing police capabilities and often resulting in army intervention. Conditions in West Pakistan were hardly better in 1958. Dr. Khan Sahib was shot and killed by an unknown assassin, and Abdur Rab Nishtar passed away in his sleep. Both individuals were unique major actors on the political stage, and both were difficult to replace. Their deaths came just as the anti-United-States demonstrations by leftists and Islamists reached crescendo proportions. Pakistan had joined the American cold war alliances with SEATO in 1954 and the Central Treaty Organization (CENTO) in 1955 and the demonstrators demanded the severance of those pacts. In the meantime, Ghaffar Khan, the "Frontier Gandhi," was calling for a war (*jung*) against the central government and had raised anew his earlier call to the Pashtuns for secession and the formation of a sovereign Pashtunistan.

Firoz Khan Noon had no control over events. Nor could he manage affairs in the parliament. Totally dependent on the military establishment, he too yearned for an end to the political charade. The promulgation of the constitution had done nothing to restrain the dissidents and their followers. The country had become unmanageable and there was no indication the rabble in the streets would opt for laws and rules that meant nothing to them. Moreover, there were increasing cries for rebellion and secession in both wings of the country. All threats were registered with General Ayub, but it was the least of the crises that moved him to action. The Khan of Kalat, ruler of a remote and barren region in Balochistan, declared he had taken personal control of his ancestral lands and that he no longer respected the ties that bound Kalat to Pakistan. Ayub, who had been patiently waiting to take direct action against what he judged to be the anti-Pakistan crowd, did not hesitate in sending his troops into Kalat.

On October 6, 1958 General Ayub ordered the army to seize the Khan's lands, depose him, and strip him of all his titles. The Khan was subsequently arrested and thrown into a Pakistani prison. The very next day the Pakistan army seized control of the radio and telegraph stations in Karachi, Lahore, Peshawar, and Dacca. Troops occupied the railway and air terminals, as well as the ports of Karachi and Chittagong. The National Assembly and provincial legislatures were closed and orders were given to the country's newspapers not to publish anything that had not been approved by military authority. Finally, the constitution, promulgated barely two years earlier, after so much delay and rancor, was abrogated. All political party activity was banned. The imposition of martial law was a reality, and given the speed with which the country was brought under army decree, it had no doubt been planned well in advance of the action.

The Kalat secession was merely the trip-wire, not the cause for the military operation. When the dust settled on that first day, it was made public that Mirza and Ayub had engineered the coup. Mirza remained President and Ayub was named the country's Chief Martial Law Administrator. Dual leadership, however, was hardly a likely prospect. Mirza now knew that Ayub had his own plan for Pakistan's future. Moreover, Mirza was successful at intrigue but not given to large-scale planning. Nor did he have the support of the army, which showed allegiance only to Ayub. Ayub Khan's role as Chief Martial Law Administrator was Mirza's major obstacle and indeed it tended to make the President redundant. Mirza therefore lost little time in attempting to separate the army high command from its commander-in-chief. The President told the nation that martial law was a temporary measure. And to Ayub's surprise he also announced he was arranging an emergency cabinet and had named General Ayub Prime Minister.

Ayub, however, was beyond flattery. The Prime Minister's office, even without the constitution, was without real power. Moreover, the personalities that occupied the office were never secure from the long reach of the Governor General, and now the President. The viceregal tradition remained the central theme of Pakistani governance. Ayub therefore refused to fall into a trap so obviously prepared. He ordered his top commanders to meet with Mirza. They were instructed to serve Mirza with a direct order to resign his office and leave the country for permanent exile in Great Britain. If he refused he would be imprisoned and tried for high crimes. His cabal having failed, Mirza accepted the offer to leave Pakistan and he was hurriedly escorted to a waiting aircraft. Subsequently, General Ayub Khan declared martial law would not be quickly lifted, nor did he have any intention of resurrecting the abrogated constitution. The country, he said, was firmly in control of the army; a new civilian government would have to wait on the passage of events.

The Ayub Khan era

Pakistan was barely eleven years old when martial law was clamped on the body politic. The politicians had lost the confidence of the rank-and-file citizen, and the bureaucracy had shown that it too was inept in mastering the political conditions. The army's intervention into the political realm was therefore greeted with considerable popular approval. It had been a long and trying decade. For most Pakistanis the belief persisted that only the army could clean the Augean stables, or offer new directions for their greater concerns. The abrogation of the constitution and the stifling of the political parties received less attention than might otherwise have been anticipated. General Ayub Khan, for a brief moment, was the country's knight in shining armor. Ayub seized the moment by declaring a period of reform and national reconstruction. He also let it be known that Pakistan was unprepared for a full-blown experiment in parliamentary government. Too much time had been wasted in meaningless debate, and too many precious resources had been squandered in projects of little national significance. Ayub declared it his intention to avoid the pitfalls of his predecessors.

The army was organized along lines that stressed discipline and unity and the General made it abundantly clear the country would be organized to follow a similar path. Tribal and ethnic divisions, vast illiteracy, and sectarian conflict militated against the parliamentary system as well as against contemporary expressions of democracy. Ayub was emphatic on this point. The nation was not ready for democracy as practiced in Western Europe and another form of democratic expression had to be found to give voice to popular longings for self-improvement. Ayub's answer to the dilemma was a system of local government that he referred to as "Basic Democracies." Although the more sophisticated elements of the population were quick to denounce the idea, the General refused to be dissuaded.

Ayub introduced his Basic Democracies System on the first anniversary of his taking power. It was a tiered arrangement. At its lowest level were the directly elected Basic Democrats who represented the local population. Essentially a rural system, Basic Democracies also involved the towns and municipalities and in large part was intended to provide the voting public with direct connection to their representatives. Denied political party affiliation, the Basic Democrats were seemingly made accountable to the electorate, whose felt needs were to be reflected in the actions taken by the lowest level union councils. Resources made available to the union councils were linked with a Works Program supported largely from funds made available from donor countries. Basic Democracies in Ayub's judgment was a method of learning the ways of self-government; it also sought to expand developmental operations at the grassroot level.

Guiding the Basic Democrats was a second tier composed of elected chairmen of the union councils and members of the civil bureaucracy. Expertise in managing projects was supposedly available at this level and it was soon clear that the professional administrators had been made responsible for the success or failure of local ventures. The third tier corresponded with district administration, with the deputy commissioner established as the chairman of a body that represented more sophisticated law and order issues as well as developmental matters. The fourth tier represented the traditional administrative divisions; this tier was clearly dominated by senior members of the civil service. The immediate criticism leveled against Basic Democracies was that the system did little to free the citizen from the control of the bureaucracy. Ayub deflected such attacks by emphasizing the need to tutor the population in political responsibility while also recruiting the masses for their own self-improvement.

Still another criticism surfaced shortly after the creation of the Basic Democracies when Ayub called for a vote of confidence in his administration and asked the Basic Democrats to cast the required votes. No one expected the Basic Democrats, all beholden to Ayub, to vote against him and thereby nullify their newly acquired influence. Despite the criticism, therefore, Ayub was overwhelmingly given his vote of confidence and Basic Democracies became a centerpiece of his administration. Ayub, however, moved on a number of fronts soon after assuming the presidency. Martial law was sustained indefinitely. Ayub promoted himself to the rank of Field Marshal and retained effective but not direct control of the Pakistan army and armed forces.

Armed with dictatorial powers, Ayub's rule was more benign than oppressive. Politicians were isolated and often imprisoned, but Ayub's purpose was to embarrass, humiliate, and neutralize, not physically punish, let alone order the execution of those deemed guilty of illicit and often criminal behavior. Ayub was not mean spirited, nor did he harbor a vengeful attitude. National solidarity was his objective, and he sought the cooperation of those whom he believed had the country's preservation as their primary interest. A student of Aligarh, Ayub imbibed much of Jinnah's teaching and although a staunch Muslim he too believed the country was better off when freed from the machinations of those in the religious community who stressed a theological definition of the state. Ayub assumed a secular stance in his contest with the Islamists and for him the country was too divided along ethnic, religious, and geographic lines to adopt an absolutist interpretation of Islam. Muslim interests had to be served because the state was formed to provide Muslims with a freedom they did not expect to enjoy in a country dominated by Hindus. But this did not mean Muslims could ignore the views of non-Muslims, nor did it mean one version of Islamic practice prevailed over others. Ayub therefore opposed sectarian expression in all its forms and displayed little patience with those measuring loyalty in the context of narrowly defined religious beliefs.

Ayub inherited a refugee problem of immense proportions. Little if anything had been done to alleviate the plight of those that had come to Pakistan from India after partition. He ordered one of his premier generals to bulldoze the slum dwellings around Karachi and Dacca and erect permanent housing for the otherwise most neglected segments of the population. Previous governments also had done nothing to reduce the corruption in the distribution of evacuee property. Venal behavior had become the pattern in the issuing of licenses, the setting of standards, and the determination of ownership of property. Ayub's administration sought to put an end to these practices and to assure the distribution of holdings would be proper and fair. Rapid industrialization, however, complicated the task of those responsible for the equitable distribution of resources. By the same token, prices for essential commodities were arbitrarily inflated and the collection of taxes from the wealthy was a virtual impossibility. The few therefore had grown rich at the expense of the many and the general public was made to suffer high prices and massive unemployment. Black markets flourished in these conditions. Food and medicine were adulterated and standards were hard to implement. Smuggling was rampant and too many government officials were found engaged in the selling of permits for imported goods.

The martial law government was called to address all these problems. It restricted the import of foreign-made products, it lowered prices on staple and essential items, and it was forceful in arresting those found exploiting the public. Public corporations were established in vital sectors of the economy, and army officers, both serving and retired, were placed in charge of their operations. The government also tried an export bonus scheme in an effort to stimulate economic growth, and those businesses involved in questionable practices were sealed or seized so that their account books could be audited for fraud and other misdemeanors. The business community decried these actions and a number of business leaders fled the country, taking their wealth with them. Nevertheless, the government uncovered hidden caches in a number of high-profile cases and the general public truly believed the Ayub government would bring an end to the huge concentration of wealth in a few hands.

Ayub also introduced land reforms and a Land Reform Commission was established with orders to break up the feudal estates in West Pakistan, especially in the Punjab. Individual holdings of five hundred acres of irrigated land, one thousand of non-irrigated land, and 150 acres of orchard land were sanctioned, and the opportunity was provided to transfer excess land to other family members. What were deemed to be surplus holdings were to be transferred to government control for distribution to the landless cultivators. Lands identified with pious endowments, however, were not included. A West Pakistan Land Commission was created to implement the reforms and in time it came to control more than two and a half million acres of farmland. The Commission paid substantial sums in compensation for the seizure of lands from about nine hundred large landlords, but the landed elite remained intact and very few peasant-cultivators experienced a change in their living standard.

Good intentions were never enough in the implementation phase. In spite of the serious effort to serve the mass public by targeting those aggrandizing themselves, Ayub's reforms fell short of their mark. In the agricultural sector, little was really done to reduce the power and influence of the country's landlords. The martial law authority was dependent on the landlords for the maintenance of law and order in their respective regions and the regime could not avoid complicity with the major feudal chieftains. Moreover, the land had been abused and misused since colonial times when barrage systems were developed to enhance the productivity of the soil. It was no coincidence that the largest and most powerful landlords were located in Punjab and Sindh provinces, the location of the most extensive barrage and irrigation systems. But the inability to properly use large quantities of water had produced a nightmare of waterlogging and salinity by the time Pakistan achieved independence. More land was removed from cultivation each year than could be replaced by improved practices. Ayub therefore leaned on both the landlords and foreign donors, notably the United States, to address the dilemma. A vast and costly project was launched to reverse the loss of land and to reclaim lands already affected, but this could not be done without the support of the feudal leaders. Ayub launched a "Green Revolution" aimed at improving agricultural yields, but the role of the large landlord class was central to its success. In the end, little was done to correct the politics of land-holding and the influence of the landed class remained virtually unchecked.

One of the first martial law regulations was aimed at identifying and eliminating corrupt civil servants. Taking bribes and other abuses of power were commonplace and tribunals were established to ferret out the worst miscreants. Numerous civilian committees were organized and provided quasi-judicial powers to try bureaucrats who had violated the public trust. By the end of June 1959, 1662 central government officials and more than four thousand provincial officers were found guilty of a variety of offenses and removed from the service. Although many dishonest officials escaped scrutiny, there was no ignoring the positive effect of the program. To assure a higher ethical standard, Ayub promoted the establishment of a number of training institutions for civil servants. The Pakistan Administrative Staff College was organized to provide in-service training for senior officials, while the National Institutes of Public Administration offered educational experience to middle managers. Rural Development Academies were also created to center administrative expertise in strictly agrarian circumstances. Ayub presided over the Bureau of National Reconstruction with its emphasis on attitudinal change and ethical behavior. Ayub called on the country's leaders to posture themselves as role models and practice probity and a genuine sense of national responsibility. Concerned with the need to transcend sectarianism, provincialism, tribalism, and rival clan behavior, the martial law government spoke of the need for socio-psychological engineering, but programs to implement such activity were as limited as the people who might be called upon to lead them.

Responsibility for all sorts of reform rested on indigenous personnel. A Woman's Voluntary Group, led by the President's wife, was formed in 1959 to encourage the development of cottage industries, but the program failed to enlist the services of the upper classes, who insisted on maintaining their peculiar lifestyles. The more affluent members of society preferred imported goods to the poorer-quality local manufactures; their buying habits stunted the growth of domestic industries. Moreover, the Ministry of Information and Broadcasting had been given overall charge of such programs and failure was often attributed to false and misleading propaganda. Similar efforts were made to improve working conditions and especially manager–labor relations. Strikes and protest marches, so common before the martial law period, were banned. The Ayub government pressured property owners to elevate pay scales as well as to make the workplace a safer environment. An Industrial Disputes Ordinance was put into force to improve communications between labor and management, and an Industrial Court was created to mediate contentious disputes. Although lacking in achievements, Ayub's administration had raised the profile of the working class and contributed to higher worker productivity. For the first time, labor abuses, particularly among the very poor and illiterate, were given consideration.

The Ayub government formed numerous commissions to investigate the legal, educational, and medical systems, as well as the role of the press. A Law Commission examined the work of the courts and recommended the establishment of Family Courts to focus attention on marriage and divorce as well as the care of children. Citing high population increases, Ayub plunged into the family planning issue, ordering the expansion of clinics concerned with the distribution of birth control information and devices. Addressing a subject that his critics argued preached a form of blasphemy, Ayub tried to comfort his compatriots, saying he had no intention of attacking Islamic teaching; that his sole concern was unlimited population growth and the threat it posed to the country's attempt to lift itself from poverty. Resistance to family planning, however, was well organized and passionate. Under pressure, Ayub pressed for acceptance of the Muslim Family Laws Ordinance that required the registration of marriages and divorce. Again insisting the Family Laws in no way contradicted the Qur'an, he said the purpose of the laws was to preserve the family by protecting the weaker female partner from an abusive husband. Although the Family Laws Ordinance was largely in tune with the more sophisticated section of the population, the overwhelming majority was constrained by more traditional practices. The laws impacted on Sunni Muslims differently from Shia Muslims, and religious divines combined forces with the Islamists to impede their implementation. Ayub's creation of a Central Institute of Islamic Research was an attempt to bypass the *ulema*'s legal commentaries and to provide more modern explanations of Islamic tradition. Acknowledged scholars of Islam were made directors of the Institute in an effort to elevate its prestige, but the intensification of the assault on the family planning program made even these individuals targets of a mounting anti-Ayub opposition.

Ayub had taken a page from the book of Mustafa Kemal Ataturk, the army leader who had played the pivotal role in the creation of the modern Republic of Turkey. Ataturk had emphasized the need to establish Turkey as a secular state and had introduced wide-ranging reforms that successfully separated the country from its immediate past. Ayub sought to imitate Ataturk, but conditions in Pakistan were not the same. Turkey had been salvaged from the remnants of the Ottoman Empire;

Pakistan was a consequence of a colonial dispensation that had little relevance to the contemporary nation-state. Turkey emerged as a sovereign and independent nation-state in wartime circumstances that assured instant national identity. Pakistan arrived on the world stage as a truncated structure, housing a diverse, disparate, and divided people. Furthermore, the British Raj officiated at a transfer of power to a political movement that had not yet established itself as a formal political party. Ayub therefore inherited the legacy of a failed political experience that was long on rhetoric and sentiment but short on the pragmatic methods of self-government.

The Muslim League bore closer resemblance to the Moghuls than to a modern political organization. Hence the League chose ruling over shared governance and failed to lay the foundation for a competitive political environment. Seeking a monopoly of power, in a few short years the League had become an anachronism, something that could be ignored, and in a short time discarded. By its own actions, the Muslim League also became the catalyst for the formation of numerous organizations, none of which truly gave the interests of the whole nation high priority. In spite of the obvious need for guidance and effective public policy, successive Pakistan governments abdicated their responsibilities and plunged the nation into deeper problems. It was these circumstances that challenged General Ayub. Given his apolitical background, it is remarkable how well he grasped the essentials of his new calling. Ataturk's experience may well have nurtured his psyche, but Ayub alone made the decision to reconstruct Pakistan.

No one, save Ayub, had given serious consideration to the kind of nation Pakistan might become. The Government of India Act, 1935 and the India Independence Act, 1947 framed the form of government that Pakistan would inherit from its former colonial rulers. No effort had been made to determine whether the political design suggested by those imperial actions was suited to Pakistan's circumstances. It was only with Ayub's seizure of power and the neutralizing of the forces that had played with Pakistan's destiny that a determined effort was made toward national reconstruction. Ayub spoke about the "genius" of the Pakistani nation and for doing so he was heavily criticized as furthering his personal interests. In fact, however, he was the first of Pakistan's leaders after Jinnah to demonstrate a vision for a country still in the process of becoming. Ayub's opponents, who derived from many circles, accused him of duplicity and self-serving behavior, of reaching for absolute power and personal glory, but these opponents never offered an alternative plan for the new nation. Ayub's role as Pakistan's principal architect derived more from the forces arrayed against him than from his own person. Nevertheless, Ayub was, by every estimate of leadership, forward looking and dedicated to steering a course that the nation could follow long after him.

It was Ayub Khan who called for the building of a new capital on the Potwar Plateau, outside of Rawalpindi. Arguing that Karachi could not remain the seat of government, Ayub cited the commercial significance of the port, as well as its vast international air terminus. Business and government required separation and ample room for expansion. Moreover, the Pakistan government required far more space than was conveniently available in Karachi. From such initial thinking came the decision to construct a new city in the Pakistani hinterland. Ayub spoke of his dream for a new capital at a governors' conference in June 1959. He described the site of the federal capital as bridging Punjab and the North West Frontier Province. He also mentioned the need for what he called a "second" or "administrative capital" in Dacca, East Pakistan. Though he was sensitive to the concerns of the Bengalis for parity, Ayub's gesture was not well received by the Bengalis and from the outset they were among the most vocal opponents of the scheme. What Ayub believed to be the extension of a helping hand was translated into a "second best" notion that did more to stir the passions than temper them. Nevertheless, ground was broken for the building of Islamabad in the early 1960s, and the second-capital project followed shortly afterwards. Critics continued to complain about the audacity of the administration and that the projects would bankrupt the nation and pit one region of the country against the others. Mindful of this opposition, Ayub nevertheless gave the order to commence operations, and construction on both "capitals" proceeded with due speed. The shift of federal offices from Karachi to Islamabad was slated for 1964, with the embassies beginning their move the following year.

In his many reforms Ayub anticipated the eventual heightening of a revitalized Pakistani identity and the bridging of the divide separating East and West Pakistan. Expectations, however, are easily dashed and so it was with Ayub Khan. For all his references to democratic enrichment, Ayub was a dictator and behaved like one, especially in the eyes of his detractors. Martial law remained in place for almost four years. The Ayub administration had sufficient time to cause distress in numerous places and among many different would-be representatives of the Pakistani nation. Ayub had argued forcefully against the reinstatement of political parties, believing they did more to diminish growth than enhance it. Controversy, Ayub believed, was acceptable so long as the result was positive and in the best interests of the country. Controversy, however, that deepened hostilities, exploited divisions, and ignored institutional compromise served no meaningful purpose and was best avoided. Pakistani society was far too subjected to ambitious leaders and their inherently violent followers to benefit from the free play of organized politics. People, he believed, needed time to develop the characteristics of citizenship and responsibility. Leaders needed to understand the significance of accountability. Education and hands-on experience in the fundamentals of self-government, as in the Basic Democracies, might have reduced politics to the lowest common denominator, but without that exposure it was doubtful the people of Pakistan could accommodate twentieth-century experience.

Ayub was dedicated to the restructuring of Pakistan. He envisaged a new constitutional order that was more suited to the genius of the nation, and he organized a Constitution Commission to take on that task. It was Ayub's objective to bury the past and at the same time to erect an edifice that reflected the nature and purpose of the country. Referred to by a distant admirer as a Solon or "Law Giver," Ayub was not yet ready to retreat from the political scene, nor was he one to yield to his opposition without a struggle. Much had been done during the period of martial law, but the real test of the Ayub era would be seen in the period that lay ahead.

Bibliography

Ahmed, Mohammad, *My Chief*, Lahore: Longman, Green, 1960.

Ali, Tariq, *Pakistan: Military Rule or People's Power?*, London: Jonathan Cape, 1970.

Ashford, Douglas E., *National Development and Local Reform: Political Participation in Morocco, Tunisia and Pakistan*, Princeton: Princeton University Press, 1967.

Choudhury, G.W., *Democracy in Pakistan*, Vancouver: University of British Columbia, 1963.

Feldman, Herbert, *Revolution in Pakistan: A Study of the Martial Law Administration*, London: Oxford University Press, 1967.

Gardezi, Hassan and Rashid, Jamil, *Pakistan: The Roots of Dictatorship*, London: Zed Press, 1983.

Jennings, Sir Ivor, *Constitutional Problems in Pakistan*, Cambridge: Cambridge University Press, 1957.

Kennedy, Charles H., *Bureaucracy in Pakistan*, Karachi: Oxford University Press, 1987.

Khan, Mohammad Ayub, *Friends Not Masters: A Political Autobiography*, Oxford: Oxford University Press, 1967.

Mahmood, Afzal, *Law and Principles of Local Government in Pakistan: Basic Democracies*, Lahore: All Pakistan Legal Decisions, 1964.

McDonough, Sheila, "Pakistan," in *Islam in Politics: A Muslim World Symposium*, reprinted from *The Muslim World*, Hartford: Hartford Seminary Foundation, 1966.

Minattur, Joseph, *Martial Law in India, Pakistan and Ceylon*, The Hague: Martinus Nijhoff, 1962.

Rizvi, Hasan-Askari, *The Military and Politics in Pakistan*, Lahore: Progressive Publishers, 1974.

Rizvi, Hasan-Askari, *The Military and Politics in Pakistan, 1947–86*, Lahore: Progressive Publishers, 1986.

Saeed, S. A., *President without Precedent: A Brilliant Account of Ayub and His Regime*, Lahore: Lahore Book Depot, 1960.

Smith, Wilfred Cantwell, *Islam in Modern History*, Princeton: Princeton University Press, 1957.

Zahur-ud-Din, Mian, *West Pakistan Family Courts Act*, Lahore: Mansoor Book House, 1965.

Zakaria, Nasim, *Parliamentary Government in Pakistan*, Lahore: New Publishers, 1958.

Ziring, Lawrence, *The Ayub Khan Era: Politics in Pakistan, 1958–1969*, Syracuse, NY: Syracuse University Press, 1971.

4

YEARS OF WAR: THE TURNING POINT

There is never a definitive answer to the question of whether individuals or events are more important in the making of history. One thing is certain, however: people and events are bundled together in a nexus that makes people either the master of events or their victims. Mohammad Ayub Khan, Field Marshal and President of Pakistan, set himself the task of salvaging what he could from Jinnah's creation. As a junior officer in the British Indian army, Ayub would have been content to serve his time in the service of the monarchy, but events decreed otherwise. Once the Pakistan Movement assumed real purpose and pointed in the direction of a Muslim-dominant state in the subcontinent, there was no question about Ayub's choice or his decision. As a Pashtun from the Rawalpindi region, there was no alternative to joining Pakistan and the Pakistan army. Events were in the saddle and Ayub rode them in the direction they were headed. A Sandhurst graduate and the scion of a family with an army heritage, Ayub was seasoned as an officer in World War II. Opting for Pakistan, he subsequently was named to the Services Selection Board by Prime Minister Liaquat Ali Khan and was a ranking officer in the Punjab Boundary Force when the province was divided between India and Pakistan. Nothing in those very early days hinted that Ayub Khan in a few short years would become the central actor in the Pakistan story. Events were in the saddle and in the tumultuous years leading up to and following partition, one could only follow what destiny had determined.

Ayub was not the most senior general in the chain of command when he was selected to become the first indigenous commander of the Pakistan army. Ayub replaced Sir Douglas Gracey after serving a tour as General Officer Commanding in East Bengal. Ayub's selection to head the Pakistan army was a consequence of two recommendations, one by Defense Secretary Iskandar Mirza and the other by Begum Liaquat Ali Khan, the Prime Minister's wife. Ayub's appointment did not sit well with some of the higher serving officers and a plot was soon launched to oust him, to take control of the army, and to dismantle the government – the "Rawalpindi Conspiracy." Ayub was alerted to an intended coup led by General Akbar Khan, and without hesitation he ordered the arrest and trial of the General and his conspirators. It was a formative moment in the professional life of Mohammad Ayub Khan and his actions demonstrated that he, not events, was in control. The experience hardened the resolve of the army commander and for the first time caused him to contemplate his new role and how it intertwined with Pakistan's future. Once in the saddle, Ayub became a maker of events and he no longer doubted that his destiny and the country's destiny were one and the same.

Ayub's appointment as commander of the Pakistan army became official in January 1951. Prime Minister Liaquat Ali Khan revealed the "Rawalpindi Conspiracy" to the Pakistani public in March. Liaquat's assassination occurred in October of that same year. These events placed Ayub in the forefront of Pakistani political life and shaped his future. While primarily concerned with the modernization of the army, he had become too involved in the political process to assume a neutral role, especially following the emasculation of the Muslim League and its displacement by members of the higher bureaucracy. Ayub was a close observer of the events that brought Ghulam Mohammad and Iskandar Mirza into the chief executive's office. He served both men loyally and faithfully but also noted their failings, and pondered the long-term effect of their administrations on the nation. Ayub had rejected Ghulam Mohammad's order to declare martial law in 1954, and he patiently gave the politicians as much time as the country could tolerate in the hope that differences could be resolved and the nation's business addressed. Only when all other remedies had been exhausted did he agree to follow Mirza's lead in dissolving the civilian government of Malik Firoz Khan Noon. Martial law was imposed on the nation reluctantly but firmly. Ayub and Mirza, however, were very different personalities, and from the outset it was obvious they could not both rule Pakistan. Confronted by still another conspiracy, and realizing Pakistan needed a new beginning, Ayub no longer waited on events. His actions in removing Mirza were swift and defining. On September 27, 1958, with Mirza on a plane bound for England, Mohammad Ayub Khan became President of Pakistan.

Once having consolidated his power, Ayub turned immediately to the work of reconstituting the political system, albeit under the limitations of martial law. Described as a dictator, the General, now a self-made Field Marshal, emphasized the need for national renewal in a country divided against itself as well as threatened by its larger neighbor. Ayub's effort to reduce tensions between India and Pakistan had been thwarted by Indian Prime Minister Jawaharlal Nehru. Nehru rejected Ayub's offer of joint defense. He also refused to entertain a negotiated settlement of their Kashmir dispute. Diplomacy was neglected in favor of increased military posturing, and the conditions that strained their relationship went unattended. Had Nehru not been in the twilight of his life perhaps he would have recognized that the man in uniform was his best opportunity for a substantive and permanent agreement. Subsequent events would reveal how tragic was the loss of that moment in 1959 when Ayub reached for the hand of his adversary, only to realize there was nothing to grasp.

Unable to move on the international front, Ayub devoted much of his energy to domestic affairs. National unity shared highest priority alongside national security. Ayub bypassed the politicians and enlisted the services of some of the brightest of Pakistan's military and civil officers, in addition to intellectuals and career specialists. Notable among his choices was a Lahore barrister, the sophisticated and well-educated Manzur Qadir. Like Ayub and his army colleagues, Manzur Qadir saw the need for a system of political order that weighed heavily in favor of the executive branch. Ayub also drafted a number of high-ranking generals to serve as ministers and ambassadors and to assume other high profile roles in the central and provincial governments. Ayub chose his confidants with care and with concern for the needs of his administration. The generals surrounding him were selected for their loyalty and discipline as well as their ability to lead. The civilians were chosen for their intelligence and sophistication and in the belief that their services to the nation would be marked and enduring. One appointment, however, proved critical. Zulfikar Ali Bhutto, the son of a pre-independence politician and one of Sindh province's most prominent landlords, had graduated from the University of California, Berkeley, and had passed the bar at Britain's Lincoln's Inn. He was brought to Ayub's attention after a brief stint as a teacher and publicist of international law. Ayub was impressed with Bhutto's credentials and youthful potential, and at the age of 29 Bhutto was admitted to the federal cabinet. It was not long before Bhutto entered Ayub's inner circle.

Bhutto's intimacy with Ayub and his special interest in international affairs drew him into army circles, where he cultivated ranking officers and appeared to share their views and concerns. He also revealed significant interest in the Kashmir dilemma and was drawn to those officers with an abiding determination to gain control over the disputed territory. Bhutto even made associations with the accused in the "Rawalpindi Conspiracy," notably its leader Akbar Khan, who in 1955 had been set free on orders of Ghulam Mohammad. Akbar Khan had joined the Awami League of H.S. Suhrawardy upon his release, but after the banning of the parties following the imposition of martial law he decided to attend law school. Akbar Khan remained a determined foe of Ayub Khan and he often stood out among those denouncing the Field Marshal as a dictator and tyrant. Ayub saw nothing wrong in Bhutto's activities, and indeed believed his ability to relate to different sectors of public opinion was an asset not a problem for his administration. By the same token, Bhutto saw no reason to alter his behavior, especially because with every new connection he expanded his personal horizon. Although the Ayub regime in time would lose virtually all its popularity, Bhutto's stock in the political process continued to grow. The young man seemed unable to do anything wrong and his political destiny could only be enhanced by Ayub's negative ratings.

Despite Bhutto's behind-the-scenes maneuvers, Ayub continued to nurture the young man. Ayub's decision to lift martial law in 1962 and to restore the political process met with Bhutto's approval, although it was obvious he disagreed with the counsel provided to Ayub by Manzur Qadir. Compared with the middle-aged Qadir, Bhutto was young, flamboyant, and dynamic, and enjoyed interacting with the public. Qadir had no interest in politics or personal power and served the President only with the thought that his services helped shape a more integrated and forward-looking nation. Qadir was the proverbial scholar, a man of grace and even temperament. Bhutto, by contrast, was passionate and mercurial and had developed a burning ambition to rule Pakistan. Qadir and Bhutto had studied abroad, each was a lawyer, but Qadir possessed none of the aristocratic airs of Bhutto. Manzur Qadir sought no personal rewards or honors. Bhutto, on the other hand, joined Ayub because the Field Marshal contributed to the realization of his aspirations. Each man became an intimate of Ayub, but each played a different role in his administration: one was a private confidant of the President, the other a public personality with a gift of oratory that was especially important with the younger generation.

The presidential constitution that Ayub promulgated in 1962 was the acknowledged work of Manzur Qadir. The decision to disallow party politics also revealed Qadir's influence. So too did the intention to emphasize Pakistan as a secular state. Moreover, the belief persisted that the politicians needed mentoring in the ways of democratic behavior, and that their party affiliations were more a formula for political instability than a representation of competitive politics. National unity was the fundamental goal of the Ayub administration and Ayub reopened the political process with what he hoped would be a system without parties. It was not long, however, before Ayub was forced to admit that the reinstatement of conventional political activity was necessary. Nor could Ayub avoid the clamor that Pakistan be identified with its Muslim yearnings. Under pressure to officially declare Pakistan an Islamic Republic, Ayub cast aside his original plan and all reference to secularism was muted.

The gathering storm

Once Ayub decided to permit parties to function again, as a sitting President he was forced to either join or form his own political organization. The result was the creation of the Conventionist Muslim League, which drew its support from those prepared to acknowledge their dependence on the Ayub mantra. It was at this juncture that Manzur Qadir decided to return to private life. Qadir's departure opened up still other opportunities for the ambitious Mr. Bhutto. With Manzur Qadir out of the picture, Bhutto gained prominence as Ayub's principal cabinet adviser. Bhutto's influence with the administration was significant, so too was his appeal to the youthful public. Ayub's unpopularity not only did not rub off on Bhutto, but also gave Bhutto's persona greater stature. Moreover, with the lifting of martial law and the promulgation of the new constitution, the political opposition became more vocal and they did not refrain from heaping abuse on the President and his administration. Ayub had insisted on and had promulgated a presidential constitution. The politicians could not be reconciled to the change, especially because it institutionalized and gave new meaning to the viceregal tradition. The politicians read in these developments a dictatorial regime that all but eliminated their role in the political process. Judged as yet another aspect of Ayub's "Basic Democracies," it reminded the dissenters of Mirza's and Dr. Khan Sahib's ruminations about "guided democracy." Concluding the system was stacked against them, the politicians resolved to sustain a campaign to have the constitution abrogated, not amended.

The constitution retained an indirect from of election for the office of President, and in 1964 Ayub announced the holding of presidential elections. The Basic Democrats were to be the only voters, however, and the presidential candidates would have to seek their votes. The opposition immediately cried foul and saw the election as a hypocritical act, tilted totally in favor of the President. Ayub's detractors vehemently protested this manner of election, but finally agreed to participate. Citing Ayub's strength and their weakness, the politicians formed a united front, soon identified as the Combined Opposition Party (COP). Also acknowledging that none in their ranks had national appeal, the leaders of the COP called upon Ms. Fatima Jinnah, the sister of the Quaid-i-Azam, to challenge Ayub. Fatima had chosen a reclusive life following the death of her brother, but publicly expressed her pleasure in 1958 when Ayub Khan forced Iskandar Mirza into exile. Now, however, after forty-four months of martial law, after the promulgation of still another constitution, and with Ayub appearing to want a lifetime presidency, she agreed to become the COP standard bearer.

The opposition also registered dissatisfaction with the President's foreign policy. Ayub had drawn ever closer to the United States. His goal remained the transformation of Pakistan and the building of a modern South Asian state. The United States relationship was seen as the key unlocking the door to medieval thinking that denied Pakistanis a view of the contemporary world. Ayub welcomed American government ideas and support as well as private investment, and Americans and American-sponsored programs were established in virtually every sector of Pakistani society. Rural development and land reclamation were given special consideration, but ample attention was given to health, education, social welfare, and good governance. The United States also made Pakistan a major recipient of military aid and Pakistan's alliances with the United States played a significant role in cold war strategy.

In 1961, Ayub was invited by President John F. Kennedy to make a state visit to the United States, where the Field Marshal delivered a major address to a joint sitting of the U.S. Congress. President Kennedy also entertained Ayub in a fashion befitting royalty. But while Ayub cut an impressive figure in Washington, it did little to elevate his popularity in Pakistan. At home, Ayub was seen as engaged in personal aggrandizement, and all his constructive works, including the building of Islamabad, were judged to be so much personal vanity. The presidential election campaign therefore centered more on what were considered the negative aspects of the Ayub administration than on any of its positive works. Ayub was reminded that he was a dictator propped up by the Americans as well as the country's civil–military bureaucracy and landlord class. Leftists and Islamists merged their political roles in an effort to convince the public that too much foreign influence combined with feudal dominance denied the people a proper role in shaping the country's future. Moreover, the country was more concerned about its larger and bellicose neighbor, and particularly India's refusal to allow the Kashmiri people to determine their own future. Ayub's failure to take advantage of Indian weakness during its conflict with China in 1962 also did not sit well with a solid portion of the Pakistani nation. American military assistance to New Delhi, following the Chinese incursion, weakened Ayub's grip on his own army, which saw the American aid program as a betrayal of alliance commitments. Furthermore, Ayub's constraint during the India–China border war, his reluctance to take advantage of Indian weakness in Kashmir, was attributed to his United States connection. Thus, the COP ignored the accomplishments of the administration, condemned it for its intimacy with Washington, and made the freeing of Kashmir a central issue in their campaign.

The rising passions in West Pakistan, notably in the Punjab and North West Frontier Province over the unresolved Kashmir dispute, could not be ignored. Nor was Ayub in a good position to address the issue. As a consequence, this task was left to Zulfikar Ali Bhutto, who had been elevated to Foreign Minister. Ayub had come to regard Bhutto as a vital element in the success of his reform program, and he unleashed the minister to address the Kashmir issue as he saw fit. That proved to be a major mistake. Unlike Ayub, Bhutto wanted distance from the United States and was determined to emphasize Pakistan's independent foreign policy. He was less interested in Ayub's nation-building program, and the Field Marshal's dependence on the United States was most discomforting. Bhutto had developed a strong antipathy toward the United States. His work among Pakistani youth had more than convinced him that the association with America had serious drawbacks. Pakistani young people were largely dissatisfied with their lot and heavily influenced by leftist ideas on the one side and Islamist callings on the other. Military alliances were no assurance of satisfaction on an emotional plane, nor did they serve Pakistan's material interest. While the rich acquired still greater wealth, poverty and illiteracy weighed heavy on the masses and, despite Ayub's record of improving the national infrastructure, little had been done to relieve their plight. The politicians therefore posed as the representatives of the misbegotten and were eager to challenge the entire range of Ayub's policies. A politician in the making, Bhutto shared the sentiments of the opposition, and, like them, he was convinced that America's support for the Ayub regime and other anti-Communist governments around the world knowingly reinforced dictatorship and seldom encouraged democratic development.

Aside from the United States, India was the *bête noire* in the minds of young Pakistanis. Hindu intransigence was equated with anti-Muslim sentiments, and New Delhi's reluctance to yield Muslim-dominant Kashmir, to allow it self-determination or union with Pakistan, was judged a blow against Islam itself. Islamist elements in Pakistan drew strength from the struggle over Kashmir and no administration, no matter how secular its performance could ignore the popular appeal, or the Islamic character of the Kashmir issue. Moreover, from the beginning the Kashmir dispute had defined the relationship between Pakistan and India, and India's rejection of U.N. resolutions, as well as international diplomatic efforts, hinted at an intractable problem that would be resolved only in a show of arms. Moreover, neither country had won its independence through armed struggle, and the Kashmir conflict offered each a chance to define its central ethos in the context of blood sacrifice. India's national identity as a secular, not a religious, state was central to the thinking of those responsible for the governance of India. In turn, the justification for Pakistan's existence as an Islamic republic was made to hinge on the liberation of India's only Muslim-dominant state. The perpetuation of the Kashmir dispute therefore meant the indefinite extension of the struggle for independence. The British had long packed their bags and returned to the mother country, but the insoluble conflict over Kashmir indicated there could be no peace for the subcontinent.

India and Pakistan squandered much of their potential by their failure to resolve the Kashmir problem. But for Pakistan this meant the obscuring of nation-building tasks. The armed forces consumed an extremely high percentage of the country's resources, but even the military could not limit the raucous activity of the narrowly defined Islamist orders, or temper the sustained regional and sectarian violence. The sustained unrest in the country prevented the construction of a viable, legitimate, and sophisticated political system. Political coherence was totally neglected. Political debate led nowhere and the politics of negativism gained supremacy. Street demonstrations, not parliamentary debate, dominated the political scene and the strenuous use of police powers did nothing for the maturation of democratic practices. Moreover, the never to be resolved Kashmir dispute sustained the role of the demagogues – and no one fitted that role better than Zulfikar Ali Bhutto.

Bhutto let it be known that without Kashmir, Pakistan would lack "full meaning." This was the message he brought to the election campaign of 1964. Bhutto exploited popular feeling aroused during the previous year when it was alleged that a hair from the beard of the Prophet had been stolen from the Hazratbal Shrine in Srinigar. The incident had precipitated widespread riots in both Pakistan and India. Tensions between the two countries also intensified, causing the United Nations Security Council to intervene in the hope of bringing a measure of calm. Bhutto had gone to New York City to present his country's case to the U.N., but, always the gifted showman, he used the opportunity to excoriate the Security Council's do-nothing posture, and then dramatically abandoned the proceedings and returned home. Arriving back in Pakistan, he met with Zhou Enlai, who was on an official visit to the country. The moment gave Bhutto still another opportunity to demonstrate to his emotional public that he was a different kind of leader. Thus when India's Prime Minister suddenly indicated an interest in discussing the Kashmir problem and ordered the release from custody of the Kashmiri leader Sheikh Mohammad Abdullah, instead of accepting the Indian offer, Bhutto took the dramatic step of inviting Abdullah to visit Pakistan. Caught off-guard, the Indian government agreed to sanction Abdullah's visit to Pakistan.

In May 1964 Abdullah arrived in Pakistan to counsel peace and called for a meeting between Ayub and Nehru. For a brief period it appeared that serious efforts would be given to breaking the impasse on the Kashmir issue. Events, however, are never predictable. In office some seventeen years, Nehru had aged and become ill. Having previously suffered a stroke, he suddenly succumbed to his illness and passed away. For Ayub, Nehru's death could not have been more consequential. No one among Nehru's successors had the status to pick up the fallen leader's mantle. No other Indian leader was in a position to compromise on the Kashmir dispute. Ayub was reminded of his entreaty to Nehru in 1959, when he had offered the Indian leader joint defense of the subcontinent and was rebuffed. Events again had conspired against the parties, leaving the demagogues to have their way. The opportunity afforded Bhutto therefore was enormous. Already the most popular political personality in Pakistan, Bhutto was able to cement his personal following. No discussions were pressed between Ayub and Nehru's successor, Lal Bahadur Shastri. Ayub entered the election campaign without the capacity to touch the masses, and his only satisfaction was the indirect nature of the election which allowed him to direct his message to a relatively small class of electors.

Bhutto used the platform provided by the presidential election, not so much to sing the praises of President Ayub Khan, but to excoriate the Americans, even to the extent of accusing the U.S. Central Intelligence Agency of favoring the COP's candidate, Ms. Fatima Jinnah. A major theme in virtually all the speeches by Ayub's ministers was Pakistan's independent foreign policy, but the essentials of that policy were left to Foreign Minister Zulfikar Ali Bhutto, who virtually on the eve of the ballot declared Pakistan was determined to liberate Kashmir from Indian occupation. In a moment of high vitriol he declared that the Pakistan government, following the election, would "take retaliatory steps to counter the Indian attempt to merge the occupied parts of Kashmir with India." By contrast, Fatima Jinnah had mentioned sustaining strong ties with the United States and although critical of India she was less aggressive in defining the issues between the subcontinent's principal rivals. Bhutto successfully shifted the campaign toward foreign policy and there Fatima's lack of experience was publicly revealed. Bhutto was less interested in what the Basic Democrats wanted to hear, however. Bhutto's audience was his mass public and he was not about to disappoint them. Moreover, Ayub was not expected to lose the election, and the Foreign Minister wanted it known that the moment to settle matters with India was fast approaching.

In the end, the Basic Democrats, by a close margin, voted to elect Ayub Khan. The Field Marshal, however, was denied a mandate and had it not been for the exploitation of the Kashmir dispute in

West Pakistan, Ayub might well have suffered a humiliating defeat. Bhutto received all the credit for the victory. Moreover, he had demonstrated that emotional issues trump solid and more meaningful debate. Ayub had endeavored to overcome the deficiencies in his government, to broaden its base, to appeal to the alienated, and to accelerate the development process, but he found himself blindsided by the Kashmir dilemma. Nothing rallied the West Pakistani masses like the call to liberate Kashmir. Bhutto had promised freedom for the Kashmiri people, and the political opposition, especially the more radical Islamists, raised the volume by calling for a return on that pledge. Ayub had no intention of going to war, but the momentum favored the four horsemen of the apocalypse and the Field Marshal was helpless to prevent them from trampling on his best-laid plans for the revival of Pakistan.

The Pakistan–India war of 1965 and its aftermath

Ayub had yielded command of the army to General Mohammad Musa soon after the declaration of martial law. Moreover, he was too preoccupied with the affairs of state to be privy to all the discussions and decisions confronting the army high command. Trusting his fellow officers, he enjoyed their loyalty, but his aloofness from their day-to-day deliberations prevented him from understanding the shift in army thinking. India's inability to effectively counter the Chinese thrust into its territory in 1962 was examined in considerable detail by the Pakistan high command. Ayub's reluctance to take advantage of India's demonstrated feebleness had been a major subject of discussion among high-ranking officers, and Bhutto's more defiant posture provided him with access to their deliberations. Bhutto had registered a commitment during the election campaign that could not be ignored, and the moment to strike in Kashmir seemed opportune while India was still licking its wounds. Moreover, the sudden death of Jawaharlal Nehru had added to India's demoralization. The Indian leadership was reported to be in disarray and unable to move on the diplomatic or military fronts. Finally, Lal Bahadur Shastri was considered a curious choice for the leadership of India. Pakistani intelligence described him as weak, colorless, ineffectual, and with little stomach for war.

In addition, in April 1965, only months after the Pakistan election, Indian and Pakistani forces had clashed in the swampy region that marked the southern border between the two countries. The Rann of Kutch was an uninhabited territory, of no serious consequence to either country that separated the two countries on the Arabian Sea. The Kutch encounter was brief, Pakistan apparently getting the better of the Indian force. And although the dispute demarcating the precise border was subsequently transferred to an international arbitration panel, Pakistan had sensed a weakness in the Indian armed forces that it believed it could exploit in Kashmir. Plans therefore went forward for precipitating a conflict in Kashmir that would finally give Pakistan the victory it had long sought.

Ayub's success in reining in his forces following the Rann of Kutch skirmish did not sit well with the more hawkish military commanders. Nor did Bhutto believe that Ayub's insistence on diplomatic solutions in Pakistan's dealings with India would work. Ayub could not challenge the argument offered by his detractors that the Pakistani soldiers were superior to the Indian, and that despite the latter's numbers Pakistani arms could prevail over India's in any serious engagement. The Rann of Kutch incident was blown out of all proportion to the actual circumstances and made to appear as convincing proof that Ayub's hesitation was uncalled for. Military strategists also pointed to the question of timing. The United States, despite Pakistani protests, had transferred weapons to India, and in due course those weapons and the training provided by the Americans could make India a more formidable adversary. Pakistan's own dependence on United States arms was not factored into this equation. Indeed, anti-Americanism was more apparent now than earlier and Pakistanis were led to believe China would be a better ally. Beijing, it was said, could supply Pakistan with needed military equipment and there was no longer a need to look to the Americans. Ayub rejected such thinking and informed his comrades there would be no shift in alliances, that Pakistan intended to maintain solid relations with both the United States and China, and that the Pakistani forces were becoming a formidable presence. A breakthrough had been in the offing just before Nehru's death, and Ayub argued that a strong Pakistan would yet bring the Indian leaders to the conference table.

Again, Ayub's conservatism was not welcome. Nor did his success in the Basic Democracies polling calm the Pakistani public or reduce the criticism directed against his administration. Ayub made every effort to turn the public dialogue to the matter of nation building and, with substantial donor aid, there was progress to report. Moreover, the private sector had shown signs of recovery and along with the expansion of the public corporations, unemployment had been reduced and a large portion of the population could access the open market. Domestic products mixed with imported goods to satisfy demand across a broad spectrum of wants, and by the summer of 1965 it appeared Pakistan had made headway in constructing a more formidable economic base. It was during this period of otherwise relative calm that information was circulated describing altercations in Kashmir that had caused an unusual loss of life. The Pakistan Foreign Ministry released a number of stories describing atrocities committed by Indian forces, although observers on the scene could not corroborate the reports. Jingoism on both sides had long been a part of the Kashmir conflict, but this time it was the Pakistani press that picked up the story and spread it countrywide.

According to Altaf Gauhar, Ayub's Minister of Information, in Ayub's absence Bhutto called a cabinet meeting in late July 1965 to inform the highest-ranking officers in the Pakistan army that a "popular revolt" had broken out in Kashmir and that the situation was desperate. He reportedly told the generals the country could not stand by and do nothing. Bhutto is said to have left the meeting before he could be questioned. The army commander, General Musa, was described as shocked by the presentation and unable to understand its source. Nevertheless, on August 8 the Pakistan army launched "Operation Gibraltar." The operation was described as an aggressive, small-unit penetration of Indian lines in Kashmir, and apparently was directed by Inter-Services Intelligence (ISI). The clandestine operation, however, was uncovered prior to the initial action and before it reached its first objective the force was repulsed. What Bhutto failed to reveal in his July meeting was now a lead story on All-India Radio. Pakistani insurgents had attempted to precipitate a conflict and all the infiltrators had been either killed or captured. Bhutto and his

Foreign Secretary, Aziz Ahmad, had planned the operation after drawing upon the expertise of Akbar Khan, the discredited general behind the Rawalpindi Conspiracy. Ayub had not been consulted about the ISI operation. Nor was he informed of Bhutto's role in masterminding the assault. Indeed, it is difficult to believe that had Ayub known of Akbar Khan's involvement he would have approved the action. Events, however, were again in the saddle. Conspired against by ambitious personalities, the events of July and August 1965 undermined Ayub's authority and seriously damaged his administration. Ayub had to accept responsibility for the setback. In addition he could not take disciplinary action against Bhutto without causing deep rifts in the army. Ayub was trapped in a "Catch 22" and unable to extricate himself from what would become an even deeper dilemma.

Despite the more secretive aspects of the Kashmir operation, the President had been given a Kashmir position paper in December 1964 which he had not thoroughly digested. The election campaign was in its final stages and all Ayub's attention was riveted on winning a major electoral victory. When Ayub finally got around to reading the document it was some months later. Gauhar reveals that he rejected the strategy as the work of uninformed lay amateurs who knew nothing about military formations and tactics. The plan, however, did not die. Bhutto tried to convince Ayub that the seizure of Kashmir would provide Pakistan with a balance of power in the region. It would also win Ayub new popularity and improve the prospects for Pakistan's development. Bhutto also addressed the need to shift dependence from the United States to a more secure alignment with neighboring China. The 1963 China–Pakistan border settlement was only the beginning of what Bhutto envisaged as a new relationship with the world's most populous nation. Understanding Ayub's aversion to joining a major cold war adversary of the United States, Bhutto tried to convince Ayub that China's proximity and friendship was a far better guarantee of Pakistani security. Bhutto's interest in the China connection, however, went even further. Pakistan, he said, would achieve greater international respect and its more formidable position would rank it at the top of all the Muslim nations. Bhutto's geopolitical vision centered on lifting Pakistan from its South Asian confines to make it an integral part of the Middle East. But the key issue in all his machinations was the liberation of Kashmir.

Bhutto's first goal was to win the support of the Pakistan army high command. His persuasive powers were so formidable that even General Musa complained to Ayub about his commanders being "brainwashed." When the decision finally was made to open the campaign in Kashmir, even Ayub found difficulty in resisting Bhutto's thesis. Apprised of an impending war, however, New Delhi was not idle. Army units were reinforced and Kashmiri dissidents likely to support an invading Pakistan army were quickly rounded up and imprisoned. If Pakistan anticipated surprise, the Pakistan army failed to grasp India's readiness or its overall strategy. Moreover, if Pakistan expected a popular uprising, that did not materialize. "Operation Gibraltar" was a complete failure. The larger "Operation Grand Slam" also met with disaster.

Ayub was not immediately informed of these setbacks on the battlefield. Nor was the Pakistani nation. To the contrary, Pakistan's propaganda machine pumped out the most optimistic statements, leading the public to believe the Indians were in retreat and that Kashmir would at long last be liberated. Ayub soon learned otherwise and tried to salvage what he could from the misadventure by reassigning the officers directing the fighting and by deploying Pakistani forces in more defendable positions. Ayub also had to contend with the American decision to assume a neutral position. President Lyndon Johnson, who had succeeded Kennedy following his assassination in 1963, placed an embargo on arms to both India and Pakistan. That decision impacted on the Pakistanis, who were totally dependent on American military supplies. India, by contrast, was unaffected because it could produce its own small weapons and also anticipated receiving heavier arms shipments from the Soviet Union. Ayub knew he could not fight a protracted war without American assistance and given the failure of the initial operations, he now had to ponder the possibility that the army could suffer major losses. Indeed, India expanded the war to include the entire frontier with West Pakistan. It had even launched air attacks against Pakistani installations in East Pakistan. To avert a terrible disaster, Ayub began looking for a way out and found it in the call for a cessation of hostilities by the United Nations Security Council.

The end of the Ayub era

With the United States opting out, and no Muslim country coming to Pakistan's defense, the Soviet Union saw an opportunity to bring Pakistan and India together. Moscow extended its good offices and called for a meeting between the Pakistani President and the Indian Prime Minister. At first Ayub was reluctant to accept Moscow's offer, but, given his lack of options, he eventually agreed to meet his Indian counterpart in Soviet Central Asia. Shastri was no more eager than Ayub to engage in peace talks. India saw a Pakistan–China axis in the making, and Beijing's threat to again invade India's northern territory was proof enough of its collusion with Islamabad. Nevertheless, India too reluctantly agreed to accept the Soviet invitation. Ayub ordered Bhutto to Moscow to prepare for the summit conference, letting the Pakistani public think Kashmir would be the subject of the talks. Bhutto said nothing about Soviet complicity in or sustained support for the Indian position on Kashmir. Nor was it ever disclosed whether this preliminary meeting had any significance in the subsequent discussions. Thus, the Pakistani public was still led to believe a satisfactory settlement would be achieved or else hostilities would resume.

Ayub arrived in Tashkent on January 3, 1966, accompanied by Foreign Minister Bhutto. In spite of Bhutto's earlier mission to Moscow, the Pakistan side did not present an agenda, and Ayub had to improvise his way through the talks. The parties quickly revealed they were more immediately concerned with the disengagement of forces and that a Kashmir settlement was not in the works. Ayub wanted a pullback of troops in order to avoid a renewal of hostilities. After achieving this objective he wanted to end the talks so that he could return to Pakistan, where his army, his administration, and his many development programs were in disarray. Ayub knew he needed time to repair the damage done to his army. He was also mindful that without a credible military, loyal to its chief, his government could not be sustained. In Pakistan, however, reports circulated that the two principals were at an impasse over the Kashmir question, that no agreement could be expected, and that Ayub would return to issue new orders to his army to resume fighting. The obfuscation was obvious but it was soon made apparent that Ayub and Shastri had not journeyed to Tashkent to accommodate each other's more abiding interests. The Soviet leaders had invested too much prestige in this meeting to allow it to terminate without an agreement of some kind. Thus, when the parties failed to find common ground, an agreement was drafted by the Soviets, and Ayub and Shastri were pressured to sign the document. The Tashkent Agreement said nothing about the status of Kashmir but it did bring an end to the Indo-Pakistani war of 1965. Ayub's minimum demands were granted when both sides agreed to pull back and reposition their forces. Military commanders from both armies were formed into a truce observation team and ordered by their respective governments to supervise the disengagement. Joint military sites were located on both sides of the line of control, but the Kashmir question still demanded a response. A final solution to the Kashmir problem would have to wait on the wisdom of future statesmen.

Not a Kashmir settlement, but rather Bhutto's decision to leave the Ayub government was the most dramatic outcome of Tashkent. Bhutto's strategy involved exploiting Ayub's weakness. Seeing that Ayub had been made more vulnerable and was not likely to perpetuate his rule, Bhutto plotted his future and meant to reap advantages from his astounding popularity. Appealing to people representing a broad spectrum of Pakistani society, Bhutto played to the crowd and made it appear that only he wanted and could achieve a Kashmir settlement. Young people were especially entranced by his rhetoric. Moreover, Ayub had no counter. Few were prepared to believe that Bhutto's audacious behavior had prompted the war, and the President held his silence on the matter. Ayub had known for some time that Bhutto's aspirations would not be appeased with service in his administration. But he also was mindful of Bhutto's importance to the regime, and he could not bring himself to dismiss him. Ayub feared that a sudden decision to dismiss Bhutto from the cabinet would only provide him with greater opportunity to damage the administration. Ayub therefore demanded that the Foreign Minister stay at his post until Ayub was prepared to remove him.

On the night following the signing of the Tashkent Agreement, Lal Bahadur Shastri suffered a heart attack and before medical assistance could be summoned he passed away. Ayub asked Bhutto to escort the body back to New Delhi. Ayub returned to Pakistan without his Foreign Minister and faced a grieving public, not because they mourned the death of the Indian Prime Minister, but because Ayub had failed to measure up to their expectations. Ayub was never the same following the 1965 war. His confidence shaken, the Field Marshal, who once believed it possible to shape Pakistan's destiny, no longer held to that opinion. For Ayub it was now a question not of whether to step aside, but of when and how. Events had overwhelmed him. Too dependent on his staff and too ready to delegate responsibility, Ayub lost the authoritarian instinct. He showed himself to be a poor judge of human character, especially in some of the men chosen to surround him. Ayub was used and ultimately abused by those who never shared his ideas. Among this group, Zulfikar Ali Bhutto was the most obvious and by far the most unscrupulous.

A March 1966 visit to Pakistan by Chinese leaders brought tens of thousands of Pakistanis into the streets to welcome them. The outpouring was described as a demonstration of appreciation for China's efforts on behalf of Pakistan during the 1965 war. The display was unprecedented. Moreover, Bhutto, still the country's Foreign Minister, had the opportunity to share in the acclaim as he rode with the visitors through the streets of Pakistan's capital. Ayub had declined to participate in the festivities and his absence from the ceremony was yet another misreading of events. The adulation heaped on the Chinese also washed over Bhutto. Bhutto seemed incapable of doing wrong and his popularity had soared to new levels when Ayub finally decided to accept his resignation. Once on his own, Bhutto was not expected to quietly retire from the political scene. On the contrary, the young man immediately searched for the political party that best represented his views. Finding none, he came under the influence of people who wanted to establish a new national party, and it was not long afterwards that he assisted in the formation of the Pakistan People's Party.

Ayub reshuffled his government following Bhutto's departure. He made General Musa governor of West Pakistan and named General Mohammad Yahya Khan as commander of the Pakistan army. His new cabinet attempted to draw upon the expertise of technicians and scholars as well as politicians but Ayub was left with one intimate, the Minister for Information and Broadcasting,

Altaf Gauhar. When Bhutto began his verbal assault on Ayub, the President had few defenses and with the exception of Gauhar no one who could represent his true intentions. In November 1966, Bhutto accused Ayub of poor administration and divisive policies. To demonstrate that he was a bridge builder and a national healer, Bhutto announced his support for Mujibur Rahman's Six Point Program, which he had earlier condemned as secessionist and calculated to destroy Pakistan. Gauhar tried to level the playing field with a ploy of his own. The Information Minister declared Bhutto continued to own vast holdings in India and was in fact an Indian citizen. Bhutto was able to deflect the charge, but the government fought back, hinting that Bhutto's embrace of Mujib associated him with a known traitor. Mujib had been arrested for what the government reported was a serious attempt to break up the country. Accused of clandestinely working with Indian diplomats, Mujib was indicted in the "Agartala Conspiracy" and threatened with either execution or a long jail term.

The Pakistan People's Party (PPP) was officially organized in 1967 by a small group of left-leaning intellectuals. Bhutto assumed the post of Chairman of the party and his General Secretary was J.A. Rahim, a former civil servant and avowed Communist. The Pakistan Communist Party had been banned in 1955, but Rahim continued to represent Marxist views. Rahim, much older than Bhutto, was a paternal figure to the young politician, and the spirit behind the PPP. It was he who convinced Bhutto to help form a new party rather than take on the baggage of one of the existing organizations. Moreover, Bhutto's enormous popularity was forecast to sky-rocket the PPP into first position among all Pakistan's political organizations. The PPP put Ayub on notice that if he intended remaining in power, he would have to confront political maneuvering never before experienced in Pakistan.

During this period of increased political activity, Ayub fell victim to pneumonia complicated by a pulmonary embolism. Though little was offered the public in the way of details, Ayub was incapacitated and questions were raised about his life expectancy. Against the odds, however, the President rallied and made what was described as a full recovery. He returned to the duties of state hardly a month after being stricken. Weak from the ordeal, however, he confided in those closest to him that he did not expect to remain head of state much longer. Policies were therefore in train to prepare the succession, and the generals jockeyed for position, believing one of their own would replace Ayub as President of Pakistan.

Ayub again had been made a creature of events. During his illness his cabinet had taken the decision to highlight the "Decade of Ayub Khan." The administration wanted to display its accomplishments in the ten years the Field Marshal had ruled Pakistan. The program was officially called the "Decade of Development" and, though in itself an innocent gesture of breast-beating, its impact on the general public was anything but positive. The political opposition questioned the expense of mounting such a celebration. They also questioned its utility and purpose. Concluding it was assembled to portray the Ayub decade as something beneficial to the nation, its only real beneficiary, they concluded, was Ayub Khan. Protest meetings opposed to the celebration took to the streets and the violence they engendered surprised most members of the administration. The politicians needed an issue to open their campaign against Ayub, and the spark for this latest example of anti-social behavior was the planned but not yet realized celebration. Confirmation that this was a broad undertaking, planned well in advance of the "Decade" being declared, came from the role played by the religious fraternity. The latter's assault on the Muslim Family Laws that had been introduced to provide protection for women and children pointed to a concerted attempt by the opposition to eliminate everything Ayub had accomplished during his tenure. The Family Laws had done much to advance the idea of equality between the sexes, as well as to provide material assistance for children and the indigent, but the Islamists still found reason to describe it as anti-Islam and blasphemous. The Islamic Research Institute also came under intense fire from the Islamists. Both the Family Laws and the administration's family planning program were condemned as counter to Islamic practices. The learned director of the Research Institute, a major scholar of Islamic jurisprudence, was targeted for advocating contraception, and because threats were made on his life he had to flee the country.

Bhutto's paradoxical behavior in all these matters was seldom questioned by those opposed to the Ayub system. Bhutto gave voice to any criticism directed against the administration, despite his long-term service as a minister in a number of key positions. Moreover, though he associated with socialist doctrines, he saw nothing contradictory in merging Islamic issues with Marxist rhetoric. The PPP Manifesto was released to frame the party's program. It avoided all references to theological matters but it was a Marxist-Leninist reminder that the party's work was centered on Pakistan's proletariat and the population's need for "bread, clothing, and shelter." Bhutto wanted it known that only the PPP represented the poor. He also wanted it known that he was a crusader who would bring an end to corruption and autocratic rule.

Bhutto claimed the power both to deliver democratic reforms and to protect the country's Islamic heritage. All things to all men and women in the country, Bhutto resisted all appeals that he moderate his rhetoric or change course. In the meantime, rioting had broken out in East Pakistan and quickly spread to the western province. Ayub called for the imprisonment of all those responsible for disturbing the peace, but it was a monumental task that neither the police nor the army was ready to tackle. Moreover, members of the army high command had decided it was time for Ayub to go. Divisions within the ranks were apparent after the 1965 war, but they were even more obvious during Ayub's illness. The time seemed opportune for a changing of the guard, and a number of key army officers believed the army's honor, sullied in the aftermath of the 1965 war, could be restored if Ayub were forced to vacate his office. Ayub, however, was not yet prepared to go.

While he tried to keep the army intact, Ayub was also concerned about the future of the political system he had given so much to construct. Convinced that the presidential system was better for Pakistan than another parliamentary experiment, Ayub wanted assurances that his wishes would be honored following his retirement. Events, however, were already beyond Ayub's control. The "Decade of Development" celebration had opened all the old wounds. In spite of the incarceration of much of the political opposition, including Bhutto, the riots continued to spread and intensify. In desperation, Ayub reversed his order and called for the release of the politicians. Even Mujibur Rahman, whose conspiracy trial was in process, saw the charges withdrawn and the case closed. Ayub called upon all the politicians to meet with him in an effort to return the country to a semblance of order. Some complied with this request, but others refused to participate in a meeting that they assumed was aimed at extending Ayub's tenure in office.

Bhutto publicly declared his vote of no confidence in his former mentor, and even Manzur Qadir was heard calling on Ayub to step aside. Ayub Khan wanted a propitious moment to yield his authority, but his physical weakness was matched by mental fatigue. Though reluctant to leave office under pressure, in the end he wanted nothing more than to leave the presidency with his dignity intact. Only when his brothers in arms no longer found it possible to pledge their unconditional loyalty did he finally agree to give up the role he had filled for more than ten years. His final decision was to transfer authority, not to an interim civilian government, but to the army commander-in-chief, General Aga Mohammad Yahya Khan. Martial law was again imposed, and Ayub Khan, after more than a decade as the supreme leader, took his leave. Ayub retreated to his home, where he would live out his last years in relatively quiet contemplation. On March 25, 1969, the nation was told it would have to endure the presidency of yet another uniformed officer.

The Yahya Khan interregnum and the civil war

Yahya Khan had been selected by Ayub to salvage what he could from the ill-fated strategy to liberate Kashmir in 1965. It was Yahya who oversaw the consolidation of the few gains Pakistan reaped from the conflict and who prevented the army from splitting into different factions. For his service, Ayub promoted Yahya to commander-in-chief of the army in spite of his junior standing among the higher-ranking officers. Commissioned in 1938, he served in the Middle East and Italy during World War II. After Pakistan was created he was instrumental in the development of the Army Staff College at Quetta. Made a brigadier at age thirty-four, he was subsequently transferred to army headquarters, where he assisted Ayub in the modernization of the Pakistan army. The youngest officer to be promoted to the rank of Major-General,

Ayub named him his chief of staff just before martial law was declared in 1958. Yahya remained at Ayub's side throughout the forty-four months of martial law and the two men developed a close working relationship. Yahya worked with American military advisers in integrating U.S.-provided weapons systems in the Pakistan army. He also was made responsible for supervising the construction of the new capital of Islamabad, having served on the commission that recommended the project and later as the chairman of the Capital Development Authority that prepared the overall plan. Promoted to Lieutenant-General for his performance in the 1965 war, when he took command of the army in 1966 he was confronted not only with healing the psychological wounds, but with repairing the physical damage done to the armed forces by a misguided group of high military officers.

Ayub selected the only officer in the Pakistan army he believed he could trust to sustain what he had started. He also anticipated Yahya would perpetuate the presidential system. Yahya, however, had his own political agenda and shortly after taking control of the government he issued an order abrogating the Ayub constitution. He also declared his preference for the parliamentary system and promised to reinstate the political parties once the country's equilibrium had been restored. He also needed time to heal the rift with the United States. Richard Nixon's ascendancy to the American presidency in 1969 and Henry Kissinger's selection as Nixon's National Security Adviser were both judged pluses for Yahya's objectives. For the moment, however, Yahya's concerns were more domestic than foreign.

On March 30, 1970 Yahya issued a Legal Framework Order, breaking up the One Unit of West Pakistan and reconstituting the original four provinces. Punjab, Balochistan, Sindh, and the North West Frontier Province (NWFP) were to have their own legislative assemblies, along with East Pakistan. A National Assembly was to be constituted that would be divided between East Pakistan and the western provinces, the former receiving a larger proportion of the seats as a consequence of its greater population. Yahya had served as the General Officer Commanding in East Pakistan and he credited himself with a peculiar sensitivity to Bengali issues. The Yahya reforms appeared to be a welcome change from the more arbitrary politics of the Ayub years, but Yahya would soon learn how his well-meaning intentions would play out in the arena of Pakistani opinion.

Ayub's Basic Democracies system was scrapped with virtually all the other institutions associated with the fallen leader. Indirect elections for the office of President went with the banishing of the Basic Democrats. According to Yahya, the people wanted accountable and responsible leaders and a political system they could readily embrace as legitimate and popular. Chastened by a bitter war and hopeful that the Kashmir issue could be placed on the back burner, Yahya saw his task as the healing of internal wounds, most of them self-inflicted. But Yahya was not an absolute dictator, nor did he stand alone among the generals under his command. More readily identified as a chairman of a board of strong military associates, Yahya found it necessary to filter his vision through an army junta representing diverse views. Among the ruling elite were those sanctioning a more liberal attitude and others who argued for firm and determined decision making. Consensus within the junta was important but it was soon apparent that the more conservative members in the ruling circle held sway over those calling for greater flexibility. Moreover, Zulfikar Ali Bhutto had become an even more imposing figure after Ayub's departure. Popularly credited with the Field Marshal's resignation, Bhutto sustained his connections with the conservative wing of the junta, and projected an even higher profile when political party activity was reinstated on January 1, 1970.

Under pressure from the politicians, Yahya announced Pakistan's first national election. It was scheduled for October 5, 1970, and a new National Assembly was to be convened shortly thereafter. Yahya had turned the clock back to 1955, some time before the Ayub era and just following the dissolution of the first Constituent Assembly. The overall idea was to provide Pakistan with a second chance at building a constitutional order based upon democratic principles and reflecting the concerns of its people, both east and west. The Legal Framework Order (LFO) had been generally well received by the politicians although some in West Pakistan wondered about the granting of a majority of National Assembly seats to East Pakistan. Nevertheless, the general impression was that Bhutto stood to gain the most from Yahya's actions. Bhutto was perceived as gaining particular advantage from the break-up of One Unit. Not only did he demonstrate impressive control over the Sindh constituency, he also had expanded his influence in the Punjab. By contrast, East Pakistan was seen as equally divided between Mujibur Rahman's Awami League and Maulana Bhashani's National Awami Party (NAP). East Pakistan's majority distribution of National Assembly seats was expected to divide between the two principal parties and even the PPP was projected to win seats there. Election forecasts therefore predicted a Pakistan People's Party victory. Moreover, the Awami League and NAP were not expected to develop a national following, nor were the provincial parties of the NWFP and Balochistan expected to transcend their immediate circumstances. Only the PPP seemed to represent national interests, and all the surveys pointed to a solid victory for the socialist organization.

Not all the generals were satisfied with the LFO. Several within the junta were opposed to granting East Pakistan majority representation in the central legislature. Nonetheless, the LFO stood, and the army officers as well as the politicians were forced to accept the reality of Yahya's reform program. Any turning back at this stage would be seen as doing severe damage to an already fragile edifice. For his part, however, Bhashani described the LFO as a "Trojan Horse," a subterfuge that would divide East Bengal and perpetuate West Pakistani dominance. Mujib also was less than assured about the Yahya proposals. Fearing Bhashani's rejection of the LFO would win the favor of a vast number of Bengalis, Mujib also demanded more from Yahya. The Bengali complaint centered on the distribution of the country's assets and especially West Pakistan's more significant development program. A more equitable share of the country's resources was one demand; another was the plea that the two wings of the country enjoy freely convertible currencies. According to Mujib, only the provincial units, not the central government, should have the power to tax their citizens.

The Awami League demands caused considerable distress within the junta. The army high command was especially unhappy with Mujib's insistence on autonomy for East Pakistan, and a central government restricted to responsibilities in defense and foreign affairs. Mujib also wanted East Pakistan to engage in international trade and to be allowed to open a separate foreign exchange account. The Awami League call for a provincial militia that would manage the province's internal security and negate the need to station large numbers of federal soldiers in the province was especially galling. The junta had never taken Mujib into their confidence and they were now even more convinced that his goal was the break-up of Pakistan. Bhutto, by contrast, was privy to the junta's deliberations and indeed the junta had even sought his counsel. Although momentarily embracing Mujib in the campaign to end Ayub's rule, Bhutto did not like Mujib and the Bengali leader had no more respect for the former Ayub confidant. Each man judged the other a crass opportunist and there was little likelihood that they would ever again find common ground.

Flooding, an annual occurrence in East Pakistan, caused the postponement of the much heralded first national elections, and the October polling was shifted to December. That postponement proved to be a fatal error. On November 12, 1970, a tidal wave described as thirty feet in height and whipped by cyclone winds of up to 120 miles per hour struck the coastal districts of East Pakistan. Described as one of the worst natural catastrophes in modern history, the storm totally destroyed the area of impact and washed out to sea an estimated more than one million people. Relief assistance was urgent and the call went out to the government in West Pakistan to lend all assistance at the earliest moment. President Yahya Khan was *en route* back to Pakistan from China when the disaster hit and his government was slow to respond to the request for assistance. In fact, Yahya had set down in Dacca but had not been fully apprised of the situation when he flew on to Islamabad.

Not only was the Pakistan government judged inept, but the Bengalis condemned what they believed was the callous indifference of West Pakistanis. By the time Yahya returned to East Pakistan to see first hand the extent of the devastation it was too late to soothe the feelings of the Bengali population. Moreover, aid sent to the most affected areas was minimal and were it not for international relief agencies little would have been done to relieve the plight of the survivors. Mujib and Bhashani were indignant and decried the overt lack of concern in the western wing. Both spoke for the Bengali nation, Mujib reasserting the imperative of autonomy, while Bhashani denounced the Islamabad government. Noting the inability of the West Pakistanis to register their humanity, Bhashani also questioned his Pakistani citizenship. In an angry address to his party members, he announced the NAP would boycott the December elections. Pakistan's first national election proved to be still another disaster. With the NAP boycotting the balloting, the Awami League of Mujibur Rahman won almost all the contested seats set aside for East Pakistan in the new National Assembly – but did not gain a single seat in any of the West Pakistan provinces. In West Pakistan, Bhutto's PPP won the Punjab and Sindh province but lost to provincial coalitions in the NWFP and Balochistan. The election results pointed to the absence of a single national party. Pakistan was a divided state and the elections revealed how deeply divided it was. Provincialism not nationalism was the essential dynamic and the years of primitive politics had taken their toll. The country's political life had been stunted, first, by the failure of the Muslim League to develop into a proper political organization and, second, by the long period of martial law and military dominance. Not only was the political process atrophied, but almost from the moment of independence feudalism, personal vendettas, sectarian strife, and provincial rivalries had limited any kind of political progress.

With the ballots counted and the Awami League holding a majority of the seats in the National Assembly, the expectation was that Yahya would call Mujib to form the new central government. Mujib's party controlled 169 of the three hundred seats in the National Assembly; Bhutto's PPP had won only eighty-one, almost all from Sindh and Punjab. Yahya had declared the substitution of the parliamentary for the now defunct presidential system, but under pressure from the junta, and especially from Bhutto, he hesitated in issuing the call to Mujib. Bhutto supported the President's reluctance to declare the Awami League the winner of the election, arguing Mujib would represent only East Pakistan if made Prime Minister. Demands emerged from the PPP that the election results be nullified and that new elections be contemplated. Yahya was trapped in a no-win situation. Forced to choose between the demands made on one side by Bhutto and his conservative generals, and Mujib and an aroused Bengali public on the other, Yahya's immediate reaction was to postpone a decision. Then Yahya called for a meeting of the principal parties. Neither Mujib nor Bhutto, however, was agreeable to a discussion. For the former, the election had been won fairly and the results were clear. For the latter, the election results would confine the PPP to an indefinite period in the opposition. Bhutto's lack of success in the frontier provinces also pointed to a possible Awami League and frontier coalition that would permanently isolate Bhutto's socialist organization. Bhutto sensed the need to press PPP policies now; to wait on events might ruin the organization's chances in the future. More important, Bhutto could lose the opportunity for national leadership. Yahya allowed himself to succumb to Bhutto's pleadings. He also recognized that the junta was equally unhappy with the Awami League victory and that the concerns of his colleagues had to be given serious consideration.

The viceregal tradition, not parliamentary procedure, was at work here. Yahya ignored his own proclamations and attempted to use the office of the chief executive to manage what was obviously a dangerous situation. The Bengalis exploded when they realized Yahya had backed away from a sacred commitment. Demonstrations were to be anticipated but no one envisaged the intensity or the immediate spread of the disorder. Police agencies were no answer to the problem. Moreover, Bengali police as well as government officials left their posts in protest, and government was paralyzed in all departments. Only the Pakistan army garrisoned in the province was in position to deal with the rioters, but even these troops were insufficient to restore peace. In the meantime, the Pakistan army made preparations to send additional soldiers to the region, and the generals least sympathetic to the Bengali cause presided over the build-up. Given the intransigence on all sides, East Pakistan's request for autonomy was transformed into a demand for secession, and the generals were determined to retain the eastern province no matter the cost in lives and property. East Pakistan's sizeable Hindu minority was placed at particular risk. The junta had spoken of Indian plots aimed at dismembering the country, and they now convinced themselves New Delhi was behind the uprising.

Pakistani troops, largely drawn from West Pakistan, were instructed to believe that in fighting the local population they were actually fighting India and a Hindu challenge to their Islamic tradition. The 1965 war was still fresh in the minds of the Pakistan army jawans, and they required little encouragement in cracking down on those they deemed to be enemies of Pakistan. Indeed, much propaganda had been directed at the Punjab following the election. Punjabis held minority status in the Pakistan constituted in 1947, and now it seemed that the proud Punjabi would have to submit to either Bengali or Sindhi rule, and neither was acceptable to those believing they were a "superior" people. In the midst of all this, the future of the country revolved around Zulfikar Ali Bhutto.

Bhutto's ambition never burned more intensely than after the resignation of Ayub Khan. The Pakistan People's Party was seen as Bhutto's transmission belt to the highest office. Having supported Mujib's autonomy program in the latter days of the Ayub era, Bhutto had completely reversed course and denounced the Six Point Program of the Awami League, describing it as anti-Pakistan. Bhutto issued an ultimatum to Mujib and indirectly to Yahya when he said he would refuse to meet with the Awami League leader if he did not withdraw his demands for greater provincial autonomy. Yahya's reluctance to call Bhutto's bluff, let alone to ask Mujib to form a government, only protracted and deepened the impasse. It seemed obvious to Mujib that Yahya had given up the notion of even-handed treatment of the two wings of the country. Yahya too, not just the members of the junta, would not permit the Awami League to form the central government. Although Mujib later agreed to accept Yahya's call for a meeting with Bhutto, he did not believe the General wanted a settlement based upon the facts.

With street demonstrations rampaging through the towns and villages of East Pakistan, high-positioned members of Bhutto's PPP journeyed to East Pakistan to meet with their counterparts in the Awami League. Led by J.A. Rahim, the party's Secretary General, they agreed a plan that would call for the drafting of three separate constitutions, one for East Pakistan, another for the provinces of West Pakistan, and still another to represent the federal character of the country. Believing such a plan was the only formula that could prevent secession, the negotiators tried to sell their plan to the army junta and to Chairman Bhutto. But before the junta could respond, Bhutto emphatically rejected the proposal. Concluding the central government could still come under Awami League control, or remain the responsibility of the army, Bhutto saw little personal loss in sustaining the impasse.

Moreover, the army was continuing to reinforce its garrison in the eastern province, and in time Bhutto believed it would have the capacity to silence the Bengalis and break the will of the Awami League. Bhutto was aware of army plans to arrest Mujib and to crush the Awami League's militant shock troops. Bhutto saw the Yahya-inspired negotiations as nothing more than a stunt, staged to buy time for the army to mobilize sufficient forces to restore law and order in the province and keep India from assisting the Bengalis. Justification for a military assault on its own civilian population was found in the Bengali attack on the refugee community lodged in the province. "Biharis" was a term attributed to all non-Bengalis living in East Pakistan, many of whom had established themselves in relatively lucrative commercial undertakings. This element of society had held managerial positions in the province's small industries. They also had been favored with government positions and other offices of distinction. Envy and rivalries between the different communities was a reality of life in East Pakistan and it was not surprising that long-term antagonisms surfaced when the province erupted after the elections. The slaughter of the Biharis therefore was a pretext for military action, and on the night of March 25, 1971 units of the Pakistan army made their assault on the Awami League and subsequently on an array of Bengali targets.

Among the first to be brutalized were students asleep in their hostels at Dacca University. Awami Leaguers were rounded up along with some of Dacca's leading intellectuals. Taken to a remote location, they were summarily executed. Mujib was arrested but taken unharmed to West Pakistan, where he was cast into a prison in the northern area of the country. Hindus were singled out from other Bengalis and killed on the spot. The army strategy aimed at eliminating anyone who it was believed could sustain resistance, but the gross and senseless killing of the innocent imposed a demand on all Bengalis to band together and to strike back. Bengali members of the Pakistan army as well as the East Pakistan militia defected with their arms to form the Mukhti Bahini or Liberation Army and, joining with their besieged brethren, employed guerrilla tactics to resist the superior West Pakistani forces. East Pakistan had been plunged into civil war and little consideration had been given to its consequences.

Internationalizing a civil war

The army attack was against the people of Bengal. Muslims were victimized as well as Hindus and no room remained for counter-argument or for recognition of Bengal's legitimate grievances. The election results were all but forgotten and the bloodletting opened wounds so deep that it was difficult to rationalize an outcome that could leave Pakistan intact and viable. Mohammad Ali Jinnah's Pakistan was on the block and neither Yahya nor Bhutto nor any of the generals or West Pakistani politicians seemed able to grasp the consequences of the egregious action taken to suppress the Bengali nation. Mujib's arrest did not leave the Bengalis without leaders, nor were Bengalis about to reduce their demands. The call now was for independence. There would be no repeat of 1954, when the results of the East Bengal provincial elections were quashed. Nor would Bengal submit to viceregal rule or the reincarnation of Iskandar Mirza. The brutal campaign against the Bengali nation elevated Bengali resolve. Bangladesh replaced East Pakistan as a government in exile, established across the border in Indian Bengal, declared the sovereignty of the new state. Bengali casualties were enormous, a consequence of the indiscriminate slaughter of civilians by the Pakistan army. This carnage, however, only increased Bengali determination to fight a protracted war.

When India cancelled Pakistan's overflight privileges, supplying the East Pakistan garrison became a time-consuming and costly venture of moving men and equipment by sea, a route that extended some three thousand miles. It was obvious Islamabad did not have the means to sustain such a venture indefinitely, and the Mukhti Bahini envisaged greater opportunities when this vulnerability became more pronounced. Complaints that Pakistan registered in New Delhi went unanswered. The junta also complained about India's asylum procedures. Moreover, India gave aid and comfort to the Bangladesh government in exile and refused to acknowledge any of Islamabad's concerns. New Delhi also publicized its own complaints, particularly the flood of East

Pakistani refugees washing across its border. Hundreds of thousands were on the move; in time millions would seek the protection of the Indian government. Many refugees were never expected to return to East Bengal. The Pakistan army focused on clearing the province of its entire Hindu population, but the flight of Muslims had reached similar proportions.

Prime Minister Indira Gandhi publicly declared that her government could not tolerate a continuation of the situation. She said the number of refugees entering India had placed a great burden on the entire nation and that resources were not sufficient to cope with the problem. Moreover, there was a limit to her government's patience and she urged Islamabad to cease the use of deadly force. Indira also warned Islamabad that India could not stand idly by if conditions were allowed to worsen. Civil wars, however, know no limits. Atrocities multiplied as the passions on both sides intensified. The killing of non-Bengali officers of the East Pakistan Rifles by deserting Bengali troops interfaced with the Pakistan army's massacre of Bengali intellectuals and professionals. The total number of dead could not be calculated but estimates ran as high as three million. Even if exaggerated, the number revealed a terribly high price had been paid in realizing the independence of Bangladesh.

Successive Pakistan governments had called for self-determination in Kashmir, but self-determination in East Bengal was never considered a reasonable demand. Bengali political consciousness was not unknown to the minions in Islamabad, but they never intended to honor the aspirations of this people who by 1971 had little if any reason to consider themselves Pakistanis. A majority of the Pakistan population, the Bengalis had long clamored for a fair share of the political process. They also believed they were entitled to a proportional cut of the economic bounty. East Pakistan's jute industry had kept the country afloat in the years immediately following independence, but few profits were plowed back into the province. Moreover, the economy had long been the preserve of the non-Bengalis and they had little desire to use their largesse for the province's impoverished multitudes. The Bengalis had come to see the government in West Pakistan as alien and another version of colonial exploitation. The Islamabad government did little to address Bengali suffering or change that perception of the government. Even Ayub's plan to construct a "second capital" in Dacca failed to excite people in the eastern province. Second best was hardly a demonstration of power or resource sharing and the scheme was ridiculed from the day it was presented. Bengalis understood what it meant to be second-class citizens, they also knew they would have to make great sacrifices to remove the colonial yoke.

After Pakistan's first national election, more attention might have been given the Bengali complaint. Instead, Lieutenant-General Tikka Khan, a soldier with a reputation for unbridled combat, was unleashed on a relatively defenseless people. Dehumanization is not uncommon in war, even civil war, and Tikka conditioned his men to see the Bengalis as unrepentant savages. But even Tikka was unable to cow the Bengali resistance or break its resolve. The war raged on as the Bengalis divided into small units and struck at targets of opportunity, often in the dead of night. With neither side in a position to win an all-out victory, the conflict deepened and the hatreds intensified. The protracted nature of the struggle meant the war became front-page headlines in distant places around the globe. No one, however, not the even the United Nations, let alone any other organization, possessed the leverage to bring the hostilities to an end.

Whatever their explanations, no nations truly attempted mediation. The United States government, caught up in a war in Southeast Asia, had little stomach to intervene in this one. The war raging in East Bengal, however, did not prevent President Richard Nixon from sending his National Security Advisor, Henry Kissinger, to Islamabad. Kissinger did not go to the Pakistani capital to offer his good offices or to bring pressure on Yahya to halt the hostilities. Kissinger's mission, with Yahya's cooperation, was to secretly travel to Beijing where he was to meet with Mao Zedong and open a new chapter in Sino-American relations. The civil war in East Bengal was not allowed to interfere with that mission, and the American administration demonstrated calculated indifference either to Bengali suffering or India's plight in caring for millions of refugees.

Only when New Delhi announced its patience was at an end did the world begin to take serious notice of the civil war. Indira Gandhi called for international recognition of Bangladesh's declaration of independence. In November 1971, Indian forces crossed into Pakistani territory and Yahya informed the U.N. Secretary General of the incursion and declared that New Delhi's objective was the dismemberment of Pakistan. If India did not halt its operations the chances of a wider conflict could not be discounted. The U.N. Security Council took up the issue but it was clear from the outset that nothing could be done to address the conflict. Too much time had passed and too many deaths had occurred for either India or Pakistan to reconsider its options. The Security Council voted to demand India's withdrawal but New Delhi was too committed to comply. By November 21, Indian forces had eliminated Pakistan's advance emplacements and several Indian divisions were poised for a massive attack against the Pakistani army garrison, now effectively cut off by air and sea blockade. Inaccessible to fresh troops or supplies, the Pakistan position was hopeless. Mukhti Bahini forces joined the Indians for a final assault on the Pakistani troops, who had been ordered to fight to the last man. Tikka had been called back to Islamabad earlier and it was another Pakistani general who faced the task of sacrificing thousands of his men or suffering the humiliation of total capitulation.

On December 3, Pakistan aircraft attacked Indian positions, and New Delhi gave the order for a full frontal assault. The second Pakistan–India war in six years found Pakistan at a gross disadvantage. India could move as many men and supplies into the struggle as it saw fit. Pakistan had only its East Pakistan garrison and the supplies still remaining after months of civil war. With the Mukhti Bahini striking at will and Indian formations rolling toward Dacca, the Pakistan cause lost its meaning. Although it appeared a fight to the death was about to occur, the Pakistani commander decided to surrender his forces. The war was over. Ninety-three thousand Pakistani soldiers were taken prisoner by the Indian army. Bangladesh became a reality. Pakistan suffered the loss of one-fifth of its territory and more than half of its population.

India played midwife to the creation of Bangladesh. Without New Delhi's support it is likely the civil war would have dragged on for years in the form of guerrilla insurgency. But that is so much speculation. Bangladesh had emerged as an independent state.

Pakistan as it was known before the civil war had ceased to exist. The dismembered country had suffered a grievous blow. Its armed forces had been humiliated. Tens of thousands of Pakistani soldiers languished as prisoners of war in Indian or Bangladeshi detention camps. Citing the magnitude of the Pakistani defeat, some Indian leaders called for spreading the war to West Pakistan. Their objective was the complete destruction of Pakistan. Less hawkish members of Indira's government were more cautious, wary of international opinion. Nonetheless, India had opened a front against West Pakistan. The Pakistan navy lost many of its frontline vessels and Pakistan's coastal installations, especially around Karachi, had been destroyed. The Pakistan airforce was outgunned and in short order neutralized as an effective weapon. No Muslim country came to Pakistan's assistance, or even decried the Indian action. The American embargo on arms to Pakistan, imposed during the 1965 war, had not been lifted, even after the Kissinger mission. Pakistan's defeat on the battlefield was complete. The Pakistani junta was left to contemplate the strategic consequences of its misguided operations in East Bengal, and to confront a desolate and demoralized nation in what remained of the country.

Although no country had come to their defense, some Pakistanis had found hope in President Nixon's decision to send the aircraft carrier *Enterprise* into the Bay of Bengal. Believing the American naval presence was meant to pressure New Delhi, it was the only positive gesture Pakistanis could point to as they wallowed in the despair of their terrible loss. India, of course, was not intimidated by the American action, and Washington admitted that the carrier force was deployed to retrieve Americans from the war zone, and not to threaten India. In effect, Pakistan had nothing positive to steel its resolve. India could strike the country at will and there was little that Pakistan's armed forces could do in its defense. Acknowledging its gross errors as well as the calumny of its actions, the junta understood the time had come for it to relinquish power.

Just before the Indian assault on East Pakistan, Bhutto had been summoned to a meeting of the military high command and had been made Deputy Prime Minister. He had urged the generals to make "total war" on India, but subsequent events proved that was an impossible prospect. Bhutto pled Pakistan's case before the

United Nations Security Council, but that too did little more than allow the PPP leader to inflate his rhetoric. At one point, Bhutto fulminated that even if Pakistan lost 120 million people it would still survive. Bhutto's exaggerated oratory was well known and few observers were surprised when in the course of a U.N. debate he suddenly announced he would return to Pakistan, where his people thirsted for his leadership. Given to high drama, Bhutto was in Dacca the night the army assaulted the students in their beds. Returning to Pakistan the following day, he remarked at the airport that Pakistan had been "saved." From Bhutto's posturing at that time, as well as during the civil war, it was apparent his ambition overrode his sense of reality. Bhutto wanted supreme power at any price and events had converged to give substance to his ruminations. On returning from New York City, Yahya resigned the presidency and in his last public act notified the nation that Zulfikar Ali Bhutto had agreed to become the new President of Pakistan. The ambitious twenty-nine-year-old in Ayub Khan's first cabinet had achieved his goal at age forty-two.

Bibliography

Choudhury, G.W., *The Last Days of United Pakistan*, Bloomington: Indiana University Press, 1974.

Feldman, Herbert, *From Crisis to Crisis, Pakistan 1962–1969*, London: Oxford University Press, 1972.

Feldman, Herbert, *The End and the Beginning: Pakistan 1960–1971*, Karachi: Oxford University Press, 1975.

Gauhar, Altaf, *Ayub Khan: Pakistan's First Military Ruler*, Lahore: Sang-e-Meel, 1994.

Inayat, M.R., ed., *Perspectives in Public Administration*, Lahore: Lion Press, 1962.

Jahan, Rounaq, *Pakistan: Failure in National Integration*, New York: Columbia University Press, 1972.

Jalal, Ayesha, *The State of Martial Rule: The Origins of Pakistan's Political Economy of Defence*, Cambridge: Cambridge University Press, 1990.

Khan, Fazal Muqeem, *The Story of the Pakistan Army*, Karachi: Oxford University Press, 1963.

Lamb, Alastair, *Birth of a Tragedy, Kashmir 1947*, Hertingfordbury: Roxford, 1994.

Mahmood, Safdar, *The Deliberate Debacle*, London: Sh. Muhammad Ashraf, 1976.

Shah, Mehtab Ali, *The Foreign Policy of Pakistan: Ethnic Impacts on Diplomacy*, London: I.B. Tauris, 1997.

Siddiqi, Aslam, *Pakistan Seeks Security*, Dacca: Longman, Green, 1960.

Zaheer, Hasan, *The Times and Trial of the Rawalpindi Conspiracy, 1951: The First Coup Attempt in Pakistan*, Karachi: Oxford University Press, 1998.

5

REDEFINING PAKISTAN

The civil war in East Pakistan and India's intervention dismembered, humiliated, and humbled Pakistan. The country created by Mohammad Ali Jinnah and his refugee based and inspired Muslim League disappeared and was replaced by another that was yet to be defined. The Pakistan that emerged from the ashes of defeat was not a country guided by optimism, but one smarting from its multiple wounds. Failure was writ large and there was enough blame to include virtually every branch of government and every sector of society. What remained of Pakistan was called to still another test, one that required tracing its traditional and mythological roots. Post-civil-war Pakistan needed recreating, not from the legacy of Mohammad Ali Jinnah, but by those who least supported the original independence movement. No longer a refugee experience, Pakistan had to be configured to represent the people of the northwestern quadrant of the South Asian peninsula. The loss of East Bengal obviated the need for bridge building between disparate communities, and centered attention on constructing a Pakistan that was more akin to Islamist doctrine and precept than that suggested by the constrained and tortured secularism of the earlier vision. Moreover, the new Pakistan required a different geopolitical orientation. No longer anchored in South Asia, it was seen as attached to the Muslim world of the Middle Eastern states.

Contests between nationalists and provincialists and between secularists and Islamists had been won by, respectively, the provincialists and the Islamists. The civil war put an end to the notion that a Muslim-dominant country could be constructed from a contemporary European formula and example. The vision of the founding father, in the absence of the founding father, could not be translated into operational programs that satisfied the people who had been called to accept Pakistani identity. That vision was from the outset challenged by a combination of local and distant Islamist forces. These understood the alchemy necessary for the legitimization of popular protest. The vision of an integrative and balanced civil society, governed by sensitive and selfless leaders, was shattered in the tragedy of Bangladesh. The failure to sustain a semblance of union between West and East Pakistan was read as the failure of a secularized Islam that encouraged but did not succeed in tempering sectarian and ethnic divisions within and between regions. Appeals to Islamic brotherhood did not prevent the slaughter of the innocent in East Bengal, and in fact the killing was intensified by distinctions made between one representation of Islamic practice and another. Who was the "better" Muslim, who was more worthy to be called a Muslim, was as much at play in the Pakistan army assault on the Bengali nation as was the effort to cleanse the region of its Hindu population. The soldiers from Balochistan, Pashtunistan, and the Punjab were convinced that their mission to kill Bengalis, of whatever persuasion, was a call to preserve the faith, even if doing so meant destroying Pakistan.

The gross inhumanity in East Pakistan was perpetrated by essentially the same elements that transformed the long-standing Kashmir dispute into a fetish of national identity. If the Kashmir issue were important in the original Pakistan, the Muslim state that emerged from the civil war and the nation's dismemberment would be even more tied to the Kashmir territory. East Bengalis, after all, had little if any concern for Kashmir. In post-civil-war Pakistan, however, Kashmir became the defining issue. Kashmir became sacred land and Pakistan's *raison d'être* was intertwined with the jihad to liberate it from the Indian non-believers. Pakistanis found in Kashmir, whether rationally or not, their rallying ground, the reason that they needed to recreate still another Pakistan. No Pakistani leader, present or future, was allowed to ignore the significance of the Himalayan territory, and especially its connection to Pakistan. All of Pakistan was made hostage to the Kashmir conundrum. Thus East Pakistan, because it represented a different ethos, could be erased from memory. The old Pakistan was pictured giving way to a "real" Pakistan that had risen phoenix-like from the debris of war, a war largely of its own making but nevertheless attributed to its neighboring nemesis.

Give Yahya Khan credit for trying to build a political structure that united the two wings of Pakistan, but also condemn him for not following through on his grand design. Yahya was responsible for the break-up of One Unit. But the reconstituting of the original provinces of West Pakistan opened up old political wounds that had hardly begun to heal, and re-established rivalries that could not be reconciled. Give Yahya credit for acknowledging the need to distribute representation in accordance with population numbers. But again he bears responsibility for denying his own creation when the national election results called for the East Pakistani winners to form the government. Yahya decided to substitute the parliamentary system for the much criticized presidential system, but in the process lost control over events. Yahya set a course he could not follow and the consequences of his political weakness imposed upon the country a savage bloodletting that, paradoxically, could be stopped only by the country's major enemy. Yahya's failure virtually ended whatever positive development Pakistan had experienced in the previous two decades. At the end of Yahya's tenure, Pakistan was even more "moth-eaten" than at the time of partition. Moreover, the proud Pakistan army, the recipient of the greater portion of development resources, lay in shambles, even more demoralized than the general population.

It would have been a proper time to rename Pakistan. It no longer resembled its former self, nor did it stand for the same values assumed at its creation in 1947. Transformed into a congeries of provincial units that were held together under the flimsiest of circumstances, the state was perpetuated by inertia not purpose. If there was a time for dissolution it was at this juncture in the history of the country. Sindhu Desh for the Sindhis, Pashtunistan for the Pashtuns, Balochistan for the Balochi – all had been common utterances in the different regions that sought release from alleged Punjabi dominance. But this was not like the break-up of the Soviet Union at the end of the cold war. This war, had it been simply a civil war, might well have had that same result. The Soviet Union dissolved because it no longer had a recognizable major enemy; not so Pakistan. The role played by India in bringing Pakistan to its knees was most important in linking the new Pakistan to the older version.

Unable to adequately defend themselves from their neighbor, the remaining provinces feigned unity in an effort to draw strength from weakness. The northwestern region of the subcontinent was of vital strategic interest to New Delhi, but India decided to contain, not seize it. *Akhand Bharat*, the Hindu militant call for absorbing Pakistan within India, would have to wait on another day. Better to allow Pakistan to redefine its independence, for the new Pakistan government to pick up the pieces and lead the country into a relationship with India that now was not expected to be different from those of Bangladesh, Nepal, and Bhutan. Never more confident than after its military victory in 1971, New Delhi anticipated a less aggressive and more submissive country on India's northwestern border. Bhutto was expected to shift course away from Pakistan's heavy dependence on military posturing, to more diplomatic engagement.

Bhutto's Pakistan: the external dimension

Bhutto was too close to the disaster that engulfed the former Pakistan to understand the significance of the dismemberment. Translating events in personal terms, he was compelled by his blind ambition to read the situation as he saw it, that is, as a conventional set of political circumstances that resulted in a military crackdown, which ultimately provoked an act of Indian aggression. It was all so simple. Bhutto bore no responsibility for the conflict, whether civil or international. It is fascinating to see the extent to which he, a bystander to events as they unfolded, became the principal beneficiary of the great débâcle. Bhutto refused to acknowledge his central position in the collapse of the old Pakistan because he could not be both the old Pakistan's executioner and the new Pakistan's singular benefactor. Bhutto's role as hero intertwined with his role as traitor, and few of his compatriots this time, desperate for a savior, were prepared to recognize this dual role. Thus the Pakistan army took the major blow and Yahya's resignation and the dissolution of the junta opened the way for a civilian to reclaim leadership of Pakistan. In the absence of genuine opposition, with the country in almost total disarray, Bhutto's oratory won the day. Bhutto formed the first government of the new Pakistan, with himself the President of the nation as well as its Chief Martial Law Administrator. Bhutto's legitimacy was supposedly rooted in the national elections of 1970. Bhutto called upon the citizenry to make the necessary sacrifices, and the people of the new Pakistan answered his call, much as they had answered the Quaid-i-Azam's plea for selfless devotion immediately after the 1947 partition.

It came as no surprise when Bhutto was acclaimed the "Quaid-i-Awam," the "Leader of the People." The popular memory of Jinnah as the founding father of the original Pakistan demanded replication and Bhutto's legitimacy appeared to hinge on the connection between himself and the once great leader of the Pakistani nation. The events that brought Bhutto to power, however, were significantly different. Although both men achieved their goals in the struggle with Hindu-dominant India, Bhutto's success was a consequence of the country's worst defeat. But even if Jinnah, in winning Pakistan, had bested India in the political struggle with the colonial authority, Bhutto could nonetheless attribute the twice-born Pakistan to a form of "liberation war." Unlike the first Pakistan, the second Pakistan was indeed a result of armed action against a hated foe, even if the military campaign was itself an abysmal failure. It must be remembered that Bhutto declared Pakistan had been "saved" on his return to Karachi from Dacca the day after the Pakistan army attacked the precincts of Dacca University.

By a statesman-like act of compromise Bhutto could have prevented the civil war. He chose not to do so, in large part because he believed that, no matter the outcome of the conflict, he and the nation were better served by the secession of East Pakistan. Moreover, considerable informed opinion had reached that same conclusion. But if it had already been decided to jettison East Pakistan, why then the ferocious army assault on Mujib and his Awami League, or indeed on the defenseless Bengali people?

The answer can only be found in the army's perception of East Bengal and the Bengalis. Trust and affection were in short supply between the two wings of the country. Had there been a different outlook, a different outcome might have been anticipated. Given the power of the military junta, it would have been a gracious action to call upon Mujib to form a government following the Awami League's enormous victory in the 1970 elections. Graciousness could not be found in the junta's dictionary. Nor was it an attribute of the leader of the Pakistan People's Party.

The army was ordered to humble the Bengalis and in the end it only humbled itself. The war in East Pakistan, however, demonstrated something even more compelling than the confused, stunted, and devious thinking of the instigators of the civil war. The original design of a single Muslim country with two distant parts, separated from one another in everything save religion, could not stand. East Pakistan, or East Bengal, the birthplace of the Muslim League, could not make its presence known, let alone respected, in the western wing of the country. After the defeat of the Muslim League in the provincial East Bengal elections of 1954, the secession of the east wing was only a matter of time. The mishandling of the results of the 1970 elections revealed that that time had come. Bhutto saw little of value in East Bengal. Shedding it, in his thinking, would avoid numerous difficulties in power sharing, resource sharing, and in defensive needs. Moreover, East Bengal was too heavily influenced by Hindu culture. Pakistan could never realize its potential as a Muslim country while connected to East Bengal. Bhutto's ambition was not only to become the supreme leader of Pakistan; he also envisaged a role as a great international figure and the major political personality in the Islamic world. To construct the new Pakistan was the first task. Building a strong, high profile nation from the calamity of a devastating war would be judged a heavy responsibility in any circumstances, but for Bhutto it was the stepping stone to still higher status.

Knowing that the Pakistan armed forces had suffered substantial losses, the new President placed himself in the center of the effort to rebuild the military. At the same time he was prepared to take advantage of the weakened army command to accrue more power to his person. As Chief Martial Law Administrator he had ultimate say over the uniformed soldiers, as he did over the general population. The time also enabled him to emphasize the role of the Pakistan People's Party, which came under his strict command. Declared the Chairman of the party, he saw his role as similar to that held by Mao Zedong in China and Kim Il-Sung in North Korea. Bhutto unabashedly clothed himself in the austere garb of the pre-eminent Chinese leader, including the familiar Mao cap and jacket. Bhutto was clear in his determination to reshape Pakistan's domestic and foreign policy, and his embrace of the People's Republic of China, as well as North Korea, was made in public view. The Chinese and North Korean models of development that called for mass mobilization intrigued him. He was convinced the more sophisticated development strategies and theories of the Western countries had little relevance for Pakistan. The people required guidance and the country needed a disciplined population, completely focused on and devoted to the tasks of nation building.

Demonstrating the need for distance from the United States, Bhutto let it be known that Pakistan's security, and its overall interests, was better served by cooperative relationships with the Communist states. It was Bhutto's view that the confrontation that Pakistan's alliances with the United States had created served only to undermine the country's sovereignty and make it more dependent on Washington. Washington's actions during and following the Indo-Pakistan War of 1965, and even the more recent 1971 war, proved the dysfunction of the Western alliance system. Arms shipments to Pakistan remained under embargo and the country had been given little if any outside assistance to warrant a continuation of alliance agreements. Moreover, with the loss of East Pakistan, Bhutto justified the severing of ties to SEATO. Not only was that alliance commitment a relic of the old Pakistan, but the independence of Bangladesh had removed Pakistan from the arena of Southeast Asian concerns. Pakistan did not withdraw from CENTO. The Central Treaty Organization represented the country's association with the Muslim Middle East, and the membership of Turkey and Iran in that alliance made such a withdrawal inopportune. The same was not true for Pakistan's membership in the British Commonwealth of Nations. Bhutto determined it was no longer in Pakistan's interest to remain in the Commonwealth – a reminder of the country's former colonial tutelage. Cutting ties to Britain was judged another demonstration of the new Pakistan's greater independence.

Confirming the new Pakistan had absolutely no intention of reclaiming East Bengal, Bhutto ordered that Mujib be freed from prison and the Bengali leader was permitted to return to Bangladesh, where he became that country's President. Although Bhutto was not yet prepared to recognize the independence of Bangladesh, his gesture was aimed at India, with which he sought improved relations. Moreover, Bhutto was under pressure from the army to gain the release of the ninety-three thousand Pakistani soldiers held as prisoners of war in Bangladesh and India. Much talk had circulated in Bengal about the trial of soldier war criminals who were implicated in the commission of atrocities during the civil war. Such trials were better avoided and the new Pakistani leader indicated a willingness to discuss outstanding issues with his Indian counterparts in an effort to prevent the trials. In April 1972 Bhutto lifted martial law and promulgated an interim constitution that suggested an attempt to return the country to normalcy. Differences between Bhutto and Prime Minister Indira Gandhi seemed to delay their agreeing to a face-to-face meeting. Bhutto nevertheless pressed Indira to accept his entreaties and to almost everyone's surprise the Indian government announced a meeting had been arranged for June in the hill station at Simla. Gone was the vitriol when the Pakistani public received the news. Anti-Indian rhetoric virtually disappeared when Bhutto journeyed to India. Unlike the public outcry when Ayub went to Tashkent, Bhutto was urged on by a tide of well wishers. Thus, Bhutto and Indira, without third party involvement, struck a deal in a short time and without rancor. India agreed to pull its forces from territory occupied during the 1971 war. The two sides also agreed to a new line of control in Kashmir. In return for Indian recognition of Pakistan's domination of Azad Kashmir, Pakistan did not question India's control of the Vale of Kashmir.

The Simla agreement was also important for what it did not include. No mention was made of the long-disputed plebiscite in Kashmir, and some observers concluded that Pakistan had finally agreed to accept permanent Indian occupation of the Muslim-dominant Vale. Of more immediate concern was Bhutto's apparent failure to gain the release of the ninety-three thousand prisoners of war languishing in Indian and Bangladeshi prison camps. Moreover, the matter of show trials of Pakistani troops remained a major interest. Under criticism when he returned to Pakistan, Bhutto called for patience and insisted he had not sold out the country or its armed forces. All the same, he faced the first serious opposition since taking up the reins of Pakistan government. Bhutto called for calm and a more realistic understanding of the parameters of his discussions with Indira and argued the need to provide time for the armed forces to rebuild their units. He declared he had reiterated Pakistan's support for Kashmiri self-determination and that that quest would be raised again when the country was better prepared to press its claim in international forums. What was important, he cautioned, was a calculated response to Indian aggressiveness which enabled Pakistan to avoid falling within India's sphere of influence. As Stanley Wolpert reported, Bhutto's opposition melted before the fire of his oratorical eloquence.

Bhutto's diplomatic skills were highlighted in his relations with India, but the Islamic Summit Conference he initiated in 1974 brought him even more plaudits. Convened in Lahore, the meeting drew together Muslim rulers and governors from all over the Islamic world. In attendance was King Faisal of Saudi Arabia, Anwar al-Sadat of Egypt, Hafiz al-Assad of Syria, Muammar Qaddafi of Libya, Yasser Arafat representing the Palestinians, and others. Prominent for his absence was the Shah of Iran, whom Bhutto had intimate relations with but nevertheless could not convince to attend. Bhutto also used the occasion of the Summit to announce Pakistan's official recognition of Bangladesh and had Mujibur Rahman appear at the meeting. The apparent rapprochement with Mujib enabled Bhutto to press the Bengali leader to release the prisoners of war and to forgo the trials of those troops accused of war crimes. Mujib complied with this request, and, with Indian assistance gained earlier, the soldiers were released and returned to Pakistan. Perhaps because he did not want to undermine his improved relations with the Indian government, Bhutto did not mention the Kashmir dispute at the Summit. Instead, he reserved his attack for the Israelis, who, he noted, had refused to return captured Arab lands to their original owners. Pakistan's solidarity with the Palestinians became a central feature of Bhutto's foreign policy, not only because it was a burning issue in the Arab states, but because the Muslim nations had shown virtually no interest in the Kashmir dispute. Given his wider ambitions, Bhutto worked at reinforcing his new relationship with India while developing greater intimacy with the Arab leaders.

Bhutto's Pakistan: the internal dimension

Despite being hailed Pakistan's new savior, Bhutto confronted serious challenges to his rule. In fact his general success in moderating the country's foreign policy ushered domestic questions to centre stage. Bhutto's Sindhi identity was seen to offer *carte blanche* to local Sindhis to resume their movement against the province's refugee or "mohajir" community. Asserting the mohajirs had monopolized the economic life of the nation and hence had intensified the poverty of the native population, Sindhi nationalists precipitated riots in Karachi and Hyderabad. The rioters targeted those Pakistanis who had fled India during the partition, or their progeny, who were still not accepted as Sindhis. Adding to refugee numbers were the more recent immigrants from Bangladesh. Karachi, Pakistan's commercial and financial capital, had been a small seaport before independence. Transformed by the mohajirs, its prosperity was a consequence of their business acumen and dynamism. Native Sindhis, however, were not impressed, in large part because they failed to reap the benefits of the city's expanding capitalism. They declared the mohajirs exploiters, moreover, their attacks on the immigrant community were costly in lives and property and required a firm government response.

Before he assumed power, Bhutto's political antics contributed to the rising tension between these communities. His exploitation of anti-refugee sentiment was aimed at winning native Sindhi support for his Pakistan People's Party, but his rhetoric was explosive and the impact extended beyond his political needs. It was Bhutto who revitalized provincial leaders like G.M. Syed, the venerable Sindhi extremist, who had long pressed for an independent Sindhu Desh. Once in power, Bhutto remained the stalwart Sindhi nationalist. He echoed and seemed to support the attack on mohajir culture. He also added fuel to the fire that the Sindhi separatists had set in decrying the dominance of the

Urdu language. Speaking on the subject of the new Pakistan, Bhutto implied that Urdu had become the national language in the old and now defunct Pakistan only because of the heavy influence of the refugee community. According to Bhutto, the new Pakistan was formed from more indigenous circumstances and it did not need to cater to distant connections. More immediate concerns were with the provinces, and Bhutto was not one to neglect their individual identity. He no longer saw Urdu as a critical unifier. The mohajirs, however, still believing they were the genuine Pakistanis, took issue with Bhutto and questioned his Pakistani bona fides in a series of public demonstrations.

At the Lahore Islamic Summit Bhutto had addressed the need for Islamic unity; nevertheless he was disinclined to promote unity at home. The country's divisive and competitive ethnic structure provided ample opportunity for a demagogue, always seeking personal political advantage, to divide one group against the other. Bhutto was reluctant to permit more Bangladesh mohajirs (Biharis) to enter the country. He also encouraged those insisting on making the Sindhi language the official language of the province. Described as the "Raja of Larkana" (Larkana was his ancestral home), Bhutto was accused of a divide and rule policy that reminded many of the colonial era. The riots that welled up and inundated the cities and hinterland of Sindh were to burden the Bhutto administration from this time forward. Moreover, Chairman Bhutto's divisive policies could not be contained.

Bhutto's strategy was aimed at breaking the back of all current and potential resistance. His only real opposition in Sindh was from the mohajir population, which had been closely identified with the Muslim League. The collapse of that party, however, did not cause the refugee community to embrace the Pakistan People's Party. Hence Bhutto's attempt to bypass them by exciting the sensibilities of the native Sindhis. The counterproductive nature of this exercise soon led to the creation of a mohajir political party that initially was called the Mohajir Qaumi Movement (MQM). Finding it necessary to fight for their freedom in yet another vista, the MQM came to dominate the politics of Karachi.

Bhutto also took issue with the main political powers in the North West Frontier Province and Balochistan: the National Awami Party led by Wali Khan, the son of Ghaffar Khan, and

Mufti Mahmood's Jamiatul-Ulema-i-Islam. The PPP entered into a tripartite pact with these organizations, but Bhutto betrayed their agreement and removed the parties as a threat to national security. Wali Khan's claim that Bhutto intended to have him murdered increased the tension. Warned not to enter the frontier provinces, and generally concerned about his personal safety, Bhutto ordered the formation of the Federal Security Force (FSF), a paramilitary organization principally made up of former army personnel and acknowledged criminal elements. Among the leaders of the FSF was Akbar Khan, the accused leader of the Rawalpindi Conspiracy and now a close associate of the President. The FSF, and the PPP People's Guards, likewise an aggressive assemblage, assumed responsibility for protecting Bhutto as he traveled the country. The FSF also was given the task of isolating and, if necessary, arresting anyone believed to be plotting attacks on the head of state or senior members of his government. With the passage of time the FSF became the central instrument of domestic political violence. Its growing power, its reputation as an intimidating force, and its delegated but nonetheless arbitrary use of violence against defenseless citizens struck fear in the population and also raised serious questions in the Pakistan army.

Bhutto failed to sustain the confidence of the Pakistani nation. His resort to extreme measures, as well as his use of questionable tactics, embittered wide sectors of the polity. Such was the case in Balochistan only a year after the PPP takeover. The provincial government of Balochistan challenged Islamabad's intrusive methods. Asserting that the Balochistan provincial government was threatened by PPP directives and actions, local Balochi leaders insisted on reclaiming their traditional autonomy. Since Balochistan's declaration as a province shortly after partition, its tribal orders continued to dominate the political life of the region. Sardars, or local headmen, were the identifiable rulers of the different areas. Their constituents were guided by tribal practices and knew little about the more sophisticated methods of governance. Moreover, the Sardars resented PPP policies that blatantly endeavored to steal their power and destroy the historic tribal order. Bhutto refused to acknowledge the tribal tradition and was concerned only with bringing the province under PPP control. His order to the FSF to remove the provincial government met with stiff resistance. The Sardars interpreted the action as a declaration of war. They ordered the mobilization of the tribesmen and called them to do battle with the agents of the PPP. Bhutto was not one to negotiate a settlement with people he considered inferior, and thus, in January 1973, he ordered regular army units into Balochistan. Recalling Ayub's success in quickly crushing the Khan of Kalat, Bhutto directed the Pakistan army to center their actions in the Lasbela region. The Balochi resistance fighters were described as "miscreants" by the central government, the same term used to describe the Bengalis. As they clashed with the army, memories of the recent civil war in East Bengal could not be avoided.

Although the struggle in Balochistan did not receive the attention of the outside world, it was nevertheless another Pakistani civil war, and another one that Bhutto had provoked. Balochistan's arid terrain, its relatively sparse population, and its remote geographic setting circumscribed a conflict of different dimensions from that of East Bengal. Still, it was the second civil insurrection to erupt in Pakistan within a period of five years, and both tragedies could be traced to the behavior and ambition of Zulfikar Ali Bhutto. General Tikka Khan, who had gained his reputation as the "Butcher of Bengal," was again called to lead a Pakistan army against its own citizens. Tikka said the army had been ordered to put down an insurgency. Pakistan's more attentive public was stunned by the action. How many more Pakistanis were to be dubbed miscreants and, worse still, traitors? How many more were to be considered secessionists when they stood in opposition to policies that denied them their character and identity, let alone their freedom? Bhutto ignored such questions and justified his actions by declaring Pakistan was at war with nefarious forces. He cited the Baloch Liberation Front as a principal source of concern. He also alluded to collusion between the Balochi governor, Mir Ghaus Bakhsh Khan Bizenjo, and Abdul Ghaffar Khan, who had returned from self-imposed exile in India and Afghanistan to receive a hero's welcome in Peshawar. The two outspoken leaders of their respective provinces were perceived as forming a Pashtun–Balochi alliance, with assistance provided by Kabul, New Delhi, and their superpower mentor, the Soviet Union.

Bhutto therefore ordered Bizenjo removed. He installed as governor Bizenjo's principal rival, Nawab Akbar Bugti. The Balochi Chief Minister was also sacked, as was the governor of the North West Frontier Province. Thus ended the earlier agreement between the PPP and the ruling parties on the frontier. When high-ranking officers in the Pakistan army began to question Bhutto's aggressive policies, the PPP Chairman accused them of "Bonapartist" behavior and dismissed the high command. General Tikka Khan was Bhutto's choice to take charge of the Pakistan army. Bhutto claimed his decisions centered on the need to establish a democratic political system in the country, to unify its people, and to stimulate the development process. Wali Khan noted at the time that the real objective of the President was absolute power and the construction of a fascist state. It was Wali Khan who addressed the PPP leader as "Adolf Bhutto." The war in Balochistan revealed little had been learned from the civil war in East Pakistan. It also demonstrated that the new Pakistan was no more secure, no more integrated, no more stable than the older version.

Pakistan suffered from a lack of national organizations as well as a paucity of national leaders. Although the Islamic religion offered a hint of unity, it was insufficient to bridge differences that were both cultural and historic. When the United Democratic Front was organized to combine Wali Khan's National Awami Party with the Sindhi Pir of Pagaro's Muslim League and Maulana Maudoodi's Jamaat-i-Islami, it proved more a desperate attempt to challenge Bhutto's power than a serious effort in promoting political integration. Bhutto ordered his Federal Security Force to neutralize the UDF. Whether he used the FSF or the Pakistan army, Bhutto's response to anyone opposing his rule was their forcible destruction. Nevertheless, Bhutto continued to emphasize the righteousness of his actions. He continued to insist that his purpose was to eliminate the enemies of Pakistan, who, he insisted, were also the enemies of democracy.

In spite of the sustained turmoil, on April 12, 1973 Bhutto presented a constitution to the new Pakistan. Although Bhutto was more inclined toward a presidential model, the new constitution was parliamentary in form and organization. Insuring that the President would be a purely ceremonial figure, Bhutto assumed the role of Prime Minister. The constitution also described a state focused on Islamic precept and practice. Article 227 noted that all laws must conform with the injunctions of Islam as laid down in the Holy Qur'an and Sunnah. No law would be permitted that was repugnant to injunctions of Islam. An Islamic Council was incorporated in the constitution but the wording of the document left important questions unanswered about its power *vis-à-vis* the National Assembly and provincial legislatures. There was no ambiguity, however, on the matter of the President being a Muslim, or whether Pakistan would endeavor to preserve and strengthen fraternal relations with Muslim countries based upon the need for Muslim unity. Article 1 described Pakistan as an "Islamic Republic," and Islam was established as the state religion in Article 2. The constitution, however, did nothing to limit the power of the PPP Chairman. In fact extraordinary powers were conferred upon the Prime Minister which reduced the National Assembly to a submissive agency operating at the will of the supreme leader. Justification for this executive-dominant form of parliamentary government was attributed to the country's sustained instability. The country required a firm hand at the helm, it was said, and the unusual times demanded a decision-making process that was both direct and enforceable.

Wali Khan addressed the concerns of the opposition when he stated the Chairman had been placed above reproach and that public scrutiny had been made impossible. The PPP majority had made the constitution possible and those contesting the excesses of the administration were left with the awareness that only in the streets could they demonstrate their distress and disfavor. Thus was created the "Imperial Prime Minister." Bhutto intended to rule Pakistan indefinitely. The constitution gave him an initial six years and, given the government's capacity to dominate its foes, no doubt another five could be projected. After that it was anyone's guess whether the Quaid-i-Awam would be prepared to step aside, or whether, instead, he would seek a life term. Bhutto needed a constitution not to limit the powers of the executive, but rather to enhance and ensure his paramountcy in the context of the country's viceregal tradition. In the absence of an effective opposition and protected by several layers of security, Bhutto seemed untouchable, his power as dictatorial as could be imagined in the South Asian milieu.

During this period word reached Islamabad that King Zahir Shah had been forced from his throne in Afghanistan by his cousin Sardar Daud. The Afghan monarchy was declared terminated and a Republic was created under Daud's leadership. With the Pakistan army continuing to operate in Balochistan and with the war spreading into portions of the North West Frontier Province, Bhutto felt it important to quickly recognize the new regime and to begin a process of normalizing relations. Cognizant that Daud was a principal author of Afghanistan's "Pushtunistan policy," Bhutto had every intention of cementing ties with the one country in a position to assist the tribal insurrection. Afghanistan was also the first Muslim country to represent a threat to Pakistan when it was established in 1947. With Daud's assurance of cooperation and with Bhutto's promise of material assistance, the Afghan President was expected to deny sanctuary and aid to the insurgents, thus making it possible for Pakistan to bring the Balochistan fighting to a conclusion. Bhutto therefore extended his hand to Daud and promised brotherly relations between their two governments. Given his own internal problems, Daud communicated his desire to accept Bhutto's entreaty. Both leaders concluded it was in their mutual interest to bring the hostilities on their border to a close.

The fall of Zulfikar Ali Bhutto

Bhutto's deftness in handling foreign issues, however, was in stark contrast to his domestic behavior. Suspicious of anyone who might question his authority, not least those immediately around him, even the very people who had supported his rise to power, after his initial year in office he concluded he no longer needed or wanted their counsel. The marriage of political personalities that organized the PPP proved to be more convenient than permanent. Little affection passed among the principals. J.A. Rahim, Mubashir Hasan, Mairaj Mohammad Khan, Mukhtar Rana, Ahmad Raza Kasuri, for all their revolutionary expression, were men of integrity and deep learning. Doctrinaire socialists, their goal was a more compassionate Pakistan that reflected the simple instincts of the majority population, catered to basic popular needs, and gave substance to ideals of social improvement. None of them coveted personal power. Bhutto was their choice because he was already a celebrated leader with a fine education and an extraordinary gift of oratory. Bhutto, they also believed, was a young man who in their judgment not only reflected their sentiments, but was open to guidance and collective decision making.

The PPP leaders proved to be right in the former expectation but so wrong in the latter. Whatever the explanation, these colleagues of Zulfikar Ali Bhutto failed or refused to see the man's driving, even irrational, ambition, or the mental flaw that distorted his vision. And though they knew something of his aristocratic breeding, they did not grasp the mindset of this Sindhi member of the *wadera* or land-holding class of Sindh province. Bhutto, for all his Western education, for all his protestations about democracy, would never be able to transcend his autocratic attitude. He did not have the personal qualities needed to transform himself into a genuine man of the people. Bhutto was predetermined by upbringing and temperament to be a domineering manager of people, never their true representative.

Cracks in the PPP leadership opened early in the Bhutto administration. Mukhtar Rana and Mairaj Mohammad Khan were too outspoken for Bhutto's taste and when they questioned his grab for total power, he had them arrested and jailed without formal charges being brought against them. Bhutto ceased being open to collegial advice, let alone opposition. He displayed little patience with those who hesitated in carrying through his orders, and, though sometimes prepared to hear the views of others, he let it be known he preferred his own guidance. Bhutto's inner circle was not pleased with the formation of the Federal Security Force and they were even more disturbed when its personnel were drawn from the darker side of society. Aware that the FSF could be used against them as well as the official opposition, they were mindful that any action or statement on their part could bring the organization to their door. The FSF by this time was linked with a series of political murders. Its operatives were also unleashed to seize the property of targeted individuals, to maintain close watch over the activities of those deemed unfriendly to the regime, to bug telephone lines, and to pressure and intimidate members of the media. Bhutto's colleagues had not envisaged the building of a police state but they were helpless to reverse course once the President's coercive system was in place.

By July 1974, Bhutto had spread his political influence into every sector of society. No institution resisted his intrusion. He had weakened the army with the civil war in East Bengal, and now further by bogging it down in a tribal war on the frontier. He had destroyed an elite bureaucracy, in place since colonial times, and had politicized its officers. He had opened the ranks of the PPP to include landlords and industrialists who otherwise would be threatened with seizures of their property. He had nationalized many of the country's key industrial units and there were indications that other private holdings were targeted. Though he still insisted he was the people's leader, his offer of shelter, bread, and clothing to the poor remained more a slogan than a reality, but Bhutto nonetheless retained the charismatic qualities that sustained the people's interest. Bhutto had little to fear from the poor and undereducated. It was the informed opposition that he feared and his attention was centered on limiting their actions.

No one within the inner circle of the PPP was more important than J.A. Rahim, the true founder of the Pakistan People's Party. Much Bhutto's senior, the elderly Rahim had believed he could mold and shape Bhutto to play the role he believed destiny had ordained. However, Rahim had begun to have serious doubts during the débâcle in East Pakistan. It was Rahim who tried to save the country from the tragedy of civil war and dismemberment. It was he who negotiated a compromise solution with members of the Awami League, only to have it rejected by Bhutto. Events were again in the saddle and the emergence of Zulfikar Ali Bhutto as Pakistan's savior could not be prevented once the Pakistan army had surrendered to Indian forces. After the transfer of power to Bhutto, Rahim tried to advise and influence Bhutto on the need to transform Pakistan into a quasi-socialist welfare state. The nationalization of major industries and utilities soon after the PPP takeover was attributed to Rahim. But Rahim knew then that it was too late to truly influence the Chairman's thinking or methods.

Bhutto had used Rahim as he had the other leaders of the PPP. They had enabled him to distance himself from the traditional political organizations, and they had helped to set Bhutto's sight on the construction of the only true national political organization in Pakistan. But given Pakistan's condition after the 1971 war with India there was no way anyone could have influenced Bhutto to take actions he believed did not serve his personal interest. And although in the early months following his assumption of the presidency a degree of collegiality was maintained, once the weight of governing Pakistan taxed his energy Bhutto no longer suffered the assistance of others, not even those closest to him. Thus by 1974 Rahim and Bhutto came to a parting of the ways. The event precipitating the separation was Bhutto's decision to choose a Minister of Defense and Foreign Affairs. During a cabinet meeting, Rahim opposed the selection. Heated words were exchanged and Bhutto ordered the older man to leave the room. That night members of the FSF invaded Rahim's residence and informed him that he had been dismissed from the cabinet and that his office as Secretary General of the PPP would be taken from him. When Rahim's son appeared to defend his father, a scuffle broke out in which the PPP elder statesman was beaten and suffered severe injury. The Pakistan People's Party was never the same following that incident. Mustafa Khar, Hanif Ramay, Mubashir Hasan, Khurshid Hassan Meer, all celebrated founders and leaders of the PPP, left the party, but not before many of them had been arrested, imprisoned, or forced into exile.

The PPP at its inception was a political organization different from all others in Pakistan's experience. It was nurtured by men indigenous to the country, professional in calling, and urbane in temperament, but it was not democratically organized or led. Leftist-thinking philosophy permeated the senior leaders, and all assumed positions in opposition to landed feudalism, religious fanaticism, ethnic divisiveness, and the overbearing bureaucratism that had dominated Pakistani politics. Although Bhutto's aristocratic background should have eliminated his prospects for leadership of the PPP, he was the only recognized political luminary with the necessary gifts and disposition to put the organization seriously into play. The PPP's original Manifesto described an intention to make the new Pakistan a model polity and home for a polyglot society that found harmony in cooperative endeavor and progressive programs. As a consequence, and with Bhutto's high profile, the PPP drew support from students, factory workers, sharecroppers, as well as the intelligentsia and professional fraternities. When he received the transfer of power from Yahya in December 1971, Bhutto could legitimately claim that he had come to power with the largest support base since 1947, the year Mohammad Ali Jinnah became the Governor General of Pakistan. With such a successful coalition, and with no less a mandate than that enjoyed by Jinnah, how did Bhutto manage to antagonize so many so soon? The answer to that question lies somewhere in the character of the man, in his essential insecurity and his overwhelming paranoia.

Bhutto's overbearing posture, his use of arbitrary power, and his assault on anyone judged to be his enemy caused disaffection in the ranks of the faithful as well as among his more intimate colleagues. The FSF had become a self-motivating operation and its aggressiveness and repressive acts won few friends for the PPP leader. Murder, torture, false imprisonment, and the forceful seizure of private property were some of the more notable concerns of the Pakistani public. Bhutto, however, neither altered his behavior nor reined in his storm troops. Moved to voice their grievances, the student population began to reconsider their loyalty to the Chairman, and when altercations erupted in the country's universities and colleges, the force used to suppress the disorder only added to the intensity of the protest. With his inner circle challenging his authority and the student community engaging in protests, the PPP began to split into factions. Difficulties in the Punjab, the most important of the Pakistani provinces, resulted in Bhutto's sacking of successive PPP provincial governments but that too did nothing to reverse the decay. Bhutto ordered that the PPP Manifesto be redrafted but that was an exercise not likely to stymie the disaffection. Bhutto looked to the religious orders and the Islamists for support, but they struck a hard bargain. From weakness not strength Bhutto had joined the Islamist front organizations that called for renewed assaults on the Ahmediyya community, a painful reminder of the Punjab riots of 1953. Long the target of the fundamentalists, the Ahmediyya were again declared a scourge on Islam. They held high positions in the armed services as well as in government, and it had long been the Islamists' objective to destroy Ahmediyya influence in the country. The Ayub and Yahya governments had repulsed such efforts. The

PPP Chairman, however, was in need of a new alliance and the Islamist orders appeared to provide him with an important base. The Ahmediyya therefore were an available scapegoat.

Bhutto brought legislation before the National Assembly declaring the Ahmediyya to be non-Muslims. The legislation also prevented the sect from observing Islamic rituals. Minaret towers that distinguished mosques from other buildings, as well as the call to Muslims to join in common prayer, were disallowed the Ahmediyya by law. Declared to be heretics, the Ahmediyya were ordered to be removed from all positions of public office or service in the armed forces. Bhutto's support for these restrictions on Pakistani citizens won the Chairman the plaudits of the most extreme fundamentalists, but it caused deeper divisions within his party, played havoc with the notion of civil society, and raised serious questions about democratic governance. Bhutto revealed he was more the autocrat and an opportunist, not the democrat he would have others believe. Moreover, given Bhutto's alliance with the landed gentry and the country's capitalist class, the new PPP Manifesto said little about the vision of a united Pakistan and much about the feverish effort to shore up Bhutto's sagging authority. Bhutto had not only been a principal in the dismemberment of the country, he was a promoter of divisiveness and domestic violence, and the central figure in the fragmentation of the Pakistan People's Party. Bhutto was the paramount contradiction. Everything he did, he argued, was in the best interest of his country and its people. The record reveals that everything he did was for personal gain, no matter the cost to the country. Bhutto's philosophy seemed to suggest the country had to be destroyed in order to be saved. Bhutto was Pakistan, and, according to such logic, what was good for Zulfikar Ali Bhutto was also good for the country.

Bhutto had generated his own enemies. Wali Khan had become the central voice of the opposition and it was he who accused Bhutto of perpetuating and deepening a state of terror in the country. The Balochistan civil war had caused thousands of casualties. Only the brute force of the Pakistan army had forced the Balochi tribesmen to retreat and find refuge in the mountains between Pakistan and Afghanistan. Bhutto accused Wali Khan of treason, of consorting with New Delhi and Kabul, and he tried to intimidate him by directing the FSF to shadow his moves. Again, the NAP leader declared Bhutto was trying to kill him. Were it not for Wali Khan's loyal supporters and vigilant bodyguard the FSF might have succeeded in doing so. There were other targets, however, and in November 1974 Ahmad Raza Kasuri, an old PPP stalwart and former member of the inner circle around Bhutto, was returning to his residence when automatic gunfire riddled his vehicle with bullets. Kasuri survived the incident but his father died amid the hail of projectiles. Kasuri stormed into the National Assembly bearing his father's bloody shirt and pointed to Zulfikar Ali Bhutto as the person who had ordered the attack. Bhutto denied complicity in the assault and declared his enemies were trying to destroy him through false accusations. The killing, however, illustrated the roiling violence loose in the country, so much of it aided and abetted by the Bhutto government.

In February 1975 an explosive device planted under a lectern at Peshawar University killed a prominent PPP frontier leader and special confidant of Chairman Bhutto. Bhutto cut short a trip abroad and returned to Pakistan to order the arrest of Wali Khan. He also ordered the dissolution of Wali Khan's National Awami Party and seized the party's assets. In the absence of the National Assembly's opposition leader, the United Democratic Front declared it would boycott assembly deliberations and immediately ordered its followers into the streets to protest the arbitrary actions of the administration. The PPP had never been a strong party in either the NWFP or Balochistan and in the circumstances there was little likelihood of the party improving its standings. Moreover, Bhutto was under pressure to hold elections that were believed necessary to reinforce his authority. He continued to function as Pakistan's supreme ruler as a consequence of the pre-civil-war elections, and it was generally believed the Chairman required a new mandate, one more representative of the new Pakistan. Bhutto's reluctance to stand for election during a period of instability and disaffection was obvious, but so too was his need for a demonstration of political legitimacy.

That opportunity came from an unexpected source. India detonated a nuclear device in 1974 that sent shock waves throughout the world. The impact on Pakistan, however, was extreme. Bhutto's oratorical skills were made for such occasions and he sought to reassure his compatriots that Pakistan would not be idle in meeting this new Indian challenge. Publicly condemning the action, Bhutto argued that Pakistan had no alternative but to launch an effort that would provide the country with a similar capability. Bhutto emotionally addressed the need for an "Islamic bomb" in so far as the Communists had their bombs, Christian nations had theirs, and now the Hindus as well. The reception in Pakistan to Bhutto's statement was immediate and overwhelmingly favorable. Envisaging such a capability a deterrent to Indian nuclear blackmail, Pakistanis in all walks of life approved of the idea and believed it would make their country more secure. Bhutto also saw atomic weapons as ensuring Pakistan's leadership in the Muslim world. Pakistanis were divided on virtually every issue, save the matter of Pakistan acquiring nuclear weapons. How far the "Islamic bomb" issue enabled Bhutto to restore some of his lost prestige is difficult to estimate, but it certainly provided a boost to his fortunes. On the other hand, there was a greater degree of fatalism in Bhutto's speeches and pronouncements after the Indian test. Not that he felt Pakistan was in imminent danger, but his state of mind had been deeply impacted. By nature he was a brooding personality, and his sense of foreboding was heightened in 1975 when word reached Islamabad that Mujibur Rahman had been gunned down with most of his extended family by disgruntled members of Bangladesh's armed forces. On another front, the state of emergency imposed by Indira Gandhi also raised questions about the durability of governments, no matter how charismatic.

In an effort to boost his dwindling support Bhutto issued a decree calling for land reform which aimed at assisting the small land-holder. Earlier reforms had permitted the holding of 150 acres of irrigated land and three hundred acres of non-irrigated land. The earlier reforms applied to individuals, not families, however, and there had been little change in the poverty of rural folk. These reforms attempted to improve their circumstances. They were also expected to bring more people into the PPP camp. Bhutto therefore launched still other reforms that would give more tangible meaning to the PPP battle cry of "Bread, Clothing, and Shelter." Bhutto attempted to reclaim a reputation for assisting the needy and his movements were orchestrated to receive maximum attention from the Pakistani masses. Public functions involved sporting events and gymnastic competitions arranged with assistance from the North Koreans and Chinese. In 1976, Mohammad Ali Jinnah's one-hundredth birth anniversary was an occasion for year-long celebrations, culminating with the Quaid's birthday in December. 1976 also was the year General Tikka Khan's tenure as commander of the Pakistani army ended. The war in Balochistan began to lose its intensity. It seemed an appropriate time to consider holding national elections and plans moved forward to allow the Pakistani people to register their faith in the administration.

In the meantime, a replacement had to be found to lead the Pakistan army. Bhutto selected General Mohammad Zia ul-Haq, a lesser-known officer who had served in Jordan on special assignment during the civil war. Zia came to the Prime Minister's attention because he was a devout Muslim, had no connection to Bhutto's past, and was not considered personally ambitious. Zia was expected not to disturb the relationship between the government and the army and to demonstrate perfect loyalty to the constitution and the Prime Minister. With the American ambassador, Henry Byroade, pressuring Washington to lift the arms embargo imposed on Pakistan more than ten years before, there was some expectation that the Pakistan army would be put through another modernization program and Zia was considered the general best able to manage the job. The Pakistan army also was given responsibility for Pakistan's nuclear weapons program, and Bhutto envisaged a close relationship between Zia and himself on matters pertaining to the assembly of scientific personnel as well as the procurement of the required materials. Finally, Bhutto wanted a man at the helm of the army who would maintain its political neutrality, especially with elections being projected for 1977. With most of the leading politicians in prison or denied participation in politics, Bhutto intended using the FSF to maintain domestic security upon their release. He wanted assurances the army would not interfere with FSF policing responsibilities and in effect would confine its activities to external defense. In Zia, Bhutto believed he had found the general to meet his needs.

However, Bhutto's expectations and the reality within the army were not the same. By the mid-1970s the officers who had been intimate with Bhutto had all retired. The new retinue of colonels and generals were not personally connected to the Prime Minister. Moreover, as veterans of the 1965 and 1971 wars these officers had developed a different perception of Zulfikar Ali Bhutto. Unlike their predecessors, they were not in awe of Bhutto's reputed brilliance or his rhetoric. Many officers had family members who had suffered losses of property in run-ins with the PPP and FSF, or had reason to question Bhutto's governing style. Some officers therefore harbored grievances with either the PPP administration or Bhutto himself. Still others saw Ayub and Yahya as good soldiers, who were somehow caused to suffer disgrace in circumstances not entirely of their making. Little of this surfaced, however, at the time Zia was sworn in as army commander.

Bhutto's political legitimacy now appeared to hinge more on his Islamic bona fides, which were never judged to be strong. Not a religious Muslim, Bhutto played at religion more than he practiced it. Nevertheless, he could not ignore the country's tendency to express itself along spiritual lines. Therefore, Bhutto made the most of the International Seerat Congress that celebrated and memorialized the life of the Prophet. Speaking at the meeting, Bhutto tried to connect his foreign policy with the Prophet's teachings. Citing his work in promoting Islamic solidarity, he portrayed Islam as the defining civilization in world history. Bhutto also used the occasion to invite the Shah of Iran and his Empress to make an appearance at the Congress. Bhutto recalled that the Shah had declined his invitation to attend the Lahore Islamic Summit because of differences with some of the participants. This gesture was an effort to bridge that circumstance. It was also an opportunity for Bhutto to express his gratitude to the Shah for the assistance Iran had provided Pakistan, especially in the management of petroleum needs during a period of escalating prices. Bhutto discussed Pakistan's effort to develop alternative sources of energy, particularly nuclear power. He also expressed his concern about India's nuclear program that had now demonstrated weapons grade capacities.

No one could forecast how the Shah's and Bhutto's personal destinies were intertwined, but it was clear from their meeting that the Pakistani Prime Minister had modeled much of his regime on that of the Shah's and that the two men were intimately tied to one another. The Shah offered to assist Bhutto in developing a more positive relationship with Sardar Daud of Afghanistan and an invitation was extended to the Afghan President. Bhutto assured him of a warm welcome from the people of Pakistan.

With Bhutto more confident given the success of his foreign policy, by September 1976 the PPP election campaign was already in high gear. Bhutto anticipated reconnecting with the coalition of forces that brought him to power in 1971. He renewed his appeal to women, to factory workers, to students, and to former servicemen. His party also prepared a book of Bhutto's quotations that resembled the "Red Book" of Mao Zedong, who had passed away that year. Showing his socialist inclinations, Bhutto extended his nationalization scheme to include government control of cotton-ginning, paddy-husking, and flour milling. He called the middlemen running these operations "bloodsuckers" and said his administration was determined to provide the farmers with a fair share of the profits derived from their labor. The seizure of property was a matter of executive will and not something subject to parliamentary deliberation. Bhutto was attacked for such high-handed actions, notably by an old PPP confidant who accused the Chairman of putting the stick to the opposition politicians while he doled out barrels of carrots to those who helped his cause. Bhutto's political opposition, however, was particularly critical of the PPP program giving young army officers choice agricultural land for the smallest fees.

Virtually all of Bhutto's political and economic policies were linked with his political survival and seldom with the country's development. Bhutto's policies forced entrepreneurs to withdraw their funds from Pakistan. Private investment under a government that stunted or destroyed incentive became impossible. All that seemed to matter to the PPP was holding the country together, and the expenditures in the use of police power left little for constructive endeavor. This was not lost on Bhutto's critics, but the Chairman continued to demonstrate that what was good for Zulfikar Ali Bhutto was also good for the nation. Bhutto truly believed he was Pakistan's benefactor and he expected those under his command, like those affected by his rule, to display the proper homage. Bhutto's speech in December 1976 questioned how he could be so misunderstood by his detractors. "A nation that grudges honor to its leaders," he declared, "is a nation that thinks little of itself."

Pakistan's previous elections had all produced negative effects. And it was not so long ago that the country's first national election was prelude to a horrific civil war that did not end until the country had suffered terrible casualties, humiliation, and dismemberment. Election experience therefore did not lend itself to positive conclusions. Nevertheless, on January 7, 1977 Bhutto announced that national elections would be held and that the imprisoned politicians would be released to compete with PPP candidates. Before the announcement, land reforms were again publicized, and this time Bhutto reduced the size of large land-holdings so that additional land could be made available to the landless tenant farmers. But though special decrees and patronage could be expected from the PPP administration, it was Bhutto's transcendent personality that was expected to carry the PPP to victory. Bhutto believed he had framed the elections so that he could finally eliminate his opposition. Although unstated, it was obvious to all observers that he intended to establish an absolute dictatorship and call it democracy. The Chairman's goal was nothing less than a mandate that would legitimate the drastic action he contemplated taking against those who dared to challenge his authority.

Confronted with this challenge the opposition politicians did the only thing left to them: they decided to combine their organizations and to present the nation with a single slate of candidates. Thus was assembled the Pakistan National Alliance (PNA), a coalition whose sole purpose was the defeat of the PPP and Zulfikar Ali Bhutto. The PNA brought together the United Democratic Front, the Tehrik-i-Istiqlal, and all the Islamist political organizations. The PNA's target from beginning to end was the personality and rule of Zulfikar Ali Bhutto. No issue of public importance would be debated. It was not an election involving rival platforms or philosophies of governing. It was all too obvious the election revolved around one man and either defeating him at the polls or suffering the consequences. The PNA therefore zeroed in on Bhutto's personal habits, his family background, and his arrogant demeanor. Here was the opportunity for all those aggrieved by the Chairman to express their concerns. So it was in Karachi, where the mohajir community joined the

PNA. In war-ravaged Balochistan the Sardars rallied their people to cast votes against PPP incumbents. On the North West Frontier, people were reminded of the tactics used to destroy the National Awami Party and of the imprisonment of Wali Khan. Even in the Punjab, former followers and mentors of Zulfikar Ali Bhutto beseeched the public to recognize the price to be paid in returning Bhutto to power.

The elections and the aftermath

Ballots were cast on March 7, 1977 by approximately seventeen million of the eligible thirty-one million voters. From the outset of the voting, cries of fraud and voter manipulation were expressed by members of the PNA. People were blocked from reaching the polls in some areas, while PPP officials facilitated access for their supporters. It was not long after the close of the voting stations that the PPP claimed a landslide victory, winning sixty percent of the vote and seventy-five percent of the National Assembly seats, more than the two-thirds necessary to change the constitution and alter the political system. Bhutto claimed his mandate but the opposition was not done. With only seventeen percent of the seats in the National Assembly the opposition realized it teetered on the brink of disaster. Moreover, Bhutto had used the army's Inter-Services Intelligence Directorate to check on all candidates and even the few candidates the PNA was likely to send to the National Assembly were blocked from taking their seats by police order. Nothing would be permitted to impede the work of the Bhutto administration. The new Assembly convened immediately after the official count. The new Pakistan of Zulfikar Ali Bhutto was now to be shaped to serve the views and ideas of the PPP Chairman.

The opposition leaders had known that the election would not be fair. Despite Bhutto's predictable victory, they knew he would not be satisfied with a simple win. Bhutto envisaged a total overhaul of the political system and he was determined to prevent anyone from again challenging his authority, let alone embarrassing him in public. When cries erupted of vote-rigging, Bhutto's first reaction was to deny the opposition claim, but he also ordered his FSF to deal forcefully with those who he claimed opposed the will of the people and the expression of the democratic process. In response the PNA called for a countrywide strike and hoped to shut down the nation. When the demonstrations degenerated into widespread riots Bhutto ordered the FSF to crush the dissenters. But by this time tens of thousands were pouring into the streets, many as a consequence of actions launched by the Islamist parties, notably the Jamaat-i-Islami, the Jamaat-ul-Ulema-i-Islam, and the Jamiat-ul-Ulema-i-Pakistan. The fundamentalist parties vilified Bhutto as a non-Muslim, accusing him of desecrating the religion and undermining Islamic practices. Moreover, the Islamists had penetrated the armed forces, especially the ISI and the army, and large numbers of troops and commanding officers had been led to believe that in opposing Bhutto they were making a sincere statement about Islam.

When the FSF found their ranks insufficient to deal with the civil unrest, Bhutto called upon the army to crush the protesters and restore law and order. It was now Zia's job to answer the call of his beleaguered head of government, but Zia had to answer to his army colleagues, and a number refused to act. Many officers believed this was the time to eliminate the paramilitary FSF, hence their decision to reject Bhutto's plea. Disenchanted army officers also cited the deteriorating economy, the uncontrolled inflation, the inability to alleviate conditions resulting from crop failures, the mismanagement of the nationalized industries, and the corruption that permeated every sector of government and society. Unemployment had sky-rocketed, sectarian and ethnic strife had made a shambles of civil society, and the heavy expenditure on government security protected the regime but did virtually nothing for the nation.

Bhutto was advised to call new elections but he would listen to nothing that would keep him from dominating events. Bhutto, unlike Ayub Khan, was a maker of events and he refused to yield to forces he believed he could control. The Chairman declared he was prepared to meet with the opposition but only with the understanding they had accepted the election results. He also warned the opposition that he would deal with them ruthlessly if they sustained the rioting and refused to rein in their supporters. Bhutto's defiance was a red flag to the angry crowds that coursed through Pakistan's cities and towns. The violence intensified with every statement made by the PPP leader and, showing no fear, the crowds locked in street battles with the FSF and police. The latter, unable to quell the surging protesters, began to desert. Many policemen abandoned their calling when shoot-to-kill orders were implemented by some members of the FSF and the dead were left to remind people why they had to sustain the fight. The scenes were reminiscent of the days leading up to the army crackdown in East Pakistan before the civil war. Only this time the army was reluctant to become committed to a conflict it had no stomach for and did not believe in. Too many Pakistanis had been murdered in order to bring Bhutto to power, and now to sustain him hundreds, possibly thousands, would have to be sacrificed. It was time to call an end to the slaughter. It was also the time to inform Zulfikar Ali Bhutto that he would no longer be permitted to construct his personal dictatorship.

As a last-minute gesture to the Islamists Bhutto declared he had placed a prohibition on the sale and use of alcoholic beverages, had banned gambling, had closed the bars, nightclubs, and movie theaters, and would move Pakistan toward the objective of a chaste Islamic state. None of the religious leaders, however, was impressed with this decree. Nor were the members of the Inter-Services Intelligence who plotted Bhutto's demise. Bhutto, nevertheless, refused to acknowledge that the army had turned against him. Instead, he publicly condemned the United States for interfering in the country's internal affairs. But this outcry was seen as a futile gesture. Bhutto played his trump card when he called on General Zia to declare martial law in Karachi, Hyderabad, and Lahore, the most populous of Pakistani cities and the sites of the heaviest rioting. Bhutto also addressed the corps commanders, insisting the country was under siege from foreign sources and that their first duty was the defense of the nation. The army command, however, had had enough of Zulfikar Ali Bhutto. The more he pleaded for their support, and the more they yielded to his demands, the deeper were the divisions within the ranks. Army discipline had now become a key element as the generals pondered their next move.

Bhutto was accused of unleashing the most violent forces in Pakistani society. The PPP Chairman had been called to bind up the nation's wounds following the devastating civil war and the Indian invasion of East Pakistan. Instead he caused the armed forces to question their capacity for good soldiering. Instead of healing a demoralized country Bhutto had continued the blood-letting. In the attempt to construct a permanent but personal power base, he had undermined all attempts at nation building, had ruined the economy, and had aggravated sectarian rivalries. Thus, when Pakistan International Airlines and the Pakistan Railway shut down operations in a display of unity with the Pakistan National Alliance, the army could no longer wait on events to take their course. On July 5, 1977, junior officers in the Pakistan army signaled to their superiors that delay was no longer an option. The army, they warned, would come apart if action were not taken to oust the Prime Minister and terminate his government. It was made clear that the choice lay in saving Bhutto or saving the army. Zia hesitated for a moment, but then agreed to save the army.

Bibliography

Ali, Akhtar, *Pakistan's Nuclear Dilemma: Energy and Security Dimensions*, Karachi: Economist Unit, 1983.

Ayoob, Mohammed, and Subrahmanyam, K., *The Liberation War*, New Delhi: S. Chand, 1972.

Bhutto, Zulfikar Ali, *Foreign Policy of Pakistan*, Karachi: Pakistan Institute of International Affairs, 1964.

Bhutto, Zulfikar Ali, *The Quest for Peace*, Karachi: Pakistan Institute of International Affairs, 1966.

Bhutto, Zulfikar Ali, *The Myth of Independence*, Karachi: Oxford University Press, 1969.

Bhutto, Zulfikar Ali, *Speeches and Statements*, Karachi: Government of Pakistan, 1972.

Bhutto, Zulfikar Ali, *Speeches and Statements*, Karachi: Government of Pakistan, 1973.

Burki, Shahid Javed, *Pakistan under Bhutto, 1971–1977*, New York: St. Martin's Press, 1980.

Hasan, Mubashir, *The Mirage of Power: An Inquiry into the Bhutto Years, 1971–1977*, Karachi: Oxford University Press, 2000.

Janmahmad, *Essays on Baloch National Struggle in Pakistan*, Quetta, Pakistan: Gosha-e-Adab, 1989.

Mascarenhas, Anthony, *The Rape of Bangladesh*, New Delhi: Vikas, 1972.

Mody, Piloo, *Zulfi My Friend*, Karachi: Paramount, 1973.

Rashid, Harun-or, *The Foreshadowing of Bangladesh: Bengal Muslim League and Muslim Politics*, Dacca: Asiatic Society of Bangladesh, 1987.

Wolpert, Stanley, *Zulfi Bhutto of Pakistan: His Life and Times*, New York: Oxford University Press, 1993.

Zaheer, Hasan, *The Separation of East Pakistan: The Rise and Realization of Bengali Nationalism*, Karachi: Oxford University Press, 1994.

Zaman, Fakhar and Aman, Akhtar, Z.A. *Bhutto: The Political Thinker*, Lahore: People's Publications, 1973.

Ziring, Lawrence, *Pakistan: The Enigma of Political Development*, Folkestone: Dawson, 1980.

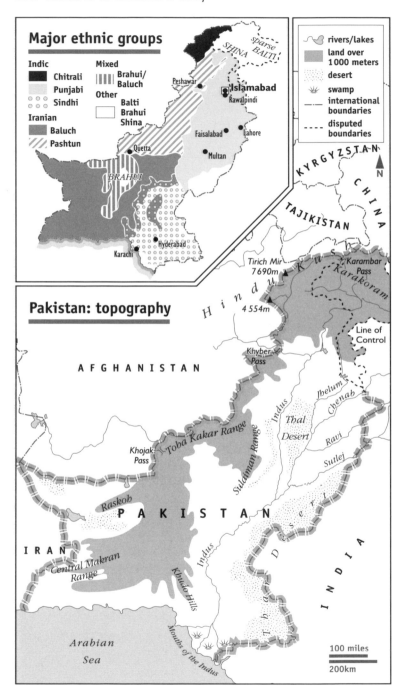

Major ethnic groups

Indic

- Chitrali
- Punjabi
- Sindhi

Iranian

- Baluch
- Pashtun

Mixed

- Brahui/Baluch

Other

- Balti
- Brahui
- Shina

rivers/lakes
land over 1000 meters
desert
swamp
international boundaries
disputed boundaries

Pakistan: topography

6

ISLAMIZATION

After a hiatus of some five years the army again assumed control of Pakistan's political process. The last period of army rule had lasted more than thirteen years and few were prepared to forecast an early return to civilian-controlled government this time. General Zia's initial statements and his treatment of the ousted Bhutto administration were relatively placid, considering the anarchic conditions that had caused the army to take over the government. Zia had stated his intention to return the army to the barracks as soon as quiet had been restored and new elections could be held. Bhutto, he said, would be permitted to stump for his party and, if successful in the projected polls, could yet again form the government. Zia's public statements, however, hardly revealed the behind-the-scenes activity among the senior officers. The troops that forced Zia's hand and had demanded the removal of the Prime Minister had no intention of permitting him to return to office. Zia, it was said, was too rooted in more conventional civil–military relations to recognize that this was no ordinary coup.

What was not detected was the transformation and birth of a new Pakistan. So much attention had centered on the person of Zulfikar Ali Bhutto, on his personal dictatorship and the peculiar manifestations of his rule, that there was little energy remaining to fathom what Pakistan had become since the civil war. Now, in the absence of Zulfikar Ali Bhutto, it was possible to see more clearly how Pakistan had been metamorphosed into a state so different from the one represented by its founders. Unlike Yahya, Zia had been reluctant to impose a junta-like government on Pakistan. Following the civil war, and after assuming his command, Zia was consumed by the need to re-establish army discipline and rebuild confidence in the ranks. Moreover, the armed forces had suffered from the cut-off of American military assistance. China had been of some benefit, but Pakistan's American-made weapons systems were either in serious need of spare parts or obsolete.

Zia had refrained from taking direct action against the Bhutto administration because of sustained disarray in the armed forces, and when he did move, it was more because he did not have complete control over his troops than out of conviction. Once he had time to reflect on his takeover, however, Zia was a different general with a different purpose. Although he had not anticipated ruling the new Pakistan, in time he came to realize there was no other alternative. He could not, as he first indicated, allow Bhutto to return to office, and he was most reluctant to call upon another civilian politician to organize a new government. Faced with a Hobson's choice, Zia decided to make the best of the situation and the martial law imposed on July 5 was extended indefinitely.

Zia did not abrogate the 1973 constitution, believing its suspension would permit him a degree of legitimacy not given the Ayub and Yahya administrations. Moreover, by preserving the document he could argue his actions were not only necessary but also legal. At the same time, Zia revealed he had some very definite ideas about Pakistan's future. Since he was a very devout Muslim, his faith influenced his actions. A more aloof observer of Pakistan's transformation following the dismemberment, the General was a living example of its consequences. Zia viewed the separation of East Bengal from Pakistan in roughly the same way he viewed the separation of Pakistan from greater India during the partition of 1947. Islam was the major concern in forming the original Pakistan, and, for Zia, Islam was the only reason for the perpetuation of the Pakistan that emerged from the civil war. For Zia the fundamentalist orders and their political organizations were no more a problem than the more conventional secular parties. Moreover, the secular parties were responsible for Pakistan's sustained instability. It was these parties and their leaders that had betrayed the nation. The secular–Islamist struggle was less a democratic–autocratic confrontation than an effort by opportunist politicians to acquire personal gain. In Zia's opinion, therefore, the Islamist orders were not nearly the threat publicized by the more secular politicians.

Zia in fact found something admirable and noble in the Islamist objective. The desire to recreate Pakistan as an Islamic state was not only more in keeping with the genius of the Pakistani nation, it also elevated the formation of Pakistan to a moral plane not experienced in the years since independence. The failure to appreciate the people's spiritual life in the mundane operations of the nation, the tendency to model the country after European example, the continuing dependence on foreign but non-Muslim assistance had prevented the development of an ethos more representative of the nation's character and purpose. Zia's surface reaction was to reject political parties as incompatible with Islamic teaching and unnecessary in circumstances that demanded adherence to precepts of Islamic solidarity. Parties were arbitrarily divisive and dysfunctional, given the basis of Islamic tradition. Therefore, shortly after declaring he would not hold elections, would sustain the ban on the political parties, and would not lift martial law, Zia began to speak about the need for a *Nizam-i-Mustapha*, a political system reminiscent of the Rule of the Prophet. Zia's reflections on the civil war involved the need to bind up Pakistan's self-inflicted wounds. It was his conclusion that Pakistanis required a true Islamic state. Anything less, he believed, would only lead to the further unraveling of the social fabric. Such an outcome he was duty bound to prevent.

Before selecting Zia to head the army, Bhutto had pondered the General's overriding and consuming Islamic practice. At the moment of decision, however, he judged it a welcome change from an earlier generation of officers raised in the British colonial tradition. Religious commitment was a more pronounced feature of military service since the civil war. The shift from a colonial-trained force to a more indigenous one was of critical importance. Before independence, and under British tutelage, Muslim units had been mixed with Hindu and Sikh components, and army discipline was a function of line and command, servicemen ascribing to a professional calling that demanded being true to one's salt. Honor among the troops was measured in obedience and a strict hierarchy of command. Dominated by Englishmen, from the lowest jawan to the most senior officer the army demonstrated its respect for the Crown and swore allegiance to the Empire. By the time of the Pakistan civil war, the generation of officers and men that comprised the earlier Pakistan army were retired or dead. A new generation emerged that possessed little if any personal memory of that earlier army. In the absence of a colonial tradition, the army's focus was not the Crown but a Pakistan state that had been forged to give voice to the Muslims of the subcontinent. Nurtured in an ambience that emphasized the spiritual under-pinnings of the country, and shorn of the colonial military tradition, this new generation of soldiers developed an entirely different outlook from that of their predecessors.

That outlook was deeply affected by the war in East Bengal. Not only was the war seen as part of a larger Indian and therefore Hindu conspiracy, but after India's invasion of the country, its defeat of the Pakistani garrison, and the humiliation suffered as a consequence of the army surrender, Pakistanis found new resolve in their Islamic faith. If Islam was declared to be in danger prior to independence, it was now judged to face an even more significant and more tangible threat. It is notable that the Jamaat-i-Islami, the primary fundamentalist party in East Pakistan at the time of the civil war, stood with the Pakistan army in its struggle with the Bengali Mukhti Bahini. The East Bengal Jamaat never criticized the brutality inflicted on the Bengalis by Pakistani forces and in fact had taken the position that the Awami League of Mujibur Rahman, like the National Awami Party of Maulana Bhashani, represented heathen forces and therefore deserved to be crushed. The apocalyptic nature of the Pakistan army's assault on the Bengali nation illustrated a classic contest between Islam and its mortal enemies. Even in defeat, the Pakistani army had fought the good fight against forces that would undo the Islamic tradition in the subcontinent. The civil war and India's intervention therefore provided the Pakistani army with its true baptism, that is, a liberation war to free Pakistan from the grip of the non-believer. In its despair and humiliation the Pakistan army, and certainly an important portion of its officer corps, found solace in their religious devotions. It was this army that Zia assumed the leadership of in 1976. Although he personally did not experience the crucible of civil war or taste the bitter Indian victory over Pakistani arms, his personal instincts were in harmony with the soldiers whose lives were forever changed by the experience.

The Jamaat-i-Islami was an unambiguous presence in the Pakistan that emerged after independence. Its attempt to recruit followers from among the younger members of the population met with considerable success. Never holding the view that it could achieve its objectives through the electoral process, the Jamaat of Maulana Maudoodi and his successors was content with the awareness that they had created an organic organization composed of elite members of the community and capable of overcoming numerous obstacles. Since they preached an austere version of Islamic practice, only the creation of a chaste Muslim state governed by *Shari'a* would satisfy their standards. Always a determined adversary of the Muslim League, the Jamaat opposed the Pakistan Movement and condemned its leaders. Beyond the range of the competitive secular political organizations, the Jamaat sustained its assault on the several governments organized to serve Pakistan during the first parliamentary period. Later a critic of the Ayub and Yahya administrations, it never accepted their secular programs or the associations they forged with the United States during the cold war. Moreover, the Jamaat's message, although not attractive to the majority of Pakistanis, nevertheless drew a large following, and particular inroads were made in the armed forces. Zia, among others, was influenced by the teachings of the Jamaat-i-Islami. Thus, when Bhutto accused Zia of linking forces with the Jamaat in an effort to destroy him, it was not an unsupported charge. More difficult to prove, however, was Bhutto's claim that the United States government had bankrolled the Jamaat, as it had the PNA, in an effort to influence the outcome of the 1977 election.

Zia's attention, however, centered on the consolidation of power. Bhutto's Federal Security Force had threatened the armed forces because it theoretically had the leverage to decimate the military ranks as well as assume responsibilities normally within the ambit of the traditional services. Moreover, a secret police agency answering only to the Prime Minister posed a threat to uniformed personnel as much as it did to the civilian population.

Federal Security Force operations targeted members of military families and the excesses of the organization were known personally to army officers. Among Zia's first decisions therefore was the destruction of the FSF. Its director, Masood Mahmood, and other high-placed officials of the agency were arrested and ordered to testify about their actions in support of the Bhutto government. Accused of intimidation, torture, and murder, FSF agents revealed what they knew about the organization's behavior and programs. Most important they implicated Bhutto in virtually all their operations. Following this testimony, Bhutto was formally accused of ordering the FSF to murder a rival politician.

The Quaid-i-Awam could not escape the avalanche of charges by members of the now abolished Federal Security Force. All crimes attributed to the FSF were linked to Bhutto's commands, and not the least of their revelations was the Prime Minister's sinful behavior. Described as having violated Islamic tradition, Bhutto was accused of womanizing, imbibing alcoholic beverages, and committing blasphemy. Bhutto's practices were publicized as an assault on Islamic tradition, and his more recent public expressions of piety were ridiculed as signs of desperation, not repentance. Zia's personal piety was juxtaposed against that of the erstwhile Prime Minister, and there is little doubt the General saw the opportunity to elevate his credentials among the fundamentalist orders by further exposing what was deemed to be the illicit behavior of the fallen leader. Bhutto became the instrument for a national catharsis while Zia gave increasing importance to the country's national genius, its Islamic tradition. Thus, religious calling merged with political aspirations, and a soldier's discipline gave resonance to the idea of personal jihad, that is, the need for self-improvement and inner transformation. Zia rejected the creature comforts of being the head of state and chose to remain in his spartan home in the army cantonment at Rawalpindi. The latter decision allowed Zia not only to portray himself as indifferent to material things, but also to maintain close surveillance of army activity. Unlike Ayub, Zia did not intend to pass command of the Pakistan army to one of his subordinates.

Zia's conservative lifestyle and his limited personal needs left little for the officers under his command to quarrel about. Moreover, the General's Islamic practices were made in plain sight and his orders to his troops to rededicate their lives to religious expression was something he already imposed on himself. Originally a reluctant coup leader, once he had assumed the responsibility of high office, Zia rose to the occasion and settled in for what would be a long reign. Agreeing with those around him that new elections would provide Bhutto with a platform from which to criticize the army high command, Zia took the decision to arrest and try him for the murder of Ahmad Raza Kasuri. Former FSF officers turned state's evidence and testified that the Prime Minister had ordered the assault resulting in the death of Kasuri. Found guilty in March 1978, Bhutto was sentenced to death. An extended appeal process followed while the condemned was confined to a prison cell. During this period Zia formally assumed the office of President of Pakistan. Appealed to from capitals around the world, Zia refused to consider pleas for mercy. Instead, the government issued a series of White Papers purporting to enumerate the crimes of the erstwhile Quaid-i-Awam. They all justified the death verdict. Bhutto pleaded his innocence from his Rawalpindi cell and spoke of dying at the hands of usurpers. No amount of pleading, however, dissuaded Zia from carrying out the court's sentence. Arguing that Islamic justice must be done, Zia rejected calls for clemency. On April 4, 1979, his appeals exhausted, Bhutto was led to the gallows and hanged.

Zia and Islamist politics

Others had played with the idea of the Islamic state and much lip service had been given to that objective, but Zia was the first to truly profess that goal as his greatest duty. Secular forces had dominated Pakistani politics and a thin veneer of sophisticated Pakistanis had influenced the course of the nation's politics. Election results, though meager and full of controversy, were nevertheless representations of secular forces. The masses of Pakistanis who were tempted to the polls seldom cast ballots as a consequence of personal preference. In an agrarian society dominated by the land-holding class, the largely rural population was more likely to vote for the wishes of the local patriarch than their own conscience. As such, the religious parties seldom had much attraction to the average voter, and their poor showing appeared to reinforce the secular characteristics of the state. Zia sought to change that condition. Under the veil of martial law Zia experienced a minimum of opposition to his policies. Moreover, Pakistan's population had already experienced so much army intervention that the situation was more the norm than the exception. The people of Pakistan made the adjustment back to army rule with little apparent difficulty, especially given the popular desire to restore society to relative normalcy. The nation had been so consumed by violence since the passing of Ayub Khan that anyone promising the restoration of law and order was a welcome addition to the political scene. Even more so if that individual leader offered a vision that reflected the genius of the larger nation.

The civil war in East Pakistan was too recent to have escaped the memory of the Pakistani people. Zia understood the consequences of that war and how it had forever changed the nation. Also aware that divisive forces continued to threaten what remained of Pakistan and cognizant that the Islamic religion was the only common denominator, Zia was convinced the building of an Islamic polity was all that stood between the nation and total anarchy. Zia therefore catered to those calling for a chaste Muslim state. He became even more mindful of the role Kashmir played in shaping the mentality of the masses, and he was determined to exploit the nation's longing for a society dedicated to the proposition that Islam not democracy was the single objective of all the country's citizens. Moreover, in emphasizing Islamic tradition, the General trod on familiar ground and had no need for foreign experts. Islamic practice came naturally to the country's illiterates and no instruction was required in defining the relationship between the rulers and the ruled.

Zia therefore ignored "Basic Democracy" experiments and avoided parliamentary governance. He rejected the political party arrangements and, especially, competitive politics. Pakistani politics had developed an overwhelmingly negative character, the goal being to outdo your rival by whatever means, irrespective of the impact on the nation. Self-aggrandizement not public service was the result of such a system and as the politicians fiddled, the people were ignored and the country was allowed to sink deeper into the morass. Zia therefore had no compunctions about abandoning traditional politics. Little, he argued, was lost and much could be gained if he were free to move the nation along a different path.

Zia's central constituency was the armed forces and especially the army, from the rank and file to the senior officer class. He especially catered to those army officers who were imbued with the Islamic tradition, who practiced their religious tenets, and who believed as he did that the nation's future pivoted on the realization of an integrated Muslim community. Zia used the 1973 constitution to press his goals, starting with the Provisional Constitution Order of March 1981, which prevented challenges to his authority. Zia's idea of a constitutional order focused less on the limitation of government power and more on the need to strengthen executive rule. The country had suffered considerable trauma and a firm hand was required to assure the populace that their government was capable of managing events. Clearly, there was no way to justify both the preservation of the constitution and the sustaining of martial law, but the obvious contradiction did not cause Zia to falter or hesitate in the pursuit of his real objective. Zia's vision had nothing to do with grand designs. His purpose was stabilizing the nation and the furtherance of goals that merged the spiritual with the temporal. Zia promised a new beginning.

In December 1982, in the course of a speech celebrating the birth anniversary of the Prophet, Zia emphasized the need to direct Pakistani life in accordance with the teachings of the Qur'an and Sunnah. The role of all Muslims, he declared, was to propagate the faith and emulate the performance of their great spiritual leader. With his government and leading members of the Islamist orders surrounding him, Zia called for a renewal of the requirement of jihad, and said that his government had been instructed to explore holy scripture in the formation of the *Nizam-i-Mustapha*. Citing the need to adopt Islamic jurisprudence, he spoke of strengthening the social fabric through a process of "Islamization." Zia cited the Islamic requirements of *zakat* (alms) and *ushr* (the tax on agriculture) that traditionally provided the state with the funds needed to assist those unable to provide adequately for themselves. Zia also described the operation of *qisas* (the right of pre-emption) and *diyat* (the laws of evidence), as well as the official establishment of *Qazi* courts that were to be headed by religious judges. Zia called for the formation of an Islamic judicial system and a form of commercial and financial practices that conformed with the principles of Islamic jurisprudence. The intended Islamic reforms were supposed to root out corruption as well as prevent the exploitation of the weaker members of society. But they also impacted on the secular legal fraternity and undermined the preserve of the country's cosmopolitan elite.

Not everyone was pleased with the implementation of the Islamization program. Wealthier entrepreneurs questioned their ability to do business across a broad international spectrum, and, rather than struggle against the government's directives, many moved their assets outside the country, while still others decided to follow their funds and took up residence abroad. Zia questioned such behavior and in an effort to prevent a mass exodus, imposed restrictions on the outflow of funds as well as on foreign travel. Zia insisted his program was not meant to antagonize the bellwethers of society, or to entrench him in power. The country, he said, suffered from moral decay, and the social fiber needed strengthening so that it would not again suffer humiliation, division, and defeat. Calling for a genuine demonstration of piety, selflessness, and the highest ethical standards, Zia envisioned a new Pakistan that he believed could become a model to all the Muslim nations. According to the General, political parties failed to contribute to this design, and hence could be ignored, if not abandoned. Parties were the bastions of would-be powerful men and had done nothing to enhance the well-being of the nation. Locked in uncompromising conflict they had already inflicted severe wounds on Pakistan, and were directly responsible for the civil war and the loss of East Pakistan. Yahya had permitted the leaders of the principal political parties to dominate him, and Zia let it be known he would not be such easy prey.

A student of Islamic tradition, Zia found nothing about political parties in its teachings and he was left to conclude they had been adopted from alien cultures. He therefore had no hesitation in rejecting them. He also understood that in banning the political parties he faced little organized opposition and thus was free to press ahead with his scheme to reconstruct Pakistan in ways that would emphasize the country's Muslim character. Another dimension of Zia's thinking was the disappearance of the country's largest minority community, which had resided in East Pakistan. Free of its Southeast Asian wing, Pakistan was truly a Muslim entity, its human composition verging on homogeneity. Though intent on moving ahead with Islamization, Zia nevertheless sustained the otherwise secular constitution from which he drew his legitimacy. Zia understood his program was more likely to appeal to the masses than the elite, but he still saw the necessity for keeping the more secular members of society in his camp. To appeal to both traditionalists and secularists was no simple task, especially when the latter saw their values and worldview so forcefully criticized. Zia therefore sought to have the constitution amended to provide the armed forces with a permanent stake in the country's governance. Citing the probity and dedication of the soldiers under his command, Zia indicated that their leadership qualities required replication in society at large. As selfless workers in the cause of God and country, the soldiers would continue to lead Pakistan long after his departure.

The realities of Zia's Islamist policy

Zia was conditioned not only by his Islamic experience and military service; he was also a creature of events, and the events that brought him to power were without question defining. The loss of East Pakistan had revitalized provincial forces, and secessionist movements were barely concealed in the violent language of those who had long struggled against the creation of Pakistan and now were even more energized by the possibilities for regional self-determination. Pakistan had been established with the belief "Islam was in danger," but the events following independence had failed to give substance to that call. Islam was never in danger and the multitudes who identified with Muslim practice continued to expand within the subcontinent as well as throughout the world. The Pakistan of 1947 was never meant to relieve those anxious about the future of the Islamic religion. Moreover, Jinnah's almost immediate portrayal of Pakistan as a home to all, whether Muslim or non-Muslim, contradicted the establishment of Pakistan as a haven for those Muslims otherwise unable to practice their faith.

Although a huge number of Indian Muslims left or were forced to leave their homes in India, an even larger number chose not to leave, suggesting that Muslims could be integrated in a largely Hindu India despite the Pakistan government's repeated declaration that the Indian government was a menace to the Muslim way of life. For this the Pakistan government fell back on the Kashmir issue, impressing upon the national psyche that the threat posed by Hindu claims to Kashmir threatened all the Muslims of the subcontinent and especially the majority Muslim state of Pakistan. Furthermore, India's rejection of the Pakistani claim to Kashmir served to reinforce a Pakistan government demand that drew particular support from those most opposed to the creation of the nation, the country's Islamist representatives. The Islamists found their destiny in the failure to resolve the Kashmir dispute. So long as that Kashmir dilemma remained, and Pakistan and India confronted one another over a dividing line that obviated the possibility of a compromise solution, the Islamists were guaranteed an audience and a following, as well as government support out of all proportion to their numbers.

The war in East Pakistan that climaxed with the independence of Bangladesh demonstrated that the struggle was never one involving Islam in danger. The brutality witnessed during the civil war, the slaughter of Muslims by Muslims, revealed the hollowness of that concern. Although Pakistanis were prone to cite the civil war as a product of Hindu and Indian machinations, there could be no getting round the charge by Muslim Bengalis that they had been maltreated, exploited, and abused by their brethren in the west of the subcontinent. India played midwife to the creation of Bangladesh, but it also brought an end to the civil strife. New Delhi was ultimately responsible for the dismemberment of Pakistan, but it was Pakistan's power seekers who created the conditions precipitating the Indian assault on the eastern province. Zia was certainly aware of these events, but Bangladesh was a reality and there was no reversing the situation when he forced Zulfikar Ali Bhutto from power and imposed his own brand of rule on the country.

Zia's task, as he saw it, was to prevent yet more ambitious power seekers from doing further damage to the nation. Not only had Bhutto played a major role in the break-up of Pakistan, but during his subsequent administration the country seemed on the verge of splitting into self-governing units. For Zia and the generals who reinforced his authority the only answer to the forces of separation was the old call of Islam in danger, and hence it was his determination to rally the nation, once again appealing to the people's abiding spiritual commitment.

That appeal assumed new dimensions when in December 1979 the Soviet Union sent its army into Afghanistan. Afghanistan had experienced several upheavals immediately before the Soviet invasion. In 1973 the Afghan monarchy was abolished. King Zahir Shah was forced into exile and his cousin, Mohammad Daud, declared Afghanistan would be a republic. Daud made himself President of the new Afghanistan, but in 1978 he too was overthrown. This time the change in government was initiated by Afghan Communists, who were no less divided over the nation's future. In the end their inability to resolve their differences precipitated the Red Army invasion. The Soviets installed their protégé, Babrak Karmal, in Kabul, but the popular resistance that had been aroused when Daud was killed now centered attention on the expulsion of the Communists. The war that ensued caused the flight of several million Afghan refugees, the majority seeking refuge in Pakistan. General Zia was hard pressed to accommodate the mass influx. Moreover, the presence of the Red Army in immediate proximity to Pakistan's frontier led Zia, like others at home and abroad, to conclude Moscow's target was not Kabul but Islamabad. In addition, Indira Gandhi was returned to office in New Delhi within weeks of the Soviet invasion, and her anti-Pakistan bias was now translated into the other arm of a pincer movement that squeezed Pakistan on its eastern border. Concerned that the Soviets and Indians were determined to exploit Pakistan's domestic problems, especially its ethnic conflicts, Zia had good reason to conclude that Pakistan faced mortal danger.

The call to Pakistani Muslims to band together, to overcome their differences, to protect their Islamic heritage now attained a resonance not experienced previously. Zia needed no further convincing that destiny had called him to serve Pakistan, to bind up its wounds, and to prepare the nation for the struggle that lay ahead. In Zia's thinking only Islam offered the integrating factor that linked Pakistanis with one another, and also Pakistan with the Muslims of Afghanistan. Although the two countries were long adversaries across a troubled Durand Line, Pakistan's assistance to the Afghan refugee community as well as to the mujahiddin resistance changed their relationship in the most dramatic manner. And if this were not drama enough, Iran too, another important neighbor of Pakistan, had experienced epoch-making changes. The Shah of Iran, and the Pahlavi dynasty that had been founded after World War I, was swept away by a revolution in 1979. In short order, that revolution became the vehicle of Islamic fundamentalists represented by the looming personality of Ayatollah Ruhollah Khomeini, a charismatic Shiite cleric. After a brief period of secular rule, Iran came under the sway of the men in black robes and the country was almost overnight transformed from the most liberal and open of Islamic societies into one of the most conservative and austere. All of these events impacted on Pakistan, and with General Zia ul-Haq at the helm of Pakistani affairs it was a foregone conclusion that his emphasis on Islamization would take on even greater urgency.

Pakistan not only became environmentally friendly to dedicated Islamists; it was now to be influenced by Muslims in the armed forces, the student population, and the circle of literati whose work was shaped by Islamic tradition. The more secular intelligentsia were sidetracked by events, their collective voice reduced to a whisper among those appealing to the spiritual dimensions of the larger society. Zia continued to confront his opposition, but he was granted a coalition of supporters that assured his durability as the country's leader. A combination of events – Zia's Islamization program, the Soviet invasion of Afghanistan, and the Iranian revolution – occurring almost simultaneously added up to the failure of the secular national state that had tracked emerging Muslim nations since the close of World War II. The rise of the Islamist state in Iran, as elsewhere in the Muslim world, was forecast in the work of some obscure philosophical writers of contemporary Islam, particularly in Egypt and Sudan. Islamic movements assumed a new dynamism during this period and all these events fueled a religious fervor that affected Muslims on a broad plane. Leaders and movements that articulated a new vision for Muslims sought to replace the heavily European-influenced past with a present filled with the glories and opportunities of Islam. Zia was caught up in an Islamic renaissance that moved from North Africa through the Middle East to South and Central Asia and on to Southeast Asia. He found himself in the hub of a wheel that radiated out in different directions, but most immediately to neighboring Afghanistan. Afghan refugees not only brought their needs to Pakistan's open door, they also flooded the country with narcotics and weapons. The tribal border region had never developed intimate ties with the central government and it had long been considered good policy to allow the tribal people as much autonomy as Pakistan's sovereignty could permit. But with a war raging to its west, Pakistan could not avoid becoming involved in the tribal belt as well as in Afghanistan. Not wanting to challenge the Soviets directly, Zia offered indirect support to the Afghan resistance, whose several organizations established their head-quarters in and around the Pakistani city of Peshawar. Pakistan did not wish to signal to Moscow that it intended to challenge Soviet power, but Islamabad refused to recognize the Babrak Karmal government in Kabul and brought the issue of the Soviet invasion to the General Assembly of the United Nations.

Pakistani aid to Afghanistan's different resistance organizations centered attention on the Islamist parties in the conflict. As early as the 1950s the Islamist movements in Afghanistan were associated with the Muslim Brotherhood of Egypt and the Jamaat-i-Islami of Pakistan. The writings of Sayyid Qutb in Egypt and Maulana Maudoodi in Pakistan were most influential, and they inspired Sibghatullah Mujaddedi, Burhanuddin Rabbani, and Maulvi Yunis Khalis, the latter two being graduates of Cairo's Al-Azhar University. The Egyptian Brotherhood and the Pakistani Jamaat were linked by their mutual struggle to realize a Pan-Islamic state and their intention to see the total transformation of Muslim society. The published works of Qutb and Maudoodi were translated into the Afghan Dari and Pashtu languages and were used to influence the thinking of other young Afghans unhappy with the plight of their country, much of which they attributed to the profligate and secular lifestyle of their rulers.

The political teaching of the Islamists could be found in Pakistan as well as Afghanistan. General Zia was himself heavily influenced by the teachings of learned and articulate contemporary Muslim theologians. Zia acknowledged the power of the Muslim faith and he did little to rein in the excesses of the *ulema*. The Soviet invasion of Afghanistan in 1979 had accelerated a movement that already had little concern for national borders nor, for that matter, any respect for national Muslim leaders who were judged too connected to Western nations, and especially to the Americans. By contrast with the liberal ideas espoused in the West, the Islamist movement, from its beginning, was demanding and oppressive and anticipated complete submission to its cause. The Islamists at Kabul University formed a Muslim Youth Organization and by 1970 this was already the most important political force in the country. Among its ranks and eventually assuming leadership roles were Ahmad Shah Masood and Gulbadin Hekmatyar. Increasing in strength, the Islamists of Afghanistan extended their influence among the *talib* (students) of the nation's madrassahs, and the most radical of the country's Islamic teachers. The Islamists supported Daud when he called for an end to Afghanistan's monarchy, but they also did everything in their power to undermine Daud's republican government. Indeed, the damage done to the Daud experiment set the scene for the Communist revolution in 1978. Daud had enlisted the services of the Parcham branch of the Communist Party of Afghanistan. In combination with the Khalq wing that attracted the more nationalist Communists, the leftists vied with the Islamists for ultimate control of the country. Daud's repression of the Islamists, the arrest of hundreds of their more active members, left the Communists with a free hand when their time came to seize control of the government. The Communists were quick to order the execution of Islamists after assuming power.

The Islamist struggle against Communist rule now reached a new level. Forming themselves into mujahiddin, the Islamists took to clandestine attacks on Communist forces. The Parcham and Khalq branches began to quarrel over strategy and find fault with one another. Mohammad Taraki, a Parcham leader operating in tandem with the Soviet KGB, was ordered by Moscow to eliminate Hafizullah Amin, the Khalqi nationalist whose policies were aimed at inflicting even greater punishment on the Islamists. Moscow had called for moderation in dealing with the religious orders, but Hafizullah Amin was not to be appeased. Hence Moscow's decision to eliminate him. On the Islamist side, the Communist government was seen as an enlarging menace. The Islamist movement also suffered from internal controversy and it fell back on its earlier factions, each led by a different leader, representing the complex ethnic and social conditions prevailing in Afghanistan. Thus, the split in the Communist ranks was matched among the Afghan Islamists. The Islamist principals in this sequence were Rabbani, a Tajik, who wanted a broad alliance, and Hekmatyar, a Pashtun Islamist intellectual, who insisted upon an aggressive armed struggle against certain Muslims as well as against infidels in and outside Afghanistan. Rabbani led the Jamiat-i-Islami, Hekmatyar's organization bore the name Hizb-i-Islami. Although they were rivals, the brutality of the Communist takeover of the country, and later the Soviet invasion, brought them into common cause, but nothing could cement their relationship.

Hafizullah Amin's killing of Mohammad Taraki and the intensification of mujahiddin attacks on Soviet operations in Afghanistan caused the Kremlin to send the Red Army across the Amu Darya in December 1979. Moscow had no intention of allowing a reversal of the Communist revolution in the country. Believing Hafizullah Amin's policies provided the mujahiddin with even greater leverage, the invading force killed the Khalq leader and established a government more favorable to the Parcham position. With both Taraki and Amin dead, the Soviets selected Babrak Karmal to head the new Afghan government. The mujahiddin, however, were not to be pacified. The Jamiat-i-Islam forces under Burhanuddin Rabbani took up arms against the Soviets in the northern areas of Afghanistan. They fought the invading force from Badakhshan to Mazar-i-Sharif. In the region of the Salang Pass and Panjsher Valley, it was the Tajik Ahmad Shah Masud who resisted the Soviet invasion. It was Masud too, along with Tajik and Uzbek commanders, who established the Council of the Northern Areas. Masud's force was the most effective fighting unit in the Afghan resistance and he answered to no one save his mentor Rabbani. Hekmatyar, many years junior to Rabbani, was the charismatic leader of the Hizb-i-Islami. More inclined to operate independently, it was less organized than

Rabbani's force and therefore less effective. More the Islamic fundamentalist, however, Hekmatyar appealed to the Pashtun tribes on both sides of the Afghan–Pakistani border. His puritanical version of Islam was more akin to the Khomeini model, but nevertheless he represented the orthodox Sunni Muslim tradition. Hekmatyar made it clear his objective was not simply the defense of Afghanistan but the creation of a purist Islamic republic, and he attracted support from a wide variety of social groups, from the Pashtun tribes along the frontier with Pakistan to the educated youth of Kabul University.

Zia was witness to these events as well as the behavior of the principals in the Afghan resistance. Because all the groups were located in the Peshawar area and drew support from the Pakistan government, Zia was in a position to determine which among them deserved more of his assistance. Moreover, two additional major actors were added to the picture within months of the Soviet invasion of Afghanistan. Pakistan had developed relations with the countries of the Arabian Peninsula and many of their leaders had found Pakistan a welcome place to vacation, to hunt, and to gain support for their international policies. Saudi Arabia was especially interested in South and Central Asia following the Soviet occupation of Kabul. Riyadh agreed to assist Pakistan with its efforts to obtain cheap fuel and to purchase armaments. It also was ready to provide the needed assistance to support the influx of Afghan refugees. Desperate for help, Islamabad was not about to shun such aid. Moreover, Zia's emphasis on Islamization was a positive element in cementing Pakistan–Saudi-Arabian ties. The two countries cooperated in numerous social programs aimed at relieving some of the tensions between the refugee and indigenous populations. Medical assistance and especially educational programs were particular gifts to the Afghan people from Saudi Arabia, and Afghan and Pakistani madrassahs along their mutual frontier received special attention.

The matter of distributing aid to the refugees, and to the mujahiddin resistance, was given to the Pakistan army. But because Islamabad was avoiding direct confrontation with Moscow, the segment of the army most involved was the more secretive and aloof ISI. More familiar with the Pashtuns and more closely identified with the Islamist philosophy of the Hizb-i-Islami, the ISI determined that they, especially the forces under Hekmatyar's command, would become the major recipient of military assistance. The Pakistan ISI therefore became Zia's extension into Afghanistan, especially in the theater of operations from Kabul to Kunar and from Kunduz to Parwan. Moreover the ISI was linked with the fighting that ensued between the Hizb-i-Islami and the other resistance groups, especially those under the command of Ahmad Shah Masud.

The ISI did not liaise with Masud, who saw the Pakistanis as interlopers more bent on capitalizing on Afghanistan's plight than assisting it in repulsing the Soviet Union. Inter-Services Intelligence agents were better disposed to the most radical Islamist causes, and in Masud's view the Pakistani intrusion was intended to spread Zia's power into Afghanistan. Moreover, when the United States decided to play a major role in support of the mujahiddin, and President Ronald Reagan ordered major military transfers to Pakistan, the ISI convinced the CIA that the Hizb-i-Islami of Hekmatyar would make the better use of American aid. Washington's concern did not take into account Hekmatyar's intimacy with revolutionary Iran, or his open invitation to domicile in Iranian Balochistan. The Americans were convinced that in choosing the Pashtuns over the Tajiks, Uzbeks, and other northern ethnic groups, they would be choosing the more dedicated fighters against international Communism.

The CIA's sole mission was the defeat of the Red Army, and the United States became party to an alliance that promoted the most aggressive form of Islamic fundamentalism. Into this mix was poured a Saudi Arabian Wahhabi Islamic program. With Khomeini preaching Islamic revolution and seemingly capable of influencing Muslims everywhere, the Saudis were determined not to lose the initiative. Saudi Arabia became a major actor in the Afghan drama as it zealously promoted the most chaste form of Sunni Islam. The Americans were too busy with the Soviets to understand the many forces shaping the region's future. In their support for Zia's fundamentalism, however, the Americans unknowingly had made a strategic decision. Consumed by the politics of the cold war, American intentions centered on forcing the Red Army from Afghanistan. What might follow such an outcome, Washington failed to factor into its analysis. For all their concern with fundamentalist developments in Iran, the Americans failed to recognize the changes sweeping the Islamic world, and most immediately Afghanistan and Pakistan.

The Zia legacy

Zia was a creature of events and he made the most of them. More prescient to the confrontation of complex forces, he reduced them all to the simple formula of Islamic renaissance. Protecting his base of operations meant working with a military junta that seldom questioned his authority. The army had taken a heavy blow in the 1971 war with India. A decade after that débâcle it was still in need of restructuring. The war in Afghanistan had provided the Pakistan armed forces with an opportunity to prove their mettle. With the extraordinary military assistance suddenly made available by the Reagan administration, the armed forces once again had an assured future. An initially hesitant Zia was transformed into a forceful and determined leader. His refusal to offer mercy to Bhutto was not lost on those around him. His determination to transform Pakistan into a true Muslim state began after Pakistan's dismemberment, but his vision took on greater meaning with the Khomeini-led revolution in Iran and the Soviet invasion of Afghanistan. Zia understood the strength of his Muslim convictions and, though he faced unprecedented challenges, he was nonetheless convinced that his spiritual foundation was secure and would sustain him. Zia was no Hamlet. Not given to contemplation or second guessing, he set a course that he did not intend to deviate from. When others were confused, or hesitated, Zia was prepared to show the way. Zia's demeanor had changed. He was eager to assume the responsibility destiny had imposed upon him. Guided by inner spiritual experience, he refused to believe he could not accomplish great goals.

Zia had become a man with a mission. Unpopular in political circles, he was reinforced in his view that the politicians were a negative element in Pakistan's design. As much as he suffered their criticism, he was just as prepared to strip them of their capacity to influence the country's development. Zia made no apologies for denying political parties the opportunity to compete in future elections. He genuinely believed political parties were inherently evil and that the politicians were not only without virtue but that they followed an alien tradition. Organizers of the Movement for the Restoration of Democracy (MRD) were therefore intimidated or arrested. When lower-echelon politicians tried to fill the political vacuum created by the incarceration of their leaders, they too were contained and their voices muted. Professional organizations and women's groups picked up the cause and demanded a lifting of press restrictions, as well as the strict accountability of men in positions of responsibility. But these demands too remained unanswered.

The MRD tried a number of tactics, at one point enlisting the services of the labor unions, but that too proved unproductive. The government's foreign policy was criticized, especially the call to sever ties to the United States and to establish Pakistan as a non-aligned state. This too fell on deaf ears. The MRD called for a mass day of protest in August 1983. Fearing the Zia-led junta was about to issue a proclamation eliminating any possibility that Pakistan would again experience parliamentary politics, the political opposition brought their legions into the streets, but that tactic also failed. Zia had already established his Majlis-i-Shura, or Muslim consultative assembly. Composed of almost three hundred members, the body was the President's answer to his political critics and their demand for representative government. The Majlis-i-Shura was an appointed, not an elected body, and its powers were defined in the presidential order that created it. It had the power to recommend laws, to suggest amendments to existing laws, and to discuss the annual budget and five-year development plan. It could also seek information from government agencies. But it was not a genuine legislature. It could not initiate laws or see its recommendations become law. Ostensibly called to advise the ruling junta, it satisfied certain Islamic traditions, but it was not given the authority to check the executive.

Zia packed the Shura with members of the *ulema* and *mashaikh* (students of Islam). He also included farmers, industrial workers, engineers, landowners, and assorted professionals. Places were reserved for women and minorities, and the government argued the assembly was more representative of the nation than anything before it. Zia also chose the speaker of the Shura, as well as its vice-chairmen. All officers were called to swear allegiance to the government under the Constitutional Order of 1981, the law that established the legal foundation of Zia's rule. Critics cited Zia's monopolization of power. They also noted the scores of politicians who had left their political parties to become members of the Majlis-i-Shura. Opportunism among politicians was a common experience and that tradition was sustained through the Zia reforms. Moreover, the fundamentalist Islamist parties like the Jamaat-i-Islami, the Jamiatul-Ulema-i-Pakistan, and the Pagaro Muslim League were not averse to the formation of the Shura, which in a way hinted at the formation of a more credible Islamic state.

The Majlis-i-Shura met in two sessions in 1982 and three in 1983. In the meantime Zia authorized the Council of Islamic Ideology to question all laws on the books that in its judgment were repugnant to Islam. He also gave new importance to local councils that had been constituted in 1979 and urged their members to avoid affiliation with political parties. Although a far cry from the Basic Democracies system of Ayub Khan, the local councils were given the opportunity to voice their concerns at the national level through connections with the Majlis-i-Shura. Here too Zia found sufficient numbers to serve on the councils, and despite the sustained criticism, the local bodies, with assistance from the bureaucracy, assumed responsibility for village agriculture, religious training, health, and sanitation.

Zia also ordered the creation of the Shariat Courts. Although these religious courts did not replace the existing secular court system, a Federal Shariat Court was established in Islamabad, not far from the country's Supreme Court. Its responsibility was described as safeguarding Islamic precepts and principles. The religious courts were supposed to formalize an Islamic legal system and to give it parallel importance to the conventional secular courts. Zia, however, went further than that with the *Hudood* Ordinance that placed emphasis on Islamic codes of behavior. Crimes against Islam or *hadd* included imbibing alcoholic beverages, attending houses of ill repute, and any form of gambling. Severe punishments were forecast for those found guilty of neglecting religious duties. Zia admonished would-be law breakers that they had best find escape in prayer and constructive social acts. Numerous individuals nevertheless suffered the severity of Islamic law. Pictures of public lashings were flashed around the world and it did not take long to convey the message that Pakistan had entered a new phase in its history. Moreover, adverse international reaction could not be avoided, and Islamic legal codes calling for corporal punishment, that is, the cutting off of limbs for theft, or stoning for adultery, were either held in abeyance or imposed sparingly. No hesitation was manifested in the case of murder convictions, however, and Bhutto's hanging was a reminder, as Zia had declared, that Islamic justice would be done.

Zia also pressed for the implementation of *zakat*, the Islamic requirement that Muslims share their wealth with the poor. *Zakat* collection was formalized and an Administrator-General who reported to the President was appointed to oversee the program. Shiite Muslim opposition to *zakat*, however, forced Zia to acknowledge sectarian differences in the collection and distribution of charitable contributions. The Shiite community therefore was exempted from the practice. Zia's willingness to treat the Shiites differently was not well received by members of the majority Sunni community. Interpreting Zia's retreat as a sign of indecision and weakness, Sunni extremists vehemently protested against the action. The ruling junta was no less disturbed, fearing Zia's decision would bring into question the whole issue of military governance. More immediately, Zia's ambivalence fueled the latent antagonism between Sunnis and Shiites, and Karachi became the venue for a series of sectarian riots.

The loss of life and destruction of property in this clash over rival religious practices highlighted the difficulty of implementing Islamic reforms. The government's difficulty in quelling the disturbances provoked a national debate about the wisdom of too much Islamization. The opposition politicians condemned Islamization as too little to do with Islamic practice and too much to do with guaranteeing Zia's hold on power. Zia was pressured as never before to defend his policies. At the same time he insisted on the rigorous enforcement of law and order. All kinds of public gatherings were banned, curfews were imposed in major metropolitan areas, and hundreds, some insisted thousands, were arrested. Zia was forced to broadcast to the nation that his government would not tolerate insurrection and that all violations of the peace would be punished.

Zia was adamant on the need to sustain Islamization, but at the same time he indicated a desire to consolidate what had already been achieved. Commenting on the paucity of Islamic scholars to fill positions in the Shariat Courts, he cited the recently enacted *Qazi* Courts Ordinance that attached religious judges to the local councils system. Reluctant to import experts in Islamic law from other Muslim countries, Zia called for the expansion of the country's madrassahs and declared his government would increase their funding in order to meet the heavy need. Zia found Saudi Arabia eager to assist in this effort to train more religious scholars. The Saudis, who were already committed to assisting the Afghan refugees, raised their contribution to expand Islamic religious schools for Pakistanis as well. Madrassahs multiplied all over the country and the more fundamentalist orders took the lead in ministering to young people who otherwise had little educational opportunity.

This was a critical period for Pakistan and the wider region. The Kashmir dispute, despite Bhutto's attempt at reconciliation, remained unresolved. Moreover, there were indications that the more militant Islamic organizations, emboldened by Zia's Islamization program, were organizing clandestine forces for a more concerted drive in the Vale. Furthermore, units in the Pakistan army and the ISI were prepared to aid and abet actions against Indian installations in Kashmir. Tensions between Pakistan and India therefore began to rise yet again. Indian intelligence units from RAW reported this intensified Pakistani activity and New Delhi signaled its intention to resist any campaign of violence when it began reinforcing its garrison in the region. Meanwhile, Pakistan was deeply committed in Afghanistan and the only hope for relief there was the work of the United Nations mediator, who continued to meet with both Pakistani and Afghan officials in Geneva. Otherwise the war continued to take its heavy toll and Pakistan's border communities could not be protected from actions spilling across the frontier. And then there was the war between Iran and Iraq that had erupted in 1980 and showed no sign of ending. With stalemate on the frontlines, Saddam Hussain had called upon Iran to cease fire, but Ayatollah Khomeini had labeled the Iraqi leader the "Little Satan" ("Great Satan" was reserved for the United States) and the conflict raged on. Pakistan led the Organization of the Islamic Conference in trying to moderate the dispute but both sides were locked in a ferocious demonstration of violence that refused to yield to diplomacy.

Through all these troubles, Zia had maintained a steady hand and though vilified as a dictator and ambitious seeker of power he nevertheless sustained his command of the army and the other services. He also had won the favor of the more conservative members of the political community, but that relationship rested on less stable ground. Zia's establishment of a *wafaqi mohtasib* or national ombudsman was an attempt to demonstrate his liberal Islamic credentials. The ombudsman, a prominent and respected jurist in the secular tradition, was given responsibility for investigating, redressing, and rectifying injustices committed against citizens by any government agency, except the courts and the judicial tribunals and commissions established by law. Giving the ombudsman a substantial budget and a secretariat, Zia let it be known he was serious about the dispensation of justice in all its forms. Although insistent that he had no intention of reversing Islamization, in 1985 Zia's hedging was more in evidence. The General-President surprised his compatriots when he declared he was prepared to dissolve the Majlis-i-Shura and begin the process of restoring conventional legislatures at the center as well as in the provinces. Holding to the belief that a strong executive was still an absolute requirement, he indicated the President would be elected by a combined vote of the newly constituted legislatures and would perform the duties of head of government as well as those of head of state.

Zia's objective was to preserve the 1973 constitution, but to amend it to meet his overall need for maximum power. The President would be the holder of absolute powers and would share nothing with the Prime Minister, who served at his pleasure. Having laid the groundwork and now assured that the constitution favored his indefinite continuance in office, in March 1985 Zia announced the holding of national elections. He also declared that martial law, in effect since 1977, would be lifted after the elections but that the armed forces would remain on station to oversee the transition to civilian government. The scheduled elections, however, were to be conducted without involving the political parties. Citing again the conflict between political party actions and Islamic practices, Zia reiterated his belief that the elections should not become the playground of opportunistic politicians. Pakistan, he opined, was an island surrounded by a sea of chaos. This was the moment for all Pakistanis to band together to meet the challenge that destiny had imposed upon them.

Zia's plea was hardly meant to placate his detractors, however. Observing how the President had amassed power, the opposition again took to the streets. Describing the country as a personal dictatorship, they denounced Zia as a charlatan and cunning despot who needed to be deposed. Apparently unprepared for the intensity of the campaign directed against him, and pressured by the Americans, who again had become a major actor in the Pakistan drama, Zia continued to retreat from his earlier more defiant stand.

Without prior warning Zia revealed he had been rethinking his opposition to political parties and was giving thought to an election that could possibly include limited and controlled party participation. If followed through on, the new plan would open a contest between the political factions, and the religious parties could not be expected to win. More important, they were likely to lose much of the leverage gained since the imposition of martial law. Moreover, whereas the conventional secular parties had been largely paralyzed by martial law, the Islamist parties had continued to function through non-governmental organizations. They tended to the masses by dispensing information and, more specifically, by meeting some of the material needs of the urban poor. These proselytizing efforts would be threatened by any introduction of traditional political party activity. Islamist parties simply could not compete with the more secular organizations and they were appalled that the President would backtrack on the Islamization program. The fundamentalists therefore vehemently rejected Zia's plan to reinstate the secular parties. The Jamaat-i-Islami had the most to lose, given its growth since Bhutto's removal. Attractive to young people, the Jamaat's student organization, the Jamiat-i-Tulaba, had developed a prominent place in society. As guardians of the Jamaat cause, they were now ordered to raise havoc in the country.

The intensity of the clash between the students and government was unanticipated. So too were its widespread character and the numbers involved. More than a thousand students were arrested as riots erupted in all of Pakistan's major cities. The government was forced to close all the universities and colleges, thus forcing more students into the streets. Nor was the unrest confined to the student community. All the more conservative Islamist parties broke ranks with General Zia. The Jamaat-i-Islami and the Jamiatul-Ulema-i-Pakistan were among the more critical of Zia's new thinking. In a desperate attempt to stem the tide of Islamist ire, Zia ordered the imprisonment of the conventional politicians he had just ordered released. He also hoped to placate the Islamists by issuing a decree depriving the Ahmediyya community, decertified as Muslims during the Bhutto administration, from using any Islamic symbols in describing their faith. The Islamists, however, were hardly appeased. They now insisted the government declare all Ahmediyya heretics, a charge that would subject them to the death penalty. Zia ignored that demand but he could not ignore a renewal of Sunni–Shiite violence in Karachi which again brought the city to a standstill and caused numerous casualties.

Zia also had to contend with an alleged army plot to overthrow the government. The soldiers implicated in this conspiracy were said to have been inspired by Indian and Libyan agents. Moreover, Zulfikar Ali Bhutto's two sons had formed a terrorist organization known as Al-Zulfikar, basing their operations in Libya. The brothers were tried *in absentia* for the murder of a Pakistani diplomat and it did not take a great deal of imagination to link them with the army plotters. Threats on Zia's life arose from several quarters, not the least of which emanated from Afghanistan, where the KGB and the Afghan KHAD were both believed to be planning his assassination. Zia, however, insisted he had little to fear. Before holding elections for the new national assembly, Zia asked for a popular vote of confidence in his administration. The referendum, however, asked the people to vote for or against the Islamization program. A vote in favor would be considered a vote for Zia; it would also extend his term another five years. Zia of course succeeded. The public voted overwhelmingly for Islamization, but Zia's critics described the President's action as a sham aimed at boosting his legitimacy.

The President's unpopularity was expressed in the National Assembly election when few people answered the call to vote. Nevertheless, there were still surprises. The voters embarrassed the General and his government by denying seats to a majority of his candidates. Although the President's power and status were unaffected, only two of nine cabinet-level officials were successful. Voters also rejected thirty candidates running for positions in the Assembly on the administration platform. The new legislature replaced the Majlis-i-Shura but it was no less an advisory body than the previous one. Zia had had the 1973 constitution amended so that even the courts could not question his extraordinary and arbitrary powers. All the martial law edicts and ordinances were declared constitutional and would remain in place after the lifting of martial law. Finally, future amendments to the constitution were made more difficult, thus ensuring there would be no challenge to the executive institution.

Zia chose Mohammad Khan Junejo, a mild-mannered Sindhi, to be his Prime Minister, knowing full well the office could not challenge his authority. Junejo's selection was aimed at gaining support in beleaguered Sindh province, the scene of so much mayhem since Bhutto's execution. The appointment was also meant to win supporters from among the Pakistan People's Party, now led by Benazir Bhutto, the daughter of Zulfikar Ali Bhutto. Benazir was Zia's most ardent and vocal critic and, although held under house arrest during the early years of martial law, she had been set free to go abroad, where she continued her verbal assaults against the regime. Junejo, it was hoped, would help reduce Sindhi bitterness and possibly dampen Benazir's campaign against the President. But if that was Zia's expectation it was not to be fulfilled. Junejo refused to be a rubber stamp. The Prime Minister publicly called for the immediate lifting of martial law. He also insisted on the reinstatement of the banned political parties and the freeing of all politicians. Zia expected as much from his chosen Prime Minister, and the alacrity with which he responded to Junejo's requests indicated he was prepared to take the necessary action. New Islamization programs were placed on hold as the more secular dimensions of the Pakistan condition were energized. An "indemnity bill", however, was rushed through the Assembly, sanctioning all acts of the military government during martial law.

As more familiar forms of politics gained prominence, reports reached Pakistan that Shahnawaz Bhutto had been found dead in his Cannes apartment on the French Riviera. Although rumors circulated that Zia's ISI had had him killed, later investigation revealed his wife had murdered him. Benazir asked Zia to permit her brother's body to be returned to Pakistan for burial next to her father. Not only was she granted her request, she also was permitted to accompany the body. Her return to Pakistan brought thousands of her supporters into the streets and she was heralded as the true heir and leader of the Pakistan People's Party. Although ostensibly in mourning, Benazir did not allow the opportunity to attack Zia to pass her by. However, the intensity of her verbal assault and the raucous behavior it engendered among her followers forced the government to re-arrest her. Imprisonment for political activity is a given in Pakistan and it certainly did not reduce Benazir's stature or the role she played in helping restore the country's political dynamics. With Benazir a looming presence, there was no way Zia could avoid his infamous "hangman" reputation, nor was he in position to win adherents. Zia received little credit for restoring the political debate because it was he who had prevented it for almost eight years. The President, however, had had enough of Benazir. After three months of house arrest, she was placed on a plane for London, where she resumed her exile. Back in England, Benazir had many admirers, especially among the expatriate community, and she immediately launched her drive to win the favor of disgruntled Pakistanis abroad as well as in Pakistan.

Martial law ended in December 1985, the longest period of direct military rule in the nation's history. Zia's presidential tenure was confirmed till 1990, and the National Assembly assented to all the laws the administration had laid before it. In January 1986 political parties were ordered to register with the Election Commission and permission to establish a party had to pass the test of national unity. Parties also had to demonstrate support for Zia's Islamization program. With political parties sanctioned, Junejo linked forces with the Pagaro Muslim League, and, almost immediately, two-thirds of National Assembly members also signed on. The Pagaro Muslim League claimed lineage back to the original pre-independence Muslim League and no other party was permitted to bear the name "Muslim League." Junejo became the party's president and Zia quickly answered his request to replace the serving generals performing as governors of the different provinces with civilians. Zia associated himself with the Muslim League, and, believing he held a winning hand, he permitted Benazir Bhutto to return to Pakistan. Benazir's arrival, however, brought even more thousands of supporters into the streets and she responded to them by declaring her mission the removal of Zia ul-Haq and the restoration of democracy. The opposition then formed the Awami (People's) Movement and selected Benazir as their leader. Her appearance in Karachi on April 10, 1986 produced crowds not seen since the days of the Quaid-i-Azam. Recognizing a tide of support in her favor, Benazir reserved all her criticism for President Zia and said nothing about Junejo or the Muslim League. Using a strategy that was intended to isolate the President, the daughter of the martyred Zulfikar Ali Bhutto anticipated putting together a political coalition that would guarantee her success in the forthcoming election.

The government, however, was hardly in retreat. The National Assembly passed legislation making Islam the supreme law. It also formally established the religious courts. The government also profited from the revival of the American assistance program. The Reagan administration acknowledged Pakistan's frontline status following the Soviet invasion of Afghanistan and aid was extended that would total more than seven billion dollars by the time Ronald Reagan left office. Given the nature of the war in Afghanistan, the Americans put aside their differences with Zia over the sacking of the U.S. embassy in 1979. The latter event had caused the death of four embassy officials and given Washington ample cause to lower its profile in the Muslim country. Strains in the relationship, however, were conveniently forgotten after Moscow ordered its forces into Afghanistan. Pakistan again became an intimate ally and the recipient of American arms shipments. The American embargo, in place since 1965, was officially terminated and Islamabad was heralded as a close and valuable partner in the cold war. Pakistan also received more than two billion dollars from the Asian Development Bank. Together these huge transfers produced improvements in the country's economy and helped re-equip the Pakistan armed forces.

The war in Afghanistan, however, was a costly venture on many fronts. Pakistan had to find the resources to meet the basic needs of more than three million Afghan refugees. The country could not prevent the war from spilling over its frontier, and Pakistanis became casualties of the war as a consequence of random bombing and shelling of villages stretched along the border. Islamabad engaged in heated exchanges with Moscow, each accusing the other of fomenting clandestine operations and indiscriminate assaults on defenseless non-belligerents. Pakistan also became a thorn in the side of the Soviets by initiating annual resolutions in the United Nations General Assembly that condemned Moscow for its operations in the neighboring state. Each vote overwhelmingly supported the Pakistani position and, through not successful in forcing a Soviet retreat, they had considerable propaganda value. Pakistan also was one of the two parties participating in the U.N.-mediated peace conferences in Geneva. Through tedious endeavor, Pakistan's patient diplomacy held out the hope of a negotiated settlement. In April 1988 an agreement was achieved and a date for a Soviet pullout from Afghanistan was approved. Zia took credit for these developments, and he also tried to achieve understanding between Iraq and Iran and to end the hostilities between the two countries. Although unsuccessful, the effort was not lost on those who previously had been reluctant to credit the Pakistani President with diplomatic skills.

Despite these achievements, Pakistan was hardly a peaceful nation. Terrorism was a rising phenomenon and Afghan-related bombings rocked the country's major cities from Peshawar to Karachi during this period. Fighting also broke out in Karachi between long-resident Pashtuns and members of the mohajir community. Into this conflict came Afghan refugees who had migrated from the frontier area to the port of Karachi and were especially active in the narcotics and gun-running trade. And if the authorities did not have difficulties enough, they also had to manage sectarian strife that periodically erupted between Shiites and Sunnis, between radical students and the police, and between Muslims and members of the small minority communities. The fact that gross domestic product increased during 1984–86 could only be attributed to the heavy role of foreign assistance, and, to some extent, to favorable weather conditions that helped increase the production of rice and cotton. Benazir and her colleagues, however, ignored the positive and accentuated only the negative. The government's failure to maintain law and order – to reduce the level of violence, or to stem acts of terror – was blamed on an inept and corrupt administration. On July 5, 1987 Zia celebrated ten years in power. The opposition, however, described the moment as "Black Day" and continued to harass the authorities for their failure to bring true peace to the nation. The bombing of the Lahore Central Train and Bus Station on that very day punctuated the politicians' complaint. A week later Lahore's main bazaar was bombed, so too the Central Bus Station in Karachi. The dead and injured were counted in the hundreds, but the perpetrators, who were accused of working with the Indian RAW or the Afghan KHAD, were more difficult to identify. The victims of terrorist attacks were largely innocent members of the population, but the target, it was all too clear, was the Zia ul-Haq regime. The administration's ineffectiveness in confronting the challenge, its failure to protect the population, raised questions about its viability and played into the hands of the opposition. A loss of popular confidence in the government could only redound to the benefit of those seeking its removal.

Terrorists had demonstrated they could strike at will, at targets of their choosing, and the government found that a counter-strike was difficult if the perpetrators could not be identified. The enemy was invisible and the government's countermeasures were futile. Some of Zia's critics found reason to believe that religious fundamentalists were behind much of the mayhem. Zia's Islamization program had energized the Islamists and they would find fault with anything more likely to enhance the power of the President than promote the creation of the true Islamic state. To that extent, the Islamists found themselves in league with more secular politicians who also derided Islamization as a charade intended to cover Zia's grab for absolute power. Islamization, it was repeated, had unleashed the forces of disintegration, not integration, and had divided rather than unified the country.

Zia's counter-argument was that he was protecting Islam against atheist Marxism, but his detractors refused to accept it.

Strong in the belief that India and the Soviet Union were conspiring to destroy Pakistan, Zia cited the Treaty of Friendship and Cooperation that those two countries entered into in 1971. The Red Army invasion of Afghanistan in 1979 was a vital part of a scenario to squeeze Pakistan from two sides. As if to confirm this perception, in 1986 New Delhi massed troops on the Pakistani frontier after claiming Islamist insurgents, encouraged by Zia's Islamization policies, had raised the level of violence in Kashmir. Pakistan answered the Indian build-up by rushing its forces to the eastern border. Hostilities between the two countries seemed imminent, when Zia surprised even his own government by suddenly flying to New Delhi. After meeting with Prime Minister Rajiv Gandhi, who had succeeded his mother following her assassination in 1984, the two leaders announced the mutual withdrawal of their troops. The event, described as "cricket diplomacy," because Zia was said to be *en route* to a cricket match, revealed once again Zia's flair for diplomacy.

But if the General anticipated credit for averting another war, it was not to be. Instead, the opposition politicians criticized him for creating the tension. More significant, however, was the complaint rumored from the ISI that Zia's intervention had ruined a clandestine campaign in Kashmir, exposed Pakistani agents, and put an insurgent force at considerable risk. The ISI had been granted a degree of independence not equaled by any other branch of the armed services, nor was it always subject to constraints imposed by the President. Zia's actions raised questions about his commitment to the Kashmir problem and how Kashmir related to Islamization. With the ISI having come under the influence of the Islamists, Zia's credentials as an Islamic reformer were brought into serious question. Zia therefore not only had to concern himself with his enemies in the political opposition, the Soviet Union and India, and the Afghan KHAD, but also had to confront the first serious divisions within the armed forces since his takeover.

In September 1987, however, Indian forces were again activated when fighting flared anew on the Kashmir front. Pakistani forces, directed in major part by the ISI, skirmished with Indian troops on the remote Siachen Glacier. From Siachen, Pakistani forces were in position to deny Indian troops in Kashmir a vital supply line, and

Pakistani intelligence secretly maneuvered its forces to thwart an Indian response. India, however, was not unaware of the action and rushed mountain troops into position to counter the action. Although New Delhi condemned Zia for breaking his non-aggression understanding with Rajiv, there was no evidence to indicate Zia had ordered the maneuver. Rather, information was circulated that the campaign had been launched to embarrass Zia and to destroy his "cricket diplomacy" initiative. Islamabad tried to play down the incident, and Zia was under pressure to remain silent about his complicity in the Siachen episode, but the loss of 150 Pakistani soldiers in the incident could not be concealed or obfuscated. New Delhi saw the action as destroying what little trust had been built between the two leaders. Moreover, India perceived more Pakistani aggressiveness on its western border. Islamabad was accused of fomenting disorder in the Indian Punjab, where it allegedly assisted Sikh separatists in perpetrating acts of terror against Indian authority. Sikh separatists had pressured India to give self-determination to the Sikh nation, and New Delhi had acted to crush what it considered an insurrection. Expressed Pakistani sympathies for the Sikhs, along with India's charge that Islamabad had provided sanctuary, arms, and training to the Sikh dissidents, all but closed the diplomatic window Zia had opened earlier.

Pakistan declared it had no interest in fueling India's Sikh problem, but it nevertheless accused New Delhi's RAW intelligence unit of aiding and abetting terrorist actions inside Pakistan. It was rumored that neither the Indian Prime Minister nor the Pakistani President controlled their operational intelligence units. Each clandestine organization enjoyed privileges that government officials were hard put to deny. It is doubtful that Rajiv directed RAW attacks on urban targets inside Pakistan, and Zia's power did not extend to controling the operations of the ISI. Zia's ability to stop secret operations had diminished with the intensification of the war in Afghanistan. Only ISI forces could be used against Soviet troops, because anything else would place Pakistan in direct confrontation with the Kremlin. Technically, Pakistan was not at war with the Soviet Union, and Moscow too was disinclined to declare war on Pakistan. As a secret and indirect force, the ISI also was free from the normal constraints imposed by the chain of command. Moreover, the success of the ISI in linking up with, and to a large extent directing, Afghan resistance forces placed them beyond the reach of General Zia. Emboldened by this autonomy, the ISI saw no reason why it could not apply the same tactics in Kashmir. If the Soviet superpower could be humbled, the Indian behemoth could also be compelled to seek a compromise solution on its outstanding differences with Pakistan. This is not to say that Zia was not fully apprised of ISI actions, it is simply to acknowledge that the army's chief intelligence unit had reason to gloat over its apparent success in Afghanistan and saw no reason to desist in its campaign against India. Moreover, the ISI had its supporters within the armed forces, especially at the highest levels.

Zia had been in power long enough to see the retirement of most of those officers who had originally sanctioned his policies. A new generation of officers had taken the reins of leadership and they were more inured in the tradition of Islamization, more accepting of Islamist orders, and more serious about Pakistan's metamorphosis as an Islamic state. Zia had pursued the goal of Islamization and although he had met considerable resistance there was little doubt he had transformed Pakistan. Zia was still commander of the Pakistan armed forces but his hold on power had diminished and the army in particular had developed a momentum that Zia did not control. Yet another factor in the changing power balance in Pakistan was the army's pursuit of nuclear weapons. Zulfikar Ali Bhutto had made the original call for an "Islamic bomb," but it was during Zia's tenure that the project received particular attention. By 1987, Pakistan had moved closer to its goal. Islamabad had refused to sign the Nuclear Non-Proliferation Treaty, as had India, and it was common knowledge that the two countries had followed a similar course in their pursuit of nuclear science. India of course had detonated a nuclear device in 1974, and since then had worked to build an effective weapon and the delivery systems for its use. Nor was Pakistan idle, or uninformed about the Indian program.

Under the cover of the Afghan war, the Pakistan government circumvented United States laws that denied assistance to a country engaged in the development of nuclear weapons. The Reagan administration year after year waived this legislation in order to service the Pakistan/Afghan resistance. Moreover, the

United States sold advance fighter-bomber aircraft to Pakistan. Such aircraft, it was acknowledged, could have nuclear weapons delivery capability. India beseeched Washington to forgo such transfers, but the plea was ignored while the Red Army remained in Afghanistan. In September 1987, a phalanx of Congressmen called upon the Reagan administration to reconsider its policies toward Pakistan, but the President ignored their entreaties and the assistance program remained in place. In the meantime, Pakistan continued its quest for nuclear weapons.

The end of the Zia era

On entering his eleventh year in power, Zia surpassed Ayub in political longevity. Zia's capacity for survival was remarkable, but Pakistan remained a troubled country, divided along ethnic, regional, and ideological lines. Zia's legacy was lengthy and complicated but it added up to a nation that had yet to construct a civil society, to express its true identity, or to chart a peaceful future. Zia had unleashed the Islamists but he had failed to provide the country with the conditions necessary to construct a viable political process. Statistically, Pakistan's economy had shown measured success, but the general population remained mired in poverty, undereducated, and hopelessly in conflict with itself. There were hints of success against the Soviet Union in Afghanistan, but the political aftermath in that ravaged country was yet to be determined. Tensions with India had intensified during Zia's tenure and the General-President, despite his personal desire to avoid war with his larger neighbor, could not impart his concerns to those under his command. The humiliation suffered by the Pakistan army in 1971 remained to be addressed and there was little doubt that after Zia more concerted efforts would be made by many of the senior officers to remedy that wound. Zia had managed power effectively but by 1988 the forces that sustained him appeared less keen to do so. The list of those who wanted him out of the picture had grown substantially.

Sindhh province and most notably Karachi had become a cauldron of discontent. Conflicting forces included both religious and ethnic affiliations. Pakistan's eagerness to become a nuclear power was more than matched by its enthusiasm for internecine bloodletting. Karachi had been transformed into one of the world's terror capitals during the tenure of Zia ul-Haq and numerous organizations were spawned there, virtually all of them with violence in their soul and unforgiving hatred in their heart. The Mohajir Qaumi Movement (MQM) was formed there in 1986 by a young scion of the original refugee community that flooded the region in the aftermath of independence. Never allowed to blend into the Sindh community, or to urge upon the indigenous population the need to fully embrace the idea of Pakistan, these refugees were joined by still others fleeing East Bengal in the midst of the civil war. Unaffiliated with the Afghan refugees who had no likelihood of adopting Pakistani citizenship, the refugees from the east had built Karachi into the commercial port city it had become. Resentment rather than grateful acceptance, however, was their reward. Because of their different background, their non-Sindhi culture, and most of all their domination of the region's economy, the fact that they shared the Islamic faith was of no importance to those who felt displaced by the more aggressive carpetbaggers. Sindhi nationalism was a product of this clash and the Zia government could neither bring peace to the area nor prevent the rivals from ruining Sindh's economy.

Sindh province was not the only region gripped by violence. Even in the remote mountain area of Gilgit sectarian strife took its toll of the innocent. Allama Arif al-Hussaini, a leader of the Shiite community in Gilgit, was murdered in Peshawar in an obvious act of revenge for the killing of Sunnis. Bombings and assassinations were commonplace and could be expected virtually anywhere in the country, especially in Peshawar, Lahore, and Karachi, but no less so in Faisalabad, Hyderabad, and Bahawalpur. In many instances the army was called in to calm the situation, to tend to the dead and wounded, to repair the damage, and most of all to trace the perpetrators of these acts. Dragnets swept up scores, hundreds, even thousands, but the mayhem continued. With the administration under severe pressure, with Prime Minister Junejo less and less comfortable with his connection to the President, with the conventional political parties sustaining their condemnation in one public demonstration after another, Zia found it difficult to maneuver or impress upon those around him that he controlled events. Releasing Junejo from his office for what he described as his opposition to Islamization, the President again tried to impress upon his colleagues that he could not be shaken in his resolve to transform Pakistan into a chaste Muslim nation. Junejo's dismissal, however, was seen as a sign more of weakness than of strength. Zia had grown desperate and more obviously frustrated.

Even the revelation on April 14, 1988 that Pakistan and Afghanistan had entered into a United Nations orchestrated agreement, and that the Soviet Union had pledged to remove its troops from Afghanistan did not bring Zia the anticipated rewards. The long war in Afghanistan had transformed the new Pakistan into an entity that could not have been forecast at the time of the 1971 civil war and the loss of the eastern province. Pakistan was very different from the Pakistan of 1947, and appeared more devoted to its religious heritage, but it was hardly a polity unified in its search for a coherent destiny. Zia believed he had the formula for resurrecting the new Pakistan when he presented his case for Islamization and then took what he believed were the necessary steps toward its realization. In the end, however, Zia had done little if anything to address the major questions burdening his people. Islam was insufficient to prevent Bengali secession and proved inadequate to meet the needs of the polyglot and violence-prone western region. Religious commitment or practice was never at issue. What hounded and burdened post-civil-war Pakistan was not religious conviction, but the converting of religious experience from an act of faith into a weapon. The Islamists were less identified with the strengthening of spiritual belief than with the use of Islam as a weapon of massive destruction. Muslims were told it was only their common monotheistic dedication that made them the equals if not the betters of those with more sophisticated economies and more substantial armed forces.

Pakistanis also were impacted by the wars in Afghanistan and the Gulf. Religious expression ran deep in both wars. Both were seen as apocalyptic contests between the forces of Allah and those of secularism. Imbedded in this titanic clash was a choice between an alien national design and one ordained by the Almighty. Islam's proud past beckoned believers to choose between the satanic forces of neocolonialism and those calling for the Kingdom of God. The Islamists now preached another form of ideological doctrine that emphasized martyrdom and the need for self-sacrifice. Rejecting the West meant challenging those who would continue to humble the Islamic world; and it followed from this that those Muslim leaders who would follow the Western design, whether politically or economically, were hardly less than apostates and hence responsible for their own destruction. Zia's performance as Pakistan's head of state had, wittingly or unwittingly, given substance to this tortured discourse. Pakistan could not escape the long shadow cast by the Khomeini revolution in Iran and that nation's protracted war with Iraq, or the fierce contest of wills that pitted a primitive fighting force of Afghans against the vast might of the Soviet superpower. Islam and Muslim sacrifice prevailed in both struggles. In both situations, success was attributed to an uncompromising commitment to God's work.

India was still another reminder that religious obligation influenced Pakistan's choice of policies. Kashmir erupted in renewed conflict in 1988. A veritable *intifada* challenged Indian rule in the state as guerrilla units began to shift their operations from Afghanistan to the former mountain kingdom. New Delhi's decision to reinforce its garrison in Kashmir was not unexpected. Some of the same foreign volunteers who had answered the Afghan call for assistance now took up the cause of the Muslim Kashmiris. The promised Soviet withdrawal from Afghanistan therefore brought little assurance that the region would finally be at peace. Cataclysmic events do not simply come and go, but rather reverberate long after the initial shock. Epochal change brings in its wake epochal transformations, and Pakistan was not far from the epicenter of nothing less than a monumental upheaval. Pakistanis therefore might have questioned the need to Islamize, but Muslims they were and Muslims they would remain. It was never a matter of what design was better or worse for the people of Pakistan – the secular or the religious – but rather what structure both satisfied the tenets of faith and met the mundane needs of a diverse and largely uninformed and malleable society.

The confusion was seen in Zia's belief that the forces of secularism were continuing to plot the destruction of his Islamization program. In June 1988 Zia decreed the implementation of the Islamic legal code that he declared would become the supreme law of the land. Superior courts were ordered to strike down laws judged to be in conflict with Islamic law. Some observers suggested that these actions, immediately following Junejo's removal from office, were signs of panic, induced in part by Zia's awareness that the Soviet retreat from Afghanistan might expose his Islamization program to increased criticism. Zia lashed out at Ayub Khan's 1961 Muslim Family Laws, which were aimed at protecting the female population of Pakistan. This action, however, only rallied the more sophisticated women to stand behind the candidacy of Benazir Bhutto and her Pakistan People's Party. Sensing his core beliefs were at risk, his power no longer supreme, his judgment more in question, Zia called for national elections to be held on November 16, 1988. Zia was in trouble or he would never have taken such a step. Moreover, the politicians certainly understood what they had to do. It was already determined that the election campaign would center on one issue: the continuing role of President-General Zia ul-Haq, his policies, and his style of governance.

Thus there was little celebration and even less relief when the Soviets agreed to pull their forces out of Afghanistan. Nor would Zia live to see the moment when the last Soviet soldier departed Afghan soil. On August 17, 1988, Zia boarded a Pakistan Air Force C-130 at Bahawalpur for a flight back to Islamabad. Aboard the aircraft were the American ambassador and most of Pakistan's highest-ranking generals. None of them reached their destination. An explosive device placed aboard the plane detonated when the craft became airborne. Zia and the others were consumed in the explosion. The era of Zia ul-Haq had ended amidst the violence and chaos that had characterized Pakistan from the day the General seized power in 1977.

Bibliography

Amin, Tahir, *Ethno-national Movements of Pakistan: Domestic and International Factors*, Islamabad: Institute of Policy Studies, 1988.

Arnold, Anthony, *Afghanistan: The Soviet Invasion in Perspective*, Stanford: Hoover Institution Press, 1981.

Binder, Leonard, *Religion and Politics in Pakistan*, Berkeley: University of California Press, 1961.

Burki, Shahid Javed and Baxter, Craig, *Pakistan under the Military*, Boulder: Westview Press, 1991.

Chopra, Pran, *Zulfikar Ali Bhutto: "If I am Assassinated ..."*, New Delhi: Vikas, 1979.

Embree, Ainslee, ed., *Pakistan's Western Borderlands: The Transformation of a Political Order*, Durham, NC: Carolina Academic Press, 1977.

Farani, M., *Tyranny and Justice in Pakistan*, Lahore: Idara Mutalia-e-Tareekh, 1993.

Government of Pakistan, *White Paper on Misuse of the Media*, Islamabad, 1978.

Government of Pakistan, *White Paper on the Performance of the Bhutto Regime*, Vols. 1–3, Islamabad, 1979.

Griffiths, John C., *Afghanistan: Key to a Continent*, Boulder: Westview Press, 1981.

Hammond, Thomas T., *Red Flag over Afghanistan: The Communist Coup, the Soviet Invasion, and the Consequences*, Boulder: Westview Press, 1984.

Hussain, Asaf, *Elite Politics in an Ideological State: The Case of Pakistan*, Folkestone: Dawson, 1979.

Inayatullah, *Pakistan Politics: A Personal View*, Lahore: Ferozsons, 1993.

Mahmood, M. Dilawar, *The Judiciary and Politics in Pakistan*, Lahore: Idara Mutalia-e-Tareekh, 1992.

Maluka, Zulfikar Khalid, *The Myth of Constitutionalism in Pakistan*, Karachi: Oxford University Press, 1995.

Schofield, Victoria, *Bhutto: Trial and Execution*, London: Cassel, 1979.

Shafat, Saeed, *Contemporary Issues in Pakistan Studies*, Lahore: Gautam, 1995.

Shahi, Agha, *Pakistan's Security and Foreign Policy*, Lahore: Progressive Publishers, 1988.

Waseem, Mohamaad, *Politics and the State in Pakistan*, Lahore: Progressive Publishers, 1989.

Ziring, Lawrence, "Government and Politics," in Richard F. Nyrop, ed., *Pakistan: A Country Study*, Washington: U.S. Government Printing Office, 1984, pp. 181–256.

7

DEMOCRACY AND HYPOCRISY

No one claimed responsibility for Zia's death, but it was reasonable to assume he died at the hands of assassins who had planned their action with great care and implemented it with even greater professionalism. The explosion aboard the aircraft was no accident and the consequences were no doubt more significant than originally contemplated. The destruction of the plane not only killed Zia, it also caused the deaths of a young and knowledgeable American ambassador, the United States Chief Military Attaché, and virtually all the top generals in the Pakistan army. The military junta that had managed Pakistan for more than a decade, suddenly and without prior warning had been blown away. The political vacuum created by the event was unprecedented. Zia's critics were now free to speak their minds. The glee of those who had opposed Zia drowned out the cries of those who mourned him. For the opposition, it was a time to set the record straight. Zia, it was said, had done great damage to the nation and it would be difficult for succeeding governments to make the necessary repairs.

Considerable attention was given to what was described as Zia's manipulation of the civil and military intelligence agencies, and the encouragement he gave to militant Islamists in their diverse ethnic and cultural views. Bhutto had raised his Federal Security Force, but Zia, in the public view, was the godfather of a host of violence-prone organizations, not the least of which was the Inter-Services Intelligence Directorate. As much as this argument had merit, it was also true that Zia, like Bhutto, lost control over those organizations. Questions remain about how much Zia imposed his authority on the ISI. Moreover, more was involved than assisting the mujahiddin in Afghanistan or the clandestine forces in Kashmir. Zia's rule, it was argued, his vaunted Islamization program, spoke more to his desire for absolute power than to his concern for Pakistan's welfare. The harshness of the criticism was to be expected, given the protracted period of political party silence, and the fact that the politicians had not enjoyed prominence since the last days of Zulfikar Ali Bhutto. But condemn as they did Zia's actions, there was no escaping the reality that Pakistan was a conflict-ridden country and that the impact of Zia's administration would be felt well into the future.

Zia's death did not signify democratic revival in the Pakistani state. Pakistan has given lip service to democracy and educated Pakistanis have articulated democratic goals, but Pakistan was not a democracy at birth, and did not develop into anything resembling democracy in the decades that followed. By the same token, for all the talk about Pakistan's Islamic genius, Pakistan was not at the outset, or later, anything measuring up to an Islamic state. No blueprint existed for such an edifice and the distant Islamic past, most notably the period of the *Rashidun* or pious Caliphs, which those opposed to everything secular attempted to reclaim, was hopelessly beyond reach. The emotional and sentimental musings of key Islamists gained attention from an unquestioning public, but even these utopian views barely concealed a play for personal power.

The question of Islam's compatibility with democracy has been analyzed by scholars and laypeople alike, but even if a linkage was believed to exist, in no way did it measure up to a popular representation of democratic expression. An act of faith demands blind obedience, and Islam speaks to the matter of submission, of personal and collective surrender to God's will. The key issue was the concept of sovereignty and the insistence by Muslims, not least Pakistani Muslims, that sovereignty can be identified only with God, never with humankind. Hence the delegation of almost absolute power to the Caliph of old, the declared vicegerent of

God on earth. God is sovereign and the earthly manifestation of God's will is the responsibility of the Caliph, who on God's behalf administers to the *ummah*, the community of believers.

The intertwining of God with notions of sovereignty reinforces the autocratic tradition. God's vicegerents are responsible for insuring that God's commands are enacted. They are by the same ordination responsible for protecting His community. The faithful accept authority unconditionally, because to challenge it is to challenge God's message. The tradition extends back to the days of the third of the pious Caliphs, when Uthman, a member of the Ummayad clan, reconfigured the Caliphate to satisfy his personal ends. The more liberal and hence more democratic rule of the first Caliph, Abu Bakr, and the second, Umar, their emphasis on *shura* and consultation, was modified to provide the temporal ruler with power that could not be challenged. The martyrdom of Ali, the fourth of the pious Caliphs and the Prophet's son-in-law, and then Ali's son, Hussain, culminated in the establishment of the Ummayad Caliphate. From that time forward into the modern era, the Caliph was more the autocratic ruler of a vast dynasty than the embodiment of Islamic precept. In the absence of a central Islamic Caliphate, abolished in 1923, lesser caliphs, that is, Muslim kings and presidents, have assumed absolute power for themselves and demanded total obedience from their subjects. From Nasser to Hafiz al-Assad, to Muammar Qadaffi, to Yasser Arafat, to the Saudi kings, indeed to Jinnah, Ayub, Bhutto, and Zia there has always been a tradition of lifetime personal rule, not predictable institutional succession.

Zia's attempt to resurrect the institution of *shura* was aimed at centralizing his authority. He was less interested in introducing Pakistanis to Islamic democracy. There must be an explanation for the absolute power sought by Muslim rulers in today's world. Clothing actions in the context of *salifiyya*, or the anticipated return to a period of "the most righteous," is meant to make "legitimate" those who have arbitrarily seized power. Islam may not *ipso facto* negate democratic objectives, but from an early period of the Islamic tradition to the contemporary era, the executive monopoly of power reveals the believer's willingness to submit to autocratic, highly centralized authority, whether theocratic or secular. Pakistanis are more familiar with regal and viceregal traditions than with pious rule. Moreover, when Pakistanis speak of democracy they are less likely to refer to their religious tradition than they are to express their experience with secular authority. Theocracies are alien to the Muslims of South Asia. They also are undemocratic. Pakistanis are creatures of mixed cultural experience, and from such a complex milieu the most circumscribed democratic expression arises. The Muslims of the subcontinent share an environment with Hindus and Buddhists, Jains, and Christians, and the nation-state embraces them all. It is in such conditions that democracy has appeal and is given direction. Learning to live with diversity is at the heart of the democratic experience. National republics that seek to be democratic also strive to become inclusive. Democracy, therefore, is a call to unity, but it also requires respect for diversity. Democracy is as much a rejection of exclusivity as it is a struggle against tyranny. Such was the secular and democratic vision of Mohammad Ali Jinnah. Vision, however, is ephemeral and no match for reality. Moreover, with the passage of time, vision fades, or is so transformed that it is only the weight of history that defines human actions and influences the future.

Political revival

The army hierarchy suffered a severe blow with Zia's death. Not only was Pakistan's longest-reigning leader gone, so too were the generals who were likely to have replaced him. The way was open therefore for civilians, long dormant, to assert themselves. The Pakistan bureaucracy had known power before but it was now their lot to fill the breach and to manage the country through the immediate crisis. An old civil servant, Ghulam Ishaq Khan, presiding officer in the Pakistan Senate, was quickly sworn in as Pakistan's President. With a personal record of service that spanned the life of the nation, Ishaq was knowledgeable in matters from finance to defense and therefore an appropriate choice in so trying a moment. More rational than Ghulam Mohammad and less ambitious than Iskandar Mirza, Ishaq was no friend of the politicians but he nevertheless quickly addressed the issue of civilian government. The new President's major concern lay not in the opportunity for building a democratic nation, but rather in stabilizing a society torn by ideological as well as cultural and economic differences. Though advanced in age, he retained sufficient vitality to assume the powers granted by his new office. His only limitation was his distance from the army that had been the essential prop of the Zia administration. Ishaq nonetheless had the Zia-amended 1973 constitution to rest his authority upon and knew full well his capacity to force legislative compliance, even if he had to deal more gingerly with the Pakistan armed forces.

President Ishaq's first act was the declaration of a state of emergency. He also played a role in appointing General Mirza Aslam Baig as the new Chief of the Army Staff (COAS). Baig's promotion was a consequence of his not having joined the other generals on the flight back to Islamabad. Returning on another aircraft, Baig consulted with General Hamid Gul, Chief of the Inter-Services Intelligence Directorate. Ishaq's state of emergency was attributed to the counsel provided by these two generals and in the rumor and conspiracy laden Pakistan society, there was much discussion about the perpetuation of military power. The formation of an emergency council composed of members of the armed forces and civilian experts in a variety of fields was sufficient indication that Ishaq and his powerful colleagues were not yet ready to announce a full transfer of power to civilian hands. At this point, however, the courts intervened: the Supreme Court declared that nothing stood in the way of full political party activity. President Ishaq did not oppose this juridical finding, in large part because he was not an Islamist and believed the conventional political parties would balance the power of the clerics.

With the Red Army in the process of evacuating Afghanistan, the matter of dealing with the Communist government in Kabul and the several Afghan mujahiddin organizations that sought to remove it was a major concern of the Pakistan army. Long committed to a solution that would favor the Pakistani cause, the ISI was in the process of reorganizing the mujahiddin for a final assault on the Najibullah Communist government. Najibullah, Babrak Karmal's replacement, had been left in place by the terms of the April 1988 U.N.-negotiated agreement. For its part, the Pakistan government had given its word that it would not interfere with the Afghan government's attempt to attract rival muhajiddin to its side, as well as neutralize those who insisted on contesting its authority. The ISI, however, never intended to keep that agreement. Operating, as the ISI always did, behind the scenes, army intelligence agents penetrated the Pashtun tribes on both sides of the Durand Line and a strategy was developed that in short order was expected to end Communist rule in Afghanistan. Working closely with the Hizb-i-Islami of Hekmatyar, the ISI was determined to establish Hekmatyar as the leader of the Afghan government. When the Jamiatul-i-Islami realized what was happening, their Uzbek and Tajik commanders issued warnings that they could not allow the more Islamist of the Pashtun organizations to monopolize power once Najibullah had been defeated.

Ishaq's experience as Secretary General in the Ministry of Defense provided him with an understanding of ISI philosophy and strategies not known by too many Pakistani civilians. The President wanted no delays in the Soviet withdrawal but he also did not want to see Afghanistan transformed into a fundamentalist Islamic state. Faced with choosing between that result and the transfer of power to more secular Pakistani politicians, Ishaq decided on the latter, despite protests from the new army high command. Ishaq, however, was all the time being second-guessed by the ISI. Seldom were external events so intertwined with domestic matters, but, given the power vacuum resulting from Zia's death, and conditions that were yet to bring the political parties back into play, the course of Pakistan's politics pivoted around the future of a Soviet-free Afghanistan. So many epoch-making changes had occurred in so short a time that no one, save perhaps Ishaq, was in a position to determine the immediate future.

Coalitions of political parties formed after it was ruled that the scheduled autumn elections would be held as originally planned. The Movement for the Restoration of Democracy, the group Ishaq favored, announced its decision to remain a united front organization. Its failure to convince Benazir to bring her Pakistan People's Party into the movement, however, meant the MRD would not have the leverage needed to win the election. Arrayed against the independent PPP was the Islamic Democratic Alliance

(IDA), which claimed to represent and perpetuate the work of the late Zia ul-Haq. Attractive to the Islamist orders, the Muslim League and its IDA coalition early on announced their intention to sustain their dead mentor's Islamization program. Ishaq, forever the secularist, wanted to slow the Islamization process, and even reverse some of its actions. The formation of the IDA, better known by its Urdu name, the "Islami Jamhoori Itihad" (IJI), thwarted that objective. The electoral contest therefore was between the IJI and the PPP.

All the parties and coalitions presented hastily prepared manifestos and platforms, the PPP abandoning all references to Zulfikar's socialism. Benazir claimed the high ground, projecting a secular image centered on the vision of a democratic Pakistan. The IJI on the other hand unabashedly adopted Zia's policies and called upon the electorate to help the movement complete the work that the dead President had begun. The divide not only separated secularists from fundamentalists; it also left the army on the side of the IJI and the bureaucracy with the PPP. The army was already too deeply committed to the Islamists to shift course now. Too much was at stake in Afghanistan following the Red Army retreat and the Pakistan army was too committed to the Pashtuns, including those Pashtuns who made up a large portion of the Pakistan army. Nor was the army in harmony with the PPP; not even a PPP led by the American and British educated Benazir Bhutto. It was the army that had hanged Zulfikar Ali Bhutto, and the army refused to sanction a government led by another member of the Bhutto family. Moreover, given the alleged acts of terrorism perpetrated by Benazir's brothers against the Zia regime, the PPP was judged unfit to govern Pakistan.

Ishaq, however, saw the crisis differently. Mindful of the need to establish stability as quickly as possible and disinclined to see the army under Aslam Baig again take control of the government, Ishaq had no alternative but to support the PPP. The election therefore would be the determining factor. The problem for Ishaq, however, was that with so many organizations competing for the parliamentary seats, it was doubtful any group or party would win a majority. And so it was. With 215 seats contested, the biggest winner was the PPP, but it won only ninety-two places in the Assembly. The IJI, despite the work of the Muslim League, achieved victories in only fifty-four constituencies. Islamist organizations never demonstrated much prowess at the polls, but their minority status was never a factor in their capacity to influence events. Be that as it may, Ghulam Ishaq was called upon to make a decision. Holding new elections was considered out of the question. Moreover, new elections might not guarantee any different result, and might precipitate an army *putsch*. Also aware that decisions had to be made with due haste, the Mohajir Qaumi Movement that dominated Karachi and the Awami National Party in the NWFP threw in their lot with the PPP. Ishaq now had his opening. The President called upon Benazir to meet with him, and shortly after their conversation it was announced that the first civilian-led government in eleven years was to be formed by a lady hardly thirty-six years old.

Bhutto insisted democracy was her goal. She called the leader of the IJI, the Punjabi Nawaz Sharif, and asked him to meet with her. When they met, the two politicians were said to have achieved a meeting of the minds: neither wanted the Pakistan army in politics, and both would center their actions on reducing political rivalries and improving the economy. That initial understanding, however, died almost as quickly as it had been established. In her first press conference Benazir lashed out at Nawaz, who had become Chief Minister of the Punjab. Calling him a "separatist," Benazir reported that Nawaz wanted to undermine her government even before it had set to its tasks. To check the IJI leader's strategy, the Prime Minister made the PPP Secretary General the governor of the Punjab. She also assigned a number of civil servants to the Punjab without consulting the Chief Minister. Nawaz interpreted the maneuver as an attempt to steal his provincial election victory, and he was reminded that Zulfikar had done similar things in the NWFP and Balochistan during his tenure. Benazir had signaled a desire to control all the provinces of Pakistan, especially the Punjab, considered the most important. Now the gauntlet had been thrown down, there would be no reconciling the two politicians.

Nawaz Sharif was ready for the struggle and he used all the leverage at his disposal to defend IJI dominance in the province. All pretence of democratic practice was ignored or forgotten. Better at democratic rhetoric, the two major contenders betrayed in their actions their true intent. Neither truly believed Pakistan was ready for a full-blown experiment in parliamentary democracy, and all their actions and counteractions proved arbitrary and vindictive. President Ishaq shuddered at the sight of the two politicians struggling in the public forum. He had gambled that Benazir's experience abroad would have tempered her actions, but her intemperate behavior revealed how wounded she was by her father's execution and how closely she resembled the character of her father, who had shown a total inability to work with people who disagreed with him. To suggest that Benazir too was touched by the feudal experience is one explanation for this clash of personalities; to understand that she felt weakness not strength in becoming Prime Minister is perhaps more germane. Benazir had achieved a plurality at the polls, hardly a mandate with which to govern a troubled and divided nation at a critical time. She knew she required more authority. She also knew that real power lay with the chief executive and army high command. Seeing confrontation not cooperation as the reality shaping her government, she preferred forcing Nawaz from office rather than trying to accommodate him.

Ghulam Ishaq was not so much a gray eminence in this battle as a man caught between two headstrong leaders representing legacies at total variance from one another. Pakistan's political scene was not only infantile, it had been stunted by years of military dominance. Benazir and Nawaz refused to regard compromise as a preferred course of action. Ghulam Ishaq could not impress upon them the need to refrain from baiting one another or, worse, seeking one another's demise. The President therefore shifted his position. No longer able to demonstrate a preference for Benazir and distressed by the antics of her PPP supporters, he assumed a more neutral stance, hoping that he could keep the army from taking matters into its own hands. In fact the army was already making gestures of its own. General Baig, never the preferred successor to Zia, demonstrated his estrangement from the Zia clique by suddenly siding with Benazir. Baig's motives were unclear but he was more the conventional nationalist and had concluded that the tilt in favor of Islamization had widened fissures in the body politic that could not be closed. Baig was a disciplinarian with tendencies toward autocratic rule, but he found the Muslim brotherhood threatening and counterproductive. Thus he frowned upon the IJI and saw in Nawaz a mediocre capitalist with false visions of grandeur.

While the Voice of America was describing Benazir as a breath of fresh air and a "symbol of the new democratic Pakistan," Benazir was struggling to ward off a variety of attacks on her government. Amidst high inflation and deepening unemployment, demands came from the private sector that she could not address. Nor could she satisfy her coalition members with her domestic diplomacy in shambles. Benazir lost the support of the Mohajir, now renamed Muttehida Qaumi Movement (MQM) as well as the National Awami Party. Virtual civil war in her native Sind province had caused her to talk publicly about a "mini-insurgency" and her use of the army to quell disturbances did not sit well with her supporters. Calls for an independent Sindhu Desh by the venerable G.M. Syed did not help the situation. Emboldened, the rioters defied the army, seized a provincial airport, and burned the Pakistani flag. Only after launching a large-scale campaign and arresting several thousand demonstrators did the army bring matters under control. Undaunted by the army action, however, separatist organizations sprang up in different areas of Sindh. Similar acts of violence erupted in Balochistan and the NWFP. The symphony of secessionist calls illustrated the fragility and essential weakness of the government in the aftermath of the Soviet departure from Afghanistan.

The last Soviet soldier left Afghanistan in February 1989, but the war did not end. Najibullah was entrenched in Kabul and determined to remain the leader of the Marxist government. Although the Americans concluded their role in the region had ended, the ISI was not about to give up the fight until the Communist government had been replaced and Islamabad had established its influence over the future Afghanistan. Lieutenant-General Hamid Gul, the ISI director, had organized a drive on the important town of Jalalabad, near the Pakistan frontier. Arranged in conventional military formation, the ISI-led fighters were soundly defeated by Najibullah's army and the reverberations of this failure rippled through Pakistan. Wali Khan, the Awami National Party leader, accused the ISI of prolonging the conflict and demanded a cessation of hostilities. The ISI, however, refused to back away. Hamid Gul, believing General Baig and Benazir were conspiring to have him removed, conferred with Nawaz Sharif and Ghulam Ishaq in an attempt to enlist their services. Learning of Gul's cabal, Benazir dismissed him, saying he had been appointed by Zia in 1987 and had outlived his usefulness. The ISI had learned a lesson, however. Acknowledging that large set battles could not be mounted in Afghanistan, the intelligence unit fell back on small unit operations. Increasing support to the Hizb-i-Islami of Hekmatyar, it believed it could rally the Pashtun tribes on both sides of the frontier, seize Kabul, and form the new Afghan government.

Benazir depended on Baig to keep her informed of ISI secret operations. But the ISI had grown accustomed to functioning outside the authority of the regular army, and, given Baig's rejection of the Zia system, even he was not informed of the directorate's plans. Moreover, Nawaz had inherited Zia's Muslim League and through the party he liaised with the special army units. Somewhat assured that he had army support despite his falling out with the army commander, Nawaz sustained his attack on Benazir. In November 1989, a motion of no confidence in the Benazir administration was brought to a vote in the National Assembly. Nawaz, along with the IJI, and assisted by the MQM, led the no-confidence vote; by doing so the Muslim Leaguer hoped to win the favor of General Baig, but the COAS refused to meet with him. When the no-confidence motion, the first in the history of Pakistan, was brought to a vote, Nawaz came up short. Benazir reveled in her victory but she also accused the IJI of trying to subvert the neutrality of the armed forces, as well as falsely vilify her administration. Defiantly, Benazir said her term as Prime Minister had only just begun and that she had no doubts about her ability to complete the course.

Benazir's confidence, however, could not conceal the fact that she was a woman in a man's world. The first Muslim woman to assume high office in a Muslim government, she was not the celebrity in her own country that she was abroad. The traditional role of women in Islamic society specified a particular subordination to men. Women were denied behavior deemed the preserve of men and from the beginning of her tenure Benazir was hounded by fundamentalists who questioned her bona fides. The Salman Rushdie episode exploded upon the Muslim world during this period, setting off violent displays in several countries, especially in Pakistan. Rushdie's *Satanic Verses* was judged blasphemous by Muslim clerics, and the Ayatollah Khomeini called upon Muslims everywhere to find and murder the author. A price was put on Rushdie's head and for an extended period he was forced into hiding in Britain. In Pakistan, demonstrations against the publication and distribution of the book resulted in a number of deaths, but Benazir was one of a very few Muslim leaders to speak out on the right of free speech. Finding fault with the Islamists, she said she would forcefully prevent all displays of anti-social behavior. Defying the extremists, Benazir defended the author's creative talents without endorsing the book. In doing so, she won the favor of members of Pakistan's literati. Her call for calm, however, did not quiet Rushdie's critics, nor did the event help her administration.

Benazir had come into office with the belief that democracy would flower under her leadership. It did not take long before that belief was substituted by another that addressed Pakistan as a failed state. Benazir continued to speak in the name of democratic institutions but she clearly had opted for the more arbitrary powers associated with her predecessors. Moreover, her husband, Asif Zardari, was a major influence on her political thinking and he convinced her that in a struggle with no rules attached, one does whatever is necessary to hold onto power. Machiaveli not John Locke dominated her governing style and when confronted with renewed rioting in Karachi in February 1990 she ordered the army to crack down mercilessly on the killers and destroyers of property. The frequent use of the army, however, did not redound to her favor. Nor could she quell the terrorists targeting the innocent. The bombing of the Karachi bus terminal took many more innocent lives, and, like all the other incidents before it, the event weighed heavily on Benazir's administration.

General Baig tried to convince the Prime Minister that only a no-holds-barred approach to root out miscreants in the PPP, the MQM, and the Islamist orders could reverse the wave of terror and bring peace to the troubled country. But the Prime Minister could not go along with the scheme, especially one that also included doing violence to her own party. The Prime Minister's rejection of the Baig proposal caused increased distress in the highest army circles. So too did Benazir's acceptance of an American request to reduce tensions with India by removing army units on the line of control in Kashmir. The generals met in secret session to discuss these and other matters burdening the state while Benazir was on tour in the Middle East. Stopping in Morocco, Algeria, Kuwait, Bahrain, and Iraq, Benazir had a publicized conversation with Saddam Hussein just before the invasion of Kuwait on August 2, 1990. Benazir was not informed of Saddam's intentions. Iraq's swift conquest of Kuwait, the termination of its sovereignty, and its transformation into Iraq's nineteenth province shocked the world. It also provoked the United States to take counteraction. Pakistan was faced with still another crisis and the army confronted still another concern.

Believing Iraq was making plans to extend its conquest to Saudi Arabia's oil fields, Washington called upon the United Nations Security Council to authorize a defense of the oil-rich kingdom. "Operation Desert Shield" was the immediate outcome and an international coalition was quickly assembled to defend the region from further Iraqi aggression. With Kuwait overrun and Saudi Arabia threatened, a number of Muslim countries declared their willingness to participate in the coalition. In Pakistan, Benazir pondered her move. General Baig had expressed his misgivings and more so his opposition to United States leadership in a matter that he believed was a Muslim affair. Benazir took a contrary position, believing Saddam had betrayed the entire Muslim world and that the international coalition was the only logical response. Benazir did not know that a decision had already been taken to remove her. Just four days following the invasion of Kuwait, on August 6, the Pakistan army, in collaboration with President Ishaq, deposed Benazir. Ishaq declared he had used the powers granted him under the Eighth Amendment and Article 58 (clause b) of the constitution. The first woman to head a Muslim government was forced to leave office hardly seventeen months into her five-year term. The National Assembly was dissolved and a caretaker government quickly assembled.

Democracy revisited?

Benazir described the President's actions as unconstitutional and arbitrary, but the decision could not be rescinded. Ishaq accused the PPP leaders of corruption and nepotism. Benazir was declared unfit for office, having failed to stem domestic violence and having allowed the economy to fall to new depths. She also was threatened with arrest for misconduct. Her husband was singled out for judicial assault, in one instance being charged with kidnapping. It was obvious from the charges that leaders of the coup did not want Benazir returned to office. She was called before the Lahore High Court to show cause why she should not be found guilty of misconduct in matters pertaining to the production of natural gas, and the dispensing of marketing rights to relatives and friends. Forced to fight the cases brought against its leaders, the PPP had little in reserve to run an effective electoral campaign. With the PPP out of the race, the field was wide open for the IJI and Muslim League coalition. The IJI manifesto issued on October 13 specified the party's central objective as the "supremacy of the Qur'an and Sunnah." The IJI wanted it known that not only did it revere Islam but it was the only genuine people's party. Exploiting latent anti-Americanism, it condemned Benazir's dependence on the United States and declared it would reappraise the country's foreign policy and identify more closely with the Islamic nations.

On October 1, the Bush administration ordered a halt to all assistance to Pakistan. Benazir's opposition, however, was not prepared to yield to American pressure. Arguing the Americans had used Pakistan's dependence on U.S. aid to force Ishaq not to dismiss Benazir, Washington's embrace of the young female Prime Minister only provided more ammunition for the political opposition to use against her. Washington, it was said, expected Benazir to put a brake on the Pakistan army's interventionist behavior and to keep the troops in the barracks. The United States also looked to Benazir to rein in the Islamists, but that too was not a popular cause and it also backfired. In retrospect, American actions provided grist to the anti-American mill, and IJI popularity rose as the PPP suffered the defection of a number of its stalwarts. Finally, the Lahore High Court ruled that the President had the legitimate authority to dissolve the National Assembly and call new elections. The court cited Benazir's failure to perform her legislative responsibilities. It also pointed to her inability to restore law and order in the country. With the powerful arrayed against her, Benazir was effectively eliminated as a viable candidate by the time the country went to the polls on October 24. The IJI coalition won the election, much as had been expected. It defeated the PPP in every province, and when splinter parties later joined its ranks it controlled 155 National Assembly seats to the PPP's forty-five.

IJI success at the polls meant Nawaz Sharif was sworn in as the new Prime Minister of Pakistan. Benazir complained about fraudulent polling, but her complaint fell on deaf ears. Nawaz quickly formed a government and Benazir had to content herself with the leadership of the opposition. Nawaz had been nurtured in Pakistan's cosmopolitan setting. A capitalist, his family's industrial activities had made him a wealthy man. He also had sufficient reason to oppose the PPP after Zulfikar Ali Bhutto had nationalized his father's property. An ardent believer in free enterprise, Nawaz criticized the threat to democracy of Bhutto's socialist program. Nawaz was also a devout Muslim. Steeped in Islamic practices, he believed the PPP's secular posture was a threat to the evolution of the Pakistani ethos. Nawaz therefore became a firm supporter of General Zia's program of Islamic renaissance.

Nawaz Sharif saw no contradiction in being a proper Muslim while at the same time promoting economic change and his own material well-being. During Zia's tenure, Nawaz accepted the position of Finance Minister in the Punjab government and achieved notable success. He also became a member of the Muslim League and was given major responsibility as an organizer and fundraiser. Quickly rising to a position of political leadership, Nawaz became an articulate spokesman for the Punjab Muslim League, and it was not long before he was tipped to be the province's Chief Minister. His conflict with Benazir, who desperately sought to control the Punjab, made Nawaz a national figure. Moreover, his dedication to the memory of General Zia stood in sharp contrast to Benazir's characterization of the dead President as usurper and despot. By retaining leverage with the army, Nawaz rode a wave of anti-PPP and anti-Benazir sentiment. Though declaring his objective was the destruction of feudalism and the flowering of democracy, the new Prime Minister was more intent on marrying commerce with religion.

The new National Assembly opened its doors on November 3, 1990. The Prime Minister declared his government would embrace all who shared the IJI philosophy and wished to work toward reconciliation and national renewal. Nawaz reached out to fundamentalists, to ethnic-based organizations, and to members of the minority communities, insisting they all could find a home in his coalition. The state of emergency was lifted the very next day and Nawaz urged the nation to join him in expanding education, improving national health, putting people back to work, and generally making life more enjoyable for all Pakistanis. Nawaz also declared it to be his government's goal to accelerate development of the country's nuclear program. Cautioning that this did not mean the pursuit of an "Islamic bomb," the Prime Minister said he wanted Pakistan to be a modern state and that the science and technology of the nuclear era were important to the country's modernization. Moreover, Pakistan needed sources of cheap energy to expand its industrial base and improve its urban infrastructure; only nuclear power, he insisted, would allow the country to achieve higher growth and greater independence.

The Nawaz formula for democratic and economic development received a positive and collective response that was unique in the history of Pakistan. Self-reliance and resource sharing were given greater emphasis. The government declared its intention to end the country's dependence on the United States, and the cut-off of American assistance was welcome in many quarters. The new administration called for tax reform, export promotion, and a vigorous industrial policy. Pakistan, noted Nawaz, wanted good relations with the United States but it wanted its independence from foreign influence even more. With the Soviets gone from Afghanistan, Washington had moved into another mode, and Pakistan no longer played much of a role in American foreign policy. Within a very short period, the country had gone from being the third-highest recipient of American assistance to receiving almost nothing. Pakistanis were inclined to find connections where they had common experiences, and even Pakistan's membership in the Gulf coalition against Saddam Hussain lacked popular appeal. A Pakistani troop contingent was sent to Saudi Arabia but its role was more symbolic than real. Protecting the holy sites of Islam was the way it was presented to the Pakistani public. General Baig, on the other hand, was outspoken in expressing the view that the royal family of Kuwait had outlived its usefulness and that Pakistan might consider a more appropriate regional policy.

The Prime Minister had no intention of following Baig's ideas. In November 1990 he made a special trip to Riyadh to meet with the Saudi royal family as well the Emir of Kuwait. Condemning Iraq's aggression, the Prime Minister said he would send additional troops to help defend the area from further assaults. Nawaz subsequently flew to the Maldives for a meeting of the South Asian Association for Regional Cooperation (SAARC) and met with India's new Prime Minister, Chandra Shekhar, who had succeeded the assassinated Rajiv Gandhi. The two new leaders addressed the old question of Kashmir, but the Indian Prime Minister accused Pakistan of instigating a new, more violent uprising in the troubled state. Nawaz nevertheless insisted on a resolution to the Kashmir problem, and that it be managed by the Kashmiris themselves. Calling again for a plebiscite to determine the future of Kashmir, he was, like those before him, rebuffed by the Indian leaders. With the war in the Gulf intensifying and the Indian–Pakistani dispute over Kashmir as far from resolution as ever, Nawaz deferred to his commanding generals. Their reach reduced by the cut-off of U.S. military supplies, the military establishment agreed to maintain a presence in the Gulf but to avoid any commitment of combat forces. Moreover, the ISI was authorized to continue operations in Kashmir and Afghanistan, where efforts to dislodge Najibullah had not yet succeeded.

Nawaz centered attention on economic stability and growth. He returned confiscated property, held since the Bhutto years, to its original owners. He tried to assure domestic entrepreneurs that their investment in Pakistan was appreciated and secure. His purpose was to rejuvenate the private sector and to balance industrial expansion with agricultural growth. Rural areas were made prime targets for agro-based industries, and government incentives promised Pakistan's capitalist class high returns. The government also deregulated the economy, attracted funds secreted abroad back to the country, and induced a higher performance of private innovation. Nawaz envisaged a number of reforms in the methods of taxation, in foreign exchange calculations, and in administrative law. Nevertheless his program of national renewal was heavily weighted in favor of the wealthy. The affluent increased their wealth, but the rank and file saw little improvement in their standard of living and it did not take long for the opposition politicians to make an issue of the discrepancies between promise and fulfillment.

In 1991, an IJI-proposed Shariat Bill became law. The legislation called for a more rigorous legal system based upon religious scripture. It also authorized the expansion of the religious schools and prescribed daily prayer schedules. The law cited the need to revise the banking system to conform to the tenets of Islam, and prevented the media from questioning religious expression. Federal and provincial laws that were deemed repugnant to the teachings of Islam were declared null and void. The country's secular opposition questioned the government's shift to a more theocratic posture, but it was the women's organizations and minority groups that stimulated more concern. Nawaz was compelled to publicly state his position on religion, but when he declared he was not a fundamentalist he brought distress to an important segment of his constituency.

Nawaz walked a tightrope strung between his business acquaintances on the one side and the Islamists on the other. He also was challenged by the "Kalashnikov culture" that permeated the major cities. Citing the frequent bombings, assassinations, and kidnappings, he called for a tough stand on law and order issues, but everyone had heard that before and the public waited to see whether the Prime Minister really intended to do anything about the problems. Recognizing citizens were safe neither in their homes nor in public, Nawaz had to find ways to deal with the brazen outlaws who took advantage of defenseless people. Moreover, gun-running and narcotics peddling had reached higher levels and government officials were implicated in the lucrative but illicit trade.

The Twelfth Amendment to the constitution approved in the summer of 1991 called for summary justice and speedy trials of those found in violation of the law. Serious efforts were launched to combat the disorder. The violence, however, continued. Nor could the police cope with the problem. Even the army offered little more than a brief respite. When more drastic measures were contemplated to deal with the situation, the critics were always ready to condemn the government for what was described as the use of arbitrary powers. Maintaining law and order proved an impossible task and the administration's apparent weakness opened it to still more criticism. Nawaz's economic program had also run into difficulty. Promises were not realized and the plight of the average citizen was judged as more not less severe than during the previous administration. It was not too long before the opposition began referring to Nawaz's economic scheme as "loot and plunder." Economic scandals drew public attention because of the changes that favored the private sector. Gaining control of energy-producing installations, telecommunications, and shipping and airlines operations, private entrepreneurs prioritized the bottom line, not public welfare. The consequences of these policies were sharp increases in the cost of basic commodities, uncontrolled inflation, and incoherent planning. Corruption was institutionalized in all sectors, including the banking industry and cooperative societies, in which innocent depositors were said to have lost their total life's savings.

What had started out as an impressive new campaign to expand and modernize the economy had in a year's time become a failed and repudiated program. Nawaz took responsibility for the shortcomings and was forced to admit his inability to transform vision to reality. He also lost the political trust needed to sustain his administration. Moreover, given defections from the IJI coalition government, Benazir, as leader of the opposition, was again active in leading the assault on the administration. Benazir sustained her argument that the IJI had stolen the 1990 election. She also charged the administration with gross inefficiencies as well as major acts of impropriety. Citing the effort to silence her and her PPP organization, she accused the government of police state tactics and seeking to convert Pakistan into a fascist state.

The Afghanistan factor

General Baig had been pressured to retire from the army in August 1991 and the new army commander, General Asif Nawaz, had assumed the post of COAS. The Gulf war had run its course by this time and although Saddam remained in power in Baghdad, his armed forces had suffered heavy losses at the hands of the American-led coalition. Baig's anti-monarchy comments in the course of the war now reverberated in the region and the Prime Minister hoped his new army commander could smooth over relations with the Gulf kingdoms, especially with the Kuwaiti royal family that had been returned to power. General Nawaz also had a major responsibility in bridging differences with the United States. The Gorbachev reforms had fizzled out in the Soviet Union, precipitating a coup that ultimately failed when Soviet army chiefs refused to go along with the coup plotters. The episode led to an implosion within the superpower which at the close of 1991 brought the startling end of the once vaunted Communist state. The Soviet Union broke up as its republics all sought and achieved their independence. The changes were felt worldwide. In Pakistan and Afghanistan the reverberations were magnified many times over.

With the termination of Soviet assistance, Najibullah's forces defected, leaving the Communist regime vulnerable on all fronts. Kabul was surrounded and fell to mujahiddin forces led by Masud, and Abdul Rashid Dostum, an Uzbek formerly loyal to the Communist leader in Kabul. On April 16, 1992, Najibullah surrendered and was placed in United Nations custody pending a determination of his fate. The swift action of the northern forces had prevented the implementation of a United Nations plan for a post-Communist Afghanistan. It also set the scene for a violent clash between non-Pashtun and Pashtun mujahiddin, especially those led by the Pakistan ISI. The ISI continued to favor Hekmatyar, whereas Masud boosted the credentials of Burhanuddin Rabbani. Dostum on the other hand was more determined to pursue his own destiny. In the circumstances there would be no peace for Afghanistan, in large part because Pakistan and its ISI had a stake in the solution.

The ISI's original orders were to neutralize Afghan meddling in Pakistani affairs. From the time of Pakistan's independence, Afghan leaders, notably Sadar Mohammad Daud, had called for the independence of Pakistan's NWFP, a region Daud referred to as "Pakhtunistan." Pakistan had warded off such threats to its territorial integrity, but during the administration of Zulfikar Ali Bhutto the issue was raised again. The Afghan government was accused of aiding secessionist forces in Pakistan, both in the NWFP and in Balochistan. During the Bhutto years the Pakistan army had been called to fight a protracted and bloody war in Balochistan, and Islamabad found enough evidence to cite the

Afghan government as a source of the trouble. The ISI therefore was infiltrated into Afghanistan to work with Islamist forces opposed to the Daud regime.

The Islamic movement in Afghanistan had been the work of Rabbani, Hekmatyar, and others, assisted by Masud, who assembled a fighting arm for the group. In time these individuals had attracted a large number of university students, as well as members of the *ulema*, and other devotees of Islam. All had dedicated themselves to the overthrow of Mohammad Daud. Daud, however, was determined to defeat the Islamists and found himself more and more in league with the Communists, who also sought his demise. Confronted by superior power, the Afghan Islamists found sanctuary in Pakistan, where Bhutto readily provided them with arms and other assistance. From this time forward, Pakistani assistance to the Islamists passed through several stages, especially after the Communist overthrow and the killing of Daud.

Inter-Services Intelligence connections with the Afghan fundamentalists were deepened with the Communist revolution in 1978 and the Soviet invasion in 1979. The ISI recognized both the weakness and potential strength in the Islamist movement in Afghanistan. Following the Soviet seizure of Kabul and the subsequent flight of the Afghan opposition leaders to Peshawar, Pakistan's army intelligence unit took on its greatest responsibility. Although the ISI did their best, in the end the ethnic divisions in Afghanistan could not be bridged. The Pakistanis therefore chose the Hizb-i-Islami as their principal change instrument in Afghanistan. They also developed intimate relations with Hekmatyar and found his message similar to their own in pressing the war against the Soviet Red Army. At the same time, the northern forces, composed mainly of Tajiks and led by Ahmad Shah Masud, assumed a more secular stance, but nevertheless were just as determined to rid the country of Communist forces. Rabbani, who opposed Hekmatyar, allied with Masud and together they formed yet another front in the war. Moreover, when Najibullah fell in 1992 it was essentially the alliance forged between Masud, Najibullah's Afghan generals, and the Uzbek militia leader Abdul Rashid Dostum that carried the day. The Pakistani ISI and the major Pashtun force associated with Hekmatyar were forced to accept a lesser role in the liberation of the Afghan capital.

It was now General Asif Nawaz's task to play diplomat in resolving differences between the different mujahiddin organizations and especially their leaders. Asif, however, had virtually no control over the ISI and the latter was not interested in a mediated settlement that left the Tajiks and Uzbeks in a dominant position in the new Afghan government. Moreover, the outflanked Pashtuns were not well disposed to the political engineering contemplated by the Northern Alliance. Northern leaders wanted to operate independent of the Pakistanis and they were opposed to sustained Islamabad influence in Afghan affairs. Efforts were made by the Northern Alliance to signal Islamabad that the Afghans should have the opportunity to arrive at an unencumbered understanding largely based upon tribal custom. In the absence of Pakistani involvement, it was said, Afghans would find common ground, and Pashtuns, Tajiks, Uzbeks, Hazara, and others would work through their differences.

The politics of chaos

Nawaz Sharif had little if any leverage in this matter. Nor did General Asif Nawaz indicate a greater capacity to deal with the main issues. Rival Afghan factions achieved an accord in Peshawar that called for a ruling council that represented all the ethnic groups. They also agreed that Rabbani would become the head of state, and Sibghatullah Mujaddedi would head the fifty-member council, composed of thirty field commanders, ten *ulema*, and ten officers from the various mujahiddin political parties. Hekmatyar was to be given the power to select the Prime Minister from the Hizb-i-Islami and the Deputy Prime Minister was to be the choice of the National Islamic Front. Ahmad Shah Masud, a leader of the Jamiat-i-Islami, was to be made Defense Minister. Although the Peshawar Accord appeared to be a reasonable compromise on who should govern Afghanistan, it did not conceal continuing bitterness among the principals and their followers. Hekmatyar was especially unhappy with Masud's decision to ally with Dostum, who was said to have betrayed the Afghans by having joined with the Communists and Soviets. The choice of Masud for Defense Minister therefore kept suspicions and animosities alive. Moreover, the interim government, weighted in favor of non-Pashtuns, led the ISI to conclude that only by their intervention could the rival forces be balanced in a way that provided Pakistan with greater security.

On January 8, 1993 it was reported that General Asif Nawaz had died. No explanation was given for his death. Nor was his family informed. What was reported was the appointment of his successor, Lieutenant-General Abdul Waheed Kakar. President Ishaq had made the decision without informing the Prime Minister, who was livid about not being consulted. Nor had he been told what had taken the life of General Asif. The Prime Minister saw a conspiracy in the making. He saw his influence with the army diminished and he also had reason to believe the ISI had gained the upper hand in driving military policy. The Prime Minister's target, however, was President Ishaq, who was operating with the special power granted his office under the Eighth Amendment. Questions were raised as to why Nawaz would challenge the supreme powers of the President at a time of parliamentary weakness. Moreover, the army command appeared unified in support of Ishaq's action, and it joined ranks against the Prime Minister. Even Benazir Bhutto involved herself in what had become a public spectacle. She publicly gave her support to the same President who had previously dismissed her. Seldom consistent to principle, Benazir hated Nawaz more than she hated presidential power.

When the widow of the dead General publicly announced her husband had been poisoned, the nation had even more reason to question the machinations of its leaders. Rumor also circulated that the Prime Minister had ordered the murder of General Asif. A shocked Nawaz rejected the accusation, and immediately assembled a three-man judicial commission to investigate the cause of the General's death. But before the panel could render its findings, Benazir publicly urged Ishaq to dissolve the IJI government, arguing the controversy threatened to tear the country apart. The mystery, she said, could not be resolved while Nawaz Sharif remained head of government. Under considerable pressure to resign, the Prime Minister chose to defend himself in a radio broadcast. He cited collusion between Ishaq and Benazir, but ignored the possible role of the army or its clandestine services in the death of the General. Instead Nawaz pointed to the President, calling him "the root cause" of all the intrigue, and by innuendo caused his listeners to conclude the President was behind the death of the army commander.

The President responded almost immediately to this assault on his integrity, declaring Nawaz Sharif had committed an "act of subversion." He embellished this remark with a scathing attack on the administration, asserting it was the most corrupt in the history of the nation. He also hinted that the Prime Minister was indeed implicated in the death of General Asif Nawaz. On April 18, 1993, President Ghulam Ishaq Khan said he had no choice but to dissolve the National Assembly and dismiss the government of Nawaz Sharif. Justifying his action, he said the peace of the country was at stake. The President insisted his major concern was the preservation of constitutional order, declaring he had no interest in power for himself, and said he was appointing Mir Balkh Sher Mazari to organize a caretaker government until new elections could be held on July 14.

Like Benazir before him, Nawaz too questioned the action of the President. He immediately appealed to the Supreme Court, asking the body to cancel the order. The Supreme Court, however, took six weeks to respond to the Prime Minister's appeal. What the jurists had to say astounded everyone. In all previous legal contests involving a head of state and a head of government, the head of state had been upheld. This time, however, the Supreme Court ruled the President had overstepped his prerogatives and had acted illegally and unconstitutionally. In an unprecedented order it called for the reinstatement of the Nawaz Sharif government.

The country was plunged into deeper chaos as Ishaq and Nawaz dueled for supremacy. Neither was successful, but together they put nearly all of Pakistan's institutions at risk. It was only when General Waheed Kakar intervened and called upon both the Prime Minister and the President to resign their positions that a modicum of stability was restored. Under pressure from the armed forces and without the institutional support needed to carry on, both men acknowledged the impasse. On July 18, 1993 they tendered their resignations. Yet another caretaker government was authorized, this one led by the Senate Chairman, Wasim Sajjad. Sajjad's first decision was to call Moen Qureshi back to Pakistan from his home in the United States. Qureshi, a former Vice-President of the World Bank, was asked to assume the duties of interim Prime Minister and to ease Pakistan over the monumental crisis its political and military leaders had created.

Bibliography

Baxter, Craig and Kennedy, Charles, eds., *Pakistan 1997*, Boulder: Westview, 1998.

Black, Antony, *The History of Islamic Political Thought*, New York: Routledge, 2001.

Burke, S.M. and Ziring, Lawrence, *Pakistan's Foreign Policy*, 2nd edn, Karachi: Oxford University Press, 1990.

Burney, I.H., *No Illusions, Some Hopes, and No Fears*, Karachi: Oxford University Press, 1996.

Butterworth, Charles, and Zartman, I. William, eds., *Between the State and Islam*, Cambridge: Cambridge University Press, 2001.

Khan, Mohammad Usman, "Tribal Politics in Balochistan, 1947–1990," Ph.D. dissertation, University of Karachi, 1997.

Lambrick, H.T., *The Terrorist*, London: Ernest Benn, 1972.

Mandaville, Peter, *Transnational Muslim Politics: Reimagining the Umma*, New York: Routledge, 2001.

Rais, Rasul Bakhsh, *War without Winners: Afghanistan's Uncertain Transition after the Cold War*, Karachi: Oxford University Press, 1994.

Ziring, Lawrence, *Pakistan in the Twentieth Century: A Political History*, Karachi: Oxford University Press, 1997.

8

THE EXTERNALITIES OF DOMESTIC CHANGE

Pakistan reached across oceans and continents for someone who it was hoped could return the country to a semblance of sanity. Moen Qureshi, an international civil servant, was summoned from an assignment in Singapore to tend to an ailing country that had just experienced the loss of both its President and Prime Minister. Qureshi's appointment as caretaker Prime Minister was a pleasant surprise to the more sophisticated and knowledgeable public who believed the country needed an erudite technician to assemble a government of reasonable probity and integrity. Qureshi was that person and he did not disappoint those who selected him, or those who put their faith in his ability to steer the nation away from the treacherous shoals of the preceding years. All of Pakistan's institutions and all of its previous leaders had failed in their service to the nation. Moreover, neither the army nor the bureaucracy was ready to fill the political vacuum. But returning the country to the "normalcy" of conventional politics after the long years of martial law and military rule proved difficult. Although the politicians had imagined themselves ready and able to assume the responsibility of good governance, not only had they failed to grow with the passage of the years, but they had regressed to a point where primitive struggle had become their calling. Neither Benazir nor Nawaz was able to rise to the occasion. Each suffered from a lack of perspective, and both inflicted considerable pain on the nation they claimed to love.

Moreover, Pakistan was less than the master of its own destiny. Influenced by events in the external world, it was forced to react in ways that were not always in its best interest. So many events crowded in on the country, events that Pakistan only partially understood and over which it had little if any say. Still unsure of itself following the civil war and the dismemberment, Pakistan was confronted by a war in neighboring Afghanistan that had been provoked by one of the two twentieth-century superpowers. The several million Afghan refugees who flooded into Pakistan were a constant reminder of the proximity of the problem. Pakistan's other western neighbor, Iran, also found itself at war, with Arab Iraq, and that bloody encounter heightened the revolutionary circumstances imposed on the region by Ayatollah Khomeini. The energizing of Islamic fundamentalism by the Ayatollah stood in sharp contrast to Iran's pre-revolutionary status as a secular nation. The successful if costly Afghan resistance as well as the protracted war in the Gulf nourished religious fervor and gave strength to the forces of radical change. Sacrifice was rewarded in the retreat and ultimately the demise of the Soviet Union. Islamic fundamentalism was reified in these circumstances and more Muslim countries saw their future in heightened Islamic identity rather than the secular European colonial dispensation that could only remind them of their previous condition of servitude.

Pakistan's Muslim character was never a matter of conjecture. Muslims' experience in an India dominated by Hindus kept spiritual distinctions in full view. Pakistan was established on the basis that Muslims required a dominant voice in their governance, and although such a state was realized in 1947, the protracted nature of the Kashmir dispute kept alive the thought that the separation from India was incomplete. Resolving the Kashmir dispute was given the highest priority in Pakistani thinking, not so much because it was about liberating oppressed Muslims, but because it justified the original partition of the subcontinent. Indeed, the quest for a resolution became more important than its actual resolution in that a protracted struggle enabled Pakistanis to renew their spiritual commitment indefinitely.

Muslim identity and renaissance were more at work in these experiences than was national purpose. The latter was sacrificed time and again by Pakistanis who were never quite convinced the nation-state served their interest or their purpose. The United States appeared on the scene almost as soon as the British departed. The nature of the American presence, a manifestation of the cold war, now with true intention to serve in the building of a new polity, was another factor beyond the ken of the region's inhabitants. How their Muslim nation could accommodate an alien force from the other side of the world, unfamiliar with South Asian Muslim experiences, was never successfully articulated. All that can be said is that Pakistan was born as a consequence of an imperial recessional. It came into a world dominated by the presence of two behemoths. Ultimately the Americans were determined to move the country in a direction it did not choose for itself. Moreover, inchoate at the time of independence and subsequently subjected to fits and starts that sapped its energy and denied institutional development, Pakistan faced its most serious challenge within itself, but, knowingly or not, outside forces also gave the nation definition and framed its self-expression.

The caretaker government

Moen Qureshi was the choice of the civil–military bureaucracy, not the politicians. Agreeing with general opinion that the politicians were the problem not the promise, Qureshi had the objective of restoring public confidence in government. Indifferent to patronage pressures and devoid of political ambition, he treated Pakistan as any other failed state. His mandate extended for three months, hardly enough time to show material achievement, but sufficient time to demonstrate what honest and purposeful leaders can accomplish. He ordered an overhaul of the economy by devaluing the rupee and by identifying those who had failed to pay their utility bills or had defaulted on their loans. Vigorous enforcement of tax obligations went hand in hand with a freeze on land distribution for political gain. To cut government expenses, he ordered the closing of fifteen ministries and ten embassies. He also imposed a levy on agriculture which was aimed to force the landed gentry to contribute to the well-being of the nation. Although all these reforms added little to the country's coffers, they nevertheless sent a message to friend and foe alike that Pakistan deserved real commitment from all sectors of society, most notably from those with the capacity to pay for the nation's development.

The Prime Minister called for sacrifices and belt-tightening measures. He also took a serious approach to drug trafficking and gun-running, and called for greater expenditure on law enforcement, health, and social welfare programs. Qureshi struck at the politicians with the same determination that he addressed miscreants and anti-social elements. He urged the politicians to pay their public debts or face a permanent ban on their political activity. Qureshi also used his United States credentials to appeal to Washington for a restoration of assistance. When he attempted to curtail the nation's nuclear program it was assumed he acted at the urging of the United States government. Although he insisted his actions were based solely on the country's needs and that Pakistanis required more medical care and education reform than nuclear weapons, his skeptics and critics were hardly convinced.

Qureshi was not all things to all Pakistanis. He was aggressive and dedicated, he was honest and selfless, but he also was an obstacle to the ambitions of many personalities in the public and private sectors. His reforms also carried negative consequences. Pakistan's inflationary problems intensified with the devaluation of the rupee. Essential commodities jumped in prices and the poor could not pay for basic necessities. Everything from wheat flour to natural gas was put beyond the reach of the masses. The Jamaat-i-Islami led the criticism against the caretaker government, but the other political parties too were not silent. Arguing it was the common folk who were most hurt by the Prime Minister's decisions, the politicians again described themselves as champions of the people. Qureshi's American connection was a ready target, as was his effort to freeze the nuclear program. The reformer therefore embittered people across the social spectrum and it was not long before calls were heard that he be dismissed from his post. Qureshi had but three months to do his work, but for many Pakistanis that was three months too many, and the call intensified for his immediate dismissal.

The caretaker government tried to remedy a serious situation but in the end it could only provide a bridge to the next election.

Qureshi returned to the United States after three brief but extraordinary months, and those experts he had asked to join him did likewise. Pakistan was returned to its traditional players and on October 6–7, 1993 elections were again held for the National Assembly. The same parties participated in the contest, a level playing field having been created between the Muslim League of Nawaz Sharif and the PPP of Benazir Bhutto. The voters showed little enthusiasm in casting their ballots and the vote split fairly evenly between the major organizations. In the end, however, the Pakistan People's Party won more seats than the Muslim League, but neither party achieved a majority. The party of Nawaz Sharif was called to accept the return of Benazir Bhutto despite the fact the Muslim League had received a higher percentage of the overall vote. Since the Islamist parties had received only a small percentage of the total vote, Nawaz had to yield to the PPP, and Benazir Bhutto was again named Prime Minister of Pakistan. Less than fifty percent of the eligible voters had actually gone to the polls and Benazir's government was constructed on softer ground than last time, but she nonetheless rose to the occasion, suggesting she had learned from previous mistakes and that this administration would be far superior to her last one.

The second Benazir Bhutto administration

During Benazir's first administration, her surviving brother, Murtaza, was permitted to return to Pakistan, and in the 1993 Sindh provincial election he won a seat for his Shaheed Bhutto Committee. Intending to play a more active role as a politician, he was shielded by his sister from those who wanted him punished for terrorist activities. At the same time he had sharp differences with Benazir which caused rifts within the family. He also shunned the PPP. Benazir shrugged off the family feud and put her efforts into forming a coalition government that could withstand the shocks that ended her earlier administration. With assistance provided by opponents of Nawaz Sharif, Benazir developed influence over the Punjab as well as Sindh provinces, but had to yield to a Muslim League coalition that drew the NWFP and Balochistan into its fold. Benazir's advantage was highlighted, however, when her candidate for the presidency, Farooq Leghari, defeated his opposition and was declared Pakistan's head of state. It was the first time the President and the head of government hailed from the same party and the development appeared to herald an era of stability and growth for the nation. The new President declared he would not interfere with the operations of government and in fact called upon the legislature to rescind the Eighth Amendment that Zia had rammed through parliament to assure his dominance of the political process. The President's sentiments found an echo in the Prime Minister's statements, and both indicated it was time that Pakistan freed itself of its colonial past, especially its viceregal tradition. More optimistic observers were quick to conclude that Pakistan had suddenly attained maturity, that a two-party system focused on competitive politics had emerged, and that a more rational and secular body politic had gained ascendancy. More battle-hardened analysts, however, were not yet ready to acknowledge a shift in Pakistani politics. The new government confronted severe economic dislocation, notably high inflation and unemployment as well as heavy debts. Pakistani society also struggled with sustained social conflict. Moreover, the level of societal violence insured the omnipresence of the civil–military establishment. The steel frame, it was said, remained the chief arbiter of the nation's ills, and hence remained a gray eminence around the Benazir government.

Nawaz Sharif had left Benazir with an economy that had not only been mismanaged but had also suffered severe debilitation from catastrophic floods and plant disease that had destroyed the cotton, rice, and sugar cane crops. Therefore much of the nation's agricultural production had been lost. Whatever gains had been made in the development of small business were lost in the failure of major enterprises. The Nawaz government had given a boost to the transport sector by inundating the country with small taxis, but this entailed the heavy expenditure of foreign exchange to pay for the vehicles. In the absence of incentives, gross investment had declined and even the subsequent actions of the caretaker government could not reverse the downturn. Fiscal management had been abominable because of the level of public and private corruption as well as the ineptitude of those charged with budgetary responsibility. National debt payments fell further behind schedule, and of course the armed services demanded so much of the national product that little was left for funding social needs. Moen Qureshi only had time to dramatize the dilemmas facing the nation. Although he made an effort to correct some of the more obvious abuses, it was left to Benazir's government to take the necessary measures that might restore a semblance of national equilibrium.

That task was complicated by Pakistan's international persona. The United States placed Pakistan on a terrorist "watch list" following increased violence in Kashmir and in India's East Punjab that was somehow linked to Islamabad. Pakistan was implicated in terrorist incidents in Europe and the United States which suggested an Afghan mujahiddin connection. Benazir also was pressured to freeze Pakistan's nuclear program. Although she refused to yield to American entreaties, the new Clinton administration sensed the Prime Minister's dilemma and sought other ways to deal with the issue. Benazir ordered five thousand Pakistani soldiers to Somalia, where they served in the United Nation's peacekeeping force. She also sent troops to Haiti and other world trouble spots, indicating her desire to assist in efforts to calm tense situations. Nevertheless, Benazir received no support for Pakistan's claim to Kashmir, nor did Clinton open channels for aid that had been blocked by the previous Bush administration. Moreover, the contest with India became more intense when the Babri Mosque, an old Mughal structure located in India, was torn down by a wild Hindu mob. Retaliation came in the form of assaults on Hindu temples and other property in Pakistan, and, in addition to communal strife, there were bombings in both India and Pakistan that were attributed to militant groups seeking vengeance. Instead of blaming extremist members of various organizations, India and Pakistan blamed each other's government for the attacks. Pakistan laid the blame on India's RAW, and India claimed Pakistan's ISI was responsible for the mayhem. Both countries expelled diplomatic personnel. They also massed troops on their mutual frontier. Skirmishes between Pakistani and Indian forces along the line of control in Kashmir also became commonplace.

Benazir had a difficult time establishing her government and addressing the nation's problems. Attacked from one side by her mother and Murtaza and on the other by Nawaz Sharif, who was still smarting from his loss of power, her defense could hardly be expected to satisfy the public. Believing she had to neutralize Nawaz, Benazir took advantage of the unstable conditions in the NWFP to prorogue the provincial government and impose governor's rule. Soon thereafter she installed a PPP government in the province and lifted the restrictions on political activity. Her opposition, however, could not remain silent in the face of this obvious effort to impose her party's rule throughout the country. Protest meetings were held from Peshawar to Islamabad and all the way to Lahore. Nawaz fought back with accusations about Benazir's dishonest political practices. He also raised questions about her personal probity, citing a banking transaction that netted the Bhutto family considerable wealth. The scandal was played up in the press and eventually it also trapped the President in an embarrassing situation. By centering attention on the excesses of Benazir and her husband, Nawaz Sharif was able to escape assaults on his own financial activity. Moreover, he managed to drive a wedge between the Prime Minister and the President.

Sensing still another attempt to force her from office, Benazir revealed that during her first administration the ISI chief had plotted to oust her, and now she implied that similar forces were trying to destroy her a second time. Benazir believed she had prevented such a recurrence by ordering the arrest of the former ISI general. Officers in the army high command, however, questioned the Prime Minister's actions and wondered if she had a genuine complaint or was simply trying to keep the military off-guard and under tight restraint. Benazir also forced the early retirement of judges of the Supreme Court and the provincial high courts, replacing them with PPP stalwarts. The arbitrary nature of this action did considerable damage to the judiciary, but Benazir knew what she wanted and paid little heed to the consequences of her decisions. Clearly, the Prime Minister was fearful of another coup and was determined to impose her will on all the branches of government.

Nawaz was not one to yield to these maneuvers. Recognizing that the army had yet to be heard from, the Muslim League leader sustained his attack on the Prime Minister. In 1994 he boarded a train in Karachi, and all along the route that proceeded north he stopped at towns and villages to berate Benazir and accuse her and her government of arbitrary and tyrannical behavior. Pakistan's survival, he declared, was in the hands of its people. Their willingness to join him in putting Benazir out of government permanently would answer the question, "whither Pakistan?" With sufficient numbers appearing to agree with his argument, Nawaz called for a national work stoppage that paralyzed a portion but not all of the country. Benazir withstood this assault, but she had ample notice that her attempt to remain in office would be difficult.

Just how difficult Benazir's course would be was seen in renewed rioting in Karachi, where the mohajirs were both the victims and perpetrators of violence. The army crackdown fell hardest on the mohajir community, however, and voices were heard insisting on the formation of "Mohajir Desh," or a separate and independent state. The exiled MQM leader, Altaf Hussain, was tried *in absentia*, found guilty of high crimes, and sentenced to twenty-seven years in prison. This action, however, was hardly the kind to bring calm to the region. The Mohajir Desh movement did not reach the proportions of the Bangladesh movement, but the army was called to action and the drastic measures taken to restore peace reminded many of the ill-fated crackdown in East Pakistan. Karachi had become the terror capital of the larger region. Bombings, assassinations, and mass murder rose to new levels. Members of the intelligentsia were singled out for no other reason than their high profile, as were members and installations of the international community. The inoperative Indian consulate was closed, but this was little more than a gesture, hardly a serious attempt to rectify the situation. It was obvious the government could not bring peace to Karachi or any other area of the country. Random murders became commonplace, as did more premeditated sectarian conflicts between Muslim Sunnis and Shiites.

Benazir's administration also was hurt by PPP defections that caused splits within the party. The only positive note was a slight rise in foreign exchange reserves and foreign investment in the energy sector. Pakistan also received assistance in the form of loans and grants from the World Bank, the International Monetary Fund, and the Asian Development Bank. In 1995, the United States Congress agreed to provide limited economic assistance and to withdraw some of the sanctions imposed in 1990. Hilary Rodham Clinton and her daughter visited Pakistan in an expression of goodwill and also as a gesture to Benazir, who was affectionately embraced by America's first family. Nothing, however, could mask Pakistan's multiple dilemmas or the shakiness of Benazir's administration.

Benazir revealed that a group within the army was again planning her overthrow. Publicly revealing they were Islamists, she said they wanted to terminate her secular government. She mentioned an unnamed major-general and several brigadiers as those leading the coup. It was their intention, she noted, to foist an Islamic state on the nation. Nothing came from this accusation, but the publicity given to the revelation highlighted the questionable status of the civilian regime. President Leghari's personal problems also caused him to distance himself from the PPP and Benazir. Complaining about the increasing influence of Asif Zardari, the President challenged Benazir to rein in her husband. He also accused Zardari of questionable business ventures in the Punjab. Moreover, because Benazir had allowed her husband to dominate PPP policy, the organization's social platform had been altered to allow for a more aggressive entrepreneurial program. This shift in PPP expression had driven many of the party's original supporters to quit the organization and form their own groups. Murtaza Bhutto and his mother also cited the change in PPP direction, arguing it did damage to the memory of Zulfikar Ali Bhutto. Murtaza promised to develop a party that resembled his father's wishes, but his Shaheed Group was not instantly popular and its existence did more to embarrass his sister's government than to firm up his personal political fortunes.

The end of the Benazir Bhutto era

Benazir's inability to reconcile friends or foes, or, for that matter, family members, only added to the mayhem coursing through the country. In 1995, in Karachi alone, more than two thousand people were murdered, and among the victims were some of the country's intellectual and artistic luminaries. Few of the perpetrators of violence, however, were identified, let alone arrested. Periodic sweeps of neighborhoods brought hundreds into custody, but the prevailing custom was to hold them briefly and then order their release for lack of evidence. Such police enforcement was hardly a deterrent to criminal acts; and the terrorists were emboldened to sustain their operations and, if anything, to increase the intensity of their assaults. Pakistan was no place to develop democratic norms, and Benazir's government was hardly in position, let alone did it enjoy the conditions, to practice democratic policy. Benazir's manipulation of the judiciary certainly was not a reflection of democratic process. Nor was the arrest in October 1995 of forty army officers, who, it was said, intended to take over the government. Again the focus was on the ISI, especially when Lieutenant-General Javed Nasir, a former head of the intelligence directorate, was declared to be the leader of the conspiracy. There was little if any evidence to implicate the accused, but the declaration of the conspiracy opened fissures within the army that forced General Kakar into retirement. He was succeeded by General Jahangir Karamat. It was unclear how the army would proceed, but observers saw the change in command as Benazir's attempt to bring the military establishment under her control.

On November 30, 1995, Benazir lashed out at what she described as the evil of tyranny. She accused the late Zia ul-Haq of so deeply wounding the country that no amount of treatment promised a cure. Identifying Nawaz Shairf as the heir to Zia's policies, she condemned what she called an "unholy alliance" of religious zealots and politicians whose sole objective was the destruction of the democratic experiment. She also offered more details about the intended coup. For the first time, she revealed the conspirators had intended killing the President, the Prime Minister, the army chief, and all the corps commanders. Saying they would have plunged the country into another civil war and converted Pakistan into a medieval representation of an Islamic state, she was grateful that the plot was uncovered before it could be implemented. Pointing to the Afghan war and the United States CIA that had armed the most radical clerics in the struggle with the Soviet Union, Benazir noted that those same radicals now wanted to control and redesign Pakistan.

Benazir's secular propensities were more in evidence following the alleged coup, but the question surfaced as to whether she was too distant from changing conditions within and just outside the country. Her tirade against the religious community came at a time when the army was torn between too much and too little emphasis on the nation's spiritual life. President Leghari's hesitation in officially designating General Karamat as the new commander of the Pakistan army was delayed until the spring of 1996 because of this dilemma. This was a critical time for the Pakistan army, especially with the ISI deeply committed to bringing order out of chaos in Afghanistan. The army's sponsorship of the Taliban, an army of madrassah-trained fighters, was just beginning to make its mark. Unleashed in Afghanistan in 1993, the Taliban was supposed to be the answer to the unrelenting blood feud between the different mujahiddin orders. The Afghans' failure to coalesce, to form a stable government following the Communist defeat, had done serious damage to an already ravaged nation. General Karamat's appointment was intended to maintain the line of succession among the Pakistan army's top officers. The President was most concerned that those officers responsible for overseeing ISI/Taliban operations not be impeded in their work. The delicate character of the situation was not lost on Benazir, but she was caught up in the need to sustain her authority and she failed to understand the gravity of the issue.

President Leghari had the greater understanding of these developments. Leghari was sensitive to the need to stabilize the army command and its control over the ISI. He was likewise concerned about the need to restore justice and balance to the political scene. Leghari replaced Bhutto's appointments to the Supreme Court with judges approved by the Pakistan Bar Association who had reputations for unfettered honesty. Benazir was not happy with the President's assertiveness, nor was Leghari pleased with Benazir's decision making. Moreover, additional allegations about a range of illicit business dealings had been made against the Prime Minister's husband. Nor was Nawaz Sharif idle. Using every opportunity to denounce the Benazir government, he found an unexpected ally in Murtaza Bhutto. And Murtaza was not the only notable to come out against Benazir. Imran Khan, a sports idol, used this moment to become a politician. Organizing the Tehrik-e-Insaaf, he too found sufficient fault with Benazir to link forces with Murtaza Bhutto.

But just as this alliance was taking form the nation was shocked by the news that Murtaza Bhutto had been killed outside his home by a police detachment. Six members of Murtaza's entourage were also shot dead, and word quickly circulated that the deaths were no accident. The young Bhutto had complained about official efforts to stifle his party as well as the arrest of seventy members of his party. But there was no evidence to prove that the police shooting was more than a response to provocation. Rumor surfaced, however, that Asif Zardari had ordered the killing. Murtaza's wife accused Zardari of arranging a contract on her husband in order to end a serious challenge to Benazir's administration. Whatever the explanation for Murtaza's violent death, the event forced President Leghari to call an end to Benazir's second administration. Leghari cited the intensification of violence in the country, Benazir's manipulation of the judicial system, her interference with administrative postings, and the rampant corruption and nepotism in her government. The President also cited the desperate economic conditions and attributed all the country's ills to the PPP's failure. Benazir made a last-minute attempt to amend the constitution to forestall her ouster but too much power was arrayed against her. On November 5, 1996 she and her government were dismissed and the National Assembly was dissolved.

Yet another caretaker government was formed, this one under the leadership of Mairaj Khalid, the aged former leader of the original PPP. Long having fallen out with Benazir, Mairaj organized a government of talents to address the country's immediate needs and to reassure the nation that the country would weather this storm as it had those before it. President Leghari functioned in tandem with the caretaker Prime Minister and ordered an overhaul of the civil bureaucracy that had been so undermined by Benazir's political intrigue. The caretaker government was granted the authority to purge the civil service of those who had colluded with the politicians. A thorough house-cleaning was forecast from the highest to the lowest levels of the administrative structure, with the purpose of restoring public confidence in government. Benazir was placed in "protective custody," a euphemism that skirted official arrest procedures, but her husband was detained on suspicion of illegal commercial transactions and on account of the need to investigate his role in Murtaza's killing. Benazir was not silenced during this latest ordeal. She accused the authorities of arbitrary actions and of kidnapping her husband. Because of the President's attempt to neutralize her, Benazir offered the thought that if anyone was responsible for her brother's death it was the President himself. Benazir wanted to know why the President included the killing of her brother in the proclamation dismissing her government. She followed this query with the thought that a pretext for dismissal had to be found, even if one had to be fabricated by sacrificing her brother.

Pakistanis were somewhat impervious to this exchange between the principal players and displayed little emotion following Benazir's departure. Conditions throughout the country were so dire that few had the inclination to express either satisfaction or anger at this latest expression of arbitrary government. Even the United States government, which had so favored Benazir, could do little more than issue a statement that noted the matter as an internal affair and said the President had acted within the terms of the constitution. Only the Pakistan judiciary could rule in Benazir's favor, but her appeal to the Supreme Court was strategically delayed to give the caretaker government the free hand needed to address the country's economic crisis and the continuing acts of social and political violence. Benazir spoke of being stabbed in the back by President Leghari, a man, she said, who had called her a sister, and a man she addressed as a brother. It was clear Benazir would not return to public office, and Mairaj declared other politicians would be placed on notice that there was no room for them in Pakistani politics, that in fact all the "feudal lords" were to be purged from the body politic.

Although the government did not declare a state of emergency, a Council for Defense and National Security (CDNS) was floated in January 1997. The CDNS included the President, the Prime Minister, the Defense Minister, the Interior Minister, the Chairman of the Joint Chiefs of Staff, the Chief of the Army Staff, the Chief of the Naval Staff, and the Chief of the Air Staff. Called an innovative approach to the constitutional system, this high-level body reflected the realities obtaining in the country. The political scene was more a charade than a true indication of real conditions.

Since the Soviet invasion of Afghanistan, Pakistan had functioned like a garrison state, the armed forces playing the central role in the country's political expression. This was certainly the case for the bulk of Zia ul-Haq's eleven years in office, and it also proved to be the case following the removal of the elected Benazir and Nawaz governments. While the politicians played at politics, the men in uniform responded to what they judged were the country's needs. Moreover, though the military avoided becoming immersed in the mundane aspects of administration, they represented the country's defense apparatus and they bore their responsibilities with considerable enthusiasm as well as confidence. Thus it was not surprising that the politicians would view the creation of the CDNS as a threat to themselves as well as to the nation's politics. Arguing that the armed forces were writing themselves into the constitutional process at the expense of the people's political representatives, they called for the order establishing the CDNS to be rescinded before it became operative.

Military power had been fused to the viceregal tradition as never before. Even though the Supreme Court upheld the constitutional legality of the Eighth Amendment that conferred special powers on the President, the formation of the CDNS meant that even without so powerful a chief executive the viceregal role could always be assumed by the generals. Zia ul-Haq had pursued a permanent place for the military in Pakistan's political life, and although he did not live to see his objective realized, those who followed him sustained the effort and now seemed poised to achieve that ambition. Crisis was not something that came and went in Pakistan. The country suffered from sustained instabilities and what at first glance might have appeared momentary had shown itself to be continuous and unending. According to the civil–military elites, it was better to write the armed forces into the system of governance than to have them act from outside the political process. The legitimacy of the military role, therefore, extended beyond the requirement of self-defense and repelling aggression. The armed forces had demonstrated repeatedly that they were the permanent guardians of domestic matters too and that their role in politics was more a necessity than an intrusion. The CDNS was designed to institutionalize that situation and to bring reality in tune with philosophy.

The second Nawaz Sharif administration

On January 16 the Lahore High Court was petitioned to rule the formation of the CDNS unconstitutional. The President also was pressured to resign for improper use of his office. On January 29, however, the Supreme Court finally declared its judgment, ruling that in removing the Benazir government the President had acted within his constitutional powers and that the country's national security was the most important reason for his action. Elections for a new National Assembly now went forward without further delay. The politicians again had their day and before the last ballot had been cast it was obvious that Nawaz Shairf and the Muslim League were the major winners. Nawaz won a significant majority in the National Assembly and did well in all the provincial legislatures. The PPP, to almost no one's surprise, was trounced, losing in every area of the country, including Benazir's own Sindh province. Nawaz Sharif's party was credited with receiving two-thirds of the total vote, and the PPP lost the leverage it had accrued in previous elections. In the space of two years Pakistan had gone from what had appeared to be a balanced two-party system, to something like a one-party dominant state. Benazir realized the futility of her situation and sought to make peace with Nawaz. Saying it was time to break the vicious circle, Benazir declared she would redefine her political activity and assume her role as leader of the opposition.

Before fading into the background Benazir called on Nawaz Sharif to beware the Eighth Amendment. Reducing the President's power, however, would not be enough. Benazir also cited the threat posed by the CDNS and she urged her former rival to neutralize this body as well. Earlier the Muslim League leader had given his support to both a strong presidency and the CDNS. Now, however, mindful of what befell Benazir, the Sharif administration began to question that position. To be head of government in fact as well as in name was the Prime Minister's greatest ambition, and achieving that status meant coming to grips once again with the real sources of power in Pakistan. Almost immediately after taking office, Nawaz moved and the National Assembly approved the repeal of Article 58 (2b) of the constitution, which gave the President the authority to dismiss the government. Adopted in a new Thirteenth Amendment the reduction of the Chief Executive's powers passed with very little debate and President Leghari signed it. Having scored a victory over the viceregal tradition, Nawaz also affirmed he would not legitimate or formalize the CDNS. Although the Pakistan army commanders still insisted their role should be written into the constitution, they were relatively content to leave the issue suspended. What seemed to matter was the military's sustained pre-eminence. For Pakistan's generals therefore the need for a formally sanctioned body like the CDNS was not worth quarreling over. Nawaz Sharif, however, interpreted army willingness to yield on the issue as a new source for his institutional power over the armed forces, and the newly elected Prime Minister took the initiative in authorizing more intense discussions with India, especially over Kashmir. The CDNS controversy and Sharif's effort at acquiring greater power, however, only obscured the rapid rise to prominence of the ISI-sponsored Taliban movement in Afghanistan.

The Nawaz Sharif government, under pressure from the army, but especially the ISI, recognized the Taliban regime that had fought its way into Kabul in 1996. By 1997 the Taliban had seized most of Afghanistan, save the northern areas where the fighting continued with rival non-Pashtu units led by a bevy of local commanders, not the least of which were Masud and Dostum. The Taliban consisted of Pashtu-speaking people who lived along the border between Afghanistan and Pakistan. Militant Sunnis, they became rigorous enforcers of the most austere form of orthodox Islam. Heavily influenced by Saudi Wahhabism and funded by Saudi Arabia as a consequence of the Soviet–Afghan war, the Taliban's ranks were swelled by Pakistani Pashtuns indoctrinated in the religious schools along the frontier. To these were added an international force composed of Arabs, Filipinos, Chechens, and others drawn from different regions of the Muslim world. Like Pakistan, Saudi Arabia and the United Arab Emirates recognized the growing and spreading influence of the Taliban, especially after Mullah Mohammad Omar, a Pashtun from the Kandahar region, declared himself the "Taliban Emir al-Mu'minin" (Commander of the Faithful). It was Mullah Omar who subsequently changed the name of Afghanistan to "The Islamic Emirate of Afghanistan."

Saudi Arabian government and business circles sent substantial sums of money to the Taliban, ostensibly to enable these austere Muslims to strengthen their Islamic state. A sizeable number of Saudi subjects also were recruited and trained to fight alongside the Taliban in their continuing struggle to dominate all of Afghanistan. The highest-profile figure among them was Osama bin Laden, a scion of one of Saudi Arabia's richest families. Bin Laden had volunteered his services to the mujahiddin in their war with the Soviet Union. In 1996 he returned to Afghanistan, where he surfaced as the leader of al-Qaeda, an organization dedicated to spreading the message of violent revolution against all non-Muslims, but particularly Americans and their supporters in and outside the Muslim states. Bin Laden moved freely between Afghanistan and Pakistan, using his wealth to attract supporters to his cause, in particular to his formation of an Islamic World Commonwealth. Soon bin Laden's al-Qaeda and the Taliban intertwined to make the Taliban a more formidable fighting force. Al-Qaeda also protected Mullah Omar, who was considered the most senior political leader of the Taliban. The Pakistan government of Nawaz Sharif, through the operations of the ISI, became a party to these developments, and thousands of Pakistanis signed up for service with both al-Qaeda and the Taliban, the two now more or less indistinguishable from one another.

Although the Taliban were credited with restoring a modicum of tranquility to areas under their control, albeit under a strict code of Islamic jurisprudence, there was no peace in the streets and villages of Pakistan, where sectarian and ethnic violence continued unabated. The rising tide of violence in Pakistan was for the moment obscured by Nawaz Sharif's success in thwarting a Supreme Court contempt of court order. The outcome of this proceeding brought the forced resignation of President Leghari and the departure of Chief Justice Sajjad Ali Shah. It is interesting to note that Nawaz had won the support, or at least the neutrality, of the army, and the latter's hands-off policy seemed to strengthen civilian rule in the country. What in fact it had done was make Nawaz Sharif more powerful than any of his predecessors and give full rein to Pakistan's more extreme Islamist organizations. Nawaz, nevertheless, had focused considerable power in the

Prime Minister's office. The Prime Minister named his own election commissioner and strengthened his legitimacy by surrounding himself with ultra-orthodox Islamic clerics. Pressing for passage of a Fifteenth Amendment to the constitution, he aimed to bypass the parliament, the judiciary, and the provincial governments by emphasizing the elevation of *Shari'a* (Islamic laws) above secular law. Unrestrained by the common law, Nawaz anticipated achieving maximum power as the leader of a Muslim people who were wholly subject to Islamic jurisprudence. Nawaz therefore had his sights on transforming Pakistan into an Islamic state only slightly different from Afghanistan under the Taliban. Talk of the Talibanization of Pakistan circulated throughout the country, much to the distress of those Pakistanis who feared a complete merger of politics with religion.

Fearing a threat to their traditional local authority, and perhaps more so a Punjabi attempt to monopolize political life in the country, representatives from Sindh, Balochistan, and the NWFP protested their loss of autonomy, and cries were heard for restructuring Pakistan along multinational lines. They called for the drafting of a new constitution that would guarantee the independence of the different regions, and twenty-eight ethnic and regional organizations came together to form the Pakistan Oppressed Nations Movement (PONM). The PONM called for a loose federation of autonomous and sovereign ethnic nations. It demanded that each be considered a "state" under the 1940 Lahore (Pakistan) Resolution and that each unit be vested with the necessary powers to function in accordance with the customs and traditions of its population. The Pakistan Oppressed Nations Movement also received encouragement from the PPP, which had joined with fourteen small parties to create the Pakistan Awami Itehad (Pakistan People's Alliance). During the same period, Farook Leghari formed his Millat Party. All these maneuvers appeared to be aimed at preventing Nawaz Sharif from emulating the Afghan Emir, Mullah Omar.

The linkage between political developments in Pakistan and Afghanistan had became clearer. With the Pakistan army straddling both countries and with Islam the central motif of their respective political systems, the objectives of the two states began to coincide. Afghanistan had demonstrated greater momentum for the realization of an Islamic state. The Taliban had been a welcome arrival for an Afghan people exhausted from almost two decades of brutal warfare. And though the Taliban imposed severe limitations on individual behavior, the vast majority of Afghans appeared to tolerate the harshness of their Islamic code. Pakistan, by contrast, had escaped a sustained assault on its territory, excepting the loss of East Bengal, one thousand miles to the east, and what remained of the western region was more a threat to itself than threatened from outside. The veneer of sophistication and civility that projected a global personality for the modern Pakistan, however, had rubbed thin with the sustained emphasis on Islamization. Forces never judged mainstream had become a mighty river and in the circumstances associated with national catharsis a different standard had been established for the measurement of Pakistani behavior.

Religious minorities were at particular risk in the new circumstances. Long the targets of majority community abuse, Ahmadiyya and Christians were prominent victims of the self-appointed purifiers of Islamic spirituality. Blasphemy laws were approved by the Muslim League dominated National Assembly which called for the death penalty against those deemed disrespectful of the Prophet, or who challenged the interpretation of scripture. In May 1997, a Faisalabad court sentenced a poor and illiterate Christian to death for misspeaking the name of the Prophet. A local Christian priest protested the court proceeding and the sentence by taking his own life, but nothing seemed to stem the violence. Punjabi villages, where minority groups had lived side by side with orthodox Muslims for generations, were almost overnight transformed into hamlets of communal blood-letting. Subject to vilification, beatings, and death, minorities looked to the government for assistance but the latter failed time and again in its mission to defend the persecuted. Not only were Christians assaulted as never before, but sectarian contests between Shiites and Sunnis attained new levels of violence. Again officials were slow to react to maintain law and order, let alone to mete out justice. The breakdown of civil society was also seen in the rising levels of criminal behavior. No one could claim security on the nation's highways or in their homes as gangs of thieves and cut-throats operated at will and without fear of retribution.

Not everyone in the Pakistan army ignored the intensification of ethnic, sectarian, and criminal violence. Nor was the army prepared to see Nawaz Sharif amass unchecked political power. Moreover, the greater the Prime Minister's quest for absolute power, the more the country seemed to slip into anarchy. It simply did not follow that an all-powerful civilian executive translated into a more secure society. Nawaz had appointed an acknowledged nobody to serve as Pakistan's President. Rafiq Tarar, who took office on January 1, 1998, was known for only one thing, his friendship with and complete subordination to the Prime Minister. Tarar's presidency meant Nawaz Sharif had a free hand in amassing the power to satisfy his needs, but it also meant the country would be left without the necessary institutional strength to deal with the multitude of national issues. Nepotism and blatant corruption were hallmarks of the Nawaz Sharif government. Pakistan's economy was allowed to decline to new depths. The only advantages accrued to Nawaz Sharif's get-rich courtiers, who lavished rewards upon themselves in open view of a semi-paralyzed public.

Democracy was nothing more than a sham. The Prime Minister and his minions operated without the intended constitutional constraints. The Pakistan Supreme Court listed government violations of fundamental rights, rule making by ordinance, and gross displays of arbitrary decision making. Although the Supreme Court tried to rectify the wrongs by judicial action, the Sharif regime did not deviate from its venal pursuits or its goal of achieving absolute power. Only the army high command was in a position to deflect the Nawaz steamroller. The task of taking on the Prime Minister therefore fell to the Chief of the Army Staff, General Jehangir Karamat. In an unusual display of candor, Karamat made a number of public statements about his personal concerns. Indicating that the Nawaz Sharif government had exposed the nation to problems that threatened its very existence, the General expressed the opinion that only the armed forces were in position to organize as an alternative.

In October 1998, Karamat raised anew the question of the armed forces and their constitutional duty: the notion of a National Security Council composed of uniformed officials and supported by the best civilian brains in the country. Karamat did not reject the Islamists, but it was obvious from his presentation that he believed the country could not survive guided by the more primitive members of the Islamic tradition. Nawaz, as those before him, had nurtured the fundamentalists and, knowingly or not, had fertilized and watered the seeds of division and blind hatred. The bitter fruit derived from internecine and sectarian conflict had caused alienation and despair. Insisting there must be a return to rational government, Karamat called for an end to mindless vendettas in the name of religion and ethnic identity. A polarized nation was a nation in conflict with itself, and he reminded his listeners that Pakistan was a dream of salvation for Muslims of the subcontinent, but it was also a positive statement about the future of the human condition. Pakistan was meant to be a national state and only a national design provided a home for diverse people. Indeed, Pakistan was created in the belief that Muslims were comfortable in a country that embraced people of different ethnic backgrounds. Karamat called for the refashioning of a professional apolitical bureaucracy with the capacity to administer a complex society. Pakistanis, he seemed to suggest, had been too long at war with one another. It was time to call a truce, and nothing would benefit the nation more than a period of extended calm. People needed to ponder what brought them to this moment so that a course more in keeping with popular need could be identified. If the Nawaz Sharif administration did not take on this responsibility, a substitute administration would have to be found. Not unexpectedly, Sharif found Karamat's presentation a serious breech of trust and demanded Karamat's resignation.

Though not oblivious to the clash between Sharif and Karamat, the army high command was too preoccupied with other matters to come to the defense of the Chief of the Army Staff. In May 1998, Pakistan entered the circle of select nuclear powers when, following India's lead, it detonated six nuclear devices. The Pakistan army also publicly demonstrated its surface-to-surface missile capability by successfully launching intermediate range rockets wholly manufactured in Pakistan. Pakistan thus signaled to New Delhi that it would no longer cow before India's military prowess. The Pakistani generals also had to weigh the international repercussions of their demonstration, including the cost to the country of the economic and military sanctions imposed by the

United States and European governments. Furthermore, the war in Afghanistan ruptured Islamabad's relations with Teheran when the latter opposed the Taliban and supported Masud's Northern Alliance. Pakistan's connection to Osama bin Laden also came under greater scrutiny. Thus, when the American embassies in Kenya and Tanzania were destroyed with heavy loss of life, the Clinton administration launched missile strikes at some of bin Laden's camps in Afghanistan and it came as no surprise that the heaviest criticism of the American action came from Pakistan.

With so much of consequence consuming the time and energy of the army commanders, Karamat's criticism of the Sharif government received scant attention. The Prime Minister's choice for the new army COAS was General Pervez Musharraf, a general in the lower tier of commanding officers, but, most important, an officer Nawaz believed he could successfully manage. Sworn in on October 7, 1998, Musharraf had been selected by Nawaz's inner circle. Sharif believed that the General, as the son of an Indian refugee, an Urdu member of the Karachi mohajir community, would be more pliable than a Punjabi or Pashtun. Moreover, Sharif was confident Musharraf would be too focused on managing the generals in his command to meddle in civilian politics. Unlike Karamat, therefore, Musharraf was expected to ally himself with the Muslim League administration.

Anatomy of a coup

Nawaz Sharif talked about democracy, but his administration was more like a Mughal court. Nawaz ignored the conventions of cabinet government: he neither held cabinet meetings nor made cabinet decisions. Surrounded by family members and a few close associates, Sharif's actions were more in tune with absolute monarchy than with representative government. A pompous and sanctimoniously self-righteous individual, he trusted few and suspected almost everyone. Without direct access to his thoughts, one can only assume he envisaged himself the fountainhead of power in a modern Sultanate rather than the elected and accountable leader of a sovereign people.

Of course, the people of Pakistan were denied their sovereignty in the early years after partition. Sovereignty belonged to the

Eternal, and only God's vicegerent was considered worthy of managing the earthly domain. By extension, therefore, the Muslim state's leaders were ordained to rule, and for the most part to rule absolutely. Sharif embodied the governing style of God's anointed; he also chose to inject a quality of mystery into his administration. Moreover, his Islamist tendencies allowed him to evoke a Pakistan guided by the spiritual instincts imbedded in the psyche of the nation. Since he allied with and encouraged the more primitive elements in the Islamic tradition, conservative orders otherwise obscured by more sophisticated and worldly ideas flowered and multiplied. Energized by the unfinished business in Kashmir and the revolutionary character of Islam in Iran and Afghanistan, as well as the emergence of the Muslim republics of Central Asia, an ambience had materialized that spoke of the death of the European-contrived national state and the rebirth of a historic Islamic order. Nawaz Sharif's perception of the world was hardly different from his perception of a future Pakistan. Pakistan was to be the central actor in the unfolding of a new and glorious chapter in the history of the Islamic people.

Jinnah had resisted the forces of fundamentalism in the years before independence, and Nawaz Sharif was no Jinnah. Moreover, although the Islamists could be ignored, as was the case from Jinnah to Yahya Khan, they could not be eliminated. The distance between the educated few and the undereducated many could not be ignored. Nor was it possible to prevent the poor and illiterate masses from seeking the services of the Islamic fundamentalists who contributed little to the establishment and sustenance of the Pakistani nation. Consumed by a mindset conditioned by extraterritorial and supernatural experience, the self-styled representatives of Islamic tradition more than the secular politicians articulated the concerns and needs of the great, unspoken-for majority. The secular symbols of independence and self-government could not be expected to compete with the expositors of religious ritual. Shunted aside by the enlightened leaders of the Pakistan Movement, the clerics saw in the formation of a Muslim state in the subcontinent not the end, but rather the beginning of a process. Pakistan's emergence as an independent state was the beginning of a transformation that would not be complete until the Islamic *ummah* had manifested itself in the tradition of the *salifiyya*, the building of a righteous and pious community of believers from one end of the Islamic world to the other.

The only institution to survive Pakistan's first half century was the Pakistan army. Denied in Kashmir and battered by the civil war in East Bengal, the army nonetheless prevailed. Humbled by the Indian army that had dismembered the original Pakistan, the Pakistan army of General Zia ul-Haq saw the opportunity to retrieve victory from defeat by emphasizing the army's Islamic bona fides. The Soviet invasion of Afghanistan indicated that Islam faced danger not only in India but in Afghanistan as well and that Pakistan could reclaim its purpose by helping the Afghan people to repel the aggressor. Followers of the Prophet could not avoid being caught up in this struggle and the Muslims who answered the Afghan call for assistance journeyed to that remote land from the margins of the Islamic world. Already energized by the Ayatollah Khomeini in Iran, Islam became the leitmotif for an ingathering of believers, all dedicated to a single cause, not just the freeing of Afghanistan, but the liberation of the Muslim *ummah*.

Thus the once contained Islamists of Pakistan were transformed into major agents of change. Roles were reversed as the more contemporary members of Pakistani society sought refuge in obscurity at home or domicile in distant lands. Nawaz Sharif's manner of governance was proof that the original understanding of democracy had lost its relevance. No Pakistani politician had enjoyed the power that Nawaz manifested at the beginning of the last year of the twentieth century. It did not matter that he had alienated the conventional politicians or had caused severe distress in the regions outside the Punjab. Not yet satiated, Nawaz Sharif connived to entrench himself in a political process that no longer represented constitutional constraints, a process that he had manipulated to satisfy his personal need for even greater authority. Only the Press appeared to challenge his grab for total power, and in January 1999 the Prime Minister called for the sacking of a number of reporters and commentators who had the temerity to criticize his government. When the Press resisted the Prime Minister's complaint, the administration found other ways to bring compliance. Charges of tax evasion and the misuse of privilege were hurled at the fourth estate, and in May prominent journalists were arrested and others were intimidated by undercover intelligence agents.

The administration's bad press disturbed more balanced members of the Pakistan Muslim League who used more conventional tactics in tackling their adversaries in the other parties. Seeking a rapprochement with the NWFP Awami National Party and Karachi's Muttehida Qaumi Movement (the revised name of the MQM), the Muslim Leaguers called for a new alliance and a power-sharing arrangement that would enhance all their policies. The opposition parties, however, were so disgusted with the Prime Minister that they refused to accept the offer. The Punjab's expanding power had come at the expense of the smaller provinces and minorities, and their Oppressed Nations Movement represented their best chance to balance the larger province's power. Moreover, some Punjabis connected with the Nawaz regime had incited religious conflict in both the NWFP and Balochistan, and the most radical of the Islamists had raised a demand for the Talibanization of the frontier region. Sindh, however, was the scene of even more intensive conflict. Governor's rule had been imposed in the province in October 1998 and by the end of the year the government had established summary military courts to mete out justice to those found guilty of violating the peace of the region. Two death sentences were carried out under these military tribunals before the Supreme Court in February 1999 declared the military courts unconstitutional. Checked by the Supreme Court, Nawaz appointed a personal adviser to be the virtual chief minister in Sindh province. This adviser, Ghous Ali Shah, appointed a council of advisers to act as a provincial cabinet, all without any reference to Sindh's elected legislature and a clear violation of provincial autonomy.

The Sindh takeover was as much a reflection of opposition disarray as it was a demonstration of the Prime Minister's power. The politicians continued to be their own worst enemies as they failed again and again to reconcile their differences or to sustain their efforts to weaken the ruling regime. The Pakistan Oppressed Nations Movement ceased to be an effective organization as member groups defected and rival politicians insisted on finding fault with their peers. The PPP too was wanting. Benazir had little option but to remain in exile after being convicted on several counts of corruption. She had been sentenced to a five-year term in prison. Without her peculiar gifts and charismatic qualities, the party could not expect to mount a challenge to the Pakistan Muslim League, and it was obvious from the statements of PPP party officials that only the Pakistan army could derail the Nawaz Sharif juggernaut.

The army, however, had more immediate problems. In May a full-scale engagement erupted in the high mountain Kargil region of Kashmir. Although Pakistan claimed the action had been initiated by Kashmiri freedom fighters, New Delhi provided a different account. India argued the Kargil operation had been launched from the highest level of the Pakistan government and army. Rumor circulated that General Pervez Musharraf had ordered the operation to demonstrate to his Punjabi and Pashtun comrades that he was committed to wresting Kashmir from Indian control. Kargil overlooked a strategic pass that India used to ferry supplies to its forces. If Pakistan gained control of the region, Islamabad believed its leverage in negotiating a Kashmir settlement would be considerably enhanced. Thus the campaign was approved and Pakistani troops, disguised as guerrillas, moved into the region. India, however, was prepared for the incursion, and from May to July its troops struggled to beat back the invading force. Both sides suffered heavy losses, but the Pakistanis took the more severe punishment and what was left of the force retreated back across the line of control. The Nawaz government was embarrassed by the failure and insisted it knew nothing about the operation. Holding to its position of denial and faced with international criticism, the Nawaz government tried to place all the blame for the Kargil operation on General Musharraf.

General Musharraf was to be Nawaz Sharif's sacrificial lamb. Replacing him, however, proved anything but simple. Senior commanders of the Pakistan army had reason to stand by their COAS. It was the Prime Minister, not Musharraf, who gave the order to terminate the Kargil campaign, and despite their losses the commanders clung to the view they could overcome Indian superiority. The Prime Minister's decision, therefore, was not popular. Karamat's dismissal now received belated attention and the move to dismiss still another COAS was judged intolerable. The generals refused to give homage, nor did they view Sharif's accumulation of power as in their interests. Determining that only they stood before the Prime Minister's intention to acquire absolute dominance, Musharraf's colleagues decided to stand by the General. Nor was Musharraf oblivious to the storm swirling around him. There was common agreement that nothing less than the future of the army was at stake, and the decision was taken to resist the Prime Minister's action. Sharif was pressured to announce that Musharraf would remain COAS until his term expired in October 2001.

Sharif, however, had no intention of keeping that pledge. He immediately moved to retire a number of generals and to shift others to different assignments. The Inter-Services Intelligence was also active in promoting the Prime Minister's wishes, and the ISI reported on meetings between Musharraf and some of the corps commanders. The generals therefore were forced to be circumspect in their actions. Not only were they dealing with a very powerful political personality; they also had to contend with the ISI and other officers who wanted Musharraf removed. While the Prime Minister and his henchmen proceeded with their behind-the-scenes maneuvers, a counter-plan was developed by Musharraf and those loyal to his command.

Musharraf left on a prearranged visit to Sri Lanka on October 9, 1999, while his brother officers planned the takeover of the country and the removal of the government. These plans were not as secret as they had wanted. The opposition parties had called for major demonstrations against the Sharif government. They had also renewed their call for the army to depose the Prime Minister. Sensing an impending coup, Sharif had sent his brother and ISI General Ziauddin to Washington with the hope of getting the Clinton administration to lift its sanctions in return for Pakistan's acceptance of the Comprehensive Test Ban Treaty and greater cooperation in the search for bin Laden. The Americans were told to ignore the complaints of Benazir Bhutto and Imran Khan and to acknowledge the threat to the democratically elected government. Thus, there was some relief in Islamabad when the U.S. government issued a series of statements calling for the preservation of stability and the upholding of constitutional principle. It was obvious that both sides were using the United States and that neither had any intention of satisfying American wishes.

Nawaz Sharif made a sudden flight to the United Arab Emirates on October 11, but left the next day. By October 12, Nawaz had returned to Pakistan and he immediately ordered Musharraf's return flight from Colombo to be diverted and prevented from landing in Pakistan. Lieutenant-General Ziauddin, the Director General of the ISI, was ushered into the Prime Minister's official residence and told he would replace Musharraf as COAS. The generals loyal to Musharraf, however, rejected the Prime Minister's action. They also prevented Islamabad television and radio stations from announcing the change. Pro-Musharraf forces immediately moved to secure the Rawalpindi cantonment as well as critical installations in the capital. Moreover, the Prime Minister's house was surrounded and Nawaz was urged to rescind his dismissal order. When he refused he was arrested along with General Ziauddin.

True to the Prime Minister's instructions, Karachi officials prevented Musharraf's plane from landing. However, the crew of the PIA (Pakistan International Airways) plane, with two hundred passengers aboard, indicated that fuel was running low and that the aircraft could not remain aloft or fly to another destination. Thanks to the pleas of the pilot, the plane was called to a landing site at Nawabshah, more than one hundred miles north of Karachi, and the authorities were alerted to arrest Musharraf as he deplaned. In the ensuing moments, word reached Karachi Corps Headquarters that Islamabad had been seized by the commanding generals and that Nawaz had been arrested along with the ISI chief. The Karachi cantonment was instantly mobilized. Units of the Pakistan army captured the Karachi airport and took into custody the bureaucrats and officials of the Nawaz administration. All of Karachi soon came under military rule, and the plane carrying General Musharraf was finally allowed to land. On the ground and surrounded by officers from Karachi Army Headquarters, Musaharraf declared the Nawaz Sharif government had been removed, that the President would remain in office, but that all government agencies had come under army control.

Bibliography

Kennedy, Charles, ed., *Pakistan 1992*, Boulder: Westview, 1993.
Kennedy, Charles and Rais, Rasul Bakhsh, eds., *Pakistan 1995*, Westview, 1995.

Magnus, Ralph H., "Afghanistan in 1997: The War Moves North," *Asian Survey*, 38 (2), 1998, pp. 109–15.

Neamatollah Nojumi, *The Rise of the Taliban in Afghanistan: Mass Mobilization, Civil War, and the Future of the Region*, New York: Palgrave, 2002.

Rizvi, Hasan-Askari, "Pakistan in 1998: The Polity under Pressure," *Asian Survey*, 39 (1), 1999, pp. 177–84.

Rizvi, Hasan-Askari, "Pakistan in 1999: Back to Square One," *Asian Survey*, 40 (1), 2000, pp. 208–18.

Shadid, Anthony, *Legacy of the Prophet: Despots, Democrats, and the New Politics of Islam*, Boulder: Westview, 2001.

Syed, Anwar, "Pakistan in 1997: Nawaz Sharif's Second Chance to Govern," *Asian Survey*, 38 (2), 1998, pp. 116–25.

9

THE POLITICS OF TERRORISM

Another military coup and another wild celebration in the streets of Pakistan. Another unpopular albeit elected government had succumbed to its own excesses, and another army commander had seized the reins of power. It had become so familiar, almost predictable. It was more than fifty years since independence but Pakistan was still in search of a political framework to contain its errant society. The country that strove to be a nation had demonstrated yet again that national unity had no more reality than half a century before. National identity remained elusive as one millennium ended and another began. After so many tests and so much tragedy there was ample evidence to prove Pakistan was meant to be but never became a nation-state. A divided people at the outset, Pakistan remained a divided country. The vast gulf separating the enlightened minority from the traditional majority, the educated from the uneducated, the contemporary achievers from those rooted in past circumstances was never bridged. So many failed personalities had aspired to lead the entity called Pakistan. So much energy had been expended, so many dreams dashed, so many promises unrealized, so much rethinking, so much maneuvering, that as the year 1999 gave way to 2000, only exhaustion and lamentations were left to remind those still caring what had been the vision and what had become reality.

No one had truly charted Pakistan's future. Too little time as well as the pressure of events denied any would-be leader from designing a program that could be embraced by all the people calling themselves Pakistanis. A creature molded by the two great wars of the twentieth century, Pakistan was born into the cold war and was never really free to imagine a destiny different from the one ordained by its colonial mentor. Made an instant adversary of its adjacent and larger neighbor by a colonial power in haste to remove itself from the burden of empire, Pakistan was destined to remain an incomplete idea rather than the living model of an oriental society transformed by global exposure. Social conflict not constructive performance symbolized Pakistan. Hostility from without defined its ethos, and penetrated the core of the nation, and as it defined relationships abroad, so too it defined the condition that would pit one Pakistani against another, separate one region from another, and do terrible violence to the national idea. The civil war devoured the idea that Muslims, no matter how disparate, how different in expression, how distant in geography, were still a single and harmonious people. The new Pakistan tried to bury the memory of that horrific bloodletting, but no matter the effort to conceal it, the legacy of internecine conflict could not be expunged. Moreover, the war in East Bengal cut more deeply than the communal strife at partition. The latter was sublimated as a price of independence, whereas the former proved to be the very denial of the country created at independence.

Pakistan's failure to accept its shortcomings, and they were legion, caused it to live with falsehood and conceal truth. It was not yet a nation, and even its status as a country was questioned. Allusions to unity and national resolve were addressed by the country's armed forces that were never far removed from their colonial origin. Repeated army intervention in Pakistan's political life was never meant to be more than the interposition of power between the forces of anarchy and those believing in a workable future. A surrogate for the departed colonial authority, the military remained in place so that the country could find time to correct course and seek an appropriate path. But the military would not be content with a mere holding action. Nor would external events permit the luxury of trial and error. Army leaders were by calling responsible for international matters, but they also became astute observers of the domestic situation. As if waiting on a maturing polity, they expected that the politicians would learn their roles and perform the tasks of governance with the same professionalism expected in the uniformed services.

Army intervention in the country's political life was encouraged, indeed welcomed. But the soldiers, it was said, remained too long. Given the frailties of Pakistan's institutions, the repeated disrespect for constitutions and the rule of law, only the army could effectively challenge runaway political power; but having called the army to such service, those who would advantage themselves from its actions would just as soon have it disappear. This the soldiers were not prepared to do. Claiming only they were capable of seeing both the international and domestic horizons, the army commanders extended their stay, outlived their welcome, and were themselves made the subject of popular condemnation. Observers of the Pakistan scene long ago convinced themselves that the army was not the answer but the problem in all that ailed the country. Pakistan's democratic growth, it has been argued, was stifled by military intrusion. Moreover, it was the military that prompted the violence that eventually overwhelmed the country. Liaisons between the armed forces and the more rabid elements in Pakistan society were seen as relationships between like-minded actors, neither of which wanted Pakistan to emerge as a democratic state. Religion not democracy was their unifying principle, and they found common ground after the Soviet invasion of Afghanistan.

But not only the Pakistan army was to blame for the failure of democracy in Pakistan. Nor did the army stand apart from society in encouraging the Islamists to play their narrow game. The Kashmir issue was made the responsibility of the army, but the dispute was neither prompted nor sustained by the men in uniform. Kashmir was a defining experience for Pakistanis before and even more so after the loss of East Pakistan. The army was called to service a demand it came to make its own, not out of ideological commitment, but as a consequence of geostrategic concerns. If the two eventually intermingled it was just as much a consequence of popular fervor as it was a calculated decision by military thinkers. The same could be said of the army's role in Islamization. As strongly committed to religious issues as they were, the soldiers were no more identified with spiritual causes than their civilian compatriots. The men who led the armed forces were just as committed to secular objectives as their counterparts in high political circles. Both addressed the mundane as much as they did the eternal, both found in the eclectic experience the merging of worldviews. Neither the one nor the other was a better representative of secular or religious calling.

Pakistan shifted course more firmly to Islamization even as it found fault with the General whose name was attached to that policy. Moreover, Islamization was as much a reaction to the civil war as it was to the deep-felt need to realize the Muslim genius in Pakistan. Islamization was also a potent weapon in the clash of arms with the Soviet Union in Afghanistan. The Soviets could not be matched as a military machine, but what advantage they gained from their superpower status was more than offset by the willingness of those resisting their intrusion to fight and die for a particular cause. Religion became the central factor in the war in Afghanistan, a war the Soviet Union did not lose, but also could not win. Pakistan, and its army, could not stand idle while Afghanistan was being assaulted. Both geopolitics and religion played important roles. Moreover, the heavy role played by the United States in sponsoring the Islamization of the war while opposing Islamization in revolutionary Iran reveals that it was not just Pakistanis who were uncertain about their course of action. Act now and worry later was a condition that permeated the struggle. But the ambivalence of Pakistan's support and the failure to effectively manage complex social issues complicated the methods of providing support. They also confused the issue of who would be the preferred recipients of that support.

Domestic violence within Pakistan had been a fact of life from the moment the country achieved independence. Terrorism was an ancient phenomenon in the subcontinent. If it was not given serious attention it was because, domestically, it was so common an occurrence and, internationally, it failed to register an impact. Terror and the use of terror to achieve goals not approached through other means were considered a law-and-order matter, and so long as terrorism could be contained or localized, its impact was considered marginal. Terrorism during the colonial period therefore represented a form of popular protest that was either containable or a matter of political leverage in achieving specific goals. But the independence of Pakistan, its inchoate nature, its sustained turmoil, its numerous struggles within itself as well as with its neighbors brought a new dimension to the subject of terrorism. An ill-defined country, containing contradictory forces, Pakistan also sought a measure of status in the wider world. Its people poor and largely illiterate, Pakistan nevertheless progressed along a scale of material and physical achievement that caused people to subsume its real condition. Technological and scientific achievements were the work of the few not the many, however, and it was the few who in 1998 ushered Pakistan into the circle of nuclear weapons powers.

The Pakistan house was in disarray, its basic infrastructure primitive and failing, but nothing had prevented the country from acquiring nuclear capability. The contrast between such scientific achievement and the pitiful economic status of most of the country's population can be compared with the quest for sophisticated democratic institutions by the few and the conception of an Islamic state for the many. It was the interfacing of future and past that elevated the terror factor in Pakistan. Militant Islamists presented themselves as the bridge between the world of the future and the world of tradition. Rejecting secular performance as blasphemous, militant Islamists adopted a form of reverse Marxism to explain their violent purpose. Marx's opiate became the Islamists' elixir. As Marx had forecast the dialectical struggle between economic classes, so the Islamists echoed a parallel refrain in the clash between the familiar Muslim religious tradition and the less familiar secular outlook. Unlike Marx, however, who addressed the dynamics of historical progress and called for the unity of the downtrodden, the militant Islamists spoke a language that described and glorified a history that centered more on distinguishing the eternally righteous from the eternally damned. Marx summoned the workers of the world to unite against their managerial oppressors and assume control of their destiny. The Islamists called on tradition-bound Muslims, the vast majority reliving through daily ritual a cherished past, to cast off those who threatened their obeisance. Marx centered his philosophy on the synthesis of all that went before; militant Islamists rejected synthesis in their effort to reclaim an original thesis. Marx was focused on a utopian future, the Islamists on a resurrected past.

Pakistan's failure to address the searing issue of mass education is writ large in the appeal of the Islamists among the general masses. Moreover, the failure of Pakistan's modernists to satisfy minimum objectives, namely the formation of civil society, is writ large in the emergence of a leadership that long dwelled in the shadows of national experience. What had been marginal, with the passage of time, and particularly with the failure of the country's modernists, had become mainstream. The Islamists had captured the imagination of the many, and the few who had represented themselves as leaders and agents of change were forced to the sidelines or pressured to follow along. The most militant among the Islamists are those who took the lead, their violent acts targeting the perceived alien flotsam of Pakistani society. The war in Afghanistan gave the Islamists a defined enemy and permitted them to network with those across the Muslim world who shared their narrow interpretation of scripture as well as their willingness to confront an identifiable enemy. Just as Afghanistan became the catalyst for an interlocking of the faithful, so too Kashmir became for Pakistani radicals and their supporters the defining issue in the destruction of the secular state.

Linkages between the Pakistan military establishment and the militant Islamists were forged in the unresolved Kashmir dispute. So closely aligned were the two that it became difficult to distinguish the one from the other. The 1999 Kargil incident was just the latest example of the blurring of lines between those professing Islamic and national goals. The Pakistan army's role in Afghanistan could not end with the withdrawal of Soviet forces. Too committed to an Islamic solution, Pakistan identified with the Taliban and the Taliban in turn joined hands with the Afghan Arabs associated with Osama bin Laden. The holy war against the chief representative of Marxism had been won, but the war against the new infidels of northern Afghanistan and elsewhere had just begun. So too the renewed struggle in Kashmir.

Pakistan's allies in the al-Qaeda and the sundry movements it spawned to make war in Kashmir were far more responsive to the military's established goals than anything experienced during the years of global cold war. In alliance with a cross-section of the Muslim world, Pakistan envisaged a payoff that could never be realized in its alliances with the United States and the West. But intimacy with militant Islamists also posed a potential link between the latter and the weapons of mass destruction the Pakistan army had so energetically made their goal. In the marriage of Islamic militancy with Pakistan army policy, there arose the possibility of the sharing of nuclear weapons capability. Terrorism had assumed new and more terrifying dimensions. It was in these circumstances that General Pervez Musharraf assumed the leadership of the Pakistan government. Not only did the future of Pakistan hang in the balance, but the future of the subcontinent, the extended region, and indeed the world would be affected by this latest Pakistan army coup.

The Musharraf factor

Born in 1943 in India, Pervez Musharraf was a member of an educated Syed family residing in Allahabad. His father, Musharraf-ud-Din, was a long-term professional in the Indian civil service, who following the partition of the subcontinent moved the family to Pakistan, where he served in the new Pakistan diplomatic service. He retired in 1974. Musharraf's educated mother was an official in the International Labor Organization until 1987. Pervez received his education at St. Patrick's School in Karachi, and subsequently Foreman Christian College in Lahore. He entered the Pakistan Military Academy at Kakul in 1961 and was commissioned an artillery officer in 1964. Musharraf led his troops in the Khem Karan, Lahore, and Sialkot sectors during the 1965 war with India and was decorated for heroism. After the war he volunteered for the Special Services Group of elite commandos, spending seven years with the force. Active in the 1971 war with India, he rose to the rank of Company Commander in a commando battalion. An expert in self-propelled artillery, he was later promoted to Brigadier and given command of an infantry brigade, and later an armored division. In 1995 he was promoted to Lieutenant-General and functioned in a variety of staff positions. Connected to the Command and Staff College at Quetta and the National Defense College in Rawalpindi, Musharraf was made responsible for the advanced training of combat officers. Later, he was appointed Director General Military Operations in the Pakistan army's General Headquarters. On October 7, 1998 he was promoted to General and made Chief of the Army Staff. On April 9, 1999 he was given the added responsibility of Chairman of the Joint Chiefs of Staff Committee.

Musharraf's distinguished military career brought him to the attention of Prime Minister Nawaz Sharif, but it was his mohajir status that convinced him the General would be pliant and hence subject to his will. Otherwise, there was nothing in Musharraf's record to indicate weakness or subservience. A disciplined soldier, Musharraf always demonstrated loyalty to the chain of command. He served faithfully under Ayub and Yahya as well as Zia. He also accepted the return to civilian-led government in 1972 and again in 1988. He was not known as a dabbler in politics. His professional bearing had brought him to the highest rank in the Pakistan army and it was anticipated he would complete his term as COAS and retire to civilian life in November 2001. Destiny, however, ruled otherwise. The Kargil fiasco and Sharif's grab for absolute power had targeted the General, who responded with the assistance of other commanding officers who did not want to see another of their own humiliated and stripped of his authority. Nor did they want the director of the ISI, much their junior, to succeed to the army's highest post. Musharraf was obviously the choice of a coterie of generals now opposed to the Prime Minister. The COAS responded to this crisis as he had to the others during his long career, with firmness and dedication.

However, Musharraf did not declare martial law. The 1973 constitution was suspended but not abrogated. President Rafiq Tarar was permitted to remain as head of state but was confined to a ceremonial role. Musharraf contented himself with the unique title of Chief Executive and he assumed all the responsibility for managing government policy. The state of emergency declared by the Prime Minister in 1998 was allowed to stand, but the political parties were permitted to function as normal. The press too was notified it was free to publish criticism so long as it did not undermine the Chief Executive's authority or threaten the security of the country. The judiciary was sanctioned to operate in accordance with its self-determined schedules and no military tribunals were contemplated. The provinces, however, came under the direction of governors appointed from the military services or from retired military personnel. Balochistan was made an exception when a former chief justice of the High Court was made governor of that province. Overall, the armed forces remained in their conventional roles and the country's civil servants administered public affairs.

Besides from the Chief Executive's office the only other unique arrangement was the formation of a National Security Council composed of the commanding officers of the different services, and a federal cabinet that reported to Musharraf as the head of government. Musharraf and his colleagues were quick to put Pakistanis on notice that elections would not be held for the foreseeable future. All efforts, Musharraf declared, would be centered on maintaining law and order, restoring national morale, balancing rival provincial interests, and reviving an economy devastated by illicit practices and blatant corruption. Musharraf also promised administrative reform, the strengthening of local self-government, and punishment of those who had violated the public trust. In a manner reminiscent of the caretaker government of Moen Qureshi, Musharraf was determined to expose those who had exploited their positions to accumulate private wealth. Tax evaders and those in arrears on bank loans or failing to pay for public services were ordered to pay what they owed or face the consequences.

Nawaz Sharif and his brother, Shabaz, were singled out along with several other officials. They were accused of actions detrimental to the country. Treason, engaging in criminal conspiracy, and aircraft hijacking were some of the major charges brought against the former Prime Minister and his colleagues. Nawaz was accused of making war on the country and initially was brought before the Anti-Terrorism Court that he himself had established. The fate of the Muslim League leader hung in the balance. Sensing a repeat of Bhutto's trial and execution, numerous governments around the world questioned the military's actions in not only deposing elected officials but threatening them with death. The United States government was especially exercised over Sharif's ouster. Washington had received assurances from the Prime Minister that Pakistan would sign the Comprehensive Nuclear Test Ban Treaty. The Americans had also been trying to prompt Sharif to find and arrest Osama bin Laden. They had resisted Indian demands that Pakistan be placed on the State Department's terrorist list and Nawaz Sharif had pledged his cooperation in identifying and neutralizing terrorist organizations. These activities as well as the war on drug trafficking seemed jeopardized by the army takeover, and considerable efforts were directed to getting Musharraf to back down and allow Nawaz to return to his post.

Musharraf, however, was not about to yield to foreign pressure. Even the suspension of Pakistan's membership in the Commonwealth, and the European Union's condemnation of the Pakistan army for again interfering in the country's politics were brushed aside. In less than two months the critics acknowledged the futility of their complaint and withdrew some of the sanctions imposed on the military government. The Indian government was the exception. With Kargil a fresh memory and Musharraf's role in the campaign indisputable, New Delhi refused to abandon its criticism. Believing the army coup signaled a worsening of relations between the two countries, New Delhi declared the situation in Pakistan a threat to peace for the entire region. Anticipating an intensification of guerrilla actions in Kashmir, India warned Pakistan that any threat to its security would be answered with the full force of the Indian armed forces. It was India's pressure that had forced Pakistan's suspension from the Commonwealth, and a meeting of the South Asia Association for Regional Cooperation scheduled for Kathmandu in November also was postponed at the request of the Indian government.

Despite the criticism at home and abroad, Musharraf settled to his task as Pakistan's Chief Executive. The Pakistan Muslim League and the Pakistan People's Party, in the absence of their main leaders, decided to limit their competitive rhetoric and instead found sufficient agreement to ally their parties in what they called a "Grand Democratic Alliance." In an alliance of weakness the political parties sought ways to protect their organizations in the face of strong executive measures. In the meantime the trial of Nawaz Sharif went forward. Although the court decided to release the others involved in the alleged conspiracy, Nawaz was found guilty and his death sentence was commuted to twenty-five years' imprisonment. The Supreme Court, not unexpectedly, ruled the army takeover a lawful act. However, the court insisted Musharraf could not remain in power indefinitely. His government was ordered to hold elections that would reinstate the national and provincial legislatures no later than October 2002. The General did not contest that order.

Musharraf's public statements continued to justify the army *putsch*, insisting there had been almost no advance planning and that his colleagues had reacted to the Prime Minister's initiatives. Rumors, however, continued to circulate that the army had moved to oust Sharif to deflect public attention from the Kargil incident. The generals nonetheless cast aside all criticism. Musharraf's argument was that the army had responded to national need and had thwarted a plan to impose a dictatorship on the country. By protecting Musharraf, the generals had also preserved the military tradition. This also meant insuring the country's security and safeguarding its nuclear stockpile. The Prime Minister's imperious behavior, his chameleon-like approach to politics, had made him a totally untrustworthy guardian of the country's major assets. Moreover, his mismanagement of public policy, the virtual ruin of the economy, and the threat posed to the country's basic freedoms could not go unanswered.

Musharraf drew support from the Islamist parties that had opposed the visit to Pakistan of the Indian Prime Minister, Atal Behari Vajpayee, in February 1999. Nawaz and Vajpayee had issued a Lahore Declaration that called on their forces to relax their vigilance in Kashmir. Nawaz was condemned by Islamist organizations for extending the invitation to the Indian leader and for agreeing to such a declaration. He also was accused of betraying the Kashmiri people. A number of army commanders shared these sentiments. By removing Sharif, Musharraf had knowingly appeased the Islamists, as well as the hawks in the army hierarchy. He also had boosted the work of the ISI operating in conjunction with Islamic militants in the disputed territory. With Nawaz in prison, Benazir in exile in Dubai, and the leader of the MQM isolated in London, Musharraf found willing allies among the Islamists, especially the Jamaat-i-Islami. He also was assured of a lessening of street demonstrations and a relatively free hand to promote his reform program.

The failed campaign in Kargil, however, continued to stalk the General. The operation was launched after Vajpayee's visit, and Nawaz's protestation that his government did not have advance word about the action was almost believable. The attack was supposedly mounted to deny Indian forces the use of the Vale–Leh road in the high mountain region that connects with the Siachin Glacier, a venue for sustained Indian–Pakistani skirmishing. For a brief period Indian troops were cut off from their supply base in Srinigar. Indian forces also suffered significant casualties when they were caught by surprise. Islamabad reported the campaign was the work of Kashmiri freedom fighters, but New Delhi gave a different account. Charging the use of regular Pakistan army units, the Indians did not rule out the presence of militant Islamists, but they were convinced the entire operation was the work of the Pakistan ISI, which, they said, had Musharraf's complete backing. New Delhi therefore reinforced its contingents in the area. It also threatened Islamabad with a wider war.

Nawaz had continued to insist his government was not privy to the action, but in the tense circumstances the Prime Minister flew to Washington for a meeting with President Clinton. On his return, he learned that the Indians had successfully countered the attack and he ordered the withdrawal of all Pakistani forces. Although it was not known how Musharraf viewed the pullback, many of his commanders were unhappy with the Prime Minister's order. The Kargil adventure, however, came to an abrupt end. India again had demonstrated its resolve as well as a capacity to defend its position. In Pakistan, however, the blame game was only beginning. The Kargil episode had ruptured relations between the civilian government and the generals. It also had unleashed the omnipresent fanatics among the religious-political orders, who were now even more eager to take up the battle with New Delhi.

Musharraf had isolated the major political parties, had neutralized their leaders, but had also allowed himself to become intimate with formerly fringe Islamic elements. The character of the Musharraf takeover, allowing parties to function, had opened the political field to the more extreme political orders while limiting it for others. Nawaz Sharif's fall from power, instead of providing greater opportunities to the national parties, had marked the decline of secular politics and conferred legitimacy on Islamist groups from Afghanistan to Kashmir. New Delhi cited this development and comments were rampant about the further Talibanization of Pakistan. Qazi Hussain Ahmed, leader of the Jamaat-i-Islami, and Maulana Fazlur Rahman, mentor to the

Jamiat-i-Ulama-i-Islam, were jubilant, and the Indian protests only galvanized their efforts. Wanting no settlement with India, they pressured Musharraf to ignore the criticism leveled against his regime by the United States, Britain, and the European Union.

Musharraf was not a welcome figure in Washington or Europe. He traveled little beyond Pakistan during his first year in power, journeying only to New York City in the autumn of 2000 to join in the millennium session of the United Nations General Assembly. Even on that occasion he failed to engage in any substantive discussions. Scheduled to meet with Bangladesh's Prime Minister, Hasina Wajid, he canceled the meeting after learning that her agenda would question the return to military government in Pakistan. Bangladesh also sought a public apology from the Pakistan government for atrocities committed by the Pakistan army during the 1971 civil war. Musharraf was not prepared to mend fences, however, and he left New York as quietly as he had arrived. Moreover, the chill in U.S.–Pakistan relations had been acknowledged in March 2000 when President Clinton spent a full week in India but barely more than a few low-profile hours in Pakistan.

Musharraf's isolation from the outer world did not cause distress among the Islamists. The Taliban had opened a new offensive against the one significant force still denying the fundamentalists total control of Afghan territory. The Northern Alliance of Ahmad Shah Masud continued to battle against great odds. Moreover, the Taliban now could count upon the support of Pakistani troops as well as al-Qaeda recruits. By the summer of 2000 it appeared that total victory was in sight for the Emirate of Afghanistan. The success of Taliban arms, however, had also caused distress in the newly independent Central Asian republics, and they now implemented more rigid dictatorial policies to counter Islamist penetration and influence. Efforts also were made to assist the Northern Alliance from Uzbekistan, and even Iran stepped up its aid to the Masud forces as well as the opposition in western Afghanistan. With concern growing about the power of the Taliban, and its spreading influence through alliance with bin Laden's al-Qaeda, only Pakistan, Saudi Arabia, and the United Arab Emirates recognized the regime of Mullah Omar. Global pressure therefore was placed on Musharraf to rein in the Pakistan army's role and especially the ISI.

Pakistan's sustained support for the austere religious order in Afghanistan had opened divisions in the Muslim world. The few Muslim countries that Musharraf visited in 2000 voiced this concern. He had to manage criticism from both Turkey and Malaysia, who questioned the course taken by the Musharraf government, notably its support of the jihadis and the violent religious extremists both in and outside his country. Musharraf discovered he could not simultaneously promote secular democratic reforms and this more violent form of Islamization. Finally acknowledging his balancing act could not work, he was forced to contend with social conditions long neglected by his predecessor regimes. Moreover, Pakistani youth in substantial numbers were attracted to the religious-political organizations and Pakistan's high birth rate had caused their ranks to swell. The undereducated and unemployed were also willing recruits for the jihadists.

The religious schools expanded during the Zia years. Supported by Saudi Arabia, and to some extent by other Gulf states, schools had drawn alienated and disenfranchised young people to their doors and they were not turned away. Moreover, the growth of the madrassahs was in stark contrast to the scant attention given to secular education, and the overall decay in Pakistan's secondary schools, colleges, and universities. The religious schools, moreover, had links with the Taliban and al-Qaeda, and they not only attracted Pakistani youth but also drew students inclined towards fundamentalism from Muslim as well as non-Muslim countries. Saudi Wahhabism was spread by these more conservative schools of Islamic jurisprudence. For Muslim youth discouraged by the course of events, denied economic goals, limited in social expression, Islam appeared a welcome path from their otherwise frustrating and more secular environment. Here too was a breeding ground for the army of al-Qaeda and Osama bin Laden, who had developed a reputation as a folk hero, especially following the U.S. missile attack on some of his camps in Afghanistan.

Musharraf therefore had little to celebrate in the millennium year. Pakistan's economy was abysmal and showed little signs of improvement. The huge external debt all but negated the country's gross domestic product and attempts to slow the inflationary spiral were still frustrated by wide-scale corruption in the market place. Foreign investment had been frightened off following the 1998 nuclear tests, and the economic sanctions imposed following that event were still more or less in place. And although Musharraf could point to greater self-sufficiency in agricultural production, the manufacturing sector, so heavily dependent on outside sources of demand, suffered from lack of international interest. The International Monetary Fund, however, mindful of an economic meltdown, indicated that restrictions on loans to Pakistan might be eased as a consequence of the government's demonstration of willingness in 2000 to repay a portion of its foreign debt. Unable to gain access to more sophisticated financial circles, Pakistan remained dependent on countries like Saudi Arabia, and on Pakistanis abroad with their remittances to families and friends. Pakistan's military establishment, however, its extension into Afghanistan, and its overall needs in ruling a country shaken by sustained violence, demanded far more in the way of resources. The staggering costs of a government that could not find peace either at home or abroad did not add up to a successful economic recovery.

Political evolution and revolution

Pakistan began 2001 much as it had ended 2000, virtually alone, save for its ventures in Afghanistan and its sustained test of India's capacity to hold the line in Kashmir. Domestically, the country was awash in violence, with both targeted and random acts of terror taking a toll of the largely innocent civilian population. Foreigners too had never been far from the violence. The intensification of the Islamist movements and their jihadi goon squads seemed to parallel the rising number of assaults on Pakistan's foreign community. Musharraf, however, continued to speak of his democratic objectives for the country. Commemorating the first anniversary of the coup in October 2000, the Chief Executive reiterated his noble quest by noting the regime's achievements during the past year. His government, he said, had improved civil–military relations, had purged and punished corrupt officials, had demanded honesty in all transactions, had kept the faith with a free press, and had given Pakistan a new profile among the world's nations. The latter claim was almost comical given Pakistan's growing reputation for indiscriminate attacks on the weakest members of society. Musharraf, however, ignored that condition. The profile of which he spoke was Pakistan's status as a nuclear power, which, in his thinking and that of his compatriots was a very notable accomplishment. Therefore, the Chief Executive called upon Pakistanis to celebrate with him and to face the future with positive resolve. But his platitudinous speeches could not conceal the country's severe economic dislocation, his own lack of political legitimacy, or the military government's connection with the chief cause of public disorder, namely the fundamentalists and jihadis who masked their activities in the guise of Islamic purifiers.

Musharraf and his supporting cast of generals and technocrats were still sorting out their options in a country that had long rejected governance from a distant central government. People were more inclined to follow the dictates of local authorities. The centralization of power was always perceived as overbearing, corrupt, and alien. Repeated efforts to overcome the preference for localized politics, prompted a variety of reforms that were never embraced by those who believed there was more to lose than gain from any of the proposed policies. In this environment Pakistan's latest rulers searched for but could not find an answer to the question of appropriate government. Moreover, not given to innovative experimentation, successive governments repeated what others had done before them. Thus similar leaders with similar ideas and mannerisms, with similar inhibitions and arguments, sustained their influence over the body politic. In fact, leaders proved more durable than institutions. Nevertheless, the passing of a particular leader also meant the discarding of whatever might be associated with his or her rule. Whether Basic Democracies or One Unit, parity formulas or federalism, Islamic socialism or separate electorates, all became relics of history in the search for national identity.

Reinventing government was not a Pakistani penchant. Two models were expressed at the moment of Pakistan's creation and neither was altered with the passage of time. Parliamentary government dominated one mode of thought; the other was the quest for the Islamic state. Successive governments were forced to try to combine the two goals, no matter how impossible the task. Moreover, failure to achieve the ideal system did not mean never trying again. So it was with Musharraf, who, for all his democratic discourse, continued to associate himself with the Muslim clerics. The clerics had to play at parliamentary politics just as much as the more secular politicians had to bolster their Muslim credentials. It had been this way since Pakistan's first days, and the only difference more than fifty years later was the Islamists's greater political leverage. If Musharraf was intent on building democracy along parliamentary lines and also promoting a political system the Islamists could identify with, his policies appeared to favor the latter over the former.

In December 2000, Musharraf entered into a confidential agreement with the former Prime Minister's attorneys and representatives which allowed the entire Sharif family to leave Pakistan for exile in Saudi Arabia. Nawaz was released from prison and flown to Riyadh. In departing, he agreed to remain in Saudi Arabia for a minimum of ten years. Musharraf's demonstration of compassion contrasted with the vindictiveness of Zia ul-Haq, who had rejected all pleas to spare Zulfikar Ali Bhutto's life. The decision to let Nawaz go left Musharraf to contemplate the political future without the Punjabi leader's looming presence. Moreover, the Chief Executive demonstrated he was not a foe of the Pakistan Muslim League, but in fact wanted to give the organization an opportunity to resurrect itself. The same attitude did not hold for Benazir Bhutto's Pakistan People's Party. Unlike the Muslim League, the PPP was too much associated with the personality of Benazir Bhutto and the spirit of her father. Representing a different calling, the PPP could not be fitted into a design that embraced both parliamentary politics and Islamic tradition. Musharraf attempted to forge alliances with secondary leaders in the PPP, but, realizing they would have to betray their leader, they rejected his advances. In so doing, they prevented any revival of their party.

The only other major party in the country was Altaf Hussain's Muttahida Qaumi Movement. Altaf Hussain's permanent exile in Britain, however, meant the MQM again would be denied its principal guide and mentor. In the absence of his leadership the MQM had to content itself with a major role in Karachi politics. Of the minor parties, the only genuinely secular organization was the Awami National Party (ANP), which had passed from

Wali Khan to his son Asfand. The ANP had lost much of its appeal on the frontier as a consequence of its anti-Taliban posture. Unlike its former allies among the Islamist orders, the ANP rejected associations with the Emir of Afghanistan and this left Asfand with a very minor role in frontier politics. The ANP defection, however, allowed Musharraf to ingratiate himself with Maulana Fazlur Rahman and Maulana Sami-ul-Haq, leaders of the major Islamist factions of the Jamiat-i-Ulama-i-Islam in the NWFP.

For a soldier who had not engaged in politics before October 1999, by the early months of 2001 Musharraf had demonstrated a political adroitness that was cause for worry among the conventional politicians. Musharraf authorized the holding of local council elections and, except for of the MQM, the parties did not prevent their members from contesting the available seats. The success of this venture also convinced the Chief Executive it was time to discard his ambiguous role and assume the title associated with the powers he actually held. Rafiq Tarar was eased out of his position as ceremonial President and in July 2001 Musharraf assumed the presidency and merged his powers with that office. Although nothing was said about the return to the viceregal tradition, it was clearly too ingrained in the Pakistani ethos to expect that the authoritarian tradition would be ignored. With Supreme Court sanction, Musharraf had made himself both head of state and head of government. So anticipated was the event that little criticism was heard from either the politicians or the Press. Declaring he had assumed the presidency to give support to the democratic process, Musharraf cited the success of the local council elections and his intention to hold nationwide elections for a new parliament and provincial legislatures much as the Supreme Court had recommended. It could be inferred that Musharraf believed all the political elements would be in place by October 2002 when those elections were to be held.

Antecedents to September 11

Building democracy in a country devoted to religious tradition has been a problem in numerous states. The founding fathers of the United States constitutional system acknowledged the problem in eighteenth-century Europe and it was their judgment that only by a strict separation of church from state was democracy attainable. Democracy was seen as a give and take of ideas and views. To live democratically meant accepting thoughts and utterances that did not always coincide and might sometimes be in conflict with one's understanding of specific religious commandments. Moreover, religion, unlike democratic expression, was not subject to compromise, and rather than rule out one's interpretation and practice of faith to please another, it was deemed best to allow all people to worship and believe as they wished without any interference from the state. This left the state to function not as an extension of spiritual expression, but as an instrument of common good, embracing all people under its jurisdiction. Unlike the piety of the religious order, the state was a legal structure that acknowledged no faith except the preservation of the nation. Pakistan emerged as an independent state with this general understanding. But the Pakistan Movement, the call to Muslims to unite behind the Muslim League's demand for a separate state, would not have been successful had the leaders of the movement insisted their goal was the creation of a secular system. The Indian National Congress had represented the cause of secularism and it was not secularism that Jinnah's followers wanted for Pakistan. Therefore, whereas India emphasized its formation as a secular state, the leaders of Pakistan, with perhaps the exception of Jinnah, muted such an idea. Pakistan's constitutional record is a poor one, but one matter is clear in each of its constitutional documents: the country was formed for Muslims and was to be guided by Muslim practices. Democracy was implied but it was never made the dominant feature.

Pakistanis were never exposed to philosophical debate about the merits of the democratic state versus the Islamic state. Jinnah was more Lockean than Jeffersonian in that he encouraged tolerance, not the parting of religion from state governance. But after him, no political leader truly emphasized toleration, let alone the separation of church and state. There is no body of political theory in Pakistan that explores the subject. Scholars were reluctant to broach the matter in public and politicians failed to see the value of such discourse. Thus, Pakistanis were left without a clear definition for their state and were forced to find explanation in their individual lives or through the voices of the more articulate literati. Moreover, the repeated failure of the politicians to satisfy citizens' expectations left little room for public flights of fancy. Few questioned their circumstances and the vast majority simply followed the forces set in train by society's leaders. It should come as no surprise therefore that the Islamists should have emerged as a potent force, or that they should vent their long and deeply held beliefs in the direction of political objectives. Pakistan may not have been the goal of the Islamists in the years leading up to the partition of the subcontinent, but Pakistan became a reality, and it seemed only right to the men of deep faith that its evolution should be defined in Islamic not democratic terms. Musharraf was challenged by this juxtaposition of faith and secular practice. So too were all his predecessors, but no one before him confronted the specific issues that impacted on Pakistan in 2001.

The events that swept the Shah from power in 1979 were only somewhat peculiar to Iran. A secular monarch prevailed over a secular if autocratic system until such time as the forces of Islamic revolution overwhelmed his once vaunted monarchy and brought forth a new order centered on religious experience. The clash of secular and religious forces was as predictable as the outcome. So too was the expansion of the Iranian experience to include the full range of Muslim nations. The Soviet invasion of Afghanistan followed within months of the Shah's ouster, an invasion little understood at the time, but organized to prevent the spread of revolutionary Islamic teaching to Central Asia. Afghanistan, at first considered the prize, was actually the pawn in a new great game, only this one was aimed to keep an Islamic tide from welling up and sweeping through the cultures of the Soviet Muslim republics. The men in the Kremlin who considered themselves the guardians of autocracy did not miscalculate their role in Afghanistan. Rather, they failed to predict Pakistan's reaction, or the American decision to supply its then alienated former ally with substantial military assistance. Moreover, Moscow never took the measure of the ISI, or foresaw the melding of ISI and CIA operations in the Afghan interior. The Soviets counted on a short, limited war, but the Islamabad–Washington decision to use Islam as a weapon against them baffled the Kremlin leaders and ultimately forced the Soviets' retreat. Neither

American military supplies nor Pakistani determination was alone responsible for the eventual outcome. All the military supplies provided would have been wasted (note the collapse of the Kuomintang despite heavy American assistance) had it not been Islamabad's strategy, with American concurrence, to replicate the passion of Khomeini's Islamic revolution in the Afghan war against the Red Army.

That strategy insinuated Pakistan's Inter-Services Intelligence Directorate directly into Afghan affairs. Pakistan could not simply remain passive as Afghan refugees flooded the country. Britain had taught the merits of a "Forward Policy" in defense of the subcontinent and the Pakistanis adopted that policy as their own. Since they were not in a position to confront Moscow directly, the use of clandestine forces was the only option and the ISI was trained and equipped to operate in Afghanistan as a surrogate for the regular army. The ISI, organized in 1948, had been shaped by the Ayub military government and was made responsible to the three major services, including the army, through the Joint Chiefs of Staff Committee. In 1975, Prime Minister Zulfikar Ali Bhutto, by executive order, created a political cell within the intelligence unit which brought it directly under the control of the chief executive. The Prime Minister used the ISI, as he used his more personal Federal Security Force, to spy on the political opposition and to make it impossible for them to challenge the authority of his government. Matters of national security, however, particularly those dealing with force levels, external intelligence, and military strategy, were channeled through the Joint Chiefs of Staff Committee. This division of function followed into the Zia administration and beyond. During Zia's rule, and especially during the several years of martial law, the ISI reported directly to the President, who doubled as Chief Martial Law Administrator. Up to the end of martial law in 1985, Zia used the ISI as he saw fit. After 1985, however, Zia's decision to unleash the politicians provided the ISI with the opportunity to skirt the President's authority. Moreover, the war in Afghanistan had taken a new turn with the assistance provided by the CIA, and the latter's intimacy with an expanded ISI.

Inter-Services Intelligence and CIA officials acknowledged the power of religious commitment and a decision was taken to supply what were deemed the more spiritually committed forces among the resistance fighters. Thus Gulbadin Hekmatyar and his Hizb-i-Islami was an early candidate for assistance. A leader of Islamic revolution in the years of the Afghan monarchy, Hekmatyar had ties to the Egyptian Muslim Brotherhood and Egyptian Islamic Jihad. Provided shelter in Pakistan during the short-lived Daud republic, Hekmatyar's connections in Pakistan were mainly with the Jamaat-i-Islami, a group favored by Zia ul-Haq. The Pakistani President therefore, apparently without CIA objection, made it possible for Hekmatyar to receive an estimated sixty-five percent of U.S. military assistance and financial aid. More secular Afghan leaders like Masud and Ismail Khan also saw a need to link forces with ISI, but they were treated circumspectly and received comparatively little of the American-proffered assistance. Abdul Hagh and other more dubious mujahiddin leaders refused to become instruments of Pakistani-directed policy and they had no choice but to look elsewhere for their support.

After Soviet acceptance of the U.N.-mediated withdrawal agreement in 1988, the ISI took on the appearance of a paramilitary force and was immediately involved in the formation of an Afghan interim government. Its powers enhanced by its success and the number of agents and military personnel in its command, it also was relatively independent of the army command structure. This became even more apparent following Zia's death in October 1988. The Director General of ISI was always a uniformed officer but the army's COAS had little influence over him. Moreover, Zia's successor as COAS, General Aslam Beg, became a suspect in Zia's death. General Beg also had reason to believe ISI was complicit in the destruction of the President's aircraft. Officially, the loss of Zia's plane was attributed to sabotage and the government was content to point to the Soviet KGB and the Afghan KHAD as the joint culprits. Thus, the ISI escaped scrutiny and was left free to continue its intrigue in Afghanistan. General Beg, however, experienced considerable difficulty in directing the Pakistan army.

ISI operations in Afghanistan also fueled the conflict between Pakistani and Iranian interests. The ISI had links with Saudi Arabia and thereby became embroiled in the rivalry between Riyadh and Teheran, each seeking leadership of the Islamic revolution. This contest provoked clashes between Afghan Sunnis and Shiites which spilled over into Pakistan, where sectarian disturbances had become an everyday occurrence. Sunni–Shiite conflict negated cooperation among the Afghan mujahiddin and prevented them from challenging the Communist government in Kabul after the Red Army withdrew. Inter-Services Intelligence actions actually impeded the creation of an interim government and allowed the Najibullah regime to remain in Kabul an additional four years. What the Afghans lost, however, the ISI gained. By this time the ISI had a force of thousands and the distribution of international aid became a major responsibility of the intelligence agency. The ISI approved or rejected requests for bases in Pakistan. It also determined which Afghan politicians would be favored and which denied, thereby prompting or aggravating rivalries that led to serious internecine conflicts. Directly or indirectly, the ISI was responsible for the assassination of Afghan officials, and for many the Pakistan ISI had assumed the role of a para-Afghan government.

Iran's desire to compete with the Pakistan ISI only further destabilized the country. Shiite Afghans from the Hazarajat central region of Afghanistan had resisted Iranian influence, but because they had difficulty in procuring Western aid, Iran continued to be a source of assistance. Iran's Sazaman-e-Italaat, the government intelligence service, Islamic Revolutionary Guard, and Ministry of the Interior also became involved in the attempt to shape Afghanistan's destiny. Afghan commanders tried to distance themselves from both the Pakistanis and the Iranians. Some mujahiddin leaders formed the National Commanders Shura (NCS) to coordinate their activities. The NCS denied the ISI a place in their organization; they also rejected an Iranian presence. The Afghan commanders were especially disturbed by an ISI plan that would have the mujahiddin forces make a combined frontal assault on the Najibullah-based Kabul government. Instead, the NCS authorized an incremental strategy that would enable them to secure the provinces and regions, thus isolating the Communist regime in the capital. The ISI plan, if implemented, would have involved heavy casualties and would have weakened rather than strengthened the Afghan commanders' forces. Suspicious that the ISI wanted a weak and divided mujahiddin army in order to press its own interests, the NCS stuck to its own plan and announced its intention to divide Afghanistan into nine separate zones, each with its own regional administration. The grand purpose of the NCS strategy was an Afghanistan in which the Afghans controlled their own destiny.

Not surprising, the ISI refused to accept the NCS plan and its agents organized defections from the NCS with Hekmatyar among the first to break ranks. With assistance from the ISI, Hekmatyar organized a rival Laskar-e-Eissar (Army of Sacrifice), which quickly opened a military campaign and succeeded in capturing the strategic border town of Khost. The NCS soon found itself riddled with dissent. Masud, however, rallied his Northern Alliance and, with Dostum's decision to join ranks, Najibullah die-hards also jumped to the Alliance. The Northern Alliance emerged as a force determined not only to replace the Communist regime in Kabul but also to stem the expanding influence of the ISI. The main struggle now pitted pro-ISI against anti-ISI forces. The combined force of the Northern Alliance and Dostum, with the help of Communist defectors, swept down from the north and quickly entered and captured Kabul against minimal resistance. They captured Najibullah as he was preparing to flee to India. The ISI force, led by General Assad Durani, was furious, first at being refused a place in the National Commanders Shura, and second when the northern force led by Masud and Dostum denied Kabul to Hekmatyar's warriors moving in from Khost. It is important to note that Kabul was entered in relative tranquility and the city was secured quickly. Following Kabul's capture by Masud's Northern Alliance, the other Peshawar-based leaders of the mujahiddin, with the exception of Hekmatyar, agreed to journey to Kabul, where an interim government was established without ISI assistance on April 29, 1992.

Following the alliance between northern and eastern Afghans, ISI's pan-Islamic policies were integrated in a new Pakistan foreign policy. Pakistan needed a land bridge to the newly independent Islamic republics of Central Asia. Masud and his Northern Alliance blocked the way. Islamabad therefore rejected the interim Kabul government before it could be established, and intrigued to form another that conformed to Pakistan's perceived national interest. The ISI also continued to promote Hekmatyar and intrigued to destabilize the new government of Mujaddidi Rabbani. Arguing the interim government aligned itself too closely with Masud, Dostum, and Ismail Khan, Islamabad provided the ISI with *carte blanche* to destabilize the new Afghan administration. Pakistan feared the interim government would open Afghanistan to advances from New Delhi, an echo of conditions prevailing before the Soviet invasion. Given the new government's anti-Pakistan bias, it was also seen as blocking Pakistan's interests in Central Asia. A related concern for Pakistan was the possible revival of an Afghan claim to Pakhtunistan, in Pakistan's northwestern territory. The ISI therefore developed a strategy that not only undermined the secular Afghan government, but also nourished the Afghan Islamist movement. The key ISI decision, however, was the formation of the Taliban and its recruitment of Pakistanis as well as Afghans. By 1993 the Tehrik-i-Taliban was a formidable force with direct ties to the Pakistan army.

The rise of the Taliban coincided with the establishment of the Clinton presidency. The new American President was advised to scale back and ultimately remove the CIA presence from Afghanistan. Najibullah had been defeated, Communism had been overturned, and Washington thought it better for the Afghans to work out their future without American involvement. The departure of the Americans left the other outsiders – the Pakistanis, Saudis, and Egyptians – to pursue their objectives without Washington's influence. Saudi efforts were joined to those of the ISI: both were devoted to building a counter-force to the mujahiddin interim government, which was falsely seen as favoring Iran. Egyptian input involved expanding the ranks of the Afghan Arabs (Arabs who joined the mujahiddin in the war against the Soviet Union) and other Muslims associated with the al-Qaeda of Osama bin Laden. Pakistan wanted an Afghanistan dominated by loyal Pashtuns, and Islamabad directed Hekmatyar's forces, reinforced by the Taliban and Afghan Arabs, to march on Kabul, where a bloody campaign was unleashed that destroyed much of what was left of the Afghan capital. From a distance the struggle for Kabul looked like an ethnic quarrel in which tribal vendettas were more significant than the continued suffering of the Afghan people. The war, however, was as much orchestrated as it was spontaneous. The ISI had used Hekmatyar and the alliance of jihadi and Islamist forces to deny the success of the interim government. But this was only the first phase of a broader plan.

The Taliban was Islamabad's answer to a third force between the Pashtun Afghans and the non-Pashtun Afghans. Raised, supported, and trained by the ISI and special forces of the Pakistan army, the Taliban was made the instrument not only to end the fighting in Afghanistan, but to bring the country under Pakistani control. The Taliban was Afghan at its core, emerging from the southern city of Kandahar and its environs, but augmented by tribal Pashtuns from Pakistan's frontier region, as well as Afghan Arabs and other more distant Muslims drawn from the Islamic world as far as Indonesia on the one side and Algeria on the other. Taliban funding was supplied by Saudi Arabia and the Gulf states. The Taliban was the instrument of an Islamic renaissance, and it seemed to serve the interests of both Islamabad and Riyadh. Religious schools had been established along the Afghan–Pakistani frontier and in the Pakistani hinterland. Primarily supported with Saudi money, these schools indoctrinated their students in the tenets of an austere form of Islam and trained them as warriors, reminiscent of the *ghazis* who had fought the Byzantine Christian *akritai* in the march lands of the expanding Islamic empire. It was the *ghazis* who established the Ottoman Empire and spread their influence through Afghanistan to medieval India. By 1994, Washington had all but accepted the Taliban as a pacifying force, concerned with disarming the rival tribes and restoring law and order to an Afghanistan desperately in need of time to repair the damage of fifteen years of constant warfare.

American support during the Reagan and Bush administrations had heavily favored the more religious orders in Afghanistan. Under the Clinton administration Washington again gave its support to Pakistan's inspired Islamic scholars. Clinton saw in the Taliban an army of dedicated Muslims who had volunteered their services to bring order out of chaos in the mountain country. The Taliban's righteous outlook and determination, it was assumed, would end terrorism, stop the cultivation and trafficking of narcotics, and unite the country under a nationally inspired regime composed of selfless individuals. Needless to say, from a geopolitical viewpoint, the Taliban would also stymie Iranian and Russian influence in Central Asia and open the region for commercial development. High on the list of such commercial activity was UNOCAL's oil and gas pipeline complex through Afghanistan. Although the Taliban were Islamic fundamentalists, the Americans were convinced that Taliban fundamentalism was very different from the political fundamentalism of Iran. Therefore, when the Taliban stormed into Kabul in 1996, routing its opposition, the United States believed that a stabilizing element had been established in Afghanistan. Moreover, with Pakistani and Saudi assistance the region could be expected to achieve a level of tranquility and development not experienced in almost two decades. Washington began to envisage the return of King Zahir Shah and the prospect that a revived and stable Afghanistan would open the larger region to growth and reconstruction.

What Washington had not foreseen was the opportunity a Talibanized Afghanistan offered to a broad cross-section of Muslims determined to end Western influence. The Taliban's success was buttressed by assistance from across the Islamic world, including from Osama bin Laden, who had declared war on the Saudi government and on the United States. A Saudi subject who had been expelled from his country when he criticized royal regime policy for allowing Western forces to operate in the kingdom during the 1990–91 Gulf War, bin Laden had returned to Afghanistan to help the Taliban consolidate their power. The Pakistan ISI acknowledged bin Laden's presence, accepted his offer of financial assistance, and did nothing to prevent him from attracting other Muslim fighters to Afghanistan, nor did they stop him from constructing training camps and bases in the country. Bin Laden became the catalyst for a network of Islamist militant organizations that were in fact aided by the ISI. The training camp of Al Badr was associated with the Khalid ibn-i-Walid that bin Laden used for global operations. Another camp, the Muawia, was of more interest to the ISI because it came under the direction of the Harkat-ul-Ansar, a Kashmiri guerrilla organization. The relationship between ISI, bin Laden, and the Taliban was undeniable, but its portents were not fully realized until 1998 when bin Laden's operatives in Tanzania and Kenya blew up the American embassies in those two countries. The Clinton administration's response to these assaults was the cruise missile strikes on some of bin Laden's training camps and the multi-million dollar reward Washington offered for Osama bin Laden's capture. Believing the Afghans could be bought, the Clinton government was surprised when there were no takers. Nor was there any indication of bin Laden's whereabouts.

The Pakistan ISI was too committed to its Afghan policy to abandon it now. Pakistani governments led by Benazir Bhutto and subsequently Nawaz Sharif were pressured unsuccessfully to yield bin Laden or his lieutenants. Except for the arrest and extradition of two terrorists, one connected with the 1993 bombing of the New York City World Trade Center and the other with an attack on CIA headquarters in Virginia, nothing was done about al-Qaeda. Nor was Pakistan's growing intimacy with Mullah Omar, the self-proclaimed Emir of Afghanistan, reconsidered. Taliban operations were allowed to intertwine with al-Qaeda's expanding legions and the spillover in Kashmir was evident in the escalation of the violence there. As elusive as bin Laden proved to be, Mullah Omar was an even more shadowy figure, refusing even to be photographed, let alone appearing at public events. Washington called upon the Emirate of Afghanistan, a state it refused to recognize, to arrange for the extradition of bin Laden to the United States, but the Taliban turned a deaf ear to the request. The United States responded with sanctions. The United Nations Security Council, at American urging, followed with limited sanctions of its own. The Taliban, however, appeared to gain strength from the publicity and the American pressure. Mullah Omar was quoted as refusing to yield a Muslim to a non-Muslim demand, no matter the alleged criminal offense. In May 2000, President Clinton cited a bomb plot supposedly planned by al-Qaeda to occur at the United States millennium celebrations. Although that period passed without serious incident, the United States government launched a multi-million dollar counter-terrorism program aimed at fanatic Islamic organizations such as al-Qaeda and the Taliban. In Pakistan, however, there was no shift in policy or intention. Islamabad continued to see positive results in the operations of the Taliban despite growing international criticism of its violation of human rights, especially its treatment of women.

Although Pakistan participated in the Six-Plus-Two Conference in July 1999, it had little interest in promoting the Afghanistan peace proposals developed by the concerned nations. The conference consisted of China, Iran, Tajikistan, Turkmenistan, Uzbekistan, and Pakistan (Afghanistan's six neighbors) plus Russia and the United States. The conference called for an end to military assistance to the Taliban and the northern legions that continued to resist its rule. The Six-Plus-Two countries called for a broad-based government, and meetings were held between the Taliban and its opposition, but without satisfactory result. While these negotiations were in train, supporters of the different groups were assisting them behind the scenes with even heavier arms shipments. From his residence in Rome, the long-exiled King Zahir Shah was encouraged to participate in renewed peace efforts. In December 1999, the King called for a world gathering of Afghans to meet with him in Rome, a call supported by the world's major nations. The Taliban regime of Mullah Omar, however, declined the invitation. Already committed to a program that included al-Qaeda and other Islamist orders, and boosted in their resolve by Saudi Arabia as well as Pakistan, the Taliban and al-Qaeda leaders could not be deflected from their now determined course to spread their radicalized Islamic vision to other regions.

A summing up

Pakistan's quest for democracy was compromised decades ago. Politicians, bureaucrats, and soldiers all failed to deliver on their promises. Successive frustrations, combined with the civil war that caused the loss of East Pakistan, led to popular despair and questioning that could only be answered by those who draw their strength from such disasters. Religion is all pervasive in Pakistan and religious leaders with political ambitions had fertile ground in which to plant seeds of discord and rebellion. A demoralized nation turned to Zulfikar Ali Bhutto after the loss of the country's eastern wing. They looked to Bhutto to lift their spirits and to revitalize a country that had been defeated by a hated enemy. Bhutto failed that test. He gave way to another General who saw in Pakistanis a longing for something closer to their genius and more workable than the oft spoken objective of an alien form of democracy. Zia was vilified for his rule and his method of governance, but his Islamization program proved timely in giving voice to a country overcome by anomie. Afghanistan's plight confirmed the utility of Islamization, and as it was used to bolster the resolve of the Afghan mujahiddin, so too it reinforced the will of the most ardent Muslims of Pakistan, who were now made to focus their attention on the liberation of Kashmir. Afghanistan's plight was linked with Pakistan's post-civil-war condition. Both countries sought to save their identities as individual nations challenged by great powers. The two were linked by Islamic tradition and each spawned political religious organizations that were prepared to use any means to realize their objectives.

The humiliated Pakistan armed forces found new strength through the work of the Inter-Services Intelligence Directorate, nurtured by General Zia to challenge the Soviet Union in Afghanistan, as well as India in Kashmir. Pakistan enjoyed logistic advantages in both areas which made those contests different from the conflict in East Pakistan. Moreover, the ISI could readily tap into those forces in Afghanistan, Kashmir, and elsewhere where service in the name of God was a potent weapon. Thus a marriage with the most militant of religious orders was forged on both fronts, and particularly with those orders that were prepared to undergo a protracted and costly struggle. For the Islamists, the collapse of the Soviet incursion in Afghanistan, and the subsequent implosion of the Soviet monolith, was a sign from God that the cause pursued by righteous Muslims was true and just. But the struggle was only half won when the Soviet retreat proved to be not quite the end of the matter. Pakistan needed to consolidate its victory in Afghanistan even if it meant denying the Afghans their cherished objective, independence. Kashmir had yet to be liberated from India, and the alliance forged between elements of the Pakistan armed forces and Islamic militant organizations was deemed to be the correct and only strategy toward that end.

Afghanistan had never experienced rule by religious zealots. Most of its history describes a people separated by tribal experience, but nonetheless capable of remarkable codes of tolerance. Different religious orders, whether Christian, Hindu, or Jewish, lived side by side with the majority Muslim population and Sufi pedagogy assisted communities to accept the rituals and ceremonies of other faiths. Buddhism enjoyed a degree of respect and the ancient archaeological sites that were reminders of pre-Islamic civilization were protected and appreciated as expressions of human diversity. The Taliban, however, believed that anything that deviated from the most conservative practice of Islamic tradition was blasphemous and should be removed or destroyed. What the Soviets began in shattering the social veneer of Afghan society, the Taliban finished. The Taliban was not only a totally new Afghan experience, it came very close to replicating the Communist aim, albeit in fundamentalist Islamic character, of re-engineering society.

The extreme form of Islam that was imposed on the Afghans made them candidates for a transformation whose roots were to be found in Saudi Arabia, and especially within the Egyptian Muslim Brotherhood, which emanated from Cairo's Al-Azhar University, the principal institution for the training of Muslim clerics. Afghan leaders like Hekmatyar, Rabbani, Rasul Sayyaf, and Sibqatollah Mujaddadi had all attended the Cairo school and it was they who formed the Afghan branch of the Muslim Brotherhood. Returning to Afghanistan on the completion of their studies, they attempted to break the hold that secularism had long imposed on the country. Failing in their initial effort to destroy Mohammad Daud's republic, they took refuge in Pakistan and gained the protection of Zulfikar Ali Bhutto. These events provided Pakistan with opportunities it would later seek to exploit.

The Soviet thrust into Afghanistan, and the threat it seemed to pose to a Pakistan still reeling from the civil war and India's role in dismembering the country, made the linkage between the Pakistan government and the Afghan Islamists an imperative of Pakistan's foreign policy. The Afghan mullahs called for a jihad against the infidel, the *monafiq*, the one who would create divisions among Muslims and thereby make war on God and His community of believers. These ideas were perpetuated even after the Soviet departure and were made more emphatic by those determined to seize control of the devastated country. The brutal internecine feuding, though tribal in character, was made to appear endemic and traditional as well as uncompromising. A clash of warlords was the general perception of the mayhem that swept Afghanistan after the Soviet withdrawal. What in fact had happened was quite different. With Pakistani assistance, the most fanatic of Afghanistan's religious leaders, joined now by fanatics from the Middle East and across the Muslim world, unleashed an assault on the traditional but secular elements of Afghan society. The fundamentalists were determined to eliminate whomever might be considered a rival and in the extended night of the long knives they murdered the more noteworthy politicians, the intellectuals and professionals, as well as the mujahiddin commanders who had been instrumental in defending Afghanistan from the Red Army.

Under the influence of the ISI, the Hizb-i-Islami of Hekmatyar and the Jamiat-i-Islami of Rabbani became the principal agents of terror. Those Afghans who could escape the carnage sought refuge in distant countries, thus denuding Afghanistan of vital citizens and setting the scene for the arrival and takeover of the Taliban. Nor did the killing end after the Taliban victory. Abdul Ahad Karzai, an Afghan politician who had found refuge in Pakistan, continued the effort to reconcile the conflicting forces in his native country. In 1999 he became the victim of an assassin. Bereft of its leaders, Afghanistan was an easy target for the Taliban and its allies. Except for the pocket of resistance represented by Ahmad Shah Masud, the entire country appeared to be unified under the Taliban Emirate. Taliban peace, however, was never meant to be moderate and forgiving. Afghanistan had been hijacked by the most extreme of Islamist militants. Assembled from distant places, they had an unfinished agenda that included targets far removed from Afghanistan. The Taliban's purpose was to purify Afghan soil, to transform the people of Afghanistan into model Muslims even if that meant cruelties and behaviors incongruous in the modern world, or even in Islamic tradition. And while the Taliban set out to reinvent Islam and impose it on a hapless Afghan people, their non-Afghan fanatics would carry the message of the new Islam to the outside world. Bin Laden's al-Qaeda was the principal bearer of that message. Although the Saudi terrorist declared war on the United States in 1998, he saw the first line of battle as being in Pakistan, where Talibanization had merged with Islamization and where an army of believers was being primed to act at the master's beck and call.

As alien as the Taliban was to Afghanistan, it nonetheless became the focus for a transformation of the Islamic world. Bin Laden was the messenger of the new Islam, a defiant and all-powerful representative of Muslim tradition capable of standing up to the most formidable global forces, notably those represented by the United States. Building upon the Mektab al-Khidmat established by his fellow Saudi mentor on Afghanistan's border with Pakistan, bin Laden formed the al-Qaeda or "base" to be the core institution in what was projected to be a long war with the infidel Americans and those associated with them. Bin Laden joined the Taliban as they conquered the region of Nangarhar province where he had established his operations. Providing the Taliban with several million dollars drawn from his personal account, he was instantly made a member of the movement and given responsibility for recruiting fighters from far away, something he had already done in the campaign against the Soviet Union. In time bin Laden became the public face of Mullah Omar, who preferred obscurity and whose interests seldom extended beyond the Kandahar region. It was therefore bin Laden who announced in 1998 the formation of the International Islamic Front for Jihad. Included in this hydra-headed organization was a litany of Islamic terrorist groups and cells. The Jamaat-al-Islamia and Islamic Jihad from Egypt, Hezbollah in Lebanon, Hammas in the Palestinian Gaza Strip, Harkat-ul-Mujahiddin and Lashkar-i-Ansar in Pakistan, Abu Sayyaf in the Philippines, the Islamic Movement of Uzbekistan, the Islamic Salvation Front in Algeria, and al-Qaeda were the most prominent. The appeal of the jihadi movement to Muslims in circumstances where they appeared to be outnumbered or oppressed was impossible to overstate.

The Pakistani ISI was not oblivious to what was happening in Afghanistan. How the ISI or the Pakistan government, under Musharraf's direction since October 1999, could have ignored the more than twenty thousand non-Afghans trained in al-Qaeda camps is impossible to fathom. How Pakistan could ignore the thousands of its own countrymen who flocked to the Taliban and al-Qaeda is another dimension of the same question. How the Pakistan government could remain oblivious to the excesses of the

Taliban, which they continued to recognize despite the known atrocities committed in its name, can be explained only in terms of fear. Nurturing Islamists had become a *sine qua non* for governing Pakistan. For Pakistanis in and out of government, the question was not how to thwart terrorism, but how to live with it. Appeasement mixed with indifference and blended with self-interest was the course taken by the Musharraf government. It can only be concluded that having waded so far, the Pakistani government now found it more difficult to retreat than to continue forward. Pakistan still had a foreign policy to pursue. Afghanistan and Central Asia remained high priorities in Islamabad, but so too was the *intifada* in Kashmir, now fueled to a greater intensity by al-Qaeda-supported Kashmiri groups like Jayash-i-Mohammad and Lashkar-i-Tayyaba. The Musharraf government, like those before it, was prepared to acknowledge the dangers of international terrorism, but nevertheless insisted on separating the struggle in Kashmir, no matter how violent, from that association. New Delhi's claim that Pakistan was a terrorist state, that its role in Afghanistan as well as its sustained support for the Kashmiri *intifada* established Islamabad's complicity in terrorist operations, was a continuing subject of debate in Washington and in European capitals. But it was not until September 11, 2001 that Pakistan's connection to worldwide terrorism became a critical concern.

Bibliography*

Abbas, Syed A., "Pakistan Coup: A Harbinger of Turmoil in the Near East and South Asia," unpublished manuscript, 2000.

Baxter, Craig and Kennedy, Charles, eds., *Pakistan 1997*, Boulder: Westview, 1998.

Hoge, James F. and Rose, Gideon, eds., *How Did This Happen? Terrorism and the New War*, New York: Public Affairs, 2001.

Malik, Iftikar, "Pakistan in 2000: Starting Anew or Stalemate?" *Asian Survey*, 41 (1), 2001, pp. 104–15.

Malik, Iftikhar, "Pakistan in 2001: The Afghanistan Crisis and the Rediscovery of the Frontline State," *Asian Survey*, 42(1) January/February 2002, pp. 204–12.

---

*Numerous internet sources were examined in drafting this chapter. See websites and authors and writers consulted at the close of chapter 11.

Nojumi, Neamatollah, *The Rise of the Taliban in Afghanistan: Mass Mobilization, Civil War, and The Future of the Region*, New York: Palgrave, 2002.

Talbott, Strobe, and Chanda, Nayan, eds., *The Age of Terror: America and the World after September 11*, New York: Perseus, 2001.

10

CHOOSING SIDES

Much is made of international pressure in the formation of self-governing political systems. Nevertheless there seems little that external powers can do to determine whether a particular political actor will become more or less autocratic, or more or less democratic. A considerable amount of intellectual energy has gone into the exercise of measuring one country's influence upon another. Studies have examined the relationship between the country to be changed and the one supposedly doing the changing. Little, however, has come from these efforts. So it is with Pakistan and the foreign influences it has been exposed to.

The country that is said to have had the greatest influence on Pakistani governance is the United States. Those exploring the relationship are more likely to conclude that the Americans have nurtured autocracy, not democracy. No state is an island unto itself, and Pakistan's history is full of instances where the United States played a pivotal role at a critical time. It is therefore not surprising that students of the subject have concluded that Pakistan's difficulty in establishing true democracy represents the failure of Americans who could have done more to promote democracy in Pakistan. The United States is said to be responsible for the perpetuation of Pakistan's viceregal tradition, for the long periods of military rule, and the resulting atrophy in the democratic process. Washington's preference for military rulers like Ayub Khan, Yahya Khan, and even Zia ul-Haq was demonstrated again in its embrace of Pervez Musharraf, especially after the calamitous events of September 11, 2001.

The utility of placing blame for a country's domestic failures on an alien power presents significant dilemmas. In reality, distant powers, no matter how intrusive, cannot be held responsible for the course a state chooses to follow. The complex character of the state is seen in the relationships of the people who are its citizens. Pakistanis have contributed to their own malaise, to their repeated failure to define who and what they really are and what they intend to become. It is so much easier to find fault with distant forces than to come to grips with the misadventures that have led many resident Pakistanis to conclude they live in a failed state. A reluctance and even fear to discuss the nation's conflicted ethos, to achieve consensus on the path to be followed, is at the core of the problem. Except for those who speak the language of division and secession, who would seriously entertain the break up and the disappearance of the Pakistani state, the obfuscation persists. Pakistani identity, more than five decades after the state's founding, remains an elusive objective, and never more so than in the present climate of social and political disorder.

Pakistan is a seedbed for extremists desperately seeking a role. The extremist frame of mind does not dwell on the future of Pakistani democracy. "Democracy," like so many other artifacts of Pakistan's experience, is an alien expression empty of all meaning for those not party to the political process. Furthermore, those in a position to play the democracy game generally hail from those segments of society touched by foreign experience. The colonial authority dealt mostly with the land-holding caste and the business element. Colonialism prompted the development of bureaucratic, not political institutions, and the ties between the ruling administrators and the feudal landlords were carefully constructed to minimize stress and maximize obedience. Acceptance of the dominant landlord had a carryover effect that permitted the magistrate or the civil service official to implement the will of the Viceroy and, most significant, to maintain law and order. Business interests were inclined to acknowledge the fountainhead of power and to pay homage to its predictable style of governance. Pakistan inherited this structure at independence, and it was this very structure that provided the country with a semblance of stability and decorum. The political party that fought for an independent Pakistan had little in the way of structure to substitute for the colonial legacy and after independence the Muslim League remained dependent on the steel frame of colonial administration.

Democracy was reduced to a contest between a Muslim League and a bureaucratic system that both served and undermined each other's interests. All the energy in this dynamic centered on the ability of the one to overcome the resistance of the other. Absent from the scene was the citizenry, more the subjects of local leaders than active participants in an evolving political process. A congeries of rural folk, Pakistanis responded to the expectations of those immediately around them, seldom to an abstract and distant authority that was neither concerned with their day-to-day needs nor sensitive to their cultures. Democracy therefore never entered their thoughts or aspirations. Religious demands always meant more to people with little if any exposure to a larger universe. Although dependent on the landlord for bodily sustenance, the rural poor found a voice in the rhetoric of the Muslim clerics who lived among them. The language of Islam was the beginning and the end of their experience. The masses answered to the Islamists, not the politicians who seemed to care little about their day-to-day needs. Thus, as politicians struggled with bureaucrats in a vain attempt to promote their notion of democracy, the masses were influenced by the *ulema* that articulated their concerns and guided them. They did not seek progressive society, but spiritual revival and righteous belief. Extremism therefore begins with the vast gulf separating the sophisticated minority, with their quest for popular self-government, and the common folk's overriding need to do God's work. The two goals were never made compatible.

With the masses either forgotten, ignored, or taken for granted, the so-called builders of democratic tradition failed to meet the test of their own making. Moreover, by their inability to structure a more integrated society, they opened the floodgates to people with a different vision and purpose. Rallying the disenfranchised became the purpose of simple, but nevertheless powerful, men in black who had every intention of shaping Pakistan in their own image. Inchoate at birth, Pakistan failed to produce the leaders needed to fill the political vacuum created by the early death of Mohammad Ali Jinnah. No one was ready for the role vacated by the Quaid-i-Azam, and the instincts of the politicians, both at the center and in the provinces, judged the bureaucracy the greater threat to their influence. Muslim League politicians tried to enlist the services of the masses in their confrontation with the ruling administrators, but in failing in this encounter they precipitated their own decline. The party of Jinnah splintered and in its fragmentation prompted the proliferation of lesser organizations. Few of the parties, however, represented national interests. Moreover, the localization of the parties exposed their weakness. It also caused them to seek the help of religious leaders who insisted on narrow agendas. Kashmir became a prominent political concern, and no politician could escape that burden. The protracted Kashmir conflict not only drove a permanent wedge between Pakistan and India; it became a prime source of religious commitment. Self-determination for the Kashmiris was given a democratic context, but Kashmir was never going to make Pakistan more democratic. The insolubility of the Kashmir dispute, and the sustained conflict with India, became the source of Islamic renewal and reification. Kashmir also legitimated a political role for the clerics, who became the spokesmen for the restoration of the House of Islam in Kashmir, as in Pakistan.

The expanded influence of the *ulema* in Pakistani politics meant clashes of political interest would focus more on the construction of the true Islamic state than on the nurturing of democratic purpose. The many had surpassed the few in both drive and enthusiasm. Mainstream political life now meant the representation of a tradition imbedded in the customs and values of a people who were Muslims long before they became Pakistanis. Into this scenario came the Pakistan army. Believing neither the bureaucrats nor the politicians could administer to the needs of a divided nation, the senior army officers assumed leadership roles formerly the prerogative of the civilian cadres.

Rejecting the politicians because of their divisive behavior, the generals reclaimed the bureaucracy and gave it a new role. Modernization and development were given special emphasis and the bureaucracy was urged to make better use of the country's human and physical resources. Elevating the general population's standard of living required a variety of reforms. There was an expectation that larger public needs could be addressed and that the masses would find a better future in a Pakistan focused on economic expansion that did more than benefit the few. Increasing awareness was expected to bring a higher level of enlightenment, and with that a more rational understanding of secular government. Although the army reformers never expected to shift the population from their traditional practices, they believed that the people would eventually transcend clerical leadership for something more progressive and personally rewarding.

Ayub Khan introduced Basic Democracies and a Works Program that promised fundamental changes in the lives of ordinary people. Political experience and self-reliance were combined to promise that people of any station could be empowered and their life experience enhanced. The bureaucratic system was interposed between the people and the *ulema*, and the nation was guided toward constructive purpose and away from ethnic and sectarian rivalries. The United States willingly supported Ayub's program in nation building with assistance that was supposed to make Pakistan the model of third world achievement. The politicians, however, shut out by the Ayub reforms and finding military rule a challenge to their calling, struck back. Their argument was simple. The army posed a mortal threat to democracy. The restoration of the democratic experiment, by which they meant a renewed form of parliamentary government, was compared with Ayub's vice-regal presidential system. In seeking an end to army rule, the politicians enlisted the services of the religious guides. Their Islamization of politics was intended to force the army back to the barracks, but after a decade of stewardship Ayub had made a permanent place for the army in Pakistan's political life. What the politicians lost, however, the Islamists won. The representatives of religious tradition saw greater gains in their association with the country's armed forces.

The 1965 war with India over Kashmir, and the civil war in East Pakistan hardly five years later, demonstrated the ephemeral nature of political and economic reform, and the ease with which a country divided into antagonistic groups could impose great harm upon itself. Both wars were fought less for territorial gain than for religious expression. The 1965 war symbolically pitted

Muslims against Hindus, and ended in virtual stalemate. One Pakistani Muslim soldier was said to be the equal of six or seven Indians, but that kind of empty bravado proved nothing on the battlefield. Kashmir remained in Indian hands. Ayub was forced to accept responsibility for what in fact had been a fiasco, a poorly planned and executed military campaign. Considerable damage was done to the Pakistani psyche, especially to the army's self-image. Ayub clung to power to the last possible moment. His successor, General Yahya Khan, sustained military rule but he also had to acknowledge it was time to return power to civilian hands.

The country's first national election was held under army supervision and although judged fair by most standards the results nevertheless unleashed a whirlwind. The politicians, out of power for a dozen years, still had not learned the basic rules of democratic government. Zulfikar Ali Bhutto, a gray eminence in the 1965 war, took it upon himself to reject the 1970 election results that had given a parliamentary majority to the East Pakistan Awami League of Sheikh Mujibur Rahman. What ensued was a weak army high command yielding to the diatribe of the Pakistan People's Party leader. Yahya and his generals allowed themselves to be manipulated by an ambitious politician. The country paid an enormous price for their timidity. The civil war that erupted in March 1971 again had religious overtones. East Pakistan's Hindu population became a principal target of the Pakistan army, but the strife impacted on the entire province, Muslims and Hindus alike. Hindu India became the Bengalis' major benefactor. Although Pakistan lost its distant province when New Delhi intervened, what remained of the country after the war was an even more elevated cry of "Islam in Danger."

Now it was the army's turn to enlist the services of the Islamic fundamentalists. Unable to best the Indian army in a conventional encounter, the embarrassed and humbled army high command looked to the militant arm of the Islamist orders to carry the fight to the enemy. Thus while Bhutto, who had now assumed the reins of a civilian government, set about transforming Pakistan into a one-party state with himself the supreme leader, the army was repairing the damage done to its forces. No less significant, the Inter-Services Intelligence Directorate prepared for a long, clandestine campaign in Kashmir, while Bhutto's diplomacy was aimed at a cessation of hostilities in the disputed territory. On the other side, Bhutto's adventures in Balochistan had forced the Pakistan military establishment to engage in still another unpopular civil war. Pulled in directions it chose not to go, and citing Bhutto's abuse of power, the army took the opportunity to strike against the PPP leader when the 1977 elections were declared fraudulent by the political opposition and the country again was caught in an agony of street violence. Bhutto was deposed and General Zia ul-Haq became Pakistan's dominant authority.

Zia confirmed how closely the military had affiliated with the Islamists. The General's Islamization program was only in its infancy when the Red Army was ordered into Afghanistan. The Kremlin's decision to invade the neighboring country, already swept by a Communist revolution, confirmed the thinking of the Pakistan military that they faced a fight not only to defend the integrity of Pakistan, but to preserve Islam and the Muslim people. Already in intimate association with the Islamists, the Pakistan ISI was given a broader mission that in time defined the limits of the struggle in and outside Pakistan. Islam not democracy was central to the mission of those defending the region against an aggressive atheist force. The subcontinent's independent Muslim state was deemed to be in mortal danger from its Indian and largely Hindu nemesis, and Pakistan's first line of defense was the country's commitment to its Islamic faith. It was that force that the Pakistani ISI harnessed to meet the perceived threat, and, because the concerns were not limited to Pakistan, aroused Muslims in distant places answered the call to jihad, to make holy war on the defilers of Islamic tradition. They did not make democracy their mission. Only the American presence hinted that the struggle had anything to do with democratic objectives. United States military transfers to Pakistan were enormous and provided Zia and the ISI with the wherewithal to gather the Afghans for a decisive struggle. A curious mixture of essentially irregular forces, i.e. Afghans of diverse tribal identity, Pakistanis, Afghan Arabs, and Muslim volunteers from other regions of the world, resisted the Red Army. It was never explained how any outcome could result in a democratic victory. To argue otherwise is to ignore the realities of the effort to defeat the Soviet behemoth.

The road to September 11

Survival not democracy was the objective of Pakistan's military establishment. In a struggle for survival, a nation, no matter how conflicted, returns to its wellsprings, and so Pakistan found energy and solace in its Islamic commitment. It also received substantial assistance, funds and manpower from around the Muslim world, especially from the Arab countries. Pakistanis, and indeed Muslims around the world, therefore could celebrate when the Soviets agreed to pull their troops from Afghanistan. The United States too marked a special victory in its long cold war with Moscow. Moreover, the Soviet retreat coincided with the passing of General Zia and his administration. Pakistan returned to civilian government, and almost overnight the discussion centered again on the democratic process. There were high hopes in elite Pakistani circles, echoed in the United States and across Europe. But the alliance forged between the Pakistan army and the Islamists was not abandoned, and proved to be just as necessary in the aftermath of the Soviet withdrawal as it had been during the long occupation. Eliminating the Communist government in Kabul and bringing Afghanistan under its control became a high priority for the ISI and its supporters in the armed services.

The unexpected implosion in Moscow that suddenly brought an end to the great experiment in Marxism-Leninism seemed to herald a new age of worldwide democracy, but in Afghanistan it only caused the Afghan Communist system to come apart. The many elements that had subscribed to resisting the Red Army now sought other avenues for their expression. Thus began the long and costly internecine conflict that reaped more havoc to the damage wreaked by the Soviet troops. In the midst of this tribal warfare was the ISI, ever trying to turn the battle in favor of Pakistan's long-term interests. The ISI were operating in similar fashion in Kashmir. In 1989, the year when the last Soviet soldier departed Afghanistan, an uprising erupted in the disputed territory. The ISI could not dodge their complicity in the guerrilla assaults on Indian installations in Kashmir. Muslim warriors were welcome to join the struggle and the forces of the jihadis became a common element in the protracted effort to make Pakistan secure and Islam an unbeatable force.

Pakistan not Afghanistan was the key for the most ambitious members of the jihadi movement. What was at stake was more a matter of Islamic renewal and purpose than a call to stable and responsible government. A vast network had emerged from the shadows of the Islamic world which linked the foes of Western secularism with the military institutions of Pakistan. Zia's Islamization program had caused the madrassahs to multiply and the output from these schools of religious instruction became the willing recruits for a steady stream of jihadis. One major consequence of this development was the formation of the Taliban, which by 1996, with significant Pakistani assistance, had seized Kabul from the warring militias and had spread its fiat to most major regions of Afghanistan. The Islamists and their jihadi shock troops were also active in Kashmir, but it was New Delhi that first noted their impact on Pakistan, citing the Talibanization of Pakistan in a period when civilian government appeared to dominate decision-making processes. There was no escaping the ubiquitous actions of the ISI and the Pakistan army. The short-lived governments of Benazir Bhutto and Nawaz Sharif could not be described in terms of democratic renewal. Their coming and going, and coming and going again, had more to do with the nexus of military and Islamist activities than with the birth pangs of Pakistani democracy. The politics of Benazir and Nawaz was little more than a sideshow. The main events were Islamabad's dominance in Afghanistan through links with the Taliban, and the intensification of the *intifada* in Kashmir.

Al-Qaeda found fertile ground in Pakistan. Although it was the Taliban in Kandahar and Kabul that provided the minions of Osama bin Laden with safe haven and bases in which to train, plan and launch their attacks on an unsuspecting Western world, it was Pakistan that, knowingly or not, facilitated their operations. Operating across a broad geographic landscape, al-Qaeda was identified with attacks on Americans in Somalia, in Saudi Arabia, in Tanzania, in Kenya, in Yemen, and finally in the United States. The ingathering of Muslims to Afghanistan and Pakistan, dedicated to the struggle with the infidel, had been initiated by the Soviet invasion of Afghanistan and it did not cease with the Soviet retreat. But whereas Afghanistan offered these dedicated fighters the remote terrain to establish their many fortresses, it was

Pakistan that provided them with access to the larger world. The events of September 11, 2001 brought these otherwise obscure connections into prominence. Al-Qaeda suicide bombers hijacked four American passenger airliners, two of which they flew into the World Trade Center in New York City. Another struck the Pentagon in Washington. A fourth crashed to earth in a field in Pennsylvania before it could deliver another lethal blow against an American target. Approximately three thousand people lost their lives in this unprecedented assault on American soil. George W. Bush, the American President since January, announced that war had been declared upon the United States, but where responsibility for the action could be laid was another matter. All trails led to Osama bin Laden and ultimately to remote Afghanistan, where the suicidal terrorists had trained among the Taliban before passing through Pakistan to their destinations in Europe and the United States.

The war on terrorism

Pervez Musharraf had served as Pakistan's Chief Executive since October 1999 and only shortly before the events of September 11 had assumed the office of President. Reluctant to return authority to civilian hands, Musharraf had talked effusively about the time needed to reclaim Pakistan's purpose and especially to construct democratic institutions. Musharraf believed it possible to bring stability and progress to Pakistan. But he also was committed to a foreign policy that gave virtual *carte blanche* to religious militants and their ISI mentors operating in both Afghanistan and Kashmir. Foreign policy trumped domestic objectives. Building Pakistani democracy never received the high priority given to achieving geopolitical goals. Musharraf therefore sustained diplomatic relations with the Taliban and gave the ISI a free hand to form alliances with Islamist groups in Afghanistan and elsewhere in the Islamic world. Pakistan's intimacy with the Taliban also meant there would be connections to al-Qaeda, and the latter exploited the relationship to maximize its global opportunities. Linkages between the ISI, al-Qaeda, and the Pakistani Jayash-i-Mohammad as well as Lashkar-i-Tayyaba were well established. Each was able to use the other's base camps, though the Pakistani militants were more inclined to operate in Kashmir than in Afghanistan. Nonetheless, Maulana Masood Azhar, leader of the Jayash-i-Mohammad, and the jihadis under his command were known to have operated in Khost and Kandahar and to have had close associations with the Taliban Emir, Mullah Omar. Both leaders had also been major recipients of Osama bin Laden's celebrated money transfers.

At the time of the al-Qaeda strikes against the Twin Towers and the Pentagon, the militants were no mystery to ISI chief General Mehmood Ahmed. The continuing disorder in Pakistan's cities and towns, the use of terror and intimidation, like the earlier bombing of the Egyptian embassy in Islamabad, had provided sufficient cause to charge the complicity of Taliban and al-Qaeda agents in the violence in Pakistan as early as 1995. The intensification of violence in the country was also cause for the informed and more secular segments of Pakistani society to demand the reining in of the ISI and the more violence-prone organizations. Neither Benazir nor Nawaz had succeeded in bringing the terrorists to book and there was some anticipation that the military government of Pervez Musharraf would act more aggressively to neutralize the perpetrators of the mayhem. It was not until August 2001, however, that Musharraf, faced with deepening sectarian conflict, banned the Lashkar-i-Jhangvi and the Sipah-i-Mohammad. Musharraf had done nothing, however, to halt the operations of the ISI and its thousands of regulars and irregulars. Torn between a desire to establish normalcy in the country and a foreign policy concerned with maximizing gains in a limited international arena, Musharraf generally seemed sincere in the former while practicing duplicity in the latter. September 11 brought that contradiction into full view.

Addressing the country on September 19, Musharraf spoke of the great dangers confronting Pakistan. He mentioned the war against terrorism that had been imposed on the United States following the tragic events of September 11. The entire Muslim world, he said, as well as the United Nations stood behind the Americans in their effort to root out and destroy the purveyors of unprovoked mass violence. Moreover, because the terrorists were judged to be al-Qaeda operators, and because al-Qaeda was entrenched in Afghanistan, the United States had asked the

Pakistan government to provide Washington with intelligence, logistic support, and the right to use Pakistani airspace for strikes on al-Qaeda targets. Although American operational plans were not yet known, the President said he had decided the situation was so critical that he had given an affirmative reply to Washington's request. To act otherwise, Musharraf declared, could spell disaster for Pakistan. Aware of Islamist opposition to his decision, he insisted only a small minority of those consulted in his National Security Council, cabinet, and among other politicians, religious leaders, retired senior officers, academic scholars, and former foreign ministers had called for denying the American request. Asserting he had tried to bring the Taliban into the mainstream of world diplomacy, he insisted he had not abandoned that quest. It was his wish that the Taliban could still be persuaded to moderate its policies. And although Mullah Omar had declared bin Laden a guest of the Afghan people and was adamant he would shelter him from the Americans, Musharraf said there might be other ways of dealing with Washington's demand that bin Laden be arrested and extradited to the United States. Echoing the Taliban, Musharraf asked for evidence that would incontrovertibly prove the al-Qaeda leader was responsible for the attacks of September 11. Musharraf's speech indicated he still wanted it both ways: he had opened the door to the United States, and he still clung to the view that Islamists and terrorists were not the same.

Musharraf's statements aimed to buy time. Sensing the Americans were mobilizing for an attack on al-Qaeda bases in Afghanistan, and possibly too for an assault on the Taliban regime of Mullah Omar, the Pakistani President endeavored to protect his country's and his army's interests in the fast-changing events. To defy the United States in the aftermath of the horrific events of September 11 would be to place Pakistan in direct association with the actions of al-Qaeda. Moreover, at this juncture there was no separating al-Qaeda from the Taliban, and Islamabad was forced to choose between being identified as a co-conspirator with the named band of terrorists, or joining the American call for the severing of ties to the regime of Mullah Omar. Musharraf was also forced to ponder the decision to neutralize the most militant of the Islamist organizations operating in Pakistan. Not without considerable hesitation and foreboding Musharraf declared he had chosen to stand with the Americans. Citing New Delhi's sustained effort to have Pakistan declared a terrorist state and President Bush's declaration that not only terrorists but those who harbor them were justifiable targets, Musharraf noted that India had offered the United States defense facilities for its war on terrorism. India's tactics, he said, were to place Pakistan in a situation where strikes could be launched at Pakistan's nuclear facilities and international support could be mustered for New Delhi's expanded war in Kashmir. Musharraf also spoke of the recent Dushanbe conference in Tajikistan, where New Delhi teamed up with Central Asian governments to increase support to the Northern Alliance, the only remaining force in Afghanistan still capable of fighting the Taliban. The Indian government, Musharraf declared, was intent on achieving a regime change in Kabul that would establish an anti-Pakistan government in Afghanistan. For these reasons, Musharraf concluded, he had accepted the American request for assistance. At the same time, he reiterated his argument that in joining with the United States in the war on global terrorism he made no connection with Pakistan's desire to see a just resolution of the Kashmir issue. Nor did he believe the Kashmiri struggle for self-determination was in any way related to the acts of terror perpetrated by al-Qaeda.

Musharraf's decision to assist the United States was condemned in conservative Muslim circles, both in Pakistan and beyond. In Afghanistan, Muslim clerics and scholars were virtually all reported to be in support of Osama bin Laden and they called upon the Taliban regime to offer him protection. Afghanistan's more extreme elements publicized the need for a jihad against the United States. Similar sentiments were heard from their brethren in Pakistan. For the Islamists, the American targeting of bin Laden was merely a pretext for a general assault on the Islamic world and they urged the Pakistan government to reconsider its support for the Americans. Nonetheless, with the United Nations Security Council calling for the immediate arrest of Osama bin Laden, and with the Iranian Foreign Minister joining other world leaders in demanding the arrest and punishment of those behind the September 11 attack, the Pakistan government had no other option. Pakistan provided the Americans with use of several military airstrips near the Afghan frontier. No longer in a position to equivocate, Musharraf had committed Pakistan to the war on terrorism.

On September 26, however, the Pakistan Foreign Minister Abdus Sattar condemned the support made available to the Afghan Northern Alliance. The Alliance's charismatic leader, Ahmed Shah Masud, had been assassinated by alleged al-Qaeda agents, pretending to be journalists, on September 9, less than forty-eight hours before the attack on the United States. Anticipating support would be made available to the Northern Alliance following the September 11 attack, the agents had killed Masud with the aim of demoralizing and causing the break-up of the Alliance. Now, however, the United States, assisted by the Central Asian republics as well as Russia and Iran, was determined not only to sustain the Alliance but to expand its operations against the Taliban. Pakistan's attempt to forestall such efforts were clearly directed at bolstering the Taliban regime in the face of an attempt by the United States to destroy not only al-Qaeda but the Taliban too. Musharraf was trapped on the proverbial horns of a great dilemma. The dynamics of the situation in Afghanistan had shifted from the Taliban and Pakistan to the Americans and the Northern Alliance. Masud was dead, but the United States had filled the leadership vacuum and the struggle for Afghanistan had taken yet another turn. Belgium's European Union leader and Foreign Minister, Loui Michel, summed up the situation best. Though understanding Islamabad's concern about a regime change in Kabul, Michel noted, "there are no good terrorists and bad terrorists." The Taliban, like al-Qaeda, he chided the Pakistanis, was a threat to the stability of Pakistan and to moderate governments all over the Muslim world. Also pressuring the Pakistan government, the United Nations called for a broad-based interim coalition government in Afghanistan. The Taliban, it was said, might have control of ninety percent of Afghan territory but it did not have the support of ninety percent of the Afghan population. The U.N. Assistant Secretary General, Fransesc Vendrell, insisted the majority of Afghans were hostages in their own country. The Six-Plus-Two organization, the Afghan Support Group, the U.N. Security Council, and the U.N. Secretary General all wanted a political solution, he said, but nothing could be done to relieve the crisis until bin Laden and al-Qaeda had been liquidated. Moreover, the time for negotiations on this matter had passed.

The American military response to the September 11 attack began with an aerial campaign against al-Qaeda and Taliban installations in Afghanistan. The intense bombing, using a variety of weapons, including unmanned as well as manned aircraft, was a prelude to the use of American special forces. First authorized to raid and return to ships in the Indian Ocean or bases in friendly countries, especially in Uzbekistan, they were later called to establish bases inside Afghan territory. Saudi Arabia and the United Arab Emirates were pressured to break diplomatic ties with the Taliban, and Islamabad was put on notice that it too would have to withdraw support for a regime it had sponsored since the early 1990s. With a considerable segment of the intelligentsia supporting the decision to sever relations with the Taliban Afghan government, the Jamaat-i-Islami and the different factions of the Jamiat-ul-Ulema-i-Islam condemned the American air strikes and the incursion into the neighboring state. Taking to the streets, the Islamist parties tried to rally massive demonstrations against the Americans, and especially against Musharraf for having yielded to a non-Muslim power. Their call had a particular impact on the Pashtuns. A Shariat Movement was organized under the leadership of Sufi Mohammad of Malakand, who attempted to raise an army to assist the Taliban in their struggle with the United States. Thousands of Pakistanis were recruited in these emotional circumstances but when Islamabad decided it was time to break with the Taliban this large group of Pakistanis found themselves on the wrong side of the fight. With limited means to withstand the American intrusion, cut off from re-supply, and faced with a quickly disintegrating Taliban organization, the Pakistani force found themselves at the mercy of the Northern Alliance and the Afghan forces that joined with it in the advance on Kabul and Kandahar.

Musharraf was forced to react to the fast-moving events on the ground. Accepting the inevitable defeat of the Taliban government, especially after the fall of Kabul, the General-President tried to salvage what he could from the Afghanistan situation by calling for a U.N. peacekeeping force to demilitarize Kabul. That effort was futile in the circumstances. Northern Alliance forces took control of the capital and the fear that Pashtun representation would be minimized in the *ad hoc* government quickly became reality. Taliban control of Afghanistan was replaced by a decentralized command structure, unified only by the international contingent led by United States special forces. But though the Americans were concerned with pressing the fight against al-Qaeda and the hardline Taliban, they were also mindful of the need to establish a semblance of governmental order in the beleaguered country. Calls went out to King Zahir Shah, in exile in Italy, and to his entourage, which included the Pashtuns Hamid Karzai and Yunas Khalis. The need to reassure the Pashtuns that Afghanistan would not be overrun by an Uzbek and Tajik dominated government was high on Washington's list of priorities. Therefore in addition to the seven thousand men the United States had inserted into the country, the U.N. Security Council authorized the sending of five thousand peacekeepers to restore law and order to Kabul and to stop rival tribal leaders from again preventing the consolidation of the nation. No amount of external support, however, could guarantee a better future for Afghanistan or an end to the terrorism associated with the jihadi movements.

Musharraf could not now retreat from his earlier decision to join with the Americans, nor could he continue to support an ISI committed to pro-Taliban operations. Leaving the pursuit of bin Laden and Mullah Omar to the Americans and their team of international forces, Musharraf turned his attention to conditions in Pakistan. The President called for and received ISI chief Mehmood Ahmed's resignation and appointed Lieutenant-General Ehsan ul-Huq of military intelligence to replace him. The new ISI head was ordered to examine ISI ranks and to purge all agents associated with the more militant Islamist associations. Moreover, the ISI was to be de-Talibanized and brought firmly under the army command structure. Word was circulated that Muslim extremists would do best to leave the government, but Musharraf's order to ferret out militants was never clearly defined in the case of Kashmir, where the Afghan mujahiddin model remained in play. Nor was it clear how the Islamist organizations that fueled the *intifada* in Kashmir were to be prevented from sustaining havoc throughout Pakistan, where minorities and foreigners were at considerable risk. And most worrisome to the Musharraf regime was the tie connecting Pakistani militants with al-Qaeda and Taliban cells secreted in Pakistan. Moreover, just as the ISI had enabled bin Laden and Mullah Omar to flee the grasp of their would-be captors, so the ISI, even under new leadership, was reluctant to curtail the operations of some of the most radical Islamist organizations.

Musharraf ordered the round-up of fundamentalists of varying significance, only to release them when it was said there was insufficient evidence to implicate them in plots to harm the country. Harming India, however, was another matter. In October, Jayash-i-Mohammad and Lashkar-i-Tayyaba were implicated in a suicide bombing of the Kashmir State Assembly which killed almost three dozen innocents. Indications pointed to connections between the actions in Afghanistan and those in Kashmir, especially those high-profile terrorist acts that aimed to demonstrate that though the militants could be assaulted they could not be silenced. If for a period the more violent fundamentalists were destabilized in Afghanistan, they had demonstrated they could still function with impunity in Kashmir. Musharraf therefore found himself not only pressured to make greater efforts to monitor Pakistan's porous border with Afghanistan, but also urged to close jihadi training camps and installations in Azad Kashmir as well as in Pakistan. New Delhi was particularly agitated, especially after Musharraf had visited the Indian capital in July in an effort to relieve the tensions caused by the Kargil incident and the constant sniping in Kashmir. Using the leverage afforded by the September 11 attack on the United States, New Delhi pointed to Pakistan government complicity in the construction of a vast terrorist network. Musharraf was thus forced to show his government, and most notably the Pakistan army, that he was no longer committed to supporting militant Islamists.

In view of the need to transform the Pakistan army and to make it more compatible with American interests in the war on terrorism, Musharraf had to do more than change the chief of the ISI. In October, the President extended his term as Chief of the Army Staff and reshuffled all the key positions in the Pakistan army. Musharraf acknowledged the price on his head, that he was a prime target for an assassin, and the army makeover was aimed at constructing the most effective and loyal team of generals, from headquarters to corps commanders to the field units. However, Musharraf also had to withstand the verbal abuse of his detractors. Former ISI chief and now retired Lieutenant-General Hameed Gul, speaking at the Lahore High Court Bar Association, declared the events of September 11 were part of an Israeli and Zionist conspiracy to create the pretext for the long-term occupation of strategic Muslim territory. Reciting the litany of Osama bin Laden, Gul insisted that Israel's American ally wanted to subjugate the Muslim world. Jihad was the only answer to this action against the Islamic people. In the twisted logic of the jihadis, Gul linked official American chicanery to the destruction of the Twin Towers and the attack on the Pentagon. The Americans, he implied, needed a *cause célèbre* to justify their actions in Afghanistan. Hence the events of September 11. Gul's description of September 11 had been circulated earlier via the web and it was hardly an original presentation. Nevertheless, it revealed obstacles Musharraf faced in reorganizing his army and strengthening his political bona fides. Gul's argument found an echo in the divisions within the pro-Musharraf faction of the Pakistan Muslim League when it failed to support the decision to provide air bases and Pakistani airspace to United States forces. Musharraf's Muslim League Party was divided on the subject of a broad-based government in Afghanistan, believing it would damage Pakistani interests. Moreover, Musharraf was put on notice that further capitulation to the Americans would destroy Muslim League chances in the anticipated general elections.

Musharraf had to wear two hats, neither of which fitted him perfectly. Reorganizing the army was a great challenge, but so too was the President's desire to transform the Pakistani political system. Musharraf's role as leader of the Pakistan Muslim League (Q, Quaid-i-Azam) needed special care as the country struggled to achieve a degree of normalcy while immersed in a major international conflict. Washington attempted to ease Musharraf's burden by not addressing the connection between Kashmir and Afghanistan. The visit of U.S. Secretary of State Colin Powell to India and Pakistan centered on playing down India's accusation that Pakistan was a sponsor of terrorism. Instead, Powell attempted to bridge the differences between the two nations, each of which was important to the war effort. Powell cited the centrality of the

Kashmir issue to improved India–Pakistan relations, but in India he also had his spokesman reiterate the strengthened bilateral ties between New Delhi and Washington. Although the pressure on Musharraf remained, and in fundamentalist circles in fact had increased, the attentive Pakistani public read in American behavior an indication that everything had changed, including the American attitude toward the Kashmir dispute. Musharraf therefore used the occasion to call for the reorientation of the country's intelligence services so that there would be diminished interest in political intelligence and more resources devoted to criminal, sectarian, and terrorist activity. The restructuring involved both horizontal and vertical changes that allowed for greater coordination between the federal and provincial levels and could provide the authorities with advance information that would assist in pre-empting terrorist actions. Reversing developments in train for almost twenty years was a gargantuan task, but the effort seemed to indicate that Musharraf was serious about turning Pakistan away from the anarchy that its flirtation with the extremists had caused. If nothing more had been accomplished, it appeared that Musharraf himself had undergone a transformation.

On October 24 an Afghan Shura was convened in Peshawar, an indication of the Afghans' desire to find stability in the mayhem that continued to swirl around them. Former King Zahir Shah was cited as a symbol of unity and it was speculated that he could head a broad-based interim government and call for the meeting of a Loya Jirga to pave the way for a more enduring peace. Although the King's representatives were not yet prepared to attend the conference, the two-day session brought together some seven hundred notables from Afghanistan's thirty provinces, representing all ethnic, communal, and political groups. Also in attendance were members of Pakistan's Federally Administered Tribal Areas (FATA). Conspicuously absent from the Shura were Gulbadin Hekmatyar and the Hizb-i-Islami faction that had denounced the United States and Musharraf. Hekmatyar had pledged holy war against those who had attacked the Taliban and al-Qaeda. Once the favorite of the ISI and hence the CIA as well, the old militant was now seen as directly connected to bin Laden. American special forces therefore were ordered to locate his whereabouts in Iran and Afghanistan, but attempts at eliminating him were unsuccessful. Nevertheless, the Shura was the necessary first round that would lead to more formal meetings in Europe where the Afghan King was expected to preside. Signaling how far the wheel of fortune had turned, Saudi Arabia publicly condemned Osama bin Laden as a heretic and declared his conduct contrary to the universal principles of Islam. Insisting he had done great harm to Islam and was no friend of Muslims, the Saudis accused bin Laden of driving a wedge between the civilizations. The Saudi ambassador to Pakistan also found fault with the Taliban, which he said had brought great misery to the Afghan people. Indicating Riyadh would increase its financial support to the Afghan people and the refugees in Pakistan, he declared his government condemned terrorism in all its forms and was prepared to give assistance to counter-terrorism in any part of the world.

In spite of these developments the Musharraf government repeated its concern that only a broad-based government in Afghanistan would be acceptable. Still concerned that Tajiks and Uzbeks could dominate a new Afghan regime, Musharraf hinted that the war on terrorism could flounder if due attention were not given to this Pakistani dilemma. An *ad hoc* body describing itself as the "Defense of Pakistan and Afghanistan Council" (DPAC) brought together a host of religious parties dedicated to the defense of the Taliban. Warning Musharraf that his intimacy with the United States was totally at odds with the Islamic people, the DPAC declared its intention to begin a vast disobedience movement on November 1. The Islamists announced they would close all major roads in Pakistan and prevent the movement of vehicular traffic. Government civil servants were called to join the effort by quitting their posts and paralyzing the government. Among the more vocal representatives of what was described as a jihadi conference were the Jamaat-i-Islami, the two factions of the Jamiat-ul-Ulema-i-Islam, the Jamiat-Ulema-i-Pakistan, the Tanzim-i-Islami, and the Harkatul Mujahiddin. Collectively the Islamists declared the Musharraf government had lost the support of the masses. Musharraf, in their judgment, had committed an act of heresy by allowing the Americans to make war on a Muslim country. The Islamists also condemned the United Nations and urged Pakistan to withdraw its membership from the world organization. On the action front, the DPAC noted the need to organize training camps and to enlist recruits for the war with the infidels. The latter call was especially associated with the leader of Tehrik Nifaz-i-Mohammadi, Maulana Sufi Mohammad. Joining his clerical colleagues, Qazi Hussain Ahmed, chief of the Jamaat-i-Islami, declared that the Musharraf government had lost the confidence of the masses and would be toppled within a few months.

Musharraf, however, had no option but to stay the course. With the Americans devastating Taliban defenses from the air, the Northern Alliance made significant progress on the ground. The Taliban government ceased to be an effective instrument and concerns turned to the establishment of an Afghan administration and the identification of an Afghan leader acceptable to the different factions in the Northern Alliance and among the Pashtun tribes. To that end, Abdul Haq, a Pashtun leader in the mujahiddin resistance against the Red Army, went on a personal peace mission, hoping to win the favor of moderate members of the Taliban who had formerly been his associates. Haq's mission, however, came to an abrupt end when he was seized by his erstwhile colleagues, tortured, and summarily executed. Musharraf was forced to deny ISI complicity in the death of Abdul Haq, insisting the intelligence directorate no longer supported the Taliban and that the Taliban representative in Pakistan, Mulla Zaeef, had been denied permission to hold a public press conference. The Taliban, however, remained dedicated to their cause. While Musharraf made a hurried trip to Teheran to get Iran's approval for a broad-based government for Afghanistan, Taliban fighters were quoted asserting there was no moderate Taliban, that they rejected all broad-based governments, including one that allowed for their representation, a possibility Musharraf had continued to promote. Cooperation with the Northern Alliance, it was said, was unthinkable. Nor would the Taliban join with King Zahir Shah. The King, they argued, had failed to do anything to assist the Afghans during their long war with the Soviet Union and they wanted no part in a government built around his return to Kabul.

As efforts were being made to assemble an interim Afghan government, Taliban fighters were forced to yield the northern Afghan metropolis of Mazar-i-Sharif. A relief column made up principally of four thousand Pakistani volunteers, organized by the Harakat Jihadi Islami, was prevented from joining up with their Taliban brethren when they came under heavy American bombing. The northern areas controlled by the forces of the Uzbek general Rashid Dostum received the surrender of hundreds of Taliban warriors. The successful campaign made it possible for elements of an American mountain division, based in Uzbekistan, to establish a presence in Afghanistan and eventually to gain control of the Bagram air base, which was made ready for American air power. Musharraf was in London while these events were happening. In a public gathering he described Islam as a religion of peace and called for a quick end to the hostilities in Afghanistan. Pakistan's decision to join the United States and the international coalition, according to the General, was deliberate and taken in pursuit of a "just course." The war on terrorism, he cautioned, could not be confined to Afghanistan. It must also take into account the problems of Kashmir, Palestine, and Chechnya. Knocking a few branches off the tree of terrorism, he opined, does not deal with the tree itself. Arguing Pakistan was a "moderate" Islamic country, he attributed the demonstrations and protest meetings depicted in worldwide television broadcasts to Afghans and other foreigners who wanted to give Pakistan a negative reputation. Obfuscation and ambivalence seemed to be the order of the day. Even the statements of the exiled Benazir and Sharif had little if any credibility. Moreover, their respective parties had fragmented in their absence and were in no position to provide guidance to their followers. The only clear political voice was that emanating from the Islamist camp that opposed Musharraf's military regime and continued to find solace in the Taliban and the personality of Osama bin Laden. Democracy was nowhere to be seen and the only matter that appeared to gain consensus was the institutionalization of the military in politics.

Terrorism and the nation-state

In April 1948, Mohammad Ali Jinnah had discussed his vision of a secular Pakistan state. Pakistan, he said, "is not going to be a theocratic state to be ruled by priests with a divine mission." In 1949, Liaquat Ali Khan repeated and elaborated on this statement. Rule by priests, he declared, was "absolutely foreign to Islam.

Islam does not recognize either priesthood or sacred authority; and therefore, the question of a theocracy simply does not arise in Islam. If there are any who still use the word theocracy in the same breath as the polity of Pakistan, they are either laboring under grave misapprehension or indulging in mischievous propaganda." On the issue of sectarian differences, Pakistan's first Prime Minister noted, "differences of opinion among his [the Prophet's] followers are a blessing. It is for us to make our differences a source of strength to Islam and to Pakistan and not to exploit them for our own interests which will weaken both Pakistan and Islam."

For those who speak of Pakistan as a failed state, it is enough to remind them that it is more an example of failed leadership. After the passing of the founding fathers there was no one to assume the responsibilities of modern governance, and this failing more than anything else produced débâcle after débâcle, finally resulting in the free-wheeling activity of the most obscurantist and irresponsible people ever to lay claim to state leadership. The Taliban found fertile soil in Afghanistan, but its creation may be attributed to Pakistan. By their abdication of responsibility at home and obsequious posturing abroad, Pakistan's leaders never rose beyond the fantasies of their polyglot population. Leaders in name only, they foisted on the people conditions that seldom permitted them to transcend the primordial. Moreover, the arrogance of officialdom plunged the country of Jinnah and Liaquat into a miasma of circumstance that blinded the people to the realities of a world changed by the engines of science and technology. Obsessed with their larger neighbor, they were always reminded by Kashmir of the conspiracy that denied them status as the world's principal Muslim power. In the absence of a realized national identity, it was left to the Islamists to articulate a message of questionable logic that mirrored the confusion of a leaderless people.

The termination of the Taliban government was received in Afghanistan with the popular excitement that can only come from a people relieved of a system that had savaged their traditions. The end of Taliban rule in no way meant an end to Islamic belief or practice. The Muslims of Afghanistan who gathered in Bonn to hammer out an agreement on an interim government took only nine days of civil discourse to achieve their initial objective. By contrast, what could be said of Pakistan, which since the time of

Zia ul-Haq had allowed itself to fall victim to the ambitions of Islamists and their jihadi shock troops? Conditioned by a Pakistan army humiliated in East Bengal, Islamabad adopted the programs of the most zealous elements in the population. All the country's energy was focused on the acquisition of nuclear weapons, on a misguided policy in Afghanistan, and on popular rebellion in Kashmir. Held hostage to these schemes and dominated by ambitious personalities, Pakistan's economy was allowed to deteriorate and its often repeated quest for democracy proved nothing more than the hollow calls of the disenfranchised. Indeed, Musharraf's reasons for joining the United States in its war on terrorism centered on these defining issues.

The events of September 11 had transformed Pakistan's foray in Afghanistan into global conflict, and in the context of superpower activity even a South Asian nuclear power had to accept the status of being a lesser entity. Nonetheless, Pakistan continued to see its security in the context of a "strategic depth" policy in its ongoing struggle with India. Pakistan's military establishment therefore envisaged a continuing role in Afghanistan. It also continued to pursue the notion that Kashmir could be pried from the stubborn clutches of New Delhi. But in reality Islamabad had to take a back seat in the unfolding events that were now truly beyond its control. The Pakistan of Pervez Musharraf had been given a new opportunity to examine its ethos and to decide what exactly it wanted for its future. The situation juxtaposed the messianic state that conceived of Pakistan as the fortress of the Islamic faith, with that other Pakistan, guided by the principles of Jinnah and Liaquat, that aimed at transforming a portion of the Asian subcontinent into a modern, secular democracy. Somewhere in the din of the war on terrorism, in the clashes of sentiment in Kashmir, and the furtive effort to give new meaning to the tribal society of Afghanistan, there existed a Pakistani yearning to achieve an enlightenment commensurate with the age of globalization.

External events had given Pakistan yet another opportunity to give substance to dreams that the Islamists had turned into nightmares. Democracy remained a goal of the more worldly segments of Pakistani society and it had become Musharraf's task to reverse the alchemy of social discourse and to redirect popular energy toward constructive projects. It was no simple matter to sever ties with the Taliban, which had become Pakistan's inspiration, guide, and benefactor. Musharraf, however, had finally come to recognize this most contemporary of Frankenstein monsters as a creature he could not control; it had metamorphosed into a menace that threatened Pakistan's survival as a nation-state. No longer a government alternative in the heart of the Muslim world, the remnants of the Taliban and al-Qaeda scattered into the mountain retreats of Afghanistan and spilled over the frontier to regroup among their brethren in Pakistan. The sustained American military campaign against the Taliban and al-Qaeda in Afghanistan could not avoid crossing into Pakistani territory. Protective of its frontier areas, the Pakistan government had envisaged Afghanistan as its final line of defense against an aggressive Indian army, and that strategy was viewed as being put in jeopardy by American forces in pursuit of al-Qaeda. Nor could skirmishes between Pakistani border troops and Americans be avoided. The Musharraf government therefore was compelled to criticize the American incursions and to insist only Pakistani forces would be used against fleeing Taliban and their terrorist compatriots.

The Taliban endeavored to make Pakistan part of a greater Afghanistan, a messianic state that eventually would encompass the whole of Central Asia. The tide of history had turned in another direction, however, but the belief of bin Laden's al-Qaeda and Mullah Omar's jihadis, that the age of *Pax Islamica* had arrived, and that it could be achieved with the Talibanization of Pakistan persisted. Musharraf finally seemed to grasp the magnitude of Pakistan's dilemma. Haltingly, he tried to reach out to India, calling upon New Delhi to assist in treating their mutual paranoia. Musharraf wanted serious dialog about their mutual but antagonistic grievances in a Kashmir that for too long had divided the two neighbors. But the Islamist militants also reached out to India, and their methods had nothing to do with diplomatic entreaties.

The terrorist assault on the Indian parliament on December 13, 2001 was attributed to Kashmiri jihadis, but by this time it was meaningless to separate one group of homicidal radicals from another. Al-Qaeda had merged with the Taliban, and the jihadis of Pakistan and Kashmir had become one and the same. In Pakistan, Lashkar-i-Tayyaba and Jayash-i-Muhammad were singled out by the Musharraf regime, but their distinctive characteristics were lost in their common use of violence. The Islamists' flagrant assault on the seat and symbol of India's secular democracy brought an instant reaction from New Delhi. India massed troops on its western border and accused Islamabad of complicity. India demanded Islamabad transfer to its charge several named terrorists and aggressively eliminate terrorist installations and cells. With the threat of nuclear war growing in the region, world leaders could not ignore probabilities of a horrific calamity. Among other leaders, Britain's Prime Minister made a hurried visit to India and Pakistan in an effort to ease tensions and stimulate another round of diplomacy. Acknowledging that the attack on the Indian parliament was aimed at weakening the Musharraf government and hence the American-led war on terrorism, New Delhi was imposed upon to resist laying all the blame on Pakistan. Musharraf publicly declared his determination to root out the terrorists. Nevertheless, he also noted he was in no position to abandon the long-held view that Kashmir must be given the right of self-determination. The two actions, however, fed upon each other.

Jinnah had held all forms of extremism in contempt. Musharraf's declared intention to follow in the footsteps of the country's founder required him to realize that sustained conflict with India over Kashmir connected with sectarian violence in Pakistan. Armed jihadi invasions of mosques and imambargahs were no different from assaults on churches and other Christian sites in the Muslim country by vengeful terrorists connected with al-Qaeda and Taliban. On December 31 the Pakistan government announced the arrest of Hafiz Saeed Ahmad, leader of Lashkar-i-Tayyaba, and Maulana Masood Azhar of Jaish-i-Mohammad for violating laws banning provocative speeches. On the same day, two dozen jihadi foot soldiers were arrested, all alleged members of Jaish-i-Mohammad and Lashkar-i-Tayyaba. New Delhi indicated guarded satisfaction with the arrests, but its troops continued to exchange heavy mortar fire with Pakistani units at the southern end of the line of control in Kashmir. A spokesman for General Musharraf reiterated Pakistan's intention to defend its integrity should Indian forces penetrate Pakistani soil.

11

DEFINING THE FUTURE

Although Musharraf wanted to focus on domestic concerns, the war on terrorism became even more compelling in January 2002. The collapse of the Taliban regime in Afghanistan and the search-and-destroy mission launched by the Americans against al-Qaeda camps and hideaways ran parallel with Musharraf's orders to cleanse the ISI of its shadowy role in Afghanistan and Pakistan. Pakistan's Supreme Court became the venue for the airing of ISI adventures that included the creation of training camps for terrorists from a variety of radical Islamist groups. Moreover, the financial connections between ISI and Pakistan's religious parties, as well as the recruitment of jihadis for both Afghanistan and Kashmir, had been undertaken in spite of an official ban on such activities. The emergence of the jihadi culture in Pakistan had become a major subject of public debate, and the questions about terrorists and freedom fighters had caused obvious divisions within the population. That debate, however, was largely moot given aggressive American military action in Afghanistan, much of it arranged from bases located on Pakistan territory. News that Mullah Omar, the erstwhile Emir of Afghanistan, had fled Helmand province pointed to complicity between jihadis loyal to the Taliban leader and Pashtuns working with the ISI. Washington was outraged that Omar had been allowed to slip away and immediately called for the arrest of the Taliban ambassador to

Pakistan, Mullah Abdul Salam Zaeef, and his transfer to American military custody. Musharraf, however, had gone to Kathmandu for the South Asian Summit and was more interested in defusing tensions with India. In the meantime, in Afghanistan, the International Security Assistance Force (ISAF) was taking shape with the arrival of approximately five hundred British paratroopers and Royal Marines and, in Kashmir, New Delhi reported killing more than twelve mujahiddin who were attempting to break through Indian fortifications. As a consequence of the continued fighting in Kashmir, India not only refused to withdraw its military build-up on Pakistan's borders, but reinforced its lines at a number of strategic locations.

On January 13, 2002, President Pervez Musharraf addressed the Pakistani people declaring his government's highest priority was the eradication of extremism, violence, and terrorism, and the re-inspiration of genuine Islamic practices. He declared his respect for the country's *ulema*, but said that he expected them to curb those elements exploiting religion for their own vested interests. Musharraf recounted how he had ordered the closing of the border with Afghanistan in January 2001 to prevent students from the madrassahs from joining the Taliban. He reminded his listeners of the February 2001 Anti-Weaponization Ordinance that was aimed at removing weapons from Pakistani society, and his speech at the June 2001 Seerat Conference in which he implored the *ulema* to avoid inciting religious extremism. He spoke of his August decision to ban the Lashkar-i-Jhangvi and the Sipah-i-Mohammad, as well as the warnings issued to the Tehrik-i-Jafria not to engage in inflammatory sectarian rhetoric. Musharraf insisted the actions taken by his government were in the national interest and not a consequence of foreign pressure. He said he had decided to join the international coalition against terrorism because it was in Pakistan's interest, and that it pained him when religious parties and extremist groups opposed his action. Referring to the protest meetings and processions that had resulted in numerous deaths, Musharraf declared he would continue to meet with religious scholars but that his government would not tolerate disobedience and threats to undermine the state. Equating the Pakistani zealots with the Taliban, Musharraf declared that they claimed their version of Islam to be the only one, whereas, he reminded his audience, Muslims practice their faith in many ways and all are acceptable in God's eyes. He beseeched his audience to beware of those who mix politics with religion and who claim their interpretation of the divine is the only true path.

Musharraf raised the question of who was responsible "for misleading thousands of Pakistanis" and sending them to their death in Afghanistan. Calling for a renewal of patriotism, the General declared, "Pakistan is our identity, our motherland. We will be aliens outside Pakistan and be treated as aliens. Pakistan is our land. It is our soil. If we forsake it, we will face difficulties. This lesson we must learn." This meant putting an end to the sectarian violence that had continued despite the banning of extremist organizations. Musharraf said it was his objective to rid the nation of its Kalashnikov culture and to move the country away from the notion of a theocratic state. Education, he insisted, involves more than religious learning and he had every intention of revitalizing Pakistan's secular educational institutions. Calling upon Pakistanis to recall the teachings of Mohammad Ali Jinnah, and especially his call for brotherhood among Muslims of all persuasions as well as those who find God in other expressions of worship, Musharraf declared that the mosque is no place for the preaching of hatred. The country's religious schools required reform and introspection, and the President announced a new madrassah ordinance that would make these schools responsible to the same codes of behavior required of secular schools. All madrassahs should be registered by March 23, 2002 and no new madrassah would be allowed to open without government approval. Religious schools indulging in extremism, subversion, or militant activity or possessing weapons would be immediately closed. New teachers would be trained for the madrassahs who were capable of teaching the standard subjects of math, science, and languages. Moreover, foreign students would not be admitted unless they were properly documented; those who had not received certification from the government were to be deported. All foreigners visiting the country were to be scrutinized and only those deemed to have appropriate business in Pakistan would be allowed to remain. Musharraf closed his speech by acknowledging that issuing ordinances and regulations was easy and that the difficulty would come in their implementation. To this end, the President revealed that Anti-Terrorist Courts would be strengthened and that Pakistan would mete out justice to its own miscreants; there would be no transferring of suspects to India, irrespective of New Delhi's demands. Musharraf called for the "land of the pure" to purify itself. He noted that Pakistan's population was ninety-eight percent Muslim and that in a Muslim state he expected the people to live as brothers and to stand as a model for the larger Islamic world.

Musharraf's speech was aimed at separating the government, and hence the Pakistan army, from its long and tragic involvement with militant Islam. In a demonstration of willingness to remove the yoke of terrorism from the country, the President ordered the banning of five organizations (Jayash-i-Mohammad, Lashkar-i-Tayyaba, Tehrik-i-Jafria, Sipah-i-Sahaba, and Tanzim Nifaz-i-Shariat-i-Mohammadi). Under partial ban earlier, the extremist organizations were now to be prevented from taking any public positions, holding meetings, collecting funds, or any other activity associated with a working group. Moreover, no new organization could assume the name of the banned parties. Mosques also were to be placed under surveillance, and loudspeaker use, a common practice, was to be used only on the Friday sabbath and for specifically religious purposes. Citing the use of Pakistan by Muslims from other countries, Musharraf let it be known that Pakistan would no longer serve as a "hub" for their nefarious actions. "No way, we will not tolerate this any more," he declared. Musharraf had set in train a policy that he hoped would nullify the former Taliban support policy that had given the Lashkars and the Jayash a free run of the country. September 11 proved the folly of that policy, and its bankruptcy in both Kashmir and Afghanistan. As one Pakistani pundit put it, "We are now paying not for our sins but our foolishness, a history of errors accumulated over the last decade. When will ISI learn its lessons?" India's response to Musharraf's address was guardedly positive; nevertheless New Delhi indicated it would wait on "concrete action" before believing Islamabad had truly changed course.

As might be expected, Musharraf's new posture on extremist fundamentalism did not satisfy everybody. In fact those who condemned the President were more numerous than those daring to publicly support the restrictions imposed on the religious institutions and their chief representatives. Among the critics, few were prepared to accept Musharraf at his word when he said his actions were taken in the name of Pakistan's national interest, not under foreign pressure. The Secretary General of Sharif's Pakistan Muslim League was one of the first on record deploring Musharraf for what was viewed as his knuckling under to New Delhi and Washington. The critics' main line was that in the name of combating terrorism Musharraf had sold out the freedom of Kashmir to the "terrorist state of India." Moreover, the increased latitude to arrest innocent people could only transform Pakistan into a police state. The religious leaders and their parties pursued the same theme, threatening to challenge in court the government order banning their organizations. Pressure emanated from provincial government leaders asking Musharraf to reconsider his decision. The Jamaat-i-Islami wanted its followers to know that no Muslim ruler since Turkey's Mustafa Kemal Ataturk had dared take such action against religious institutions and that Musharraf was not in a position to transform the country into a secular state. Musharraf, however, ignored the protests and the government announced the closing of 254 offices and the arrest of more than one thousand activists, all allegedly members of the banned organizations. In the meantime New Delhi maintained pressure on the Musharraf regime by declaring there would be no reduction of forces on the Pakistan frontier until cross-border terrorism totally stopped. Indian newspapers, however, were more excited by the prospects of tranquility, calling Musharraf's speech and subsequent actions "a watershed" in India-Pakistan relations. The *Times of India* referred to Musharraf's presentation as a "milestone" and called upon the Vajpayee government to reduce the troop build-up on the border and give Pakistan a chance to find its way back to being a "modern, vibrant and confident" nation. Also sounding a positive note from exile in Dubai, Benazir Bhutto described the U.S.-led war in Afghanistan as the catalyst of the resurrection of democracy in Pakistan. A new era was forcing itself on Islamabad whether Pakistan's military rulers were prepared for it or not, she said.

The Musharraf reforms?

However, soon after Musharraf's strong statement on the subject of Islamic extremism and his insistence that there be a clear separation between the mosque and the state, the General began to backtrack. Blasphemy laws passed earlier subjected people to cruel penalties, including capital punishment. Musharraf, despite pleas from the country's literati and conventional legal fraternity, refused to declare the blasphemy laws inhumane or violations of human rights. Nor did he seek to pardon those sentenced to death for simply discussing issues deemed sensitive to the most fundamentalist orders. No less significant was an interview the President gave to a journalist for the American weekly magazine *Newsweek*. In noting that his guide, mentor, and role model was Mohammad Ali Jinnah, Musharraf cited the Quaid's desire to see Pakistan develop as a secular not an Islamic state. The comment was quoted in the religious press and Musharraf was vilified and accused of putting words in Jinnah's mouth. Jinnah's vision for Pakistan, it was said, did not speak of secularism as a Pakistani goal. Instead of holding to his position, Musharraf was advised to deny having made the statement and imply that the reporter had taken liberties with his interview rather than give a true depiction of the exchange. Musharraf's spokesman insisted the General never used the word "secular." Pakistan's vernacular press used the English word "secular" to imply irreligious behavior. In Urdu and some of the other more regional languages "secular" was construed in the pejorative. Given Musharraf's position, some-where between the secular and the spiritual, and forced to acknowledge the growing influence of the Islamists, it was considered wise to tilt toward the religious interpretation. Although the controversy was weathered, it nevertheless showed up the difficulty of moving Pakistan away from its tryst with the Islamic state and hinted that Musharraf's beating the drum of democracy was likely to resonate in ways he did not intend.

In 1999 Musharraf had tried to link his name with that of Ataturk, but he also expressed the belief that Pakistan was more Muslim in its practices than the successor state of the Ottoman Empire. Finding Ataturk too liberal a thinker and too active a secular reformer for Pakistani tastes, Musharraf subsequently adopted the memory of Jinnah, but here too he ran into difficulty. Jinnah's bold statement that Pakistanis could represent any religion, caste, or creed, and that neither ethnic nor religious differences had anything to do with the state may have sounded plausible to Pakistanis of his era. But Musharraf was a Pakistani man of the twenty-first century and an exclusive not inclusive view of society was the popular focus of attention. Carried to a powerful conclusion, Pakistan was a state created for Muslims and therefore it was deemed to be a state guided by Islamic practices and, in particular, by those whose religious practices were the least flexible. As a member of the refugee community from India, Musharraf had to tread lightly; his ambivalence on the matter of where his thoughts were rooted indicated his difficulty in being true to his philosophy, though not to his religion. In late January an American reporter forced Musharraf to come to grips with his official role as President of Pakistan as well as his personal sentiments. Daniel Pearl, a journalist for the *Wall Street Journal*, was kidnapped while pursuing a lead related to the war on terrorism. The kidnappers audaciously publicized his incarceration by sending out email messages and photographs of Pearl's desperate circumstances. All efforts to trace the whereabouts of his kidnappers failed, although the authorities were fairly certain from the outset which group they belonged to. Several weeks passed before the captors released a video that revealed in graphic detail Pearl's hideous death. It all added up to the vengeful actions of a terrorist cell that claimed to have perpetrated the killing as a religious duty. Expressing his profound grief, Musharraf ordered the arrest of the group suspected to have carried out the act. The Pakistan Ministry of Foreign Affairs offered its "profound condolences" to Pearl's widow and described the murderers as devoid of all humanity and their act as barbaric and a stain on Islamic society. The kidnappers had played with the sentiments of Pakistani society by describing Pearl as a CIA operative and then as an Israeli intelligence agent. Indeed, Pearl, who was Jewish, before being beheaded was forced on video to declare his Jewish identity. Daniel Pearl, one of his captors later exclaimed, was "anti-Islam and a Jew."

The Pearl case tested Musharraf's resolve irrespective of his vacillation on his secular propensities. By early February the major culprits in the kidnapping and killing were in custody. The leader of the band of cut-throats proved to be a British-born Islamic militant, Ahmad Omar Saeed Sheikh, who confessed during what was described as intense interrogation. Despite this confession the affair was put to a formal trial under less than public circumstances. Musharraf attempted to deflect world public opinion from the Pearl case by citing India's plans to detonate more nuclear weapons. Although New Delhi insisted it had no intention to detonate more nuclear devices, the two antagonists continued to mass troops on their mutual border and with this threat of a new Indo-Pakistan war the Pearl case faded into the background. Islamabad, however, continued to hammer away at Indian intransigence on the Kashmir issue and, with the global community sufficiently aroused, there was no let up in the demand that India open the door to Kashmiri self-determination.

In February the *Pakistan Herald*, a popular magazine among the English-speaking middle class in Pakistan, revealed the results of a poll it had taken asking the Pakistani public what was the country's most pressing problem. The response said much about the government's religious dilemma: thirty-one percent declared unemployment to be the key issue, and twenty-one percent said it was fear of another war with India. Fifteen percent cited inflation and various economic problems. When asked about the unending Kashmir conflict, hardly four percent registered concern. As one renowned Pakistani columnist put it, "so much for Kashmir being in our blood." Kashmir, it was said, cost Pakistan no less than four billion rupees each year to subsidize the Azad Kashmir government. And that sum was a pittance compared with the billions expended in the perpetual confrontation with India.

Of such stuff was Pakistan's Islamic revolution made. Moreover, Musharraf's attempt to rein in the jihadis, and Pearl's killing had done nothing to restore equilibrium to Pakistani society. In late February, the Pakistan government issued a warning that other Americans could be targets of militant Islamists. American diplomatic installations were placed on high alert and U.S. firms doing business in Pakistan were told to examine their security measures. The Pakistan Interior Ministry issued a statement noting "the way the kidnappers executed him [Daniel Pearl] shows they have made up their mind that they do not care about their own future." Martyrdom had taken on even greater significance among the jihadis, and the revelation that one of the suicide bombers that had killed the Afghan Tajik leader, Ahmad Shah Masud, was a young man with a European education came as no surprise to those called to combat terrorism. The dance of death that the jihadis had accepted as their ultimate expression was also the supreme ritual in their act of faith. That the living were expected to draw something positive from this display of contemporary human sacrifice was difficult to comprehend except among those who fervently believed that their cause was the destruction of a world they had no part in making. Attention was drawn to the spreading influence of al-Qaeda and bin Laden's formation of the International Islamic Front for Jihad. That umbrella organization included, among others, the Pakistani Harkat-ul-Mujahiddin and Jamaat-ul-Fuqra, the latter a Pakistani organization with roots inside the United States through Shaikh Mubarik Shah Gillani, long associated with the ISI. Gillani's disciples were reported as living in at least twenty-two American states. Gillani was another example of the blind leading the blind. Speaking of a conspiracy against the Islamic people, Gillani claimed there were documents that proved the aim of the "Zionists" was to divide Pakistan into four republics. If Gillani was speaking of separate states for Punjabis, Pashtuns, Sindhis, and Balochis, it remained to be explained how that would benefit Israel. Gillani also spoke of the American inquisition against Muslims and said that the growing Muslim population in America was seen as a looming threat to Washington and its war on terrorism. The United States, he declared, wanted to stop the flow of Muslims and purge society of its Muslim members. When it came to the uses of terror, he opined, the Americans were the most adept.

But it was in India that the keepers of the Islamic flame faced their most immediate challenge. Communal warfare was nothing new to India and riots between the religious communities, notably the Hindu and the Muslim, had been a constant since the days of partition. In late February, however, the Indian province of Gujarat exploded in a mad display of indiscriminate violence. This latest example of uncivilized behavior was precipitated by a band of Muslim zealots attacking a train carrying militant Hindus back from Ayodhya, where a mosque had been destroyed to make way for the construction of a Hindu temple. In retaliation Hindus attacked the Muslim community, particularly those living in Ahmedabad. Before the mayhem subsided weeks later almost a thousand people had lost their lives, most of them Muslims. The instigators of the action could no doubt guess the consequences in attacking the train, but, given their efforts at destabilization, the loss of innocent life was a small price to pay, no matter how many innocents were sacrificed. At the very same time, terrorists described as activists by the Pakistan government attacked a Shiite mosque in Multan, slaughtering the worshipers at prayer. Those detained by the police linked responsibility for the assault to the Lashkar-i-Jhangvi and the Jayash-i-Mohammad, the very organizations banned and supposedly disbanded a few weeks earlier. Another Shiite mosque was attacked in Sialkot; the noted scholar Baqir Hussain Shah was one of the victims. By early March, Pakistani police had in custody more than two thousand Muslim militants, the majority from the banned organizations. The Ministry of the Interior was given responsibility for determining who was innocent and who dangerous. The government announced they could hold the detainees no more than three months. If charges were not then brought against them within that period, by law they had to be released. But even before the expiration of the detention order the government decided to release leaders of the Jamaat-i-Islami and the Jamiat Ulema-i-Islam. Most of the lesser figures who had been detained were released soon after.

Law enforcement in Pakistan left much to be desired. Following Musharraf's speech on January 12, the level of violence rose to even higher levels. Sectarian clashes between Sunni and Shiite Muslims were especially bad. Almost every day since the start of the government's get-tough policy, slayings and maimings of Shiites were reported in the daily newspapers. Particular targets were members of the Shiite professional and business community. Motorcycle assailants were noticeably active, directing their fire on shopkeepers and pharmaceutical workers, and academics and medical doctors. Another Shiite mosque was attacked in Rawalpindi and again the death toll was in double figures. In a display of unusual unity Shiites and Ismailis along with concerned Sunnis drew up a petition that was addressed to President Musharraf and was also supported by frightened members of the Christian, Hindu, Parsi and Buddhist communities. The petition called upon Musharraf to take the necessary action to put an end to the killing and disorder: "We ask you General Musharraf: are you able to sleep in peace surrounded by this ever widening pool of blood of Shia Pakistanis...?"

Musharraf's oratory had yet to be matched by his actions. Courageous journalists pointed out that too many criminals had been provided safe haven in Pakistan simply because they professed an extreme attachment to Islam. It was their argument that the commitment to faith did not give Muslims the right to kill. Sheikh Omar Sayeed, the confessed murderer of Daniel Pearl, had been released from a jail in India as part of a deal that ended the 1999 hijacking of an Indian airliner. He had served five years in jail for kidnapping. His violent proclivities were well known to the Pakistani authorities; nevertheless he was allowed to remain in Pakistan to perpetrate further crimes, simply because he said he had found the "true" meaning of religion. It was by such reasoning that the leader of Jayash-i-Mohammad, also a leader of the terrorist organization Harkatul Mujahiddin, could justify the assault on the Indian parliament. Arrested only to be released due to "lack of evidence," the would-be violent defenders of faith were clearly a group that the Pakistani authorities were reluctant to deal with forcefully. Inter-Services Intelligence links with terrorist organizations had been well documented, but little if anything had been done to break the network of government and non-governmental terrorist organizations working in the name of religion. Terrorism flourished wherever the writ of the state was weak and ambivalent, and it remained shrouded in strained religious discourse. Musharraf may have had a life-changing experience and at least in his public pronouncements he had reversed the course of Pakistan's government, but there was no mistaking Pakistan's immersion in a high tide of calumny and intrigue.

Realizing the need for concerted action, in March Musharraf ordered the army, the police, and the intelligence services to act more aggressively in ferreting out terrorist cells. On March 8 four such groups were exposed in Karachi and quickly linked with religious and sectarian killings. Information was also uncovered about the targeting of Shiite medical doctors in Karachi. The next day the government announced it intended to expel thousands of

Arab and other foreigners allegedly studying at religious schools in the country. According to the authorities, there were thirty-six thousand foreign students in the country, seventeen thousand from Arab countries. Pakistan was home to more than six hundred religious institutions with a combined student population of approximately six hundred thousand. With such a vast pool from which to draw recruits, it was hardly surprising that hundreds, even thousands, had been attracted to the many jihadi organizations. Perhaps sensing their honeymoon days with the Pakistan government were fleeting, the terrorist cells, heretofore nurtured by agencies like the ISI, revealed they would not be intimidated. A Protestant church frequented by American diplomats and their families in Islamabad was invaded by grenade-wielding militants who killed a number of worshippers. The U.S. government advised all Americans in Pakistan to practice caution, noting the increased risk and the impossibility of determining in advance the terrorists' next target. Subsequently, Washington ordered all non-essential diplomats in Pakistan to leave the country. Americans, however, were not the only ones at risk. On March 19 another motorcycle attack, this time in Lahore, took the lives of a Sunni scholar and a Shiite leader. Again the government's response was an expressed determination to identify and eliminate the terrorists, but, as one government official put it, "every inch of the country's land cannot be monitored." United States CIA director George Tenet seemed to echo that thought when he announced the war on terrorism had entered a new and more difficult phase, saying the terrorists had adopted small-unit operations in "a classical insurgency format."

Under constant verbal abuse from New Delhi for his failure to effectively neutralize the jihadis, Musharraf lashed out at the Vajpayee government and in an emotional response declared that New Delhi might well examine and control its own Hindu extremists. Describing Indian assaults on his government as "offensive," Musharraf declared that Pakistan would not tolerate being treated "like dirt, as if we are some kind of scum, a very weak country, which cannot handle itself." Under pressure from the sustained Indian build-up on Pakistan's frontier, the continuing war in Afghanistan and its spillover effects, and the frustrating war against terrorist cells in his own country, Musharraf was forced to shatter all ties with the militant Islamist orders, including those operating in Kashmir. The government revealed that Islamabad and Washington were working on more intimate ties between the United States FBI and CIA and Pakistani intelligence services. American use of high-tech surveillance equipment, unavailable to Pakistan law enforcers, had been tracking al-Qaeda and Taliban agents, many of whom had found refuge in Pakistan. These data were now being used by Pakistani intelligence and assault units ordered to encircle and seize alleged terrorists. An indication that the closer working relationship was beginning to show rich dividends was the capture in Karachi of Abu Zubaydah and Ramzi bin Al-Shaiba, members of bin Laden's inner circle. Both al-Qaeda leaders were quickly transferred to American custody.

The real Musharraf reforms?

For a brief period in April terrorism took a backseat to politics. Insisting on holding onto his multiple roles and having already extended his term as Chief of the Army Staff, General Musharraf called for a referendum on his status as the country's principal political leader. Following in the tradition of Field Marshal Ayub Khan and General Zia ul-Haq, Musharraf announced the holding of a national referendum to give him an additional five-year term as President and Chief Executive. The October 2002 poll for the national and provincial legislatures would not change the outcome of this referendum. Challenged by criticism from every quarter, the General deflected all opposition to his plan, arguing that the country needed his brand of leadership and that his administration had much to do to restore Pakistan's political system to a level of equilibrium. Describing himself as a "democrat," Musharraf stressed his determination to restore true democracy in the country. Again arguing that Benazir's and Sharif's governments had failed to promote an equitable political process, had exploited their high office for personal gain, and had destroyed the people's confidence in competitive politics, the General-President said there was no alternative to his remaining in power. With the country challenged by militant Muslim extremists, only the combined efforts of the country's security forces could hope to bring an end to the havoc, and he was in the best position to lead that struggle.

With the referendum scheduled for April 30, Musharraf met with many of the country's active politicians to review the law and order situation and to explain the need for a "legal" extension of his authority. Sensitive to criticism, however, the General was not ready to listen to dissenting views, especially from officials in his administration. As he made the rounds to stump for support, a rally in Faisalabad turned ugly when journalists covering the event were pummeled by the police. The Punjab governor, a protégé of the President, was accused of ordering the manhandling of the newspapermen. In response the governor criticized the press for what he believed was its mendacious reporting. The journalists, however, had the last word when their influential unions condemned the police baton charge and the bloodying of a number of their colleagues. The journalists declared the government could not have both a free and a gagged press at the same time. Musharraf was heavily criticized for his apparent decision to thwart an independent assessment of the referendum. Moreover, because of the attack on the press, all the political parties, previously paralyzed by the military government, had been given an open invitation to condemn the projected referendum. Musharraf, however, was not about to alter his plans. Arguing that his government had already empowered people at the grassroots, had stimulated a lackluster economy, had strengthened national unity, and had enhanced Pakistan's prestige in the world community, he now wanted the population to indicate their support for a continuation of his policies. Asserting the referendum was a constitutional act, the General believed the people would see through the diatribe of his detractors and vote for the restoration of democratic government by giving him another five years.

Musharraf's timing was significant. The country had in fact seen an improvement in its economy. Foreign reserves had risen from U.S.$0.5 billion to U.S.$5.5 billion and Musharraf said never again would government officials be allowed to plunder the country's wealth. Claiming his was a selfless administration, he noted that previous elected governments had looted the treasury and contributed nothing to the well-being of the people. For too long the country had been made subject to a feudal leadership that nurtured corruption and nepotism. Those days, said Musharraf, would not return. Democracy meant nothing if its benefits were directed only at the few. His administration, he declared, was centered on reducing poverty and this meant helping the masses of poor. The referendum that he had ordered was meant to bring the people into good relations with the government and to seek popular support for the policies already in train. As a demonstration of his resolve Musharraf announced the granting of proprietary rights to landless farmers wherever state land was available. He also declared that villages not yet electrified would be given high priority. Musharraf also stressed the need to repair barrages and canals and to improve the country's irrigation systems. The President said it was his expectation that all development targets would be met before his new five-year term in office expired. However, Musharraf's forecast of economic success depended on the funds made available by the Asian Development Bank, the World Bank and International Monetary Fund, and the United States, which had offered to compensate Pakistan for much of its costs in the war on terrorism. This the General did not wish to publicize.

Musharraf could not understand why there was so much opposition to the referendum, in particular the fear registered by the informed public that the referendum would not be a free expression of the people. His critics had convinced much of the population that the referendum was not democratic practice. Put forward by the military government, it could only enhance the dictatorial powers of the General-President, who might, if given the opportunity, make himself President for life. The politicians complained that the October elections could produce a legislature and a Prime Minister, but they would be so weak and their powers so confined that together they would be little more than a rubber stamp for the Musharraf government. Musharraf had spoken of the need for a system of checks and balances. His critics saw his program as more check and virtually no balance at all. Even before the referendum could be held, Musharraf spoke of amendments to the constitution that were intended to restructure the political system. Citing among his critics Benazir and Sharif, who he said were "sitting outside Pakistan ... trying to destabilize the system," Musharraf said he deplored confrontational politics, believing it to be counterproductive. The country, he said, could no longer tolerate conflict between the government and the President and it was his intention to secure the presidency against those who would weaken it. A reminder of Ayub Khan's preference for the presidential over the parliamentary system, Ayub spoke of the "genius" of the Pakistani people and their unfamiliarity with democratic practice. Like Ayub, Musharraf wanted to separate the masses from the politicians' intrigues, and hence he acknowledged the legislature's role in making law but rejected its claim to executive powers.

Despite the protest meetings and petitions calling for the rescinding of the referendum, it was held on schedule on April 30; those casting ballots gave Musharraf the expected resounding victory. With politicians calling upon their constituents to remain at home and with the MQM officially boycotting the election, voter turnout was low but nevertheless Musharraf won a stellar victory. The government claimed that of the 61.90 million eligible voters seventy percent had gone to the polls, a number disputed by the opposition but nevertheless the only figure readily available. Thus out of a total of 43.39 million said to have voted, Musharraf received ninety-eight percent of the votes polled: 40.02 million. As stated under the Referendum Order of 2002: "If the majority of votes cast in the referendum are in the affirmative, the people of Pakistan shall be deemed to have given [a] democratic mandate to General Pervez Musharraf to serve the nation as President of Pakistan for a period of five years." The period of five years was to be computed from the first meeting of the Majlis-i-Shura or parliament that was to be elected in October 2002. Constitutional lawyers therefore questioned whether the President's term could be made official without the validation of parliament, or else the Supreme Court. Cynics argued that the President would never tolerate a negative vote by the national legislature and that the question of a future parliament approving the referendum was moot. Musharraf therefore still faced the task of demonstrating whether democracy could be restored to the beleaguered nation. The General's insistence that the National Security Council would be given ultimate authority to approve or reject the President's mandate also appeared to make a sham of the democratic process. What Musharraf meant by democracy therefore remained unclear, but certainly parliament's powers were to be circumscribed and in no way would it be allowed to frame a challenge to the Chief Executive. Ayub Khan had tried "Basic Democracy" and Bhutto had made some reference to "People's Democracy," but Musharraf wanted neither of those systems. Given the army's central role in the ongoing political process, it was obvious that the democracy of which he spoke had more to do with the guardians in Plato's *Republic* than the representative government of Locke's *Second Treatise*.

The higher bureaucrats and army generals had demonstrated their contempt for the politicians since the early years of independence. That perception had only been reinforced with the passing decades. Military rule was a consequence of the failure of the country's political leaders to address the major issues of provincialism, corruption, and nepotism, and Pakistan had paid a high price in blood and wealth as a result of leadership failure. The generals who interposed themselves between the politicians and the people of Pakistan fared no better and generally acted no more selflessly or professionally than the politicians, but the frequency of military takeovers had over the years blurred the lines between the army generals and the politicians. Given the intimate association of the one with the other a point was reached in the 1990s when it was believed best to provide the military with a formal role in the political process. Instead of assuming that the politicians represented democracy, and the army autocracy, it seemed a propitious time to accept the intertwining of the one with the other. Neither had an absolute claim on democracy, nor did either show a greater tendency toward authoritarianism.

The proposal for the creation of a National Security Council (NSC), composed mainly of the highest-ranking officers of the armed forces, was rejected when initially proposed, but the realities of Pakistani politics did not allow it to disappear. It took the Musharraf coup of October 1999 and the events of September 11, 2001 to give the NSC substance and the necessary momentum to make it an integral part of Pakistan's constitutional system. With a war on terrorism likely to continue indefinitely and the nation's politicians far too limited in ability and government experience, the military had to maintain its proactive political role, with or without Musharraf. Moreover, if democracy, or a manifestation of it, was to be pursued as a national goal, it was beginning to dawn on Pakistanis that the army might become less the periodic disturber of the democratic process and more a positive force in constitutional development. Ayub Khan in the 1960s expressed the view that Pakistan was not prepared for the Western model of democracy but that the country could begin to manage a democratic process that reflected its condition and time. Some four decades later, and as a consequence of the global struggle with terrorism, that view had finally acquired a modicum of acceptance.

Punctuating this issue, after the referendum an MQM strike shut down Karachi and disturbances produced bombings in the city that forced the army and paramilitary forces to respond. The politics of violence had long swirled around the activities of the MQM and this latest disruption was just one more example of the failure of political parties to reinforce civil society in the country's largest metropolis. Still another indiscriminate act of violence was the killing, this time in Lahore, of Dr. Murtaza Malik, another noted religious scholar, who was gunned down as he left his home. In addition to his death were those of Dr. Nishat Malik, Mustafa Kamal Rizvi, and school principal Zafar Zaidi, all residing in Karachi. The newspaper *Dawn* in an opinion piece on March 18 cited the killing of more than one hundred medical doctors by unidentified assassins. The column also spoke of the killings of Christians in Bahawalpur and Islamabad and the total inability of the government to protect the innocent. As the purveyors of violence continued to target the most sophisticated members of Pakistani society, a more publicized act of terror occurred on May 8. Suicide bombers drove their car into the side of a bus that was ferrying French technicians and engineers to and from the Karachi port facilities, where they were assisting in the construction of three French-designed Pakistani submarines. The event occurred in broad daylight, outside the Sheraton Hotel in the central part of the city. Eleven French citizens lost their lives in that attack, allegedly the work of al-Qaeda and Taliban cells. Following this latest incident Musharraf called a meeting of the National Security Council and heads of the different intelligence services. Federal Interior Secretary Tasnim Noorani reported that approximately three hundred al-Qaeda and Taliban suicide bombers had infiltrated the country and that many of them were expected to unleash themselves on the public. Acknowledging that still more concerted action against terrorism was necessary, Musharraf announced there would be more cooperation with American, British, and French intelligence agencies and that the country's borders would have to be tightened further, if necessary in concert with American and other international forces operating in Afghanistan. He said that sixty thousand regular Pakistan army personnel had been deployed on the Afghan border, and that the number was to be increased to the extent it did not jeopardize Pakistan's defenses along the border with India. Although invitations to foreign intelligence and military units were not popular in Pakistan, the Pakistani generals were compelled to admit they could not alone expect to neutralize a multiple ongoing threat.

The United States asked for Pakistan's permission to send its special forces into the Pashtun tribal areas, generally off limits even to Pakistani regular forces. Washington had received intelligence that al-Qaeda was operating in Waziristan, and there was even speculation bin Laden had been given refuge there. The region was already seething with anti-American sentiments, and so penetration of the mountain fortifications, in official Pakistani opinion, was not worth the increased hatred that would be stirred up. Islamabad signaled Washington that it would be better to monitor movements in Waziristan from Pakistan, where al-Qaeda agents would be more exposed. Indeed, al-Qaeda and Taliban activists were allegedly paying smugglers huge sums for entry into Pakistan. The killing of four terrorists in Multan on May 14 underlined the utility of that strategy. Believed to be al-Qaeda and associated with Lashkar-i-Jhangvi, within this cell, according to Pakistani authorities, was an assassin wanted for the killing of an Iranian diplomat. Acknowledging the closer cooperation between United States and Pakistani intelligence, U.S. Defense Secretary Donald Rumsfeld publicly praised Islamabad's contribution and hinted that larger efforts were in the offing.

The May issue of *Fortune* magazine, however, indicated the cooperation between Washington and Islamabad was still insufficient for the test imposed on the nations combating global terrorism. Pakistan was said to have the largest number of terrorists in the world, and informed Pakistanis were the first to admit that the country had been so long exposed to terrorist activity that rooting it out would require resources not yet imagined. It was nevertheless perplexing how successive Islamabad governments had allowed such conditions to develop. Afghanistan may have been the beginning of Pakistan's current dilemma, but the problem of Afghanistan was compounded by myopic Pakistani officials, too many of them in uniform, who saw Afghanistan as a proxy partner in the war with India. In creating the Taliban, Islamabad had enhanced bin Laden's legions, not Pakistan's national security. If Islamabad at one time had tried to influence the course of Afghanistan's history, by 2002 it was all too obvious Islamabad's Forward Policy had rolled back on itself. It was now left to the Americans and the European nations, working with Musharraf, to salvage what they could from the ghost of Pakistan-past. Informed Pakistani opinion mused that the American presence in the region had given Musharraf the opportunity to re-chart Pakistan's future.

With an estimated one million Indian troops massed along Pakistan's frontier, New Delhi was seemingly eager to take advantage of the war on terrorism to strike at alleged terrorist bases in Pakistan and Azad Kashmir. More than Pakistan's nuclear deterrent, it was again the United States that appeared to hold back a vengeful Indian onslaught. Pakistan's strategy in Afghanistan in shambles, its armed forces split between its two hostile borders, Pakistan, like India, had cited the horrors of nuclear war *ad nauseum*. Nevertheless, in a statement made at the United Nations, Pakistan's ambassador declared his government could not promise a "no first strike" policy if India precipitated an attack and Pakistan could not effectively respond with conventional forces. With Pakistani and Indian forces on high alert, no one could forecast outcomes. Moreover, Islamabad's efforts to convince New Delhi of the necessity for withdrawing forces from forward positions were fruitless. New Delhi pointed to the almost daily terrorist attacks in Kashmir and on each occasion attributed the sustained assault to Islamabad's actions and policies. Thus despite the ongoing war against terrorism and the increased cooperation between Islamabad and Washington, New Delhi did not see how any of the registered successes against al-Qaeda and the Taliban benefited India's situation in Kashmir.

In the face of what Pakistan regarded as Indian intransigence, Musharraf's Information Minister, Nisar Memon, called upon all Pakistanis, from all political persuasions, to rally behind the President and the Pakistan army. Arguing this was not the time for politics as usual, he cautioned the opposition not to fall prey to Indian machinations. The inference was that Pakistan was in a fight for its survival and that these critical conditions demanded the suspension of partisan criticism. An All Parties Conference (APC), comprising twenty-four political and religious organizations, was convened in Lahore on May 19, but it was not the meeting the government had called for. Rather, the APC condemned both Musharraf and India and called for the establishment of a caretaker government that would present a more formidable challenge to New Delhi. Calling for a "full-time" Chief of the Army Staff, the politicians wanted Musharraf out of government and out of the army. The APC's more vocal organizations were represented by the Alliance for the Restoration of Democracy and the Muttahida Majlis-i-Amal. The religious leaders were especially provoked, insisting on the removal of Musharraf and arguing that Pakistan's security would be enhanced if the General stepped aside. Musharraf, they declared, was indispensable to the Americans, not to Pakistan. In its principal resolution, the APC declared that Musharraf "stands discredited and lacks the stature and moral authority to deal with the current threat to national security and territorial integrity of Pakistan." The conference also questioned why Pakistan maintained thousands of troops on the border with Afghanistan if in fact the country was threatened by an imminent attack from India. Finally, referring to Benazir and Sharif, the APC wanted the government to explain how it could speak of fair and unfettered elections when major political party leaders had been denied the right to participate.

Musharraf's fundamentalist political opposition refused to acknowledge the war on terrorism as a Pakistani affair. Convinced that the Americans had foisted the war on the region for purposes that served their own interests, the Islamists insisted Musharraf had joined Washington because this alliance provided the needed façade behind which the General-President could sustain his personal accumulation of power. Seeming to argue they had nothing to fear from either al-Qaeda or the Taliban, the Islamists' immediate concern was the removal of the U.S. presence. In the absence of the United States, Musharraf would become irrelevant. The Americans, according to the jihadi sympathizers among the politicians, stood not for the restoration of democracy but for the reinforcing of autocratic government and the stifling of the voice of the Pakistani nation. Even when strong evidence was collected demonstrating al-Qaeda's shift to Pakistan, few Pakistanis were greatly aroused, so blinded were they by their hatred of Musharraf. Only a few were prepared to recognize suicide bombing or other violent acts of terror as something forbidden (*haram*) in Islamic teaching. Also given the fundamentalists' hatred for the United States, there was ample evidence to suggest that al-Qaeda agents escaping from Afghanistan would find sufficient numbers of Pakistanis prepared to conceal and support them. It was not surprising therefore that twelve Arab members of al-Qaeda were taken from upper-class dwellings in Hayatabad and University Town in Karachi on May 29. Aided by the American FBI agents who had tracked the men, the Pakistan special forces transferred all of them to American custody after their capture. The captives were said to hail from Jordan, Sudan, Somalia, Syria, Iraq, Kuwait, Palestine, and Algeria. A number of Pakistanis were also arrested for complicity in harboring dangerous criminals.

One indication that the frontline in the war on terrorism had shifted from Afghanistan to Pakistan was the election in Afghanistan on June 2 to select delegates to attend the Loya Jirga. With American special forces and support aircraft striking at suspected remaining al-Qaeda bases on Afghanistan's extreme eastern and southern frontier, and with a multinational force of peacekeepers providing a semblance of tranquility in Kabul, Afghanistan was able to proceed with its stabilization policy. Nevertheless, U.S. forces had not yet been given permission to strike at possible terrorist camps on the Pakistani side of the frontier. Pakistan therefore provided friendlier ground for the remnants of al-Qaeda and the Taliban. Pakistani intelligence officers living among the tribal people were known to provide safe passage to Taliban officials – like that granted the Taliban Deputy Foreign Minister, Abdul Rahman Zaid, and General Jalil Yousafzai, a senior Defense Ministry official. Both men were allowed to attend a social function in the Pakistani tribal belt and then disappear. Moreover, reports circulated about other wanted terrorist officials who were living comfortably in Quetta and Peshawar. One of this number, Maulvi Agha Jan, a Taliban defense official, brazenly announced that he considered Osama bin Laden a "a true patriot" and that despite their efforts the Americans would never be able to catch him. Bin Laden simply had too many allies among the tribal Pashtuns and they would never betray him, no matter how much money was offered for his arrest.

Al-Qaeda and the Taliban thus drifted into and regrouped in Pakistan, and others moved their operations to Kashmir. On June 4, speaking in Kazakhstan, Indian Prime Minister Atal Bihari Vajpayee warned of this shift in the war on terrorism, noting that his country was close to the epicenter of religious extremism and its attendant violence. Focusing his eyes on General Musharraf, who was also present for this summit meeting of South and Central Asian leaders, the Indian Prime Minister excoriated the Pakistani President for failing the keep his promise to halt cross-border terrorism. Russian President Vladimir Putin, also present at the meeting, was obliged to warn both South Asian leaders that their failure to begin a process of reconciliation was threatening the entire region. Moreover, because they were nuclear powers, if they failed to submit their grievances to dispute resolution, the consequences of their actions could be disastrous for the entire world. Picking up on Putin's concern, Musharraf left the meeting with an offer to Vajpayee to open an unconditional dialog. Vajpayee's response was direct: New Delhi had nothing to discuss until Pakistan destroyed the ability of the terrorists to use Pakistani soil for their attacks in Kashmir. Britain's Foreign Minister and the U.S. Deputy Secretary of State also applied pressure on the two disputants, but it was Musharraf who was forced to accept the greater burden. In response, the Pakistani President offered another proposal, this time for an international patrol to function along the line of control. New Delhi rejected that idea as well. Later, however, India offered joint patrols of the line of control, but now it was Islamabad's turn to reject the proposal. While Pakistan and India remained poised for war, King Zahir Shah, after a twenty-nine-year exile, returned to Afghanistan, and on June 10 fifteen hundred delegates from across Afghanistan gathered in Kabul for their Loya Jirga. The Loya Jirga's goal was the establishment of a more secure transitional government that could begin the long process of reconstruction in the war-ravaged country. After several days of speechmaking and raucous politics, Hamid Karzai, the interim Afghan leader, was elected Afghanistan's head of state.

In Pakistan, however, it was business as usual. Not in any way subdued by Musharraf's actions against the Islamists and their jihadi colleagues, the Muttahida Majlis-i-Amal took the opportunity to meet with Musharraf to discuss what they deemed to be a shift in his government's Kashmir policy. The Islamists not only came with a list of demands for continued and substantial support for the Muslim guerrillas in Kashmir, but also wanted specific constitutional issues addressed. They called upon Musharraf to dismiss his chief election commissioner and to replace him with an unbiased officer of the Pakistani bar. They also asked for the lifting of restrictions on the parties and on those politicians denied the opportunity to participate in the October elections. Maulana Fazlur Rahman, leader of one faction of the Jamiat-Ulema-i-Pakistan, however, argued that the franchise must be denied to members of the Qadiani community, especially if they insisted on voting as Muslims. The Islamists also condemned Musharraf's decision to invite assistance from the United States and Europe; they hinted that the General's actions verged on blasphemy.

The Islamists displayed no remorse when on June 14 a car bomb was detonated outside the American consulate in Karachi, causing significant loss of life. Deemed the work of the Harkatul Mujahiddin al-Alami, an order was issued for the immediate arrest of the group's leaders. The U.S. Secretary of Defense, Donald Rumsfeld, had met with President Musharraf in Islamabad only the day before the suicide attack. It appeared the bomb was meant to send a message to both leaders that their war on terrorism was not succeeding and that the Americans would be wise to leave the country. The more conventional party leaders denounced the bombing and instead directed their fire against the ISI. The PPP, in particular, condemned the intelligence agency for harassing and intimidating politicians as well as providing support for candidates prepared to do its bidding. The ISI was also condemned for influencing the outcome of local council elections and for trying to convince party members to defect to the Musharraf Muslim League faction. Citing the ISI's failure in Kargil, in Afghanistan, and in Kashmir, the PPP held the directorate responsible for the threat of nuclear war that hung over the country.

In July, speaking for the government, Brigadier Mukhtar Sheikh noted the "lethal alliance" between local militants and al-Qaeda terrorists. Calling for the need to alter the public perception, he also said the government had awakened to the necessity of painting the terrorists in "their true colors." For the first time declaring jihadi groups like Lashkar-i-Jhangvi "terrorists" not "freedom fighters," he appealed to the public to recognize the danger they posed to the country. The connection between the militant organizations and the Islamist parties was not mentioned but the implications were obvious. The Islamists had to be taken seriously. It was the public's sentimental support for the causes they represented that drew large numbers of the Pakistani population to identify with them. Nevertheless Musharraf's policies were aimed at neutralizing the more conventional politicians, who were more likely to challenge his authority. On July 8 a ban was imposed on third-term aspirations for politicians who had already served two terms as head of the federal government or head of a provincial government. The government's justification for the action was the need for "new blood," but the ban was fashioned specifically with Benazir and Sharif in mind. Under no circumstances did Musharraf want Pakistan's leading national politicians competing with his own slate of officers. Sharif's Muslim League and Benazir's PPP were outraged by the decree. Saying no individual could personally amend the constitution, PPP spokesmen declared the Qualification to Hold Public Office Order 2002 *mala fide* and commented it was a crude attempt to subvert the will of the people. Moreover, the order violated fundamental rights of the individual seeking office and denied the voter a legitimate preference. It was also a violation of the principle of parliamentary government. Stating that only Articles 238 and 239 of the 1973 constitution provided procedure for amending the constitution, they said that the order, rather than opening the political process to political normalcy, threatened the foundations of the state.

Musharraf's attempt to marginalize the conventional parties while encouraging Pakistanis to abandon the Islamists made sense to himself, but it remained to be seen how the war on terrorism could be managed and at the same time democracy could be revitalized. Musharraf's dubious and contradictory posture depended on the support he received from his military–technocrat power base and the success of the Americans in neutralizing al-Qaeda, strengthening the Hamid Karzai government in Afghanistan, and holding the Indians at bay. The Musharraf administration issued still other edicts – the Political Parties Order 2002 and the Election Order 2002 – that added further obstacles to politicians attempting to ply their trade. One provision laid down a minimum educational qualification of a college or university baccalaureate for anyone wishing to serve in the national or provincial assemblies. The Supreme Court unanimously upheld this requirement. Petitioners had argued violation of their fundamental rights as guaranteed under Article 17 of the constitution. Accusing the military regime of attempting to create an "aristocratic class" of legislators, the opposition declared the government wanted to control a parliament without serious competition. The Court's decision was final; no reasons were given for its judgment. It was pointed out that in a country with a high illiteracy rate only 1.32 percent of the total population possessed academic degrees and most college graduates resided in the urban areas. The Court ruling meant that seventy-nine members of the National Assembly and twenty-two Senators, including Benazir Bhutto, who obtained an Oxford Diploma but did not earn a B.A. degree, failed to meet the test.

It was not surprising therefore that the political opposition would warn against the military's deeper role in Pakistani politics. The numerous edicts as well as the decision to proceed with the formal establishment of the National Security Council pointed to a Pakistani military with a permanent place in the political process and a position far superior to that of the elected politicians. A protest procession in Multan organized by the Alliance for the Restoration of Democracy attempted to air grievances with the Musharraf administration, but the police blocked their path. As they attempted to get around the police cordon, a number were arrested, but not before they had registered their dissatisfaction with the regime. Calling for Musharraf's resignation, the protestors demanded the immediate formation of an interim government and the withdrawal of the restrictions imposed on politicians. Musharraf ignored their plea. It was difficult to see how he intended to win the support of the conventional parties or restore democratic practices in the country.

On July 12 Musharraf made a two-hour address to the nation in which he declared the country had been put back on to the road of progress and prosperity. He emphasized his government's independence in eliminating threats to the country's security. He also spoke of economic matters that were causing distress among consumers. He assured the nation that the new Prime Minister would enjoy full powers without interference from the President or the armed forces. At the same time, the President declared he did not intend to act as a rubber stamp and that his powers would extend beyond the ceremonial. The Prime Minister would be subject to the scrutiny of the people, and beyond that to the National Security Council acting in consultation with the President. Moreover, the NSC would include political leaders, including the leader of the opposition, so that a consensus could be arrived at on major national issues. Article 58(2)(b), providing special prerogatives to the President, would be restored but subject to the constraints imposed by the NSC. Saying the Prime Minister would have the capacity to set his or her own foreign and economic policy, Musharraf said the purpose of the constitutional amendments was to ensure good governance, not to usurp the powers of the head of government or weaken the democratic process. Musharraf declared he was not "power hungry" and that he sought a system of checks and balances that would obviate the need to impose martial law in the future. If successful, his amendments would prevent the army from again interfering in the country's political affairs. Musharraf assured those afraid of the NSC that it would not be a super-constitutional body or have dominance over the legislature and executive. Its prime task would be to maintain a working relationship between the army, the President, and the Prime Minister.

Responsibility for announcing the new amendments to the constitution was given to the National Reconstruction Bureau, which made several presentations in mid-July. Twenty-nine constitutional amendments had been developed to give substance to Musharraf's vision of a more effective, more stable, more forward-looking political system. Under the terms of the amendments the President was granted the power to dismiss the parliament. The National Security Council was formally established to oversee the functioning of parliamentary government and to work in concert with the President and the armed forces. Moreover, the Prime Minister and parliament would be prevented from rearranging the system to the detriment of the Chief Executive. The opposition parties were not pleased and their cries of "Dictatorship" and "Fascism" were loud and clear. The Muttahida Majlis-i-Amal rejected the entire package, saying the amendments would do the reverse of what Musharraf intended – would unleash a confrontation between the government and the President. Arguing that the amendments humiliated the entire nation, the Amal refused to permit any "individual with his coterie of experts ... [to] bind the coming generations." Commenting on the weakness built into the Prime Minister's office, the Islamists angrily declared that the head of government would be nothing more than a hostage of the country's military Chief Executive. The "rug could be pulled from his feet anytime."

Although Musharraf turned a deaf ear to these complaints, on July 22 the government announced it had amended the Political Parties Order 2002 to remove the college degree requirement for those seeking or holding political office. This reversal was hardly soothing balm to those depressed by the state of affairs. Believing that the United States secretly approved of Musharraf's *putsch*, the regime's critics declared Pakistan was headed for a "a Hosni Mubarak-style or Suharto type of military-cum-civilian dispensation." The United States, it was said, "likes pliant regimes and the one now holding the Pakistani flag has been more pliant than most." Some political pundits called for a union between Sharif's Muslim League and Benazir's PPP. Their idea included isolating the "Beards of the Muttahida Majlis-i-Amal." They also hoped to force Musharraf and the generals to come to grips with a defiant, sophisticated, and unified political opposition. The mere thought that salvation for Pakistan lay in the return of the two discredited politicians revealed the extent of the political bankruptcy burdening the nation.

It was clear from the ensuing debate that few in Pakistan bought Musharraf's argument that a permanent place for the armed forces in the country's political system was in the best interest of the nation. Nor did they believe it was the only way to satisfy democratic aspirations. By the end of July all the political parties had rejected Musharraf's proposed constitutional package and the Political Parties Order 2002. In a surprise announcement, however, Musharraf declared that nothing had been finalized and that he now contemplated implementing only the essential and immediate amendments. The others, he said, would be left to the future parliament to deliberate. Explaining he had been listening to the people, Musharraf declared that a cross-section of the Pakistani public were in favor of the reforms, despite the well-publicized disdain of the political opposition. Therefore it was with the people in mind that he had decided to forgo ruling on all the amendments. However, he did not delay action on the National Security Council or its role in working with the Chief Executive to assure a strong presidency. At the same time Musharraf wanted it understood that he would not interfere in the work of the new Prime Minister and that he expected the head of government to dominate all state matters. Again he tired to convince Pakistanis that as President he would act against a Prime Minister only in time of crisis and then only with the full knowledge, support, and approval of the National Security Council. Prime Ministers were not interfered with in the past until their behavior endangered the nation. Martial law was the ultimate result. Musharraf's plan sought to assure honest and effective administration. It was also intended to prevent the frequent imposition of military rule. Musharraf clearly assumed an integrity in the men in uniform which made them fit guardians of the country's political system as well as its territorial integrity; given popular suspicions concerning past experience with generals in politics, however, people had ample reason to be skeptical.

Prelude to an election

Sidetracked by the President-General, the Islamists poured their energy into attacking the Musharraf government, especially for its crackdown on the religious schools. Government reforms called for changes in the recruitment of students, course instruction, and extra-pedagogical activities, namely, exercises in the use of firearms, bomb making, and guerrilla training. Intent on curbing religious extremism, the government insisted on higher standards of education and on teacher responsibility as well as overall probity. In reaction, the religious parties called for demonstrations and protest meetings in Islamabad and urged the public to vote for them in the October elections if they wanted ever to regain control of their schools and country. Only the religious parties, they said, would repeal the anti-madrassah decrees, and if given a popular mandate the Islamists promised to force the government to withdraw all restrictive ordinances. A reminder of what lay behind the madrassah reforms had been again demonstrated in the killing of nine German tourists by Islamic militants who attacked their bus while they were touring archaeological sites on the North West Frontier. The government attributed the assault to al-Qaeda or Taliban elements that they said were determined to point up the weakness of the Musharraf regime.

The religious organizations also expressed dissatisfaction with decisions taken at a meeting of the Association of South East Asian Nations (ASEAN). The Association had pointed to Pakistan's aggressive tactics in Kashmir and called for an end to terrorism there. The organization's spokesperson announced acceptance of a comprehensive pact with the United States that aimed at combating terrorism worldwide. No mention, however, was made of India's use of terror in retaining control of the disputed state. Pakistani Islamists demanded a distinction be drawn between those fighting for self-government and those engaged in random acts of violence. Although seeking to separate itself from the more militant Islamists, Islamabad was compelled to make the same argument. The Musharraf government questioned how ASEAN could point to Pakistan's responsibility in the continuing violence in Kashmir, but could so completely ignore New Delhi's tactics in denying the Kashmiris their political and human rights. India's capacity to avoid criticism and the minimal attention given to communal riots in Gujarat were yet another indication to Pakistanis that a double standard applied. It was almost as if India could do no wrong whereas Pakistan could do nothing right. Thus even though Musharraf had thrown in his lot with the

United States in the war on terrorism, there was still little to impress the Pakistani public. India could proceed with its Kashmir elections, it could also threaten to deny its airspace to Pakistani aircraft, but there was little Islamabad could do other than display its defiance. When India's Kashmir Chief Minister, Farooq Abdullah, declared on August 7 that India had no alternative but to strike at militant camps across the border in Pakistan, Pakistani resolve was more in evidence. Musharraf not only repeated his government's official policy about there being no terrorist camps in Pakistan, but said that any overt action by India on Pakistani soil would be met by a swift response. The hardened nature of India's claim to Kashmir prevented Musharraf from fully separating himself from the jihadis, and the jihadis were content to keep the Kashmir pot boiling and leave Musharraf to wonder what he might do next.

Musharraf's dilemma surfaced again when in August another Christian church, this one in Murree, not far from Rawalpindi and Islamabad, was attacked and six people were killed. Although all the dead were Pakistanis, the incident once more pointed to a chain of violence that led directly to the militant Islamists. No target was off limits, no installation or institution was sacred, and no life was worth preserving. The purveyors of violence were all of the same character and all intertwined, and none among them was prepared to question their behavior or the enormous damage caused. In an editorial linking the Murree attack to so many others the newspaper *Dawn* noted that "terrorism is now Pakistan's foremost problem. Without rooting out this menace in all its forms, the economy cannot pick up, nor can political stability be achieved, whether the government is military or democratic." This was the way the international network of terrorists punished Pakistan for joining the United States in the war against terrorism. The perpetrators of the Murree attack allegedly acted on instructions from the global network. Soft targets like churches were now preferable in sowing disorder and uncertainty. Mosques too were targeted to cause Muslims to question the inability of government to protect them and to raise new questions about Islamabad's ties to Washington. Dedicated to the art of psychological warfare, the terrorists aimed to strike terror in the minds of ordinary people.

Countering such a strategy became the primary concern of the Pakistan government. A meeting in early August of Afghan security officials with a delegation led by Pakistani corps commander Lieutenant-General Abdul Quadir not only aimed to improve policing of their mutual frontier, but also signaled a sea change in Pakistan's foreign policy. Discussions centered on the need to control al-Qaeda and Taliban passage into Pakistan. The reported killing by Afghan security forces of twelve Pakistanis and one Kyrgyz national, all affiliated with al-Qaeda, illustrated the more determined efforts on both sides. Pakistan, noted General Quadir, had entered into a new era of relations with Afghanistan, and Islamabad was now in full support of the Hamid Karzai government. Pakistan intended a close relationship with the Afghan authorities. A start was with the Pakistan-proposed Chaman–Kandahar road to promote commerce. The meeting ended with both delegations committing themselves to the war on terrorism and announcing their respective governments' intentions to sign two international conventions on combating terrorism.

Islamabad established a Special Investigation Group (SIG) in its Federal Investigation Agency for the exclusive purpose of countering terrorism and sectarian violence. The SIG not only limited the role of the ISI, but was expected to coordinate the activities of all other law enforcement agencies. Its agents would focus efforts on the identification and location of the "most wanted" terrorist groups and individuals. Agents were to be empowered to arrest and prosecute terrorists and the new agency would help to close the lacunas arising out of the division of responsibilities between different enforcement and intelligence organizations. An Economic Crime Wing was to investigate money laundering between banks and offshore accounts, and would be especially trained to deal with extralegal Islamic transactions such as *hundi* and *hawala*. Another organ of the SIG aimed to control the entry into and exit from the country of suspected and known terrorists. A cyber-crime wing was also contemplated. A sign of a more serious attitude toward terrorism, the announcement also revealed the growing sophistication of the government in confronting the violence as well as the evolution of greater Pakistani–American cooperation.

Anti-terrorist organizations were late in forming, however, and the criminals and anarchists retained the initiative. On August 9 a grenade attack on a chapel at the Christian Hospital in Taxila, near Islamabad, killed four people, including three nurses and a paramedic. Many more were wounded. The assailants, later identified as connected to the outlawed Lashkar-i-Jhangvi and Jayash-i-Mohammad, threw grenades at people departing from a church service. It was not known if the attack was related to a band of thirty Buddhists from Japan, Central Asia, and Russia who were in Pakistan to engage in a cross-country "peace march" aimed, they said, at ridding the world of nuclear weapons. Nevertheless, the Musharraf government believed the attack was another example of terrorist resolve, and of their shift in tactics to softer targets. Such attacks on vulnerable sites, well outside the urban centers, represented a low-cost effort to damage Pakistan's international profile and hence further undermine the country's economy and political system. Moreover, there was reason to conclude that the earlier attack at the Murree church and this one in Taxila were connected. In the course of their investigation the authorities identified the formation of a new terrorist cell composed almost exclusively of suicide squads. This unit, the Lashkar-i-Omar, was said to have direct links with al-Qaeda, and more assaults on the innocent were expected.

Maulana Fazlur Rahman, leader of the Jamiat-i-Ulema-i-Islam, used the occasion of Pakistan's fifty-fifth independence day celebrations to declare that he could never support Musharraf's war on terrorism or his association with the United States. The purpose of his party's participation in the October elections, he said, was to win sufficient seats in the national parliament to begin the process of transforming Pakistan into a "sovereign Islamic State." Noting that his struggle with Musharraf was over ideology, the Maulana said he and the other members of the Muttahida Majlis-i-Amal would not rest until Pakistan became the true spiritual state that its founders sought to create. Distinguishing the Amal from the Taliban, he declared the latter was a response to the anarchy of Afghanistan and had no relevance to Pakistan. Pakistan was an established state with its own character. Its people, he indicated, dreamed of living in an ideal Muslim community, not a secular state, and his movement aimed to realize that objective. By innuendo and declaration, therefore, the Islamists claimed to be the true representatives of the Pakistani ethos and said that it was incumbent on them to end the secularist usurpation of power. As much as Musharraf attempted to build bridges between himself and the Islamists, it was obvious the hard-core elements never contemplated giving him their support. According to the Islamists, because Musharraf had allied himself to the United States and made war on the latest Muslim superheroes, namely bin Laden and Mullah Omar, there could be no peace.

The immediate answer to Musharraf's dilemma, therefore, was building bridges not with the "true believers," but rather with those traditional politicians that his regulations, edicts, ordinances, and decrees had so completely hamstrung. Jihadi militants had demonstrated their capacity to express themselves by killing and maiming the innocent. With hardly two months remaining till the parliamentary elections, the time seemed to call for the revitalizing of more sophisticated competitive politics. The people of Pakistan had consistently supported the more secular politicians over their fundamentalist rivals. If Musharraf was serious about the development of democracy in Pakistan, it was time to formally acknowledge the army's failed policy in Afghanistan and the futility of sustaining the Kashmir dispute with India. Neither situation was winnable. Both had played into the hands of the militants, had drained the country of its limited resources, and had made a mockery of the pursuit of modern government. Moreover, Pakistan was a nuclear power and it was time for the country to demonstrate the maturity and responsibility that comes with the possession of such awesome power.

Although it had taken the horrendous events of September 11, 2001 to engage the Americans, they were now deeply committed in Central and South Asia. Pakistan's military leaders had been forced by the same events to choose between continuing to pursue a failed course, and thus completely identifying themselves with the jihadis and al-Qaeda, and reversing positions taken many years earlier. The United States did not declare "formal" war on terrorism until after the devastating assault on its territory on September 11, 2001. Its subsequent assault on Afghanistan was also a response to the Taliban's harboring of the forces of Osama bin Laden, the perpetrators of the attack on American soil. Washington could not ignore the calamity of September 11, but its action in Afghanistan was measured and restrained. Al-Qaeda's admission of guilt for the 9/11 attack did not place the United States at war with Islam, although that was the intention of those who perpetrated the attack. When the Islamist organizations called this tragedy a fabrication by Washington to impose its writ in vital Muslim territory, they ignored reality. When the Americans abandoned the region after the end of the Soviet misadventure in Afghanistan, they had no intention of returning. Moreover, Musharraf's overthrow of the Sharif government was an internal affair and it was only because of the United States' long relationship with Pakistan that Washington initially registered its support for the elected Muslim League government.

But Pakistan has always been the master of its own destiny. The decision to abandon the Taliban and join the world was calculated to make the best of a miserable situation. It is strange that these tragic events and the reaction to them should provide Pakistan with an opportunity to reclaim its vision of becoming a secular and democratic nation. It seems that nothing less than the upheaval caused by the airliners slamming into the World Trade Center and the Pentagon could have moved Musharraf to rein in those bent on terrible deeds. Musharraf must now rethink the course of Pakistan's future. If he truly wants to reconstruct Pakistan, then he has no choice but to invite the free and open play of all the politicians. They are, after all, Pakistan's politicians, nurtured in the ambience of a country with considerable promise but too often ill-informed as to their true roles. If the Islamists are to be tolerated in the Pakistan of the future, then certainly this is no time to deny a voice and a place to all those wishing to take part in Pakistani politics. The country has endured much that is ignoble. It is time to accept the failures along with the frailties and to nurture a generation of leaders unencumbered by blind doctrines. A new generation waits off stage in the wings of obscurity. That generation wishes to see the Pakistan of the twenty-first century realize its potential for greatness, not only as a Muslim nation but as a country that represents the better instincts of humanity.

Benazir and Sharif are to be welcomed back to their country. Whatever their offenses, this is not only a moment for clemency, but a time to learn what the politicians are prepared to offer in return for renewed popular support. Pakistan has to begin somewhere. The resurrecting of the political process cannot start with a prohibition on the main contenders for political office. The process must be allowed to find its own level; it cannot be stifled even before it begins. Let the parties rebuild and restore their credibility. It is a time not for diktat but rather for diverse views and public discourse. Musharraf will need the politicians and the Majlis-i-Shura to validate the country's quest for true democracy. It is they who hold the only possible answer to those who promote hate and violence. Only a genuine experiment in modern living can expose the militants for what they are, not the bearers but the enemies of Islam. Musharraf is secure in his multiple offices and he would yield nothing in allowing the politicians to enter the fray. Moreover, the General needs the voices of those who find Islamist argument one-dimensional and hence ill-suited to Pakistan. Pakistanis can retrieve their religion from those who hold it hostage to obscurant and discursive argument. Islam is not in danger, in Pakistan or elsewhere, and it is a time to represent Muslim concerns and objectives in contexts that center on reconstruction and positive thinking. Sectarianism and terrorism are demonic, not Islamic, and strategies to combat them require the input of the best and the brightest.

Musharraf's success as a leader will depend on his capacity to transform vision into reality. His greatest challenge lies in leading his nation away from the dangers of its collective and self-imposed "Catch 22." The parliamentary elections demonstrated that Islamist and conventional party platforms are totally at odds. The former emphasized the theocratic state whereas the latter continued to stress contemporary democracy. Although neither of the two forces could expect a perfect application of its ideas, the choice between the two was made apparent by the events that brought the Taliban to power in Afghanistan. The short-lived rule of the Taliban provided Pakistanis with the opportunity to see what their future would be under clerical rule. Pakistanis have also experienced representations of secular democracy; although flawed and primitive, these nevertheless have revealed what needs to be done and undone. In the democratic tradition at least it is possible to try again. Musharraf's reforms may be aimed at respecting all shades of political opinion, but the General cannot be faulted for his hesitation and desire to harmonize the rhetorical with the substantive. The integration of the military into Pakistani governance may resemble politics in Egypt and Indonesia to some observers, but it would be remiss for those wanting to see the flowering of democracy in Pakistan not to acknowledge the failure of previous elected governments.

Pakistan is neither Egypt nor Indonesia and the comparisons are of questionable value. Pakistan, despite its sorry record, still has the possibility of building a worthwhile future. Pakistani generals have shown themselves to have feet of clay; their mistakes of judgment have caused monumental harm. But this does not exonerate the politicians, who have yet to demonstrate that their belief in Pakistan is greater than their pursuit of self-interest. Pakistan is not in search of a savior. Pakistanis rejected Ayub and Bhutto, and they had no reason to feel endeared to Benazir or Sharif. Nor is Musharraf a gift from on high to the Pakistani nation. Leaders, in Pakistan as elsewhere, are fallible people, often assuming burdens too heavy to carry. But life goes on. Musharraf has offered Pakistanis a glimpse of their future. In the final analysis, however, it is the Pakistani nation that must select the path it is to tread. The nation stands at the crosscurrent of history. A choice has to be made not only on the question of more or less freedom, but also on the primordial question of life or death.

Electronic sources and writers consulted for chapters 10 and 11

http://www.hgmp.mrc.ac.uk/~npanjwan/PAKnewslist.html
http://bambi.acc.ncuu.edu/~nkhan/news.html
http://www.angelfire.com/nm/gta2hh/news.htm
http://frontierpost.com.pk
http://www.msnbc.com/news
http://www.phonewallas.com/indo-pak_papers.htm
http://www.dawn-usa.com/pakistan.shtml
http://faridi.net/news
http://www.dawn.com
Shafiq Ahmad, Aftab Ahmed, Hasan Akhtar, Zulfikar Ali, Rafaqat Ali, Ayaz Amir, Khalid Mahmud Arif, Raja Asghar, Maqbool Ahmad Bhatty, Shahid Javed Burki, Ardeshir Cowasjee, Masood Haider, Ihtashamul Haq, Faraz Hashmi, Ahmad Hassan, Khalid

Hasan, Raza Hassan, Irfan Hussain, Anwar Iqbal, Zafar Iqbal, Qazi Muhammad Jamil, Irshad Abdul Kadir, M. Ismail Khan, Sayeed Hasan Khan, Shujaat Ali Khan, Mahmood Khattak, Omar Kureishi, Iffat Malik, Iftikhar H. Malik, Nasir Malik, Hamid Mir, Ashraf Mumtaz, Jamaluddin Naqvi, Jawed Naqvi, Kuldip Nayar, Hafizur Rahman, Arman Sabir, Shamim Shamsi, Ayesha Siddiqa-Agha, Tahir Siddiqui, M. Arshad Sharif, Anis Shivani, Rahmatullah Soomro, Jafar Wafa, Mohammad Waseem, Haider Zaman.

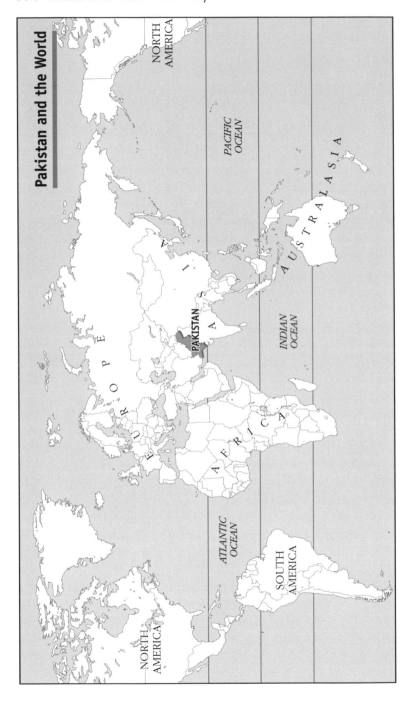

Pakistan and the World

12

STILL ANOTHER CROSSROADS

General Musharraf's desires to stabilize the country and to reopen the democratic process had earlier proved to be incompatible objectives. Pakistan had had repeated difficulties hitching the election horse to the democratic wagon. Pakistan's first national election in 1970 resulted in civil war. Its second produced the army coup that not only dismissed the Prime Minister but led to his trial, conviction, and hanging. Subsequent elections produced civilian governments only to have them short-circuited by army intervention, the Musharraf takeover in October 1999 being only the most recent in a long series of extra-constitutional military actions. In October 2002, Pakistanis went to the polls again, ostensibly with the restoration of democracy their objective, but with a degree of cynicism conditioned by so much past history.

Musharraf and a large portion of the Pakistani public were at odds on the military *putsch*, the war on terrorism, the Legal Framework Order reforms, and the future of the political process. All these elements intertwined during an electoral campaign that was anchored more in coping with religious violence than in the nation's economic development. Musharraf had demonstrated his distrust of the prevailing political process by making himself President, by ordering a referendum that granted him another five-year term, and by insisting on the prerogative to dismiss a government that failed to meet his test of national integrity. Nevertheless, his repeated statements about Pakistan's future as a viable democracy compelled him to press for a new round of elections. Although denying any intention of shaping political outcomes, Musharraf authorized a plan that was aimed at providing him with a mandate to control the political process, and thus with the capacity to influence the organization of the next civilian government. But like Yahya, who believed the 1970 election campaign would turn in his favor, Musharraf miscalculated the consequences of holding an election in the disturbed conditions wrought by the events of September 11, 2001.

The American intrusion in Pakistan and Afghanistan, Washington's role in destroying the Taliban government of Mullah Omar, and its sustained attack on Taliban and al-Qaeda remnants in both countries had embittered more than just Pakistan's fundamentalist orders. A wide array of political and professional organizations denounced the American action. Their anger only added to the rage exhibited by the Islamists and their jihadi adherents. There was considerable sympathy, and in many cases practical support, for the terrorists associated with Emir Omar and bin Laden, especially in the frontier area where the heaviest fighting continued.

The aim of removing United States forces from the region, therefore, was sufficient reason for the otherwise rival Islamist political organizations to create a united front. Six of Pakistan's principal fundamentalist parties agreed to create the Muttahida Majlis-i-Amal (MMA), and this coalition characterized their campaign with anti-American slogans. But the heaviest criticism was reserved for Musharraf, for his temerity in submitting to Washington's demands for bases and cooperation. Musharraf's long-standing unpopularity in the frontier region, and indeed his mohajir status, exacerbated the distaste for his actions. Despite his long and faithful service with the Pakistan army, Musharraf's refugee credentials were never more glaring than when he accepted and aided the American decision to dismantle the Taliban Islamic state. Musharraf's pronounced secular behavior, according to the fundamentalists and their jihadi faithful, was blasphemous; it was their objective to destroy the General and reverse the course his policies had set in train.

Curiously, however, although Musharraf was the Islamists' *bête noire*, he was also their savior in the election campaign. Although they rejected the secular state and its democratic processes, the Islamists were ready and willing to play a game that broadened and legitimated their program and gave them an unprecedented opportunity to achieve formal political power, a goal never before within their reach. Musharraf's policies had hollowed out the more secular political parties. By denying a direct role to Benazir and Sharif, he had prevented the country's principal political parties from mounting an effective campaign. Moreover, Musharraf had caused the split in the once dominant Muslim League and seemed to identify with one of its factions. He also caused the splintering of the Pakistan People's Party, especially on the frontier, where a Sherpao group had found it impossible to follow the old party line. Musharraf's faction was known as the "Pakistan Muslim League (PML) (Q)," which the opposition and members of the literati quickly dubbed the "King's Party." However, all the political parties had been reduced to rump status by the military government's determination to prevent any threat to its authority, and it was assumed the PML (Q) would gather more votes than any of the other organizations contesting the elections.

Even Musharraf had not counted on the religious parties coalescing. He did not believe their power would carry beyond a benign status in the frontier provinces. Musharraf had not targeted the Islamists as he had the conventional politicians. Still appealing to spiritual sentiments, Musharraf continued to believe his reputation as a devout Muslim would sustain his relationship with the clerics. But he had underestimated the depth of hatred caused by his association with the United States, his strict law and order methods, and his attempt to reform the country's religious schools. Seen as determined to stifle religious expression in return for American assistance, the General had made himself anathema to the clerics and their disciples. Musharraf simply could not have it both ways. He could not pretend to speak for religious Muslims and at the same time join with the United States in what the zealots argued was a direct assault on the Islamic world. The Muttahida Majlis-i-Amal therefore was the Islamists' answer to the challenge represented by what many in Pakistan had come to see as an alien intrusion into their lives.

In spite of the passionate character of the campaign, the election was conducted as originally scheduled. The total vote cast on October 10 was reported to be higher than in the previous two elections, won by Benazir and Sharif respectively. A high voter turnout in the rural areas was especially surprising and revealed the organizational ability of the politicians at the grassroots. Nevertheless, of approximately seventy million registered voters, only about thirty million actually cast ballots, a figure the government described as forty-one percent of the electorate. A low urban turnout was attributed to voter apathy and the prevailing view among city dwellers that the election results were of little consequence given the army's overriding dominance. The PML (Q) secured the favor of 7.33 million voters and won 118 seats in the new national parliament of 342 seats. This was not enough to dominate the assembly, or form a government. The election results in fact denied any party the right to declare victory. Benazir's People's Party organization won the next highest number of seats, eighty-one, and in fact had garnered the greatest number of votes, but it was the Muttahida Majlis-i-Amal that caused the biggest stir.

The six-party Islamist coalition not only established itself as the maker or breaker of national coalitions, but had all but eliminated the more established secular parties in the frontier states. The MMA had placed itself in position to name a new Prime Minister if it could form a coalition with other major winners. Perhaps even more significant, the fundamentalists held the advantage in forming future provincial governments in the North West Frontier Province and Balochistan. Energized by their success and finding themselves wooed by the PML (Q) and all the other parties, the MMA sought to reduce Musharraf's dictatorship to an administration with neither legitimacy nor power.

In the weeks after the elections none of the major organizations indicated an interest in propping up Musharraf's government. Joining forces with the "King's Party" was declared tantamount to pulling Musharraf's chestnuts from the fire of defeat. Nevertheless the PML (Q) refused to become a rubber stamp for the President and it successfully resisted his attempt to select a Prime Minister. But even this display of independence did not permit the party to advance the process of forging a coalition government. Therefore the convening of the new parliament on November 1 was postponed. Rescheduled for November 5, the date was put off till November 8 and then November 15. Finally, the government insisted the parliament would be convened on November 16.

On November 16, 2002 General-President Pervez Musharraf took the oath of office under the newly amended 1973 constitution in a ceremony in the Aiwan-i-Sadar witnessed by ministers, ambassadors, high military officials, and his wife and mother. Departing from the tradition that the President after being elected by members of parliament and Senate took the oath of office in front of the National Assembly, this more regal oath-taking was another demonstration that Musharraf had separated himself from the legislative body and answered to a different constituency. While this event was occurring the National Assembly was convening and the newly elected parliamentarians were sworn in by the former speaker. Although the legislators insisted on following the format laid out in the original 1973 constitution, the speaker convinced them that the oath in the Musharraf-amended constitution was exactly the same as that in the older document. The convening and the signing ceremony completed, the parliament was adjourned and scheduled to meet again on November 19 to elect a new speaker and deputy speaker. Thus after more than a month of political maneuvering, with the new government yet to be formed, the politicians were now in place and ready to test the revised political system that President Musharraf had imposed upon them.

On schedule, the parliament reconvened to elect the speaker and deputy speaker and both offices were won by members of the Pakistan Muslim League (Q). Chaudhry Amir Hussain, a former Law Minister in the government of Nawaz Sharif, was elected speaker by a narrow margin. The PML (Q) also won the deputy speaker seat. The runners-up in both instances were the nominees from Benazir's Pakistan People's Party and the Muttahida Majlis-i-Amal. On November 21 the parliament convened to elect a new head of government and selected Mir Zafrullah Khan Jamali to be the Prime Minister. Jamali, also a PML (Q) leader, had won 172 of 329 votes cast in the 342-seat parliament. His nearest rival was the nominee of the Muttahida Majlis-i-Amal, who won eighty-six votes. The PPP candidate received seventy votes and along with the MMA candidate had to be content with a role in the opposition. In a speech to the nation Musharraf declared he had returned the management of government to civilian hands and that he expected the new government to learn the lessons that had caused the army to terminate previously elected administrations. Though informed opinion had anticipated a greater and more immediate Musharraf victory, there was no denying that the General had kept his word to reopen the democratic process.

Further confirmation of Musharraf's desire to improve his credentials as a democratic leader was the holding of elections to the Senate, the upper house of the parliament. The elections were held in two phases in late February 2003, when the one-hundred-seat body also came under the influence of the Pakistan Muslim League (Q) with a slim majority fifty-three seats. The two opposition coalitions, one the fifteen-party Alliance for the Restoration of Democracy led by the Pakistan People's Party Parliamentarians, and the other the Muttahida Majlis-i-Amal divided most of the remaining Senate seats. PML (Q) dominance was nevertheless assured when these main opposition coalitions, the ARD/PPP and the MMA, failed to agree on matters of policy, particularly foreign policy and Musharraf's sustained ties to the U.S.-led international coalition against global terrorism.

Election Results of October 10, 2002

Party	Seats
Pakistan Muslim League (Q)	118
Pakistan People's Party	81
Muttahida Majlis-i-Amal	60
Pakistan Muslim League (N)	19
Muttahida Qaumi Movement	17
National Alliance	16
Pakistan Muslim League (F)	5
Pakistan Muslim League (J)	3
Pakistan People's Party (Sherpao)	2
Balochistan National Party	1
Jamhoori Watan Party	1
Pakistan Awami Tehreek	1
Pakistan Muslim League (Z)	1

Pakistan Tehreek-I-Insaf	1
Muhajir Qaumi Movement Pakistan	1
Independents (including twelve from the Frontier Area Tribal Agency)	14
Pending	1
Total	342

Source: Associated Press Pakistan, November 3, 2002

Immediate and long-term consequences

Although the MMA leaders publicized their dissatisfaction that Musharraf had not called the parliament into session earlier, and exploited the delay by threatening dire consequences if the Assembly did not meet, the Islamists had really viewed the situation as a win–win opportunity. The deeper the impasse the more time the MMA enjoyed to pursue its goals. Moreover, the fundamentalists knew full well that their cause was also that of a huge section of the body politic. The army had too often imposed its will on the public and a broad spectrum of Pakistani society was eager for a return to civilian rule despite their memories of the politicians' many past failures. Thus the MMA was destined to gain stature and credibility as well as legitimacy by articulating the sentiments of Pakistanis, few of whom were otherwise enamored with fundamentalist programs and policies. The key issue according to Maulana Fazlur Rahman, the MMA's nominee for Prime Minister, was the Legal Framework Order and Article 58(2)(b) of the constitution, which conferred upon the President the discretion to dismiss a government he did not agree with. The MMA also denounced Musharraf's National Security Council, which oversaw the operations of the government, and the method Musharraf had used to extend his presidency an additional five years. The MMA continually cited the supremacy of the parliament in all matters of government and repeatedly demanded Musharraf's resignation from his high army post if he expected to remain President. The two positions, they argued, were incompatible with democratic governance.

Musharraf felt the pressure of other members of the political fraternity, but none was more forceful than the MMA. Benazir's and Sharif's long-distance criticism of the Musharraf regime could not register the same impact on Pakistani society. Operating from an inside position and riding a tide of popular dissatisfaction with the administration, the MMA knew Musharraf would not cast aside his uniform for a full-time position as President given the ease with which Presidents had been forced to retire when confronted by military power. Though Musharraf spoke of the popular yearning for democracy and claimed to have made it his principal objective, it was obvious he could not relinquish control over the levers of power. Pakistan remained unprepared for democratic experience, and it would take more than an election to convince the men in uniform that the country's politicians could manage the complex affairs of state and confront the war on terrorism at the same time.

Nonetheless, in this sixth decade since independence the least likely segments of Pakistani society had made themselves the torchbearers of democracy. First the army, the epitome of centralized authority, demanding total obedience to the chain of command, had addressed the need for another form of tutored democracy. And now the Islamists, the self-proclaimed religious conscience of the nation, whose ethos embodied complete submission to God's vicegerent on earth, Emir Omar, the self-declared *Khalifah* of the Islamic state, also insisted their objective was the realization of democracy. That these contrary forces had become the supreme claimants to Pakistan's democratic heritage spoke volumes for the shambles that had been made of the political process. Musharraf, the spokesman of the army, called for a democracy he had never experienced, while the MMA, the counterfoil of military governance, claimed the high ground not only by flaunting its spirituality, but by arguing its interposition between the army and the public's desired democratic goals. That these should be the two forces to articulate Pakistan's quest for popular self government in the twenty-first century revealed much about a nation still in search of a *raison d'être*.

Washington had always been more comfortable with Pakistani generals than politicians, although among the latter Benazir Bhutto had challenged the conventional wisdom and had forged sentimental associations with American public opinion. But given the war on terrorism in Pakistan and Afghanistan, it was not extraordinary that the United States should prefer Musharraf to lead Pakistan. So the United States therefore was again singled out as the major obstacle to Pakistani democracy. This remained a particular argument of the Pakistani intelligentsia in spite of the fact that none of them had a good word for any of the politicians. "Greed," "corruption," "superego" were words applied to all the politicians, especially those in positions of power. Lacking confidence in past leaders, no one was ready to speak a kind word for the current crop of opportunists and self-seekers. Moreover, the politicians never had kind words for one another; if the public displayed their lack of confidence in their political leaders, it was only an echo of how the seekers of political office perceived one another. In more than five decades of uninterrupted political chaos there was no one past or present to measure up to the stature of the Quaid-i-Azam.

This was the army's conclusion in the days of Ayub Khan and nothing had happened since then to shift opinion in a more positive direction. With the intensification of the rivalry with India, especially over Kashmir, but in the production of nuclear weapons as well, it was the Pakistan army that was called to meet New Delhi's challenge. It was the army that developed and held control over Pakistan's nuclear arsenal. It was the army that flashed the nuclear deterrent in the 2002 face-off with the Indian army along the Pakistan–India frontier. And it was Musharraf who trumpeted the success of the army's strategy when New Delhi, after almost ten tense months, finally announced its decision to withdraw thousands of its frontline troops. From Islamabad's position, the nuclear deterrent worked even if the conflict over Kashmir continued to simmer. For all its passion, the Kashmir dispute remained a subject for rational inquiry, but how did the nuclear question factor into the war on terrorism? The sustained confrontation over Kashmir prompted world leaders to take another look at the problem and even to offer mediation. World leaders viewed with trepidation the connection between Pakistan's nuclear deterrent and the domestic conditions within the Muslim nation that had nurtured the Taliban and al-Qaeda. Pakistan's central role in the war on terrorism and its position among the world's nuclear powers meant the country would never again find itself on the margins of global events. The March 2003 capture in Rawalpindi by a joint task force of Pakistani and

American counter-terrorism agents of al-Qaeda's reputed central architect for the September 11 event was still another reminder of the close operations between the Musharraf government and U.S. agencies. (Note too, in April 2003, Washington's decision to write off $1 billion in Pakistani debt.) The arrest of Khalid Shaikh Mohammad and a number of his colleagues was not only heralded as an important event in the war on terrorism, but also raised anew concerns that a number of Pakistan's Islamist leaders continued to aid and abet the operations of the Taliban and Osama bin Laden. Moreover, the pattern of raids on terrorist hideaways and the apprehension of significant terrorist leaders in Pakistan reinforced the view held by a growing number of political personalities, in and outside the Pakistan government, that the haboring of wanted terrorists in the homes of important Pakistanis was an assault on the integrity of the nation. Shortly after Khalid Shaikh Mohammad's arrest rumor circulated of direct links between al-Qaeda and Jamaat-i-Islami, the central organization in the Muttahida Majlis-i-Amal.

If the United States preferred Musharraf to Pakistan's politicians, it was because Pakistan had become the contemporary pivot of history: if the threat posed by unbridled political activism in the name of religion were not contained, more than Pakistan's democratic objectives would be at risk. Pakistan had already come too close to being Talibanized. It was no longer possible to ignore the possibility that an indigenous political movement with an obscurant agenda could gain control of the government and in the course of events link up with an ambitious army officer of similar persuasion. Observed from that position, the war on terrorism takes on even more complex dimensions.

To ward off a more critical phase in Pakistan's history, sophisticated Pakistanis have by and large risen to the present-day challenge and have demonstrated genuine resistance to the forces of chaos. Many Pakistanis, not just Musharraf, have generally acknowledged that the times will not permit the nation to separate itself from the American presence any more than it can divorce itself from the specter of the Taliban or al-Qaeda. In the prevailing conditions and for the foreseeable future, Pakistani society will be compelled to choose between an army-dominated but secular political system, or an army-dominated government guided by theocratic ruminations. Neither can satisfy Pakistan's attentive, worldly and educated public, let alone their desire for a functioning democracy. But other alternatives are not now in the stars, or in Pakistan's future. Hardly six decades after independence, Pakistan stands at a crossroad. But unlike earlier crises, the road it now chooses to follow is not only critical to its role as a modern Muslim nation, but inevitably must impact the extended world of nation-states.

INDEX

371